# THE REGULATION OF PRODUCT STANDARDS IN WORLD TRADE LAW

This monograph has two central purposes. The first is to provide a critical analysis of how governmental, private and hybrid product standards are regulated in the GATT/WTO legal framework. The second purpose is to explore – both positively and normatively – the impact that WTO disciplines may have on the composition, function and decision-making process of various standard-setting bodies through the lens of a series of selected case studies, including the EU eco-labelling scheme; ISO standards; and private standards such as the FSC. The book analyses what role, if any, the WTO may play in making product standards applied in international trade embody not only technological superiority but also substantive and procedural fairness such as deliberation, representativeness, openness, transparency, due process and accountability.

Whilst it has been long recognised that voluntary product standards drawn up by both governmental and non-governmental bodies can in practice create trade barriers as serious as mandatory governmental regulations, a rigorous and systematic inquiry into the boundary, relevance and impact of WTO disciplines on product standards is still lacking. Providing a lucid interpretation of the relevant WTO rules and cases on product standards, this book fills this significant gap in WTO law literature.

Definitive and comprehensive, this is an essential reference work for scholars and practitioners alike.

**Studies in International Trade and Investment Law: Volume 23**

**Studies in International Trade and Investment Law**

**Series Editors**

Gabrielle Marceau
Krista Nadakavukaren Schefer
Federico Ortino
Gregory Shaffer

This series offers a forum for publication of original and scholarly analyses of emerging and significant issues in international trade and investment law – broadly understood to include the whole of the law of the WTO, the public international law of foreign investment, the law of the EU common commercial policy and other regional trade regimes, and any legal or regulatory topic that interacts with global trade and foreign investment. The aim of the series is to produce works which will be readily accessible to trade and investment law scholars and practitioners alike.

**Recent titles in this series:**

*Free Trade and Cultural Diversity in International Law*
Jingxia Shi

*Tied Aid and Development Aid Policies in the Framework of EU and WTO Law: The Imperative for Change*
Annamaria La Chimia

*Balancing Human Rights, Environmental Protection and International Trade: Lessons from the EU Experience*
Emily Reid

*Public Procurement and Labour Rights: Towards Coherence in International Instruments of Procurement Regulation*
Maria Anna Corvaglia

*The China-Australia Free Trade Agreement: A 21st-Century Model*
Edited by Colin Picker, Heng Wang and Weihuan Zhou

*Regional Economic Integration and Dispute Settlement in East Asia: The Evolving Legal Framework*
Anna G Tevini

*The EU, World Trade Law and the Right to Food: Rethinking Free Trade Agreements with Developing Countries*
Giovanni Gruni

*Patent Games in the Global South: Pharmaceutical Patent Law Making in Brazil, India and Nigeria*
Amaka Vanni

*The Nationality of Corporate Investors under International Investment Law*
Anil Yilmaz Vastardis

# The Regulation of Product Standards in World Trade Law

Ming Du

•HART•
OXFORD • LONDON • NEW YORK • NEW DELHI • SYDNEY

HART PUBLISHING
Bloomsbury Publishing Plc
Kemp House, Chawley Park, Cumnor Hill, Oxford, OX2 9PH, UK
1385 Broadway, New York, NY 10018, USA

HART PUBLISHING, the Hart/Stag logo, BLOOMSBURY and the Diana logo are trademarks of Bloomsbury Publishing Plc

First published in Great Britain 2020



A catalogue record for this book is available from the British Library.

Library of Congress Cataloging-in-Publication data

Names: Du, Ming, 1976– author.

Title: The regulation of product standards in world trade law / Ming Du.

Description: Oxford, UK ; New York, NY : Hart Publishing, an imprint of Bloomsbury Publishing, 2020. | Series: Studies in international trade and investment law ; volume 23 | Includes bibliographical references and index.

Identifiers: LCCN 2020025302 (print) | LCCN 2020025303 (ebook) | ISBN 9781509931132 (hardback) | ISBN 9781509931156 (Epub)

Subjects: LCSH: Foreign trade regulation. | General Agreement on Tariffs and Trade (Organization) | Production standards—Law and legislation. | World Trade Organization.

Classification: LCC K4600 .D86 2020 (print) | LCC K4600 (ebook) | DDC 343.07/5—dc23

LC record available at https://lccn.loc.gov/2020025302

LC ebook record available at https://lccn.loc.gov/2020025303

ISBN: HB: 978-1-50993-113-2
ePDF: 978-1-50993-114-9
ePub: 978-1-50993-115-6

Typeset by Compuscript Ltd, Shannon

# *Acknowledgements*

RECOGNITION OF THE debts incurred on the intellectual path from which this book emerges would require a heartfelt thank you note to many mentors, friends and colleagues. Writing this book would not have been possible without their warm encouragement, insightful advice, and generous support. My interest in trade law was first sparked at Tsinghua University School of Law when Professor Che Pizhao offered a seminar on Advanced Issues in International Economic Law and later kindly involved me in several research projects supported by the Ministry of Commerce. This experience led me to pursue a DPhil at Oxford University where my supervisor, Professor Dan Sarooshi QC, taught me the nuts and bolts of WTO law and challenged me to think more clearly in his office at Queen's College on numerous one-to-one supervisory meetings. Since I embarked on an academic career after years of legal practice, I have been learning almost daily from conversations, comments and debates with my superb colleagues at the Chinese University of Hong Kong, Lancaster University, the University of Surrey and my recent new home, Durham University.

I owe special thanks to the editors and staff at *International and Comparative Law Quarterly*, *Journal of International Economic Law*, *World Trade Review*, *Journal of World Trade*, *Chinese Journal of International Law*, *Legal Issues of Economic Integration*, *European Journal of Risk Regulation*, *Chinese Journal of Global Governance* and *Manchester Journal of International Economic Law*, all of whom helped edit and publish my prior articles that in some form fed into various chapters in the manuscript. I am also grateful to the series editors for including this book in *Hart Studies in International Trade and Investment Law*.

This work could not have been completed without the outstanding help of Hart Publishing team. Roberta Bassi has overseen the whole process of my writing this book. From my first inquiry email to Hart to the submission of final manuscript, she has constantly encouraged me with patience and gently nudged me to ensure that I would not be off track because of mood swings and delays, the usual by-products of many evenings and weekends with a computer. Linda Staniford, Emma Platt, Rosemarie Mearns, Chris Harrison, Richard Cox and others have demonstrated impeccable professionalism and attention to detail managing the publication of this book.

Finally, I wish to thank my parents for their unflinching support through the long years of research and writing. I owe apologies to my son, William. I cannot really make up for all the lost time I should have been with him. This book is a belated present for his 12th birthday.

I have made every effort to state the law and major developments as they stood on 1 April 2020.

Ming Du
*Durham, UK*
*August 2020*

# *Contents*

# *Table of Cases*

## A. GATT Cases



## B. WTO Cases

## C. European Union Cases

# 1

# *Introduction*

THE WORLD TRADE Organisation (WTO) and its predecessor, the General Agreement on Tariffs and Trade (GATT), have been extraordinarily successful in liberalising trade between WTO Member States. The process of liberalisation has entailed a series of negotiations resulting in reciprocal commitments to reduce or eliminate tariffs, quotas and other traditional instruments of protectionism.[1] However, if reciprocal trade liberalisation commitments at the border can be neutralised by creating the same protective effects through domestic measures, such as heterogeneous product standards purportedly for legitimate regulatory objectives, confidence in the world trade system will likely be weak. Indeed, negotiated tariff liberalisation may even create an incentive for states to pursue 'policy substitution', when deviation from tariff bindings becomes more difficult.[2] Accordingly, the predominant concern of international trading community has shifted from border measures to standards and technical regulations that exist behind the national borders, which Pascal Lamy, the former WTO Director General, called 'the real 21st Century trade issues'.[3]

Product standards specify or pin down the characteristics of a product. These characteristics can include design, size, weight, safety, energy and environmental performance, interoperability, material, and even the process of production, and they may be embodied in marking, labelling, packaging, testing, inspection and quarantine, and information requirements.[4] Food standards, for instance, may specify maximum pesticide residue levels on fruits and vegetables that are considered safe for human consumption or prescribe methods for laboratory testing of milk for fat content so that labels provide reliable and comparable information to consumers. Product standards are ubiquitous in modern life. Over the past few decades, a great number and wide range of product standards have been applied to international trade. The annual number of notifications of new technical measure made to the

[1] WTO Trade Report, *Trade and Public Policy: A Closer Look at Non-Tariff Measures in the 21st Century* (2012) 37.

[2] RW Staiger and AO Sykes, 'International Trade, National Treatment, and Domestic Regulation' (2011) 40 *Journal of Legal Studies* 149, 153–5.

[3] S Donnan, 'EU and ASEAN to pave way for trade pact talks', *Financial Times* (6 September 2004).

[4] World Trade Report, *Exploring the Links between Trade, Standards and the WTO* (2005) 29.

WTO Secretariat under the Agreement on Technical Barriers to Trade (TBT Agreement) has increased markedly from 364 in 1995 to 2,074 in 2019.[5] During the same period, the annual number of new notifications under the Agreement on the Application of Sanitary and Phytosanitary Measures (SPS Agreement) has increased from 189 in 1995 to 1,118 in 2019.[6] Increased standardisation activity reflects, among other factors, demand by consumers for safer and higher quality products, rising living standard, technological innovations, the expansion of global economic integration and the increased concern paid by many governments and non-governmental organisations (NGOs) to social issues and the environment.[7]

As will be analysed in detail in the next section, the term 'standards' differ from 'technical regulations' in the GATT/WTO legal terminology in that the use of, and compliance with, a standard is not mandatory.[8] Nevertheless, for business purposes, what is legally voluntary may be financially and practically necessary. Standards often elicit compliance from business enterprises in practice for various reasons, ranging from the wish to be responsive to consumer concerns to practical considerations of compatibility of products and insurance/liability incentives.[9] Often companies have little choice but to comply with these voluntary standards as non-adherence would in practice make it much more difficult, if not impossible, to sell their products.[10] Colombia's experience of its flower-growing industry with regard to private environmental labels is a telling example. To address concerns about the environmental aspects of flower production in Colombia, several voluntary labelling programs were proposed to Colombia by the German NGOs such as the 'Colombia Flower Declaration' and 'Flower Label Program'. Consequently, while global flower exports showed an upward trend, exports from Colombia to Germany declined markedly.[11] During the Uruguay Round, the European Community argued in the TBT Committee that standards drawn up by non-governmental bodies can, when used on a nation-wide basis, in practice created barriers to trade as serious as if they were mandatory technical regulations drawn up by central government bodies.[12] Given their similar economic effects, the term 'standard' is widely used

[5] Technical Barriers to Trade Information Management System www.tbtims.wto.org accessed 1 March 2020.

[6] Sanitary and Phytosanitary Information Management System www.spsims.wto.org accessed 1 March 2020.

[7] World Trade Report (n 4) 29.

[8] Annex 1(1) and (2) of the TBT Agreement.

[9] T Buthe and W Mattli, *The New Global Rulers: The Privatization of Regulation in the World Economy* (Princeton University Press, 2011) 148–159.

[10] P Van den Bossche and W Zdouc, *The Law and Policy of the World Trade Organization* 4th edn (Cambridge University Press, 2017) 853.

[11] WTO, 'Environmental Labels and Market Access: Case Study on the Colombian Flower-Growing Industry', G/TBT/W/60 (9 March 1998).

[12] Proposal by the European Economic Community, 'A Code of Good Practice for Non-Governmental Bodies in the Agreement on Technical Barriers to Trade-', GATT Doc TBT/W/110 (7 July 1988), para 2.

in a broader sense to cover both mandatory and voluntary technical standards outside the WTO context.[13]

Product standards are an integral part of a national regulatory framework in modern society just as crucial as hierarchies and markets.[14] They play an important role in ensuring the functioning of the market, increasing economic efficiency, correcting market failures and fostering innovation.[15] To begin with, standards may provide a superior solution to a technical problem. The cost savings of a superior technology can bring about convergence on a single standard by atomistic economic actors without any need of government intervention. Second, standards help overcome the problem of asymmetric information about product quality, enhance compatibility between complementary goods, and mitigate negative production and consumption externalities where the market, left to itself, would fail to provide the optimal level of a good or service.[16] Empirical evidence has demonstrated that companies benefit about 0.5 per cent to 4 per cent of their annual sales revenues from using standards.[17] Third, first mover advantages in standardisation are substantial incentives for firms to innovation. Absent some form of standard setting, technological progress would miss an important instrument for benchmarking and capitalising on technology advances.[18] Next, social pressure or political-legal incentive from third parties may induce a company to comply with standards that are seen as embodying 'best practices'. For example, direct pressure from activist NGOs has led many businesses to commit at least rhetorically to various 'fair trade' standards.[19] Finally, one of the hallmarks of the modern regulation era has been the shift from state-centered, command-control approaches to market forms of voluntary standards.[20] States concede part of their powers to other non-state actors that can act more effectively and swiftly due to their expertise, focus and smaller size. A particular standard developed by a private body may also be referenced or incorporated in laws or regulations. For example,

[13] AB Villarreal, *International Standardization and the Agreement on Technical Barriers to Trade* (Cambridge University Press, 2018) 78–79.

[14] N Brunsson and B Jacobson, *A World of Standards* (Oxford University Press, 2002) 1–2.

[15] European Commission, *A Strategic Vision for European Standards: Moving forward to Enhance and Accelerate the Sustainable Growth of the European Economy by 2020*, EC Communication COM (2011) 311 Final (June 1, 2011) 1–3.

[16] T Buthe and W Mattli, 'International Standards and Standard-Setting Bodies', in D Coen, W Grant and G Wilson (eds), *The Oxford Handbook of Business and Government* (Oxford University Press, 2009) 441, 443.

[17] ISO, *Economic Benefits of Standards: International Case Studies* (2011) 8.

[18] D Acemoglu et al, 'Competing Engines of Growth: Innovation and Standardisation' (2012) 147 *Journal of Economic Theory* 570, 573.

[19] B Cashore, 'Legitimacy and the Privatisation of Environmental Governance: How Non-state Market-Driven Governance Systems Gain Rule-Making Authority' (2002) 15(4) *Governance* 503, 529.

[20] AC Aman, 'The Limits of Globalisation and the Future of Administrative Law: From Government to Governance' (2001) 8(2) *Indianan Journal of Global Legal Studies* 379.

as part of the US federal law, Public Law 104-113, the National Technology Transfer and Advancement Act, and the accompanying Administrative Circular requires federal agencies to consult with, participate and use technical standards developed by voluntary consensus standards bodies for both regulation and procurement.[21]

Product standards vary sometimes tremendously among countries, and very often for good reasons such as different levels of development, technology, environmental requirements and preferences. For example, absent any regulatory measures, the level of risk posed by the same product may differ when in different countries. This may be simply because of differences in local conditions, eg, climatic or geographical conditions, so that some countries will be more exposed to risk than others.[22] On other occasions, average income and the income distribution will have considerable influence on citizen preferences. Consumers in developed countries with higher per capita income are more willing to bear additional costs to ensure a higher level of product safety and quality.[23] The difference may also come from the cultures and experiences of citizens in different societies. A nation that has experienced a serious health issue may exhibit a stronger demand for stringent standard of a particular sort. National constituencies that are less comfortable with markets and more sanguine about government intervention may prefer more intrusive regulation. Likewise, some societies have a greater awareness of, and sensitivity to, ecological concerns than other societies. Due to these differences, the desired standards that states choose to afford their citizens will also differ. In the same vein, we may also expect that risk-reducing measures necessary to achieve a given level of desired risk will differ among countries for the same reasons. For example, some governments may consider the 'controlled use' of a hazardous substance sufficient to protect human health, while others may believe that an outright ban should be in place.[24]

Despite many benefits that product standards bring to our society, they are not always applied to secure these benefits. Economic literature has told the story of how product standards may be captured by well-organised interest groups or narrow constituencies at the expense of the general interests of the whole society at large.[25] Such capture can readily produce regulatory heterogeneity and

[21] 14 U.S.C.§3701 et seq. (1996); Revised Office of Management and Budget Circular A-119 (January 27, 2016).

[22] MJ Trebilcock and JA Soloway, 'International Trade Policy and Domestic Food Safety Regulation: The Case for Substantial Deference by the WTO Dispute Settlement Body under the SPS Agreement' in DLM Kennedy and JD Southwick (eds), *The Political Economy of International Trade Law* (Cambridge University Press, 2002) 537.

[23] AO Sykes, 'The (limited) Role of Regulatory Harmonisation in International Goods and Service Markets' (1999) 2 *Journal of International Economic Law* 49, 57.

[24] WTO Appellate Body Report, *European Communities – Measures Affecting Asbestos and Asbestos-Containing Products (EC – Asbestos)*, WT/DS135/AB/R, adopted 5 April 2001, para 173.

[25] S Peltzman, 'Toward a More General Theory of Regulation' (1976) 19 *Journal of Law & Economics*, 211–240; DM Sturm, 'Product Standards, Trade Disputes, and Protectionism' (2006) 39 *Canadian Journal of Economics* 564, 577.

associated impediments to international trade. Indeed, the tendency to misuse standards for trade protectionism purposes is inevitable in a world where the commercial interests of foreigners have little or no representation in the political life of the state enacting the standards.[26] Consequently, product standards may be designed to the effect of discriminating the imported products vis-à-vis domestic like products.[27] For example, in *US – Gasoline*, under the banner of environment protection, the US required that all imported gasoline comply with a specific emission standard, while put either no restriction or a less stringent standard on domestic gasoline.[28]

Even though a product standard may be applied in a prima facie non-discriminatory way to both domestic and imported goods, the immediate cost impact of the standard may be non-uniform, with higher costs falling on imported goods.[29] This may be accomplished, for instance, by requiring the use (or non-use) of technologies, processes or ingredients in which domestic firms have a proprietary interest, or at least in which they have a cost advantage.[30] The US requirement of a larger minimum size on vine-ripened tomatoes (mainly imported from Mexico) than on green tomatoes (mainly grow in Florida) was a typical example.[31] In *EC – Hormones*, the EC prohibited the importation of all beef treated with artificial hormones purportedly to protect human health and it turned out that the domestic producers never apply artificial hormones and, as such, the burden of complying with the regulation fell solely on the foreign exporters.[32]

Moreover, even if product standards are not intended to provide protection to domestic producers, these standards may be opaque, poorly designed, badly implemented, or simply unreasonably burdensome on trade. Despite their acclaimed benefits, they put a disproportionate burden on international trade while the benefits achieved from the standards may be minimal. For example, in 1968, the US implemented a regulation related to automobile headlights, requiring two settings: one for high beams and one for low beams. Recently, some automakers have developed new technologies that allow adaptive self-dimming rather than a separate 'high' and 'low' setting. While the new technology has the potential to reduce the risk of crashes by increasing visibility without increasing

[26] RE Hudec, 'GATT/WTO Constraints on National Regulation: Requiem for an "Aim and Effects" Test' (1998) 32 *Int'l Lawyer* 619.

[27] J Karbowski, 'Grocery Store Activism: A WTO-Compliant Means to Incentivise Social Responsibility' (2009) 49 (3) *Virginia Journal of International Law* 727, 750.

[28] WTO Appellate Body Report, *United States – Standards for Reformulated and Conventional Gasoline (US – Gasoline)*, WT/DS2/AB/R, adopted 20 May 1996, 4–6.

[29] Sturm (n 25) 565.

[30] Sykes (n 23) 60.

[31] R Piermartini and M Budetta, 'A Mapping of Regional Rules on Technical Barriers to Trade', in A Estevadeordal, K Suominen and R Teh (eds), *Regional Rules in the Global Trading System* (Cambridge University Press, 2009) 250, 251.

[32] WTO Panel Report, *EC Measures Concerning Meat and Meat Products (Hormones), Complaint by the United States (EC –Hormones)*, WT/DS26/R/USA, adopted 13 February 1998, as modified by Appellate Body Report WT/DS48/AB/R, paras II 6–10.

glare and has been used in other markets such as the EU, it is not allowed in the US due to the standard requirement enacted in 1968.[33]

Finally, heterogeneity of product standards itself brings economic inefficiency as they may generate costs that burden international trade, including information costs of identifying and understanding multiple certification and testing requirements or approval procedures; specification costs of complying with divergent and duplicative regulatory standards, and conformity assessment costs of demonstrating compliance with standards in order to get a product approved for sale.[34] These requirements increase companies' compliance costs thereby decreasing their economies of scale. One often repeated example is that of a US light truck manufacturer planning to sell a popular US model in Europe required 100 unique parts, an additional $42 million in design and development costs and incremental testing of 33 vehicle systems, all without any performance differences in terms of safety or emissions.[35]

Though effects of heterogeneous product standards on international trade are difficult to quantify, there is strong evidence supporting the proposition that they could potentially constitute substantial barriers to the increased international flow of goods.[36] This is especially the case for small and medium-size enterprises in the developing countries.[37] Empirical research shows that 44 per cent of firms have to carry out significant duplication in testing in order to export. The multiplicity of standards and technical regulations not only decrease the share of exports in firms' total sales but also the likelihood that firms export to many countries.[38] Francois estimates that the average trade cost from TBT measures is 21.5 per cent for US goods exports to the EU and 25.4 per cent for EU goods exports to the US.[39] Even worse, if product standards do not serve any legitimate regulatory purposes but are covert trade barriers, they will cause additional deadweight losses that make them more inefficient than other instruments of protection such as tariffs, quotas and subsidies.[40] Moreover, the level of

[33] EA Taub, 'Smart Headlights to Inch Closer to American Road', *New York Times* (21 November 2018).

[34] OECD, *International Regulatory Cooperation and Trade: Understanding the Trade Costs of Regulatory Divergence and the Remedies* (2017) 16–18.

[35] SI Akhtar and VC Jones, 'Proposed Transatlantic Trade and Investment Partnership (TTIP): In Brief', Congressional Research Service (11 June 2014) 8.

[36] L Fontagne, G Orefice, R Piermartini and N Rocha, 'Product Standards and Margins of Trade: Firm Level Evidence', WTO Staff Working Paper ERSD-2013-04 (2013) 4; I Sheldon, 'North-South Trade and Standards: What can General Equilibrium Analysis Tell us?' (2012) 11(3) *World Trade Review* 376, 388.

[37] KE Maskus, T Otsuki and JS Wilson, 'The Costs of Complying with Foreign Product Standards for Firms in Developing Countries: An Econometric Study', World Bank Policy Research Working Paper No 3590 (2005).

[38] OECD (n 34) 20–21.

[39] J Francois, 'Reducing Transatlantic Barriers to Trade and Investment: An Economic Assessment', CEPR Final Project Report (March 2013) 20.

[40] AO Sykes, 'Regulatory Protectionism and the Law of International Trade' (1999) 66 *University of Chicago Law Review* 1, 5.

trade restrictiveness imposed by product standards takes on special significance in contemporary international trade, which has been increasingly conducted through global supply chains. Since a global supply chain requires semi-finished goods to move back and forth across international borders more than once, the adverse trade effects of product standards are compounded.[41] WTO Members' concerns about product standards are notably reflected in a surge in the number of specific trade concerns raised in the WTO TBT Committee, which rose from 146 in 2006 to 605 in 2019. In 2019 alone, Members reviewed a total of 35 new trade concerns, a new peak in the TBT Committee.[42]

In view of the significant adverse trade effects brought about by product standards, the societal returns to international legal constraints on product standards seem to be greater, other things being equal, than the societal returns to constraints on other protectionist instruments.[43] The World Economic Forum estimates that convergence in the cost of enforcing a set of trade-related regulations and standards to that observed in the most efficient countries would increase global GDP by nearly 5 per cent and trade by 15 per cent.[44] Rocha at al shows that when preferential trade agreements comprise commitments to address technical measures, trade tends to increase by 7 per cent on this account alone.[45] The significant welfare gains from actions to reduce product standards costs explains the negotiation of the GATT Technical Barriers to Trade during the Tokyo Round and the addition of separate TBT and SPS Agreements to the WTO treaty during the Uruguay Round. Under the 'single package' approach, WTO Members are obliged to adhere to a set of disciplines such as the national treatment obligation, least trade restrictive means, the use of international standards as a basis and transparency when they set national product standards.[46] The new WTO regulatory landscape largely reflects the commitment of international trade community to reduce unnecessary product standards and call for greater harmonisation so as to reduce their adverse effects on trade.

However, the shift of WTO's regulatory focus from border measures to behind-the-border product standards has raised important legal and policy questions. The standardisation bodies come in many shapes, forms and legal categories. Some are public agencies, others are private standards development

[41] MJ Ferrantino, 'Using Supply Chain Analysis to Analyze the Costs of Non-Tariff Barriers to Trade and the Benefits of Trade Facilitation', WTO Working Paper ERSD 2012-02 (2012).

[42] Note by the Secretariat, 'Twenty-Fifth Annual Review of the Implementation and Operation of the TBT Agreement', G/TBT/44 (19 February 2020) 21.

[43] Sykes (n 40) 5.

[44] World Economic Forum, *Enabling Trade: Valuing Growth Opportunities* (Geneva 2013) 13.

[45] G Oreficea, R Piermartinib and N Rocha, 'Harmonisation and Mutual Recognition: What are the Effects on Trade?', 15th Annual Conference on Global Economic Analysis (Geneva 2012) 12.

[46] G Marceau and JP Trachtman, 'A Map of the World Trade Organisation Law of Domestic Regulation of Goods: The Technical Barriers to Trade Agreement, The Sanitary and Phytosanitary Measures Agreement, and the General Agreement on Tariffs and Trade' (2014) 48(2) *Journal of World Trade* 351–432.

organisations and most are public-private hybrid.[47] They set product standards to protect important social values of the highest level such as human health and safety, consumer welfare and environment protection. All types of standardising bodies, both at national and international levels, have legitimate and widely accepted roles to play in the transnational regulatory space.[48] The underlying tension between trade liberalisation and ensuring legitimate regulatory space of standardising bodies has posed enormous challenges to the GATT/WTO regime, especially its much-admired dispute settlement system. If WTO rules are applied too strictly, a broad intrusion into the regulatory space of all sorts of standardising bodies might transform the WTO dispute settlement system into a routine reviewing court, placing undue limits on non-protectionist standards. As a consequence, legitimate policy decisions and value choice of domestic consumers will be thwarted. On the other hand, if WTO disciplines are applied too laxly, a failure to consider seriously the possibility of covert protectionism arising from the proliferation of product standards undermines the integrity of trade disciplines, providing a ready means of cheating with impunity on explicit trade commitments.[49] Therefore, how to strike a delicate balance between trade liberalisation and legitimate regulatory space of standardising bodies may represent one of the most important questions to the international trade regime.[50]

This book is precisely intended to address this research question: to what extent should WTO disciplines penetrate into the regulatory space of WTO Members, non-governmental bodies and other international standardising bodies (ISBs) in setting product standards solely based on their alleged trade concerns? Although extensive literature is available on technical regulations, the compliance with which is mandatory under the WTO law, it is widely acknowledged that voluntary product standards remain a severely underexplored topic, despite their increasingly important role in global trade governance and the fact that WTO Member States have imposed disciplines on such standards since the 1970s.[51] This book is the first of its kind to address comprehensively and

[47] H Schepel, *The Constitution of Private Governance: Product Standards in the Regulation of Integrating Markets* (Hart Publishing, 2005) 4.

[48] S Bernstein and E Hannah, 'Non- state Global Standard Setting and the WTO: Legitimacy and the Need for Regulatory Space' (2008) 11 *Journal of International and Economic Law* 575, 607–8.

[49] Hudec (n 26) 620.

[50] JH Jackson, 'Afterword: The Linkage Problem- Comments on Five Texts' (2002) 96 *American Journal of International Law* 118, 119; Consultative Board to the Director-General Supachai Panitchpakdi, *The Future of the WTO: Addressing Institutional Challenges in the New Millennium* (WTO, 2004) 29–34; DC Esty, 'Good Governance at the Supranational Scale: Globalizing Administrative Law' (2006) 115 *Yale Law Journal* 1490, 1543–44.

[51] Aspects of voluntary standards are addressed in the existing literature. For example, on international standards, see Villarreal (n 25); P Delimatsis (ed), *The Law, Economics and Politics of International Standardization* (Cambridge University Press, 2015); HZ Schroder, *Harmonization, Equivalence and Mutual Recognition of Standards in WTO Law* (Wolters Kluwer, 2011). On private standards, see A Marx, M Maertens, J Swinnen & J Wouters (eds), *Private Standards*

exclusively the regulation of voluntary standards in both the GATT/WTO law and regional trade agreements (RTAs). By offering a comprehensive answer to the overall research question, this book has two research objectives. The first is to provide a comprehensive and critical analysis of how governmental, private and hybrid product standards are regulated under GATT/WTO law. The second purpose is to explore, both positively and normatively, the implications of regime interaction between the WTO and other standard-setting bodies. In short, the purpose of this book is to map out how product standards are regulated in the GATT/WTO legal framework as well as to explore what impact WTO disciplines may have on the composition, function and decision-making process of standard-setting bodies when they set standards that affect international trade.

*and Global Governance: Economic, Legal and Political Perspectives* (Edward Elgar, 2012); J Kirton and M Trebilcock (eds), *Hard Choices, Soft Law: Voluntary Standards in Global Trade, Environment and Social Governance* (Ashgate, 2004). A Kudryavtsev, *Private-Sector Standards as Technical Barriers in International Trade in Goods: In Search of WTO Disciplines* (Wolf Legal Publishers, 2015).

# 2

# *An Overview of Product Standards in International Trade*

## I. THE DEFINITION OF 'STANDARDS' IN THE TBT AGREEMENT

Annex 1(2) of the TBT Agreement defines 'standard' as:

> A document approved by a *recognised body*, that provides, for common and repeated use, rules, guidelines or *characteristics for products or related process and production methods*, with which compliance is *not mandatory*. It may also include or deal exclusively with terminology, symbols, packaging, marking or labelling requirements as they apply to a product, process or production method.

The TBT Agreement makes a clear distinction between a 'standard' and a 'technical regulation', with the latter defined as 'a document laying down product characteristics or their related processes and production methods with which compliance is *mandatory*'.[1] As the WTO Appellate Body (AB) observed in *US-Tuna II*, the definition of standard is textually very similar to that of technical regulation.[2] It is therefore reasonable to draw inspiration from the AB's interpretation of technical regulation to understand what is a standard.

In *EC – Asbestos*, the AB set out a three-prong criterion to define technical regulation.[3] Following *EC – Asbestos*, four elements must be fulfilled to meet the definition of standard. First, a standard must provide rules, guidelines or characteristics for products or related process and production methods (PPMs). Second, a standard must be approved by a 'recognised body'. Third, a standard must apply to an *identifiable* product or group of products. Finally, the compliance with a standard must not be mandatory. The criteria of the definition are cumulative, and there is no particular order of analysis that a panel needs to follow in assessing whether the measure at issue is a standard.

[1] Annex 1(1) of the TBT Agreement.

[2] WTO Appellate Body Report, *United States – Measures Concerning the Importation, Marketing and Sale of Tuna and Tuna Product (US – Tuna II)*, WT/DS381/AB/R, adopted 13 June 2012, para 187.

[3] WTO Appellate Body Report, *European Communities – Measures Affecting Asbestos and Asbestos-Containing Products (EC – Asbestos)*, WT/DS135/AB/R, adopted 5 April 2001, paras 66–70.

### A. Product Characteristics

For the first element, product characteristics include not only any objectively definable features and qualities *intrinsic* to a product, such as a product's composition, size, hardness, flammability and density, but also 'distinguishing marks' of a product, such as the means of identification, the presentation and the appearance of a product.[4] Terminology, symbols, packaging, marking or labelling requirements are good examples of the latter category. Moreover, product characteristics may be prescribed in either a positive or a negative form.[5] The document may provide, positively, that products must possess certain characteristics, or negatively, that products must not possess certain characteristics.

In *EC – Asbestos*, the measure at issue was a French ban prohibiting any use of asbestos. There are two distinctive features about the French measure. First, it banned not only asbestos fibres but also *products that contain asbestos fibres*. The AB agreed that the prescription of product characteristics must be distinguished from a total ban on a product, as a prohibition of market access for a given product *as such* does not prescribe any product characteristics.[6] Since the French measure covered products that contain asbestos fibers, the AB held that, formulated negatively, the measure effectively prescribed certain objective features of all products, that is, they should not contain asbestos fibres.[7] Second, the French measure was not a total prohibition of asbestos fibres. It contained certain exceptions, permitting the use of certain products containing chrysotile asbestos fibres. The panel analysed the prohibition part and the 'exception' part of the French Decree separately. The AB reversed the panel and held that they should be considered as a unified whole because the exceptions define the scope of the prohibitions and they would have no legal meaning unless they operated in conjunction with a general prohibition.[8] Viewing the measure as an integrated whole, the AB held that the French measure laid down product characteristics for all products that contain asbestos.[9]

The AB usually had no difficulty in holding that the measure at issue set out product characteristics until *EC – Seal Products*.[10] At first sight, the structure of the EU seal regime was very similar to the French measure in *EC – Asbestos* in two aspects. First, the EU seal regime prohibited the placing on the EU market of both pure seal products and products containing seals. Second, the EU seal regime was not a total prohibition, but included both prohibitive and permissive elements. In essence, the EU seal regime prescribed that the placing on the EU market of seal products shall be allowed only if they met certain conditions, such

[4] Ibid, para 67.
[5] Ibid, para 69.
[6] Ibid, para 71.
[7] Ibid, para 72.
[8] Ibid, para 64.
[9] Ibid, para 75.
[10] WTO Appellate Body Report, *European Communities – Measures Prohibiting the Importation and Marketing of Seal Products (EC– Seal Products)*, WT/DS400/AB/R, adopted on 18 June 2014.

as seal products obtained from hunts traditionally conducted by Inuit and other indigenous communities (IC exception); seal products obtained for purposes of marine resource management (MRM exception); and seal products brought by travellers into the EU in limited circumstances (traveller exception). Even though there was not an explicit general ban on seal products like the French ban on Asbestos, the EU seal regime operated to the same effects, ie, seal and seal-containing products would be prohibited unless one of the exceptions applied.

Following *EC – Asbestos*, the panel in *EC – Seal Products* highlighted the fact that 'the prohibition on seal-containing products under the EU seal regime lays down a product characteristic in the negative from by requiring that all products not contain seal'.[11] To many WTO commentators' surprise, the AB reversed the panel.[12] The AB emphasised that the determination of whether a measure constitutes a technical regulation must be made in the light of the characteristics of the measure at issue and the circumstances of the case. A panel must carefully examine the design and operation of the measure while seeking to identify its 'integral and essential' aspects. It is these features of the measure that are to be accorded the most weight for purpose of characterising the measure.[13]

Applying this overall analytical approach to the facts, the AB pointed out that the panel's error was that its conclusion rested on its assessment of a single component of the measure, ie, the prohibition of seal-containing products laid down a product characteristic in the negative form. The panel, however, failed to conduct a holistic assessment of other relevant parts of the EU seal regime, particularly the permissive elements of the EU seal regime.[14] As described earlier, the prohibition of seal products was subject to conditions based on criteria relating to the identity of the hunter, or the type or purpose of the hunt from which the product was derived. Different from *EC – Asbestos*, where it was uncontested that the exceptions part of the French ban laid down product characteristics, the permissive elements of the EU seal regime, such as permitting Inuit killing seals, could not be viewed as product characteristics.[15] Another argument against the panel's analysis is that it makes the reference in the first sentence of TBT Annex 1.1 to 'product characteristics or their related processes and production methods' pleonastic because, following the panel's approach, *any* PPM would lay down product characteristics.[16] Moreover, it is indisputable that another aspect of the EU seal regime, the prohibition of pure seal products, did not prescribe any product characteristics.[17]

[11] Ibid, para 5.25.

[12] R Howse, 'WTO Seals: What is it really that makes the AB think that TBT doesn't apply?' http://worldtradelaw.typepad.com/ielpblog/2014/05/wto-sealswhat-is-it-really-that-makes-the-ab-think-that-tbt-doesnt-apply.html accessed on 1 March 2020.

[13] *EC – Seals* (n 10) paras 5.19.

[14] Ibid, para 5.25.

[15] Ibid, para 5.43–5.45.

[16] PI Levy and DH Regan, 'EC – Seal Products: Seals and Sensibilities (TBT Aspects of the Panel and Appellate Body Reports)' (2015) 14 *World Trade Review* 337, 355.

[17] *EC – Seals* (n 10) para 5.35.

Being a multi-faceted measure, the EU seal regime contained both prohibitive and permissive elements. While some elements laid down product characteristics, others conditioned market access on factors not related to product characteristics. How then to decide whether or not the EU seal regime has laid down product characteristics? The AB analysed the weight and relevance of the 'essential and integral' elements of the measure and made and following conclusion:

> When the prohibitive aspects of the EU seal regime are considered in the light of the IC and MRM exceptions, it becomes apparent that the measure is not concerned with banning the placing on the EU market of seal products as such. Instead, it establishes the conditions for placing seal products on the EU market based on criteria relating to the identity of the hunter or the type or purpose of the hunt from which the product is derived. *We view this as the main feature of the measure.* That being so, we do not consider that the measure as a whole lays down product characteristics.[18]

It is probably only apparent to the AB why the main feature of the EU seal regime was to establish market access conditions unrelated to product characteristics, rather than to lay down product characteristics in the negative form with some exceptions. The AB concluded that the prohibition on the products containing seal was *derivative* or *ancillary* of the three (IC/MRM/Travelers) market access conditions.[19] But this judgment seems to be rather arbitrary. As the AB acknowledged, the purpose of the EC ban on seal products was to prevent EU citizens' moral outrage at seal suffering. However, the purposes of the exceptions were to allow the preservation of Inuit culture and so on. Then, how can the purpose of public moral protection be derivative or ancillary of other purposes? Isn't it more plausible that the EU *first* conceived of the ban to address the moral concerns about inhumane killing of seals, and only then realised that it wanted the IC exception? If, as the AB argued, the exceptions which established the conditions for placing seal products on the EU market were the main feature of the EU seal regime, then why should the necessity test in GATT Article XX be assessed in relation to the public moral objective of the ban, rather than directly in relation to the objectives of the exceptions such as the IC hunts?

The AB provided several reasons to support its conclusion, mainly through identifying different features of the EU seal regime and the French ban in *EC – Asbestos*. For example, in *EC – Asbestos*, asbestos-containing products were regulated because of their carcinogenic properties. By contrast, the EU seal regime did not prohibit seal-containing products because they contain seal as an input. The difficulty of verifying precisely whether a particular product contains seal as an input was understood by the AB as suggesting that the regulation of the seal-containing products was not an equally important feature of the EU seal

[18] Ibid, para 5.58.
[19] Ibid, para 5.41.

regime in operation as the case for the regulation of products containing asbestos in *EC – Asbestos*.[20] But it is difficult to see how these differences concealed arguably the most important effect of the EU seal regime: seal-containing products, which constituted the majority of imported seal products, were not permitted to access the EU market unless they met certain criteria relating to the identity of the hunter or the type or purpose of the hunt. Moreover, as the AB acknowledged in the necessity analysis under Article XX, despite the fact that IC and MRM hunts also led to inhumanely killed seals which contradict the asserted animal welfare purpose, the EU seal regime has made a net positive contribution to reducing EU and global demand for seal products and the incidence of inhumanely killed seals.[21] The prohibitive and permissive elements of the EU seal regime are really the two sides of the same coin and the characterisation of the measure could be made either way, depending on the perspective of the beholder. It is not entirely clear why the AB emphasised the permissive element of the EU measure, whilst regarding the prohibitive elements as derivative or ancillary to the former.

The AB report of *EC – Seal Products* shows that the regulatory scope of the TBT Agreement is likely to be narrower than people previously thought.[22] According to the AB, mainly because the exceptions part of the EC seal regime (permissive elements) does not lay down product characteristics, the EU seal regime as a whole does not lay down product characteristics. This may mean that, assuming PPM issues are not implicated, the exceptions part may also have to lay down at least some product characteristics in order to fall into the ambit of the TBT Agreement in future disputes.

### B. PPMs and Labelling Requirements

The term 'PPMs' originated in the GATT Agreement on Technical Barriers to Trade and it referred to product standards based on production methods rather than product characteristics.[23] In the trade policy context, PPMs are usually divided into product-related PPMs (PR-PPMs) and non-product-related PPMs (NPR-PPMs).[24] PR-PPMs have an impact on the physical characteristics of the goods in question. The use of pesticides in agriculture, as long as it leaves residues on the final product, can be defined as a PR-PPM. NPR-PPMs, by contrast, do not affect or change the nature, properties, or qualities of (nor discernible traits

[20] Ibid, para 5.42.

[21] Ibid, para 5.254.

[22] R Howse, J Langille and K Sykes, 'Sealing the Deal: The WTO's Appellate Body Report in EC-Seal Products' (2014) 18 (12) *ASIL Insights*.

[23] S Charnovitz, 'The Law of Environmental "PPMs" in the WTO: Debunking the Myth of Illegality' (2002) 27 *Yale Journal of International Law* 59, 64.

[24] OECD Secretariat, 'Processes and Production Methods (PPMs): Conceptual Framework and Considerations on Use of PPM- Based Trade Measures' (1997) OECD/GD (97) 137, 10–11.

in or on) a product, ie, not bearing on their physical characteristics.[25] Examples include the requirement that the furniture should have been made from wood sourced from a sustainably managed forest or the amount of CO2 generated in the process of producing a product must not exceed a certain limit.[26] PPM-based standards have presented some challenging questions to international trade law. On the one hand, consumers or governments in an importing country may care about the way in which an imported good was produced, for instance, because they care about the environmental impact of the production process. On the other hand, as production processes may be unique in each country and typically not traded, they are only indirectly relevant to the WTO system. This indirect nexus explains why a WTO panel finds it difficult to deal with PPM standards, in particular the legality of extraterritorial application of PPM-based trade measures.[27]

It remains unsettled to what extent PPMs fall under the purview of the TBT Agreement. Annex 1.1 provides that a technical regulation covers not only product characteristics, but also '*their related PPMs*'. The AB interpreted the phrase as indicating that the subject matter of a technical regulation may consist of a PPM that is related to product characteristics. To make such a determination, a panel will have to examine whether the PPM at issue has *a sufficient nexus* to the characteristics of a product.[28] In *EC – Seal Products*, Norway argued that the EC seal regime has laid down a related PPM through the IC and MRM exceptions. The AB refused to consider the issue because the panel had made no findings on it. The AB also warned that 'the line between PPMs that fall, and those that do not fall, within the scope of the TBT Agreement raises important systemic issues'.[29] Since the AB sidestepped the PPM debate in *EC – Seal Products*, it remains to be seen how broad this 'sufficient nexus' between PPMs and product characteristics might be interpreted in future disputes.

A textual reading of Annex 1.1 may indicate that both PR-PPMs and NPR-PPMs are covered in the definition of technical regulation so long as they are related to product characteristics.[30] Indeed, nothing in the text of Annex 1.1 shows that product characteristics only refer to physical characteristics, but not non-physical characteristics.[31] Still, since only 'related' PPMs are covered

[25] Communication from Canada, 'Labelling and Requirements of the Agreement on Technical Barriers to Trade: Framework for Informal, Structured Discussions' (2003) WT/CTE/W/229, para 14; M Joshi, 'Are Eco- Labels Consistent with World Trade Organisation Agreements?' (2004) 38 (1) *Journal of World Trade* 69, 73–4.

[26] OECD Secretariat (n 24) 11.

[27] GATT Panel Report, *United States – Restrictions on Imports of Tuna (US – Tuna I)*, DS21/R, 3 September 1991 (unadopted) BISD 39S/155; GATT Panel Report, *United States – Restrictions on Imports of Tuna*, DS29/R, 16 June 1994 (unadopted).

[28] *EC – Seal Products* (n 10) para 5.12.

[29] Ibid, para 5.69.

[30] E Vranes, *Trade and the Environment: Fundamental Issues in International Law, WTO Law, and Legal Theory* (Oxford University Press, 2009) 342.

[31] M Du, 'What is a "Technical Regulation" in the TBT Agreement?' (2016) 6 (3) *European Journal of Risk Regulation* 396, 398.

in the definition of technical regulation, one necessary inference must be that not all NPR-PPMs are covered, as some of them may not be related to product characteristics.[32] Arguably, prescriptions of harvesting methods for tuna, which do not leave physical traces, qualify as a 'related PPM'. By contrast, management systems such as ISO 9000 and ISO 14000 and general policy considerations such as labour standards or human rights conditions that are not specifically related to the production of specific products would not qualify as 'related PPMs'.[33]

However, this broad interpretation is at odds with the prevailing view that the phrase 'their related' intentionally qualifies the scope of PPMs to cover only PR-PPMs.[34] The latter view seems to be corroborated by the negotiating history of the TBT Agreement. During the Uruguay Round, Mexico proposed to insert 'their related' before 'the processes and production methods' in the definition of technical regulation. In introducing its proposal, Mexico made it clear that the intent was to exclude NPR-PPMs from the coverage of the TBT Agreement.[35] Mexico's proposal was adopted in the final TBT text. In line with this understanding, requirements that products should be harvested in a certain way to meet environmental standards would not be technical regulations since they have no impact on the physical or performance quality of the product.

Similarly, it is argued that NPR-PPMs also fall outside of the definition of 'standard' in Annex 1.2 of the TBT Agreement. In the final TBT text, only the word 'related' was inserted before 'the processes and production methods' in the definition of 'standard'. Some argue that the lack of the word 'their' renders the scope of a standard broader than that of a technical regulation, insofar it also encompasses measures defining PPMs which do not refer to product characteristics.[36] But the negotiating history shows that the omission of 'their' does not imply an expansion of measures covered by the definition of standard. Indeed, Mexico proposed to align the definition of standard with that of technical regulation towards the end of Uruguay Round. All but one of the delegations involved that expressed an opinion stated that they were prepared to accept Mexico's proposal as an improvement to the text.[37]

[32] A Herwig, 'Too much Zeal on Seals? Animal Welfare, Public Morals and Consumer Ethics at the Bar of the WTO' (2016) 15(1) *World Trade Review* 109, 116.

[33] B Hoekman and PC Mavroidis, 'Regulatory Spillovers and the Trading System: From Coherence to Cooperation', E15 Task Force on Regulatory Systems Coherence Overview Paper (April 2015) 6.

[34] WTO Secretariat, *Trade and Environment at the WTO* (Geneva, 2004) 17; CR Conrad, *Processes and Production Methods (PPMs) in WTO Law: Interfacing Trade and Social Goals* (Cambridge University Press, 2011) 381.

[35] WTO Secretariat, 'Negotiating History of the Coverage of the Agreement on Technical Barriers to Trade with regard to Labelling Requirements, Voluntary Standards, and Processes and Production Methods Unrelated to Product Characteristics', WT/CTE/W/10 (29 August, 1995) para 146.

[36] E Partiti, 'What Use is an Unloaded Gun? The Substantive Disciplines of the WTO TBT Code of Good Practice and its Application to Private Standards Pursuing Public Objectives' (2017) 20 (4) *Journal of International Economic Law* 829, 833.

[37] WTO Secretariat (n 35) para 150.

Although the negotiating history appears to support the position that only PR-PPMs are covered in the definition of standard, it is not clear whether the AB will adhere to such a narrow interpretation. To begin with, if NPR-PPMs were not covered by the TBT Agreement, then both standards and technical regulations based on NPR-PPMs would be scrutinised under the GATT 1994. The irony of this exclusion is that subjecting such measures to the TBT Agreement would actually allay concerns over their protectionist effects or unilateralist abuse.[38] Second, the AB seldom resorts to *traveaux préparatoires* in practice because they are only a supplementary means of interpretation.[39] Taking a strong textualist approach set forth in the Vienna Convention on the Law of Treaties (VCLT), standards based on NPR-PPMs could be regarded as being 'related' to product characteristics.[40]

The second sentence of Annex 1.2 deals with 'terminology, symbols, packaging, marking or labelling requirements as they apply to product, process or production methods'. One view holds that even though the word 'related' was omitted, the second sentence is only illustrative of the first sentence and NPR-PPMs are excluded from both the first and the second sentences.[41] This interpretation is contested by an opposite view that the TBT Agreement applies to all labelling requirements, without regard to the nature of PPMs. The second sentence is additional to the first sentence and not merely illustrative.[42] This debate also took place in discussions of Item 3(b) on the agenda of the WTO Committee on Trade and Environment (CTE) working program which focuses on eco-labelling schemes and measures and their relationship to the provisions of the TBT Agreement.[43]

This debate has become increasingly irrelevant in practice. With the purpose of clarifying the coverage of the TBT Agreement with respect to labelling requirements, the TBT Committee took the decision that mandatory labelling requirements were subject to TBT notification provisions regardless of the kind of information provided on the label. Similarly, in the First Triennial Review of the TBT Agreement, the TBT Committee agreed that:

> … without prejudice to the view of Members concerning the coverage and application of the Agreement, the obligation to publish notices of draft standards containing voluntary labelling requirements under paragraph L of the Code of Good Practice is *not dependent upon the kind of information provided on the label.*'[44]

[38] J McDonald, 'Domestic Regulation, International Standards, and Technical Barriers to Trade' (2005) 4 *World Trade Review* 249, 255.

[39] E Partiti, 'The Appellate Body Report in *US- Tuna II* and Its Impact on Eco-Labelling and Standardisation' (2013) 40 *Legal Issues of Economic Integration* 73, 79.

[40] Vranes (n 30) 342.

[41] EP Bartenhagen, 'The Intersection of Trade and the Environment: An Examination of the Impact of the TBT Agreement on Ecolabelling Programs' (1997) 17 *Virginia Environmental Law Journal* 51, 74.

[42] Communication from Canada (n 25) para 6.

[43] The CTE Committee, 'Eco-Labelling Programmes', WT/CTE/W/23 (19 March 1996) 17.

[44] The TBT Committee, 'First Triennial Review of the Operation and Implementation of the Agreement on Technical Barriers to Trade', G/TBT/5 (19 November 1997) para 12.

In practice, many WTO Members have notified the WTO eco-labelling programs based on NPR-PPMs.[45]

The WTO case law has also confirmed that labelling requirements, regardless of the information contained, should be scrutinised under the TBT Agreement. In other words, the labelling scheme *as such* constitutes a product characteristic and is covered by the TBT Agreement.[46] In *US – Tuna II*, the US 'dolphin-safe' labelling requirements were based on the NPR-PPM criteria of fishing processes. However, the AB supported the panel's evaluation that the US labelling scheme fell within the scope of the TBT Agreement.[47] In *US – Cool*, country of origin labelling requirements that did not bear any connection with physical characteristics or PPMs were also considered as falling under the TBT Agreement.[48] By implication, voluntary labelling schemes are also within the scope of the TBT Code of Good Practice.

## C. Recognised Body

There is no definition of what constitutes a 'recognised body' in the TBT Agreement. In interpreting the term 'recognised body', useful references may be drawn from the AB's interpretation in *US – Tuna II*. In *US – Tuna II*, the AB held that either WTO Members or their official national standardising bodies must recognise the standardising body in question.[49] Evidence of recognition by the informed public will not suffice. Otherwise all standard- setting bodies may claim legitimacy and exert de facto normative force on exporters in international trade, which is clearly not the case.[50] Both a governmental body and a non-governmental body could be a 'recognised body' for the purpose of Annex 1(2).[51] The meaning of the term 'recognise', as the AB reasoned, ranges from a factual end to a normative end.[52] The factual dimension of recognition would appear to require, at a minimum, that a WTO Member is aware, or have reason to expect, that the body in question is engaged in standardisation activities.[53] For the normative dimension of the concept, evidence such

[45] The TBT Committee, 'Draft Minutes of the Meeting Held on 20 October 1995', G/TBT/W/15 (22 November 1995) para 31.

[46] Panel Report, *EC- Trade Marks and Geographical Indications*, WTO/DS290/R, adopted 20 April 2005, para 7.451.

[47] *US – Tuna II* (n 2) para 199.

[48] Panel Report, *United States- Certain Country of Origin Labelling (COOL) Requirements*, WT/DS384/R, adopted 18 November 2011, para 7.212.

[49] *US – Tuna II* (n 2) para 363.

[50] H Ward, 'Trade and Environmental Issues in Voluntary Eco-labelling and Life Cycle Analysis' (1997) 6 *Review of European Community and International Economic Law* 139, 143.

[51] J Pauwelyn, 'Rule-Based Trade 2.0? The Rise of Informal Rules and International Standards and How They may Outcompete WTO Treaties' (2014) 17 (4) *Journal of International Economic Law* 739, 750; *Partiti* (n 39) 91–93.

[52] *US – Tuna II* (n 2) para 361.

[53] Ibid, para 362.

as a WTO Member's participation in a body's standardising activities or the recognition of the resulting standard could suggest that a body is a 'recognised body'.[54] A body that develops a single standard could still be a recognised body if other evidence suggests that the body's standardisation activities are recognised. It is not necessary that the preparation and adoption of standards is a principal function of the body in question.[55] The evidence that this body follows the Code of Good Practice (CGP) in Annex 3 to the TBT Agreement and the *TBT Committee Decision on Principles for the Development of International Standards, Guides, and Recommendations with Relation to Articles 2, 5 and Annex 3 to the Agreement* ('TBT Committee Decision') in standard development may be relevant to determine whether it is a 'recognised body'.[56]

## D. The Identifiable Requirement

For the 'identifiable' requirement, it does not suggest that those products need to be named or otherwise expressly identified.[57] Even though a product standard does not expressly identify products by name, they may be still identifiable through the characteristic that is the subject of the standard. In *EC – Sardines*, the EC required that only preserved *Sardina pilchardus* could be named 'Preserved Sardines'. The preserved *Saridna sagax* were, by virtue of the EC regulation, prohibited from being identified and marketed under the term 'sardines'. The EC argued that since the preserved *Sardinop sagax* was not specifically mentioned in the EC regulation, it was not an identifiable product. The AB rejected the EC's argument because *Sardinop sagax* was prohibited from using the term 'Sardines' and the EC regulation had already been enforced against preserved sardines made from *Sardinops sagax*.[58] In other words, *Sardinops sagax* was an identifiable product.

## E. The Voluntary Requirement

The last element of a product standard is that the compliance with a standard is voluntary. This is the main criterion differentiating it from a technical regulation in the TBT terminology.[59] The voluntary/mandatory distinction has been

[54] Ibid, para 392.
[55] Ibid, para 394.
[56] Ibid, para 376.
[57] *EC– Asbestos* (n 3) para 70.
[58] WTO Appellate Body Report, *European Communities – Trade Description of Sardines* (*EC – Sardines*), WT/DS231/AB/R, adopted 23 October 2002, para 185.
[59] AE Appleton, 'The Agreement on Technical Barriers to Trade', in PFJ Macrory, *The World Trade Organization: Legal, Economic and Political Analysis* (Springer 2005) 379.

most contentious in cases involving labelling requirements.[60] In *US – Tuna II*, the preference of US consumers for dolphin-friendly tuna is so intense that all major American retailers no long sell tuna caught by setting on dolphins.[61] The US 'dolphin-safe' labelling scheme prescribed that tuna harvested in the Easter Tropical Pacific Ocean (ETP) by a vessel using purse-seine nets may be labelled 'dolphin safe' only if certain conditions were met. The issue before the panel was whether the US 'dolphin-safe' labelling provisions and its implementing regulations were voluntary.

As the US and one dissenting panel member forcefully argued, there are strong reasons why the 'dolphin safe' labelling scheme should be categorised as a voluntary standard. First, any labelling scheme must set out mandatory parameters to be satisfied in order to use a particular label. If products that fall short of meeting the criteria could use the label, then the label *ipso facto* is denied of any raison d'être.[62] Thus, a labelling requirement, in itself, cannot be dispositive of the proper characterisation of the measure. Both a technical regulation and a standard could embody a labelling requirement.[63] Second, the 'dolphin-safe' labelling requirement is mandatory if its use is a necessary condition to market tuna in the US.[64] In this case, nothing made the right of access to the US market conditional on the label. Importers retain the option to disregard the label and to market tuna without making any claim about dolphin safety.[65] Finally, even if the US measure prohibited any alternative labels, this would not modify its essentially voluntary nature, as it was simply a usual enforcement method to prevent misleading or false declarations.[66]

However, the AB adopted a different analytical approach to interpret 'mandatory'. Rather than focusing solely on whether compliance with the dolphin-safe labelling scheme was a prerequisite for market access, the AB emphasised that the characterisation must be made in the light of the characteristics of the measure at issue and the circumstances of the case. In particular, it requires an analysis of whether the measure consists of a law or a regulation enacted by a WTO Member; whether it prescribes or prohibits particular conduct; whether it sets out specific requirements that constitute the sole means of addressing a particular matter, and the nature of the matter addressed by

[60] A Davies, 'Technical Regulations and Standards under the WTO Agreement on Technical Barriers to Trade' (2014) 41 (1) *Legal Issues of Economic Integration* 37, 47.

[61] Panel Report, *US – Tuna II*, WT/DS381/R, para 7.352.

[62] PC Mavroidis, 'Driftin' too far from Shore- Why the Test for Compliance with the TBT Agreement Developed by the WTO Appellate Body is Wrong, and What Should the AB have Done Instead' (2013) 12 (3) *World Trade Review* 509, 523.

[63] *US – Tuna II* (n 2) para 187.

[64] AO Sykes, *Product Standards for Internationally Integrated Markets* (The Brookings Institute, Washington, 1995) 2.

[65] Panel Report, *US – Tuna II* (n 61) para 7.146; LJ Ankersmit and JEC Lawrence, 'The Future of Environmental Labelling: *US – Tuna* II and the Scope of the TBT' (2012) 39 *Legal Issues of Economic Integration* 127, 133.

[66] Ibid, para 7.153–7.158.

the measure'.[67] The AB proceeded to highlight three distinctive features of the US 'dolphin-safe' labelling scheme that rendered it mandatory in nature. First, the US labelling provisions and its implementing regulations were not private acts by firms or NGOs. Instead, they constituted legislative or regulatory acts of the US federal authorities. Second, the US measures established *a single and legally mandated* set of requirements with respect to the broad subject of dolphin-safe tuna products in the US. Any producer, importer, exporter, distributor or seller of tuna products must comply with the criteria in order to make *any 'dolphin-safe' claim.* Third, the US measure provided for *specific enforcement mechanisms*, which treated any statement on a tuna product regarding dolphin safety that did not meet the conditions of the US labelling scheme as a deceptive practice. In doing so, the US measure prescribed in a broad and exhaustive manner the conditions that apply for making any assertion on a tuna product as to 'dolphin-safe'.[68]

Despite all the criticisms levelled against the AB's characterisation of the US 'dolphin-safe' label,[69] the AB's nuanced approach to the mandatory/voluntary distinction is compelling. The fundamental reason why the AB views the 'dolphin safe' label mandatory appears to be the second feature of the labelling scheme: it is designed and implemented in an overbroad and exclusive manner. In effect, it covers the entire field of what 'dolphin-safe' means in relation to tuna products. Any other labels and statements regarding dolphin safe are, in themselves, a violation of law. Implicitly, the AB suggested that the functioning of the US labelling scheme in the real world was de facto mandatory.[70] By contrast, the first and the third feature of the US labelling scheme, taken separately, are not distinctive features of a technical regulation. It is entirely possible for a government to promulgate a voluntary labelling requirement and enforces general laws against deceptive practices, such as the US Energy Star Programme and the EU Ecolabelling scheme. After *US – Tuna II*, in addition to the conventional wisdom that the compliance is mandatory when a label is required for market access,[71] an 'exclusive' label, in the sense that it is the only way to meet the requirement and is enforced by the governmental power, will transform what would otherwise be a 'standard' into a 'technical regulation'.[72]

[67] *US – Tuna II* (n 2) para 188.

[68] Ibid, para 199.

[69] Mavroidis (n 62) 522–523; M Kim, 'The 'Standard' in the GATT/WTO TBT Agreements: Origin, Evolution and Application' (2018) 52 (5) *Journal of World Trade* 765, 785–788.

[70] A Kudryavtsev, 'The TBT Agreement in Context', in T Epps and M Trebilcock (eds), *Research Handbook on the WTO and Technical Barriers to Trade* (Edward Elgar, 2013) 32.

[71] GATT, *Report (1992) of the Committee on Technical Barriers to Trade*, L/7107 (3 Nov. 1992).

[72] H Schepel, 'Between Standards and Regulation: On the Concept of 'de facto mandatory standards' after Tuna II and Fra.bo' in P Delimatsis (ed), *The Law, Economics and Politics of International Standardization* 199 (*Cambridge University Press*, 2015) 211.

In the last analysis, it does not really make much difference how to categorise the US labelling scheme. Had the AB held that the US labelling scheme was a 'standard', the complainant Mexico would then be limited to an Article 4.1 claim which requires WTO Members to ensure that their central government standardising bodies accept and comply with the CGP in Annex 3 to the TBT Agreement, and to claims under the GATT 1994.[73] As will be analysed in detail in Chapter 3 of this book, at least for standards adopted by central government standardising bodies, the TBT Agreement does not materially distinguish them from technical regulations either in terms of the content of substantive obligation or the manner of review and enforcement.[74] The outcome of the case would therefore not be any different even if the US labelling scheme were classified as a standard.

The *US – Tuna II* dispute is a good example of the real-world entanglement of public authority and private actors in the functioning of a particular labelling scheme.[75] In a world where the distinction between public and private, mandatory and voluntary is increasingly blurred, and that government involvement through monopolising certain labelling criteria is particularly susceptible to discrimination against foreign exporters, the AB's case-by-case approach by analysing the characteristics of the measure at issue and the circumstances of the case leaves the AB some room for maneuver in future disputes.

Finally, it should be pointed out that the current definition of 'standard' in the TBT Agreement is unique and WTO-specific. It is an original creation solely for the purpose of the GATT/WTO system. For example, the term 'standard' is defined in the ISO/IEC Guide 2: 2004 as:

> Document, established by consensus and approved by a recognised body, that provides for common and repeated use, rules, guidelines or characteristics for activities or their results, aimed at the achievement of the optimum degree of order in a given context'. Note: Standards should be based on the consolidated results of science, technology and experience, and aimed at the promotion of optimum community benefits.

Compared to the definition of 'standard' in the TBT Agreement, the scope of the ISO/IEC definition is both broader and narrower. It is broader because it covers both mandatory and voluntary standards, as well as services. It is narrower because it only covers documents adopted by consensus while the TBT also covers documents that are not based on consensus.[76]

[73] G Shaffer, 'United States – Measures Concerning the Importation, Marketing and Sale of Tuna and Tuna Products' (2013) 107 *American Journal of International Law* 192, 198; J Norpoth, 'Mysteries of the TBT Agreement Resolved? Lessons to Learn from Climate Policies and Developing Country Exporters from Recent TBT Disputes' (2013) 47(3) *Journal of World Trade* 575, 584.

[74] Davies (n 60) 62.

[75] MA Crowley and R Howse, '*Tuna – Dolphin II*: A Legal and Economic Analysis of the Appellate Body Report' (2014) 13 (2) *World Trade Review* 321, 325.

[76] AB Villarreal, *International Standardization and the Agreement on Technical Barriers to Trade* (Cambridge University Press, 2018) 127.

## II. PRODUCT STANDARDS AND INTERNATIONAL TRADE: ECONOMIC PERSPECTIVES

Outside the WTO context, the term 'standard' is widely used in a broader sense covering both voluntary and mandatory standards. In particular, economists do not distinguish between technical regulations and standards by their binding effects as WTO lawyers do, but generally refer to both types as standards because they have very similar economic effects.[77] In some recent bilateral FTAs, such as the Korea-Canada FTA, 'standard-related measures' cover both mandatory and voluntary measures. Given their similar economic effects, the term 'standards' in this section is used broadly to cover both voluntary standards and technical regulations.

### A. Market Failures and the Functions of Product Standards

Though product standards could be significant non-tariff barriers, it is naïve to argue for their elimination in international trade. Due to a range of market imperfections such as network externalities,[78] information asymmetry,[79] and negative externalities,[80] markets do not necessarily deliver the most efficient outcomes.[81] Standards are in essence public goods used by governments and private firms to address market failures, improve welfare and achieve public policy objectives.[82] The following are some typical examples of market failure in which product standards can solve and thus enhance market efficiency.

First, in so-called network industries, such as information and communication industries, the utility that a consumer derives from the consumption of the product does not depend only on the quantity and quality of the product itself, but also on the availability and variety of complementary goods and/or the number of the people using the same product or compatible ones. For example, the value of a mobile phone for a consumer increases when she buys compatible mobile phones that she can communicate with other people, and when the variety or quality of complementary goods, such as apps that can be used on the mobile phone, increases. Economists call such phenomenon 'network externalities'.[83] It is usually in the interest of consumers to

[77] Ibid, 78–79.

[78] Network externalities are the effects on a user of a product or service of others using the same or compatible products or services.

[79] Information asymmetry occurs when producers have information about the characteristics of goods they produce which users do not have when purchasing these goods.

[80] Negative externality arises when an agent's economic activity generates costs to others that the agent does not fully absorb, such as pollution.

[81] WTO Trade Report, *Trade and Public Policy: A Closer Look at Non-Tariff Measures in the 21st Century* (2012) 53.

[82] Villarreal (n 76) 78–79.

[83] O Shy, *The Economics of Network Industries* (Cambridge University Press, 2001) 3.

purchase the most popular product in the market in order to capture positive network externalities, because the increase in the sale of a given product results in lower prices, better quality and greater variety of its complementary goods. However, network industries are characterised by potential problems of coordination. Lack of information, different preferences and firms' marketing actions may lead to inefficient outcome of too many varieties of products being supplied and network externalities not captured.[84] In that case, a compatible standard solves the problem of coordination among consumers and firms. It can increase welfare because it promotes network effects by increasing the network of users adopting the same goods or compatible ones. The compatibility of standards is particularly important in supply chain trade, which involves a large number of firms in different locations who produce parts and components and then are assembled before being distributed to the final consumer. Standards therefore represent an important way to ensure the compatibility of inputs, parts and components from a host of suppliers. Moreover, standards play an important role in the diffusion of new technology in network industries. For example, it was not until 1999 when major companies of wireless technology agreed on a common standard that the Wi-Fi market took off, although vendors began to develop their proprietary wireless equipment as early as 1985.[85]

Second, product standards help to overcome the problem of asymmetric information about product characteristics both between suppliers and consumers, and among producers serving the same market.[86] Information asymmetry occurs when producers have information about the characteristics of goods they produce which users do not have when purchasing these goods, for example the quality of food or washing machines. In the case of credence goods such as the amount of fluoride in toothpaste or the amount of calories in a snack, consumer may not learn the quality of the goods even after their consumption.[87] In these cases, information asymmetry may significantly hamper the efficient functioning of markets. The most typical example of such inefficiency is the undersupply of quality products because consumers are not able to distinguish the better quality goods and tend to buy the cheapest on offer. Product standards can solve the information asymmetry problem and enhance efficiency. Take product safety standards as an example. The standards can prescribe many types of requirements to ensure safety, from design to ingredients and from

[84] PA David and S Greenstein, 'The Economics of Compatibility Standards: An Introduction to Recent Research' (1990) 1 *Economics of Innovation and New Technology* 3, 13–14.

[85] *The Economist*, 'A Brief History of Wi-Fi' (June 12, 2004).

[86] World Trade Report, *Exploring the Links between Trade, Standards and the WTO* (2005) 51.

[87] Credence goods refer to goods and services whose quality cannot be determined before, during, or sometimes even after their use. The usual examples are services – medical, legal and financial services – where the consumer is largely dependent on the expertise and counsel given by the provider of the service. See MR Darby and E Karni, 'Free Competition and the Optimal Amount of Fraud' (1973) 16 (1) *The Journal of Law & Economics* 67–88.

manufacture process to performance. Mandatory standards in such a scenario act like minimum standards and rule out the supply of unsafe products below the required quality level determined by the standard. If the government has strong reasons to ban certain sub-quality products from the market, for instance in order to protect the health of consumers, the government will choose mandatory standards. By contrast, voluntary standards in combination with a label do not rule out the supply of lower quality products, but they allow the consumers to appreciate higher quality products and ensure that high quality products are not pushed out of the market. Voluntary standards will therefore be preferred to mandatory standards if the risks involved are considered to be acceptable to society.[88]

Third, standards may help to mitigate instances of externalities or market imperfections where the market, left to itself, would fail to provide the optimal level of a good or service. Take environmental externalities as an example. Environmental externalities are a form of market failure that arises because the use of environmental resources such as air and water is not properly priced. Therefore, producers may make use of these resources at a rate that is not socially optimal.[89] The costs arising from serious environmental degradation may outweigh the benefits obtained from producing more goods. In this case, emission standards help to address the pollution externalities problem by obliging firms to internalise the costs of maintaining an acceptably low degree of environmental damage.[90]

## B. The Trade Effects of Product Standards

The effects of standards on the volume and direction of trade flows tend to be complex and there is only rather limited empirical literature on the subject. An important point emerging from both economic theory and empirical evidence is that there is no monotonic relationship between standardisation and trade flows. Standards can be both trade creating and trade hampering.[91] It is thus important to distinguish different types of standards and to analyse their effects on trade flows on a case-by-case basis.

Take compatible standards as an example. The adoption of incompatible standards both in domestic markets and across countries works as a market segmentation device and reduces trade. Compatible standards allow for the realisation of economies of scale and network externalities to be captured.

[88] WTO Trade Report (n 86) 42.

[89] M Fairbrother, 'Externalities: Why Environmental Sociology should Bring them in' (2016) 2(4) *Journal of Environmental Sociology* 375, 376.

[90] WTO Trade Report (n 86) 50.

[91] RL Pinto de Andrade, 'The Positive Consequences of Non-Tariff Barriers' (2009) 43(2) *Journal of World Trade* 363, 363–378.

When network externalities are large, countries have an incentive to harmonise standards or make them compatible so there will be even more international trade.[92] The available empirical evidence shows that intra-industry trade can be spurred by greater standard-setting activity in industrial sectors, suggesting that standards play an important role in increasing compatibility. On the other hand, compatibility standards can also be a source of market power. This is the case, for example, when a firm standard is adopted as the de facto standard in the information technology sector. When a de facto standard conveys market power, it will limit competition and act as a deterrent to trade.

The trade effects of product standards also depend on whether they address genuine market failures. If a standard is applied for the purpose of protecting domestic producers, both trade and welfare in the importing country decrease. However, even if a standard corrects an existing market failure, its trade effects are ambiguous. A standard may increase trade, decrease it or leave it unaltered. The specific outcome will to a large extent depend on the standard's effect on the relative costs of domestic and foreign producers.[93] To comply with standards typically increases producers' costs. They may imply a fixed cost when producers switch from producing one product variety to another product variety, an increase in production costs when additional product lines are required to produce products that meet the standard and costs related to conformity assessment procedures. If a standard affects marginal costs, trade will tend to decrease if the cost increase for foreign producers exceeds that experienced by domestic producers. Theoretically this is the most likely scenario as in the course of developing standards, governments will be most responsive to domestic producers' concerns.[94] But the outcome also depends on many other factors, like the level of competition in exporting and importing countries and the willingness of consumers in different countries to pay higher prices. For example, although compliance with product standards can raise producer costs, if compliance with the standard resolves uncertainty about the quality or safety of the imported product, consumer costs are reduced and greater consumer confidence can increase the demand for the item. Trade will increase or fall depending on whether the positive effects on demand is greater than the negative effect on supply.[95]

It is important to note that the trade effects of standards and their welfare effects may diverge because many product standards mitigate market failures and therefore involve social benefits that will not be fully captured by trade flows. For example, a standard adopted to improve consumers' information or

[92] N Gandal and O Shy, 'Standardisation Policy and International Trade' (2001) 53 (2) *Journal of International Economics* 363.

[93] World Trade Report (n 81) 62.

[94] AL Hillman and HW Ursprung, 'Domestic Politics, Foreign Interests, and International Trade Policy' (1988) 78(4) *The American Economic Review* 729, 730.

[95] World Trade Report (n 81) 136.

reduce the negative effects of environmental externalities may increase domestic welfare of the standard-adopting country, but with negative trade effects.[96]

Notwithstanding the different theoretical models and their limitations, the existing empirical literature finds that, at the aggregate level, product standards may not be associated with lower trade.[97] The disaggregated trade data further show that the effects of product standards depend on the type of sector. Specifically, import-specific national standards have a negative impact on imports in the non-manufacturing sectors, in particular in agricultural products.[98] By contrast, product standards have positive impact on imports in the manufacturing sector[99] (including oils, chemicals, manufacturing and machinery), electronic products[100] and instruments for measurement and testing.[101] This is because information costs are high in these sectors. Standards provide exporters with valuable information about market preferences and reduce transaction costs. Therefore, the reduction of information costs outweighs adaptation costs of adjusting to new standards and trade increases in these sectors.[102]

Product standards also appear to have a negative effect on export market diversification. Small firms and firms that outsource their immediate inputs, in particular if they are in developing countries, appear to be most affected by product standards.[103] In contrast, exports from developed countries to other developed countries are not significantly impeded by standards. Moreover, there is a wide variation across developing countries. For example, examining the trade effects of notified TBT and SPS measures adopted by major developed countries including the US and the EU, Disdier and others found that exports from African, Caribbean and Pacific (ACP) countries and Latin American countries are most negatively affected by such measures both in terms of the

[96] J Beghin, A-Celia Disdier, S Marette and F Van Tongeren, 'Welfare Costs and the Benefits of Non-tariff Measures in Trade: A Conceptual Framework and Application' (2012) 11(3) *World Trade Review* 356, 357.

[97] P Swann, P Temple and M Shurmer, 'Standards and Trade Performance: The UK Experience', (1996) 106 (438) *The Economic Journal* 1297, 1311; P Temple and G Urga, 'The Competitiveness of UK Manufacturing: Evidence from Imports' (1997) 49 (2) *Oxford Economic Papers* 207, 224–5.

[98] Y Li and JC Beghin, 'A Meta-analysis of Estimates of the Impact of Technical Barriers to Trade' (2012) 34 (3) *Journal of Policy Modelling* 497, 511.

[99] J Moenius, 'Information Versus Product Adaptation: The Role of Standards in Trade' (2004), 25 https://ssrn.com/abstract=608022 accessed on 1 March 2020; L Fontagne, M Mimouni and J-M Pasteels, 'Estimating the Impact of Environmental SPS and TBT on International Trade' (2005) 22(9) *Integration and Trade* 7, 19.

[100] J Moenius, 'Do National Standards Hinder or Promote Trade in Electrical Products' (2006) International Electrotechnical Commission Centenary Challenge Papers 54 (2006) 59.

[101] K Blind, 'The Impacts of Innovations and Standards on Trade of Measurement and Testing Products: Empirical Results of Switzerland's Bilateral Trade Flows with Germany, France and the UK' (2001) 13(4) *Information Economics and Policy* 439, 458–9.

[102] Moenius (n 99) 25–26.

[103] MX Chen, T Otsuki and JS Wilson, 'Do Standards Matter for Export Success?' (2006) World Bank Policy Research Working Paper 3809, 24.

number of products and the magnitude of the trade effect, while the impact on Asian countries appears insignificant.[104] Furthermore, larger exporters from developing countries gained trade shares as they are better able to comply with standards, while smaller exporters are less able to comply with standards leading to trade losses.[105]

## III. A TAXONOMY OF PRODUCT STANDARDS

From a trade law perspective, if the term 'product standard' is used in its broad sense, it is possible to categorise product standards pursuant to four criteria, ie, (i) the issue of government involvement (whether the scheme is administered by public authorities or privately sponsored); (ii) its legal effect (whether standards are mandatory or voluntary); (iii) its scope (whether it applies to product-related characteristics and PR-PPMs only, or NPR-PPMs are also covered and (iv) the institutional setting where standards are drawn up (national, regional or international standards).[106] Accordingly, product standards could be categorised as public standards and private standards, mandatory standards and voluntary standards; product standards and PPMs; and national, regional and international standards.

It must be stressed that the line separating these pairs of concepts is not always clearly drawn. Standards are almost never either wholly public or wholly private, and neither are standards bodies.[107] Even where public authorities decide to set product standards themselves, it is very rarely the case that they do not enter into consultations or even negotiations with private parties. Indeed, many public standards are based on technical specifications and initiatives from private standard-setting organisations. Conversely, even where standards are set by private parties for voluntary use, government has frequently participated in their development through public-private partnerships, or exercised some influence over the content and use of these standards through approval of the standards. The question thus arises as to whether such standards should be considered public standards or private standards.[108] On the other hand, some private standards may be considered as public standards because their adoption should be attributed to the government in view of the governmental incentives

[104] A-C Disdier, B Fekadu, C Murillo, SA Wong, 'Trade Effects of SPS and TBT Measures on Tropical and Diversification Products' (2008) ICTSD Issue Paper No 12, 92.

[105] SM Anders and JA Caswell, 'Standards as Barriers Versus Standards as Catalysts: Assessing the Impact of HACCP Implementation on U.S. Seafood Imports' (2009) 91(2) *American Journal of Agricultural Economics* 310, 319–320.

[106] E Vranes, 'Climate Labelling and the WTO', *European Yearbook of International Economic law* (Springer, 2011) 211–213; WTO Trade Report (n 86) 76–85.

[107] H Schepel, *The Constitution of Private Governance: Product Standards in the Regulation of Integrating Markets* (Hart Publishing, 2005) 4.

[108] WTO Trade Report (n 86) 32.

for private actors to act in a particular manner.[109] Similarly, though product standards are legally voluntary, they may be de facto mandatory in international trade in the sense that companies have little choice but to comply with them as non-adherence would in practice make it extremely challenging to sell their products in a particular market.[110]

Nor are these classifications mutually exclusive. For example, product standards administered by public authorities can be either mandatory or voluntary. In the case of mandatory standards, only standardised products are allowed to circulate the market and they are called technical regulations in the TBT Agreement. Public voluntary standards, sometimes referred to as 'optional laws', are standards that are created by public bodies but whose adoption is voluntary.[111] Even those products not conforming to the standards can be supplied to the market. If standards are only voluntary, it is not easy for consumers to distinguish between different types of products in many cases. Labels are then necessary to support the voluntary standard policy.[112] Lastly, both mandatory and voluntary standards can prescribe either product standards or PPMs.

As this book is mainly about voluntary product standards, I will focus on three types of standards: voluntary standard administered by central government standardising bodies (Chapter 3), international standards (Chapter 4) and standards sponsored by non-governmental bodies (Chapter 5) with case studies in Chapter 6.

## IV. THE GATT/WTO LEGAL FRAMEWORK OF PRODUCT STANDARDS

### A. The Negotiating History of Product Standards in the GATT/WTO System

#### *i. The Tokyo Round*

The GATT contracting parties did not specifically address the issue of non-tariff trade barriers (NTBs) until the closing sessions of the Kennedy Round (1963–1967).[113] Soon after, the Committee on Trade in Industrial Products (the Committee) was established to work on NTB negotiations. The Committee classified the entire NTBs into six categories, one of which was 'standards involving import and domestic goods', including industrial standards, health and safety standards, weights and metrics, product content requirements,

[109] Panel Report, *Japan-Measures Affecting Consumer Photographic Film and Paper*, WT/DS44/R, adopted 22 April 1998, para 10.49.

[110] WTO Trade Report (n 81) 211.

[111] A Hammoudi et al (eds), *Food Safety, Market Organisation, Trade and Development* (Springer 2015) 79–80.

[112] WTO Trade Report (n 86) 33.

[113] GATT Sub-Committee on Non-Tariff Barriers and Other Special Problems, TN.64/3/Rev.2 (3 Nov. 1966).

labelling and container regulations, processing standards, marking requirements, and packaging requirements.[114] It was clear by then that contracting parties' concerns over multiple and divergent product standards increased. The Committee concluded that technical barriers were mainly caused by regulations, standards, and their enforcement, and trade restrictiveness was largely attributable to disparities in those measures across countries. Specifically, it was observed that de facto mandatory standards were interrupting market competition.[115]

Interestingly, almost from the start of negotiations on technical barriers to trade, the GATT contracting parties emphasised the need to draw a clear distinction between mandatory regulations, which were issued by the governments, and voluntary standards, which were usually issued by private organisations on a national, regional or international basis. This distinction was deemed important because it affected the possible scope of government action to address the relating trade concerns.[116] In 1973, the Committee prepared a draft code entitled 'proposed GATT Code of Conduct for Preventing Technical Barriers to Trade' (the Draft Code) even before the official launch of the Tokyo Round (1974–1979).[117] In the Draft Code, the term 'standard' was broadly defined to embrace voluntary standards, mandatory standards, test methods and testing specifications. However, PPMs and company standards for the company's own production or purchasing purposes were explicitly excluded from the definition. Mandatory standard was defined as 'a standard with which it is obligatory to comply by virtue of an action by an authority endowed with the necessary *legal power*' whilst there was no such legal obligation to comply with a voluntary standard.[118] Thus, voluntary standards cover all standards that are not legally obliged to comply with, including both law-based non-compulsory standards and de facto mandatory standards.[119]

As the term 'standard' was used to denote both mandatory and voluntary standards in the 1973 Draft Code, different obligations regarding preparation, adoption and use of standards were considered for three categories: mandatory central government standards, mandatory local government standards and voluntary standards. For mandatory central government standards, first level mandatory obligations were imposed on the GATT contracting parties. By contrast, second level obligations were specified for the other two categories of standards: ie, GATT contracting parties were only obliged to use all

[114] GATT Doc. MTN/3B/3, Part 3 of the Inventory of Non-Tariff Measures: Standards Involving Imports and Domestic Goods 11 (14 Feb. 1974).

[115] GATT Doc. COM.IND/W/36, Summary of Proposals in Reports of the Five Working Groups on Non-Tariff Barriers 2–3 (1970).

[116] Committee on Trade in Industrial Products – Report to Council, L/3496 (10 Feb 1971) 54.

[117] GATT Doc. COM.IND/W/108, Group 3 on Standards: Report (25 June 1973).

[118] Ibid, Annex 1.3.

[119] Kim (n 69) 773.

reasonable means within their power to ensure that the relevant obligations were met.[120]

Despite the conceptual 'mandatory' and 'voluntary' standard distinction, it made little difference to distinguish the two from a regulatory perspective except the different obligations imposed on GATT contracting parties. This is because the Draft Code required both mandatory and voluntary standards to be non-discriminatory, least-trade-restrictive, preferably based on performance rather than design, and based on international standards. Contracting parties were encouraged to actively participate in international standardisation in respect of all standards. Transparency obligations applied to both, with the only exception that central governments had to notify all mandatory standards, not voluntary standards, to the GATT.[121] These features remained unchanged even in the WTO TBT Agreement.

The following Tokyo Round gave center stage to the negotiation of improved and expanded rules on non-tariff measures. The main outcome was the conclusion of the Agreement on Technical Barriers to Trade (the Standards Code). The Standards Code operated with respect to trade in industrial and agricultural products but did not apply to standards in government procurement and private standards.[122] Neither did it directly regulate PPMs. However, it provided that a party could invoke dispute settlement procedures if obligations under it were being circumvented by PPM requirements.[123] The Standards Code marked the most significant advance in the GATT/WTO system's efforts to deal with product standards since the GATT rules were first negotiated after the Second World War.[124]

Compared to the 1973 Draft Code, the Standards Code has made a number of significant amendments. First, the TBT subgroup observed that the terms and definitions proposed in the 1973 Draft Code, such as 'mandatory standard' and 'voluntary standard' were either substantially different from, or no corresponding term could be found in the definitions established by the UN Economic Commission for Europe (ECE) and International Standardisation Organisation (ECE/ISO) joint group.[125] In particular, the meaning of 'standard' was more limited than the corresponding ECE/ISO definition since it excluded company standards, standards relating to services and codes of practice. This could potentially cause a great deal of confusion and uncertainty. Consequently, the TBT subgroup agreed to harmonise the terms by adopting the general application of ECE/ISO definitions whilst modifying certain terms to meet GATT purposes.[126] After the amendment, the

[120] WTO Secretariat (n 35) 15.
[121] Art 2 of the 1973 Draft Code.
[122] Arts 1.3, 1.4 and Annex 1.1 of the Standards Code.
[123] Ibid, Art 14.25.
[124] World Trade Report (n 81) 42–3.
[125] GATT Doc. MTN/NTM/W/14, Definitions: Working Paper by the Secretariat (26 June 1975).
[126] Note by the Chairman, 'Meeting of January/February 1976', MTN/NTM/12 (24 Feb 1976).

original terms 'standard', 'mandatory standard' and 'voluntary standard' in the 1973 Draft Code were replaced by 'technical specification', 'technical regulation' and 'standard' respectively. As a result, the term 'standard' was defined as 'a technical specification approved by a recognised body for repeated or continuous application with which compliance is not mandatory'. A 'technical specification' was defined as

> a specification contained in a document which lays down characteristics of a product such as levels of quality, performance, safety or dimensions. It may include, or deal exclusively with terminology, symbols, testing and test methods, packaging, marking or labelling requirements as they apply to a product.

However, technical specifications prepared by an individual company for its own production or consumption requirements were still excluded from the definition of 'standard'.[127]

Second, the Standards Code introduced a new system where the regulatory framework was exclusively based on standardisation bodies, ie, central, local and non-governmental bodies. It discarded the previous standard-and-body linkage in the 1973 Draft Code such as mandatory central government standard. This change removed explicit conceptual link between a measure and a body.[128] For example, it was no longer necessary for technical regulations to be enforced by a public body with legal authority, as the definition for 'non-government body' stipulated that it could have the legal power to enforce a technical regulation.[129] Instead, Article 2 of the Standards Code combined under a single section the disciplines on technical regulations *and* standards by central government bodies, and first level of mandatory obligations were imposed on these bodies.[130] This change was based on the perception that voluntary standards prepared by central government bodies should be dealt with separately from those prepared by other bodies, such as local government bodies and non-government bodies. Article 3 and Article 4 adopted a similar structure, addressing technical regulations *and* standards by local government bodies and non-government bodies respectively. For these two categories of standards, only second level of best efforts obligations was imposed.[131]

### *ii. The Uruguay Round*

The Standards Code was a plurilateral agreement to which only 43 countries, a third of the GATT membership, opted to sign. In the decade following the Tokyo Round, a consensus emerged that the Standards Code had failed to stem

[127] Annex 1.3 Explanatory Note of the Standards Code.
[128] Kim (n 69) 778.
[129] Annex 1.8 of the Standards Code.
[130] Art 2 of the Standards Code.
[131] RW Middleton, 'The GATT Standards Code' (1980) 14 *Journal of World Trade* 201, 211–212.

disruptions of trade caused by proliferating technical restrictions due to its disintegrated structure.[132] This consensus resulted in the adoption in the Uruguay Round (1986–1993) of the TBT Agreement, which is implemented universally binding on all WTO Members. The TBT Agreement sought to further improve, clarify and expand the Standards Code, with a particular emphasis on clarifying its regulatory boundary and enhancing implementation by local and non-governmental bodies.[133]

First, after the Tokyo Round, since the ISO/IEC Guide 2 revised its definition of standard in 1986, the GATT negotiating parties suggested that the definitions contained in Annex 1 of the Standards Code be amended on the basis of the new ISO definitions. Consequently, the WTO TBT Agreement completely removed the term 'technical specification' and only the definitions of 'technical regulation' and 'standard' remained. Elements of the previous definition of technical specification now become core parts of technical regulation and standard. Second, recognising a general tendency that PPM-related requirements were increasingly used in industrial and agricultural production, the Contracting Parties decided for the first time to extend explicitly the TBT Agreement's regulatory coverage to PPMs.[134] Third, it was clarified that no matter what may be printed on the label, labelling requirement itself would be considered as either a technical regulation or standard.[135]

Finally, one of the main concerns during the negotiations was that the Tokyo Standards Code had a fundamental implementation problem on the part of local and non-government bodies. The GATT contracting parties had very different domestic constitutional and regulatory systems and thus might face inequality of obligations under the Standards Code. For example, countries where private bodies play leading roles in national standardisation, central governments had far less power to bring the activities of those bodies into conformity with the Standards Code, and were less likely to achieve the level of implementation that governments in centralised systems could do. This problem was aggravated by a worldwide shift towards a greater use of standards drawn up by non-governmental bodies and a lesser use of technical regulations drawn up by central government bodies.[136] To address such concerns, the EC proposed that disciplines pertaining to 'non-governmental standards bodies' be clarified. For this purpose, it proposed the CGP for non-governmental standardising bodies as an annex to the TBT Agreement. The EC clarified that acceptance of the

[132] D Roberts, 'Preliminary Assessment of the Effects of the WTO Agreement on Sanitary and Phytosanitary Trade Regulations' (1998) 1 *Journal of International Economic Law* 377, 380.

[133] Note by the Secretariat, 'Agreement on Technical Barriers to Trade: Aspects of the Agreement Proposed for Negotiation', MTN.GNC/NG8/W/83/Add.3 (23 July 1990).

[134] Note by the WTO Secretariat (n 35) 37–45.

[135] Committee on Technical Barriers to Trade, 'Decisions and Recommendations Adopted by the Committee since 1 January 1980', TBT/16/Rev.5 (18 November 1992) 23.

[136] Proposal by the European Economic Community, 'A Code of Good Practice for Non-Governmental Bodies in the Agreement on Technical Barriers to Trade', TBT/W/110 (7 July 1988).

CGP would be voluntary, subject to the parties taking all practicable measures to ensure acceptance and adherence to the CGP by non-governmental standardisation bodies within their territory.[137] Following extensive discussions, the EC further proposed that the regulatory scope of the CGP be expanded to cover all standardising bodies, including central government bodies, local government bodies, regional governmental bodies, as well as non-governmental bodies.[138] The disciplines on standards were to be separated from those relating to technical regulations. Whereas technical regulations are subject to Article 2 of the TBT Agreement, the CGP, along with a newly proposed Article 4, constitute the main disciplines for preparation, adoption and application of standards, to be discussed below.

## B. Mapping the WTO Legal Framework of Product Standards

To deal with the problems presented by the heterogeneity in product standards, conceptually, policymakers have a range of possible responses and these options range along a continuum.[139] At one end is complete autonomy. National standardising bodies set whatever standards they deem fit for their purposes with no restraint from the international level. This option is out of step with the reality of international trade law. Since the Tokyo Round, complete autonomy has become an illusory objective that no WTO Member can pursue. At the other end of the spectrum lies full harmonisation, in the sense that WTO Members adopt standards that are identical in both the policy objectives and the detailed technical provisions, or there is some supranational polity to enact standards applicable to all Members. This is also rare at the global level.

Between the two extremes lie many alternatives that impose greater or lesser constraint on standard-setting autonomy while still affording some opportunities for variation across members. Along the order of intensity towards full harmonisation, the first one is 'policed decentralisation'. WTO Members are free to fulfil any legitimate objective, but are prohibited from adopting discriminatory standards so as to reduce adverse trade effects to the minimum. This approach is generally categorised as 'negative integration' and was largely adopted in the GATT 1947. The second one is to recognise as 'equivalent' the exporting country's product standards to the importing country's domestic standards. Recognition can be either unilateral or be achieved through mutual recognition agreements (MRAs). If mutual recognition works, each firm only

[137] Ibid.

[138] Revised Proposal by the European Economic Community, 'A Code of Good Practice for Non-Governmental Bodies in the Agreement on Technical Barriers to Trade', MTN/GNC/NG8/W/71 (20 Feb 1990).

[139] AO Sykes, 'The (limited) Role of Regulatory Harmonisation in International Goods and Service Markets' (1999) 2 *Journal of International Economic Law* 49, 50.

needs to comply with its home country regulations regardless of the markets in which it sells.[140] The third one may be termed as 'partial harmonisation'. WTO Members are requested as a rule of thumb to follow international standards, but are allowed to deviate from them with valid reasons.[141] A variation of partial harmonisation is to harmonise only essential requirements while mutually recognise each other's specific technical standards such as the EU's 'new approach'.[142] Since mutual recognition and partial harmonisation require or encourage WTO Members to be active in facilitating international trade, they are generally called 'positive integration'.[143]

The GATT/WTO regime has rejected the two extreme positions as well as the EU's 'new approach', but has adopted other options in various degrees. In addition, the sophisticated WTO legal framework includes other effective means to curtail adverse effects of diversified product standards on international trade such as transparency provisions and special committees. As will be discussed in more detail below, Article 1.1, III:4 and XX of the GATT 1994, the TBT Agreement and its Annex 3 Code of Good Practice, and the SPS Agreement constitute the core WTO disciplines on product standards.[144] The search for the right balance between trade liberalisation while protecting important social values has characterised the evolution and interpretation of WTO disciplines on product standards.

### *i. GATT 1994*

Under the GATT 1994, product standards are not addressed specifically but are treated in conjunction with other non-tariff internal regulations and subject to the same restrictions and exceptions.[145] The central provisions are nondiscrimination principle prohibiting discrimination among trading partners (Article 1), between foreign producers and domestic producers (Article III) and general exceptions (Article XX).

Product standards, as non-fiscal domestic regulatory measures, are potentially subject to Article III:4. Article III:4 provides that 'the products ... of any contracting party ... shall be accorded treatment no less favorable than that

[140] Art 2.7 of the TBT Agreement and Art 4 of the SPS Agreement.

[141] R Lawrence, *Regionalism, Multilateralism, and Deeper Integration* (The Brookings Institute, Washington DC, 1995) 5.

[142] PA Messerlin and D Palmeter, 'Technical Regulation and Industry Standards', in T Cottier, PC Mavroidis and P Blatter (eds), *Regulatory Barriers and the Principle of Non-Discrimination in World Trade Law* 245 (University of Michigan Press, 2000) 250–252.

[143] F Ortino, *Basic Legal Instruments for the Liberalisation of Trade: A Comparative Analysis of EC and WTO Law* (Hart Publishing, 2004) 12.

[144] G Marceau and JP Trachtman, 'A Map of the World Trade Organisation Law of Domestic Regulation of Goods: The Technical Barriers to Trade Agreement, The Sanitary and Phytosanitary Measures Agreement, and the General Agreement on Tariffs and Trade' (2014) 48(2) *Journal of World Trade* 351–432; Sykes (n 139) 57–86.

[145] World Trade Report 2012 (n 81) 40.

accorded to like products of national origin in respect of *all laws, regulations and requirements* …'. Thus WTO Members are required to apply product standards in an even-handed and non-discriminatory manner, precluding the application of more stringent requirements to imported like products s than to domestic products. Mandatory technical regulations and conformity assessment procedures (CAPs) clearly fall within the scope of Article III:4. But WTO panels have consistently refused to read the phrase 'all laws, regulations and requirements' in a restrictive manner, preferring a functional approach instead. In *Canada-Autos*, the panel held that 'Article III:4 applies not only to mandatory measures, but also to conditions that an enterprise accepts in order to receive an advantage, including in cases where the advantage is in the form of a benefit with respect to the conditions of importation of a product'.[146] In other words, voluntary government standards are not exempt from the scrutiny of Article III:4, in particular if there are advantages from the government by complying with the standard.[147] Whether private standards are covered is dependent on whether they can be contributed to the state, when they are influenced through incentives and disincentives to act in a particular manner.[148]

The WTO does not require its Members to observe non-discrimination and market access obligations all the time and under any circumstances. There are some important exceptions contained in Article XX of the GATT 1994. Article XX entitles WTO Members to utilise trade restrictive measures incompatible with the GATT to pursue overriding public policy goals, for example to protect public morals or to conserve exhaustible natural resources, to the extent such inconsistencies are unavoidable. At first glance, Article XX has opened the door to all manners of trade restrictions in the name of protecting high-minded non-economic objectives. In practice, however, the scope of Article XX is much more restricted.[149]

### *ii. The TBT Agreement and the Code of Good Practice*

#### a. How is the TBT Agreement 'additional to' the GATT 1994

The bifurcated GATT structure proved inadequate to tackle the rise of product standards in international trade over time. A number of intransigent disputes arose over what constitutes 'like products' or 'discrimination' and over the sincerity of appeals to Article XX exceptions. It also became increasingly clear

[146] Panel Report, *Canada- Certain Measures Affecting the Automotive Industry*, WT/DS139/R (11 February 2000), para 10.73; Panel Report, *EEC – Regulation on Imports of Parts and Components*, BISD 37S/132, adopted on 16 May 1990, paras 5.20–21.

[147] J Karbowski, 'Grocery Store Activism: A WTO-Compliant Means to Incentivise Social Responsibility' (2009) 49 (3) *Virginia Journal of International Law* 727, 762.

[148] Panel Report, *Japan-Film* (n 109).

[149] L Bartels, 'The Chapeau of the General Exceptions in the WTO GATT and GATs Agreements: A Reconstruction' (2015) 109 (1) *American Journal of International Law* 95.

that nominally non-discriminatory standards could afford protection to domestic firms when they have a cost advantage in compliance.[150] Accordingly, the GATT contracting parties were dissatisfied with the national treatment (NT) obligation as the sole textual basis for disciplining product standards, and developed additional disciplines contained in the TBT Agreement.[151]

The TBT Agreement covers not only standards and technical regulations, but also CAPs. CAPs are defined in Annex 1.3 of the TBT Agreement as 'any procedure used, directly or indirectly, to determine that relevant requirements in technical regulations or standards are fulfilled', and they are subject to a different set of rules in the TBT Agreement.[152] The Explanatory Note to Annex 1.3 provides a non-exhaustive list of CAPs, including procedures for sampling, testing and inspection; evaluation, verification and assurance of conformity; registration, accreditation and approval as well as their combinations. Nowadays TBT measures account for 37 per cent of all non-tariff barriers notified to the WTO.[153]

The TBT Agreement recognises that technical regulations and standards may be adopted to attain legitimate objectives such as protection of human health or safety and the environment. But they should not be more trade-restrictive than necessary to fulfil such a legitimate objective (Article 2.2). Article 2 of the TBT Agreement further provides a set of principles that are to be adopted in the preparation, adoption and application of technical regulations by central government bodies. These include the most-favoured-nation and NT treatment (Article 2.1); using relevant international standards as a basis for technical regulations (Article 2.4); accepting as equivalent technical regulations of other Members if these regulations adequately fulfil the objectives of their own domestic regulations (Article 2.7); preference for product standards based on product requirements in terms of performance rather than design or descriptive characteristics (Article 2.8); informing other WTO Members in advance of a proposed technical regulation, publication of adopted measures and the explanation, upon request, of the justification for the regulatory intervention at hand (Article 2.9).

In *EC – Asbestos*, the AB stated that the TBT Agreement is intended to further the objectives of GATT 1994 through a specialised legal regime that imposes obligations on Members that seem to be *different from*, and *additional to*, the obligations imposed on Members under the GATT 1994.[154] However, the AB did not elaborate on this observation. This is disappointing

[150] AO Sykes, 'Regulatory Consistency Requirements in International Trade' (2017) 49 *Arizona State Law Journal* 821, 822.

[151] RW Staiger and AO Sykes, 'International Trade, National Treatment, and Domestic Regulation' (2011) 40 *Journal of Legal Studies* 149, 194.

[152] Panel Report, *EC Trade Marks and Geographical Indications*, WTO/DS290/R, adopted on 20 April 2005, paras 7.512–7.514.

[153] WTO Trade Report 2012 (n 81) 44.

[154] Appellate Body Report, *EC– Asbestos* (n 3) para 80.

because completing this analysis is the key to understanding the nature of the TBT obligations.[155] As observed by the AB in *US – Clove Cigarettes*, the TBT Agreement and the GATT 1994 have similar objectives and that the GATT is relevant context for the interpretation of the TBT Agreement. At the heart, they both aim at striking a balance that the AB described as 'on the one hand, the desire to avoid creating unnecessary obstacles to international trade and, on the other hand, the recognition of Members' 'right to regulate'.[156] Moreover, the two Agreements encapsulate the same trade liberalisation tools such as the NT and the least trade restrictive test to fend off protectionism. Despite the similarities, a few textual differences exist between the GATT and the TBT Agreement. For example, the GATT is only applicable to mandatory government regulations but does not apply to voluntary product standards and conformity assessment measures unless the government plays a significant role in their development and application. By comparison, the TBT Agreement explicitly covers voluntary product standards. Even on similar provisions, the TBT Agreement has made some modifications over the GATT. For instance, Art XX of the GATT refers only to a limited and exhaustive list of policy objectives, whilst Art 2.2 of the TBT Agreement provides an open-ended list, indicating that a much wider range of legitimate policy objectives may be justified.

Moving beyond textual differences, there are some fundamental and structural differences between the TBT Agreement and the GATT. First, the TBT Agreement has considerably reduced the inherent pro-trade bias embedded in the bifurcated structure of the GATT.[157] Article XX is structured as a general exception under the GATT even if it is designed to protect some legitimate public policies. It is only *after* the measure is found in violation of substantive GATT provisions such as the NT obligation that legitimate regulatory objectives in Article XX will be considered. This bifurcated structure reflects a normative hierarchy between substantive trade obligations and national regulation priorities, and the latter is subordinated as 'exceptions'.[158] By contrast, the TBT Agreement does not have a 'general exceptions' provision comparable to GATT Article XX. The legitimate regulatory objectives, such as the protection of environment, are not degraded to an inferior status as 'exceptions'. Instead, it is a WTO Member's inherent 'right' to achieve a legitimate regulatory objective. This unitary structure means that trade and non-trade values will be considered at the same time and no narrow interpretation of exceptions is envisaged in the TBT Agreement.

[155] Mavroidis (n 62) 515.

[156] Appellate Body Report, *United States-Measures Affecting the Production and Sale of Clove Cigarettes*, WT/DS406/AB/R, adopted 24 April 2012, para 96.

[157] M Du, 'Domestic Regulatory Autonomy under the TBT Agreement: From Non-Discrimination to Harmonisation' (2007) 6 (2) *Chinese Journal of International Law* 269, 280.

[158] DM McRae, 'GATT Article XX and the WTO Appellate Body' in M Bronckers and R Quick (eds), *New Directions in International Economic Law: Essays in Honor of John H. Jackson* (Kluwer Law International, 2000) 226.

Second, there are virtually no constraints on product standards that accord with the NT obligation in the GATT even if the standards raise the costs of foreign suppliers disproportionately and thus have the effect of insulating domestic firms from foreign competition.[159] Precisely because of this reason, the TBT disciplines move beyond the NT principle. For example, Art 2.2 requires that a technical regulation shall not be more trade restrictive than necessary to fulfil a legitimate objective. Even if a product standard is non-discriminatory both in purpose and in effect, it may still violate Art 2.2 simply because it unreasonably burdens international trade for the attainment of a legitimate policy objective.[160] In addition, the TBT Agreement has moved beyond the NT obligation and incorporated positive integration tools such as harmonisation, mutual recognition and equivalence.[161] For example, Art 2.4 requires WTO Members to use relevant international standards as a basis for their municipal technical regulations unless they are inappropriate or ineffective. By doing so, the TBT Agreement has employed an external source of transnational regulation to provide a harmonised, if not common, set of rules capable of limiting trade barriers stemming from divergent national laws.

Third, many provisions in the TBT Agreement are procedure-oriented, focusing on the *process* of 'preparation, adoption, and application' of product standards.[162] For example, the TBT Agreement contains comprehensive and specific transparency obligations, going beyond those found in the GATT.[163] This procedure-oriented nature of the TBT Agreement ensures the transparency and integrity of the standard-setting process, and minimises the possibility that trade partners are adversely affected by unexpected standards.

In *EC – Asbestos*, the panel considered the order of application between the GATT 1994 and the TBT. The panel concluded that if the measure at issue falls into the category of technical regulation, standard or CAPs, it should be dealt with under the TBT Agreement first because it deals 'specifically, and in detail' with such measures.[164] On the other hand, obligations under the GATT and the TBT are cumulative and WTO Members must comply with both agreements simultaneously.[165] A finding of consistency with the TBT Agreement would not

[159] JJ Barcelo III, 'Product Standards to Protect the Local Environment – the GATT and the Uruguay Round Sanitary and Phytosanitary Agreement' (1995) 27 *Cornell International Law Journal* 755, 761; DC Esty, *Greening the GATT: Trade, Environment, and the Future* (Institute for International Economics, Washington, DC, 1994) 45.

[160] J Neumann and E Turk, 'Necessity Revisited: Proportionality in World Trade Organisation Law after *Korea – Beef*, *EC – Asbestos* and *EC – Sardines*' (2003) 37 *Journal of World Trade* 199, 217.

[161] HZ Schroder, *Harmonisation, Mutual Recognition and Equivalence of Standards in WTO Law* (Wolters Kluwer, 2011) 3.

[162] JO McGinnis and ML Movsesian, 'The World Trade Constitution' (2000) 114 *Harvard Law Review* 512, 597.

[163] D Prevost, 'Transparency Obligations under the TBT Agreement', in Epps and Trebilcock (n 70) 122.

[164] WTO Panel Report, *EC – Asbestos*, WT/DS135/R, adopted 5 April 2001, paras 8.15–8.17.

[165] Appellate Body Report, *Korea – Definitive Safeguard Measures on Imports of Certain Dairy Products*, WT/DS98/AB/R, adopted 12 January 2000, para 81.

automatically lead to the conclusion that it is consistent with the GATT.[166] In *US – Tuna II*, the AB criticised the panel for engaging in an exercise of 'false judicial economy' by assuming that the obligations under TBT Article 2.1 and Article I:1 and Article III:4 of the GATT are substantially the same.[167] Still, it is highly unlikely that a measure consistent with the TBT can be found inconsistent with GATT 1994.

### b. The Code of Good Practice

The CGP sets out the substantive disciplines for all standardising bodies which are active within a WTO Member. Article 4 of the TBT Agreement has imposed different levels of legal obligations on WTO Members depending on the nature of standardising bodies. For central government standardising bodies, WTO Members have mandatory obligations to ensure that they accept and comply with the CGP. By contrast, WTO Members shall take 'reasonable measures' as may be available to them to ensure that local government and non-governmental bodies accept and comply with the CGP. Up to date, the CGP is somewhat a neglected component of the WTO Agreements. Neither its scope of application nor the extent of the obligations imposed on WTO Members, have been the subject of interpretative guidance from WTO adjudicatory organs.[168] Nevertheless, two general observations of the CGP are in order. First, substantive CGP obligations that apply to voluntary standards are the same principles that apply to technical regulations. For example, paragraphs D (non-discrimination), paragraph E (the necessity obligation), paragraph F (obligation to use international standard as a basis) and paragraphs J and L (publication and notification of draft standards) of the CGP are closely comparable, although not identical, to their counterparts such as Article 2.1, 2.2 and 2.4 of the TBT Agreement respectively. Second, Article 4.1 of the TBT Agreement provides that Members *shall* ensure that their central government standardising bodies accept and comply with the CGP for the preparation, adoption and application of standards. This provision converts the CGP into a fully enforceable instrument in respect of central government standards, similar to central government technical regulations.[169] By contrast, for local government and non-governmental bodies, WTO Members shall take 'reasonable measures' as may be available to them to ensure that they accept and comply with the CGP. This is a soft law obligation in the sense that the scope of a WTO Member's

[166] A Mitchell & T Voon, 'Regulating Tobacco Flavors: Implications of WTO Law' (2011) 29 *Boston University International Law Journal* 383, 392–3.

[167] Appellate Body Report, *US – Tuna II* (n 2) para 405.

[168] Partiti (n 36) 831.

[169] Davies (n 60) 43.

obligations under this provision is member-specific and must take into account the legal and constitutional arrangements of a particular WTO Member.

There is evidence that the CGP has played an important role in regulating how standards are set at both national and international levels. Between 1995 and 2019, 192 standardising bodies from 144 Members or observers have accepted the CGP.[170] The non-government standardising bodies that accepted the CGP include not only those which enjoy a government franchise/mandate to coordinate standards in their respective countries and even to represent their countries at ISBs such as the American National Standards Institute (ANSI), but also private industry consortiums such as CalConnect in the US, a non-profit partnership between vendors and users of collaboration system and tools, in particular calendaring and scheduling and Seafood Services Australia Ltd established by the Australian seafood industry.[171] At the international level, many ISBs such as the International Organisation for Standardisation (ISO), the Forest Stewardship Council (FSC) and the ISEAL Alliance have revised their standardisation procedures or their code of good practice to incorporate the principles outlined in the CGP.[172]

### c. The TBT Committee Decision

The TBT Agreement and its associated WTO case law jurisprudence do not exhaust the institutional architecture of the TBT Agreement. Article 13 establishes the TBT Committee to carry out the functions necessary to implement the TBT Agreement and to further its objectives. One of the important functions of the TBT Committee is 'norm elaboration' through guidelines, recommendations and decisions.[173] One prominent example is the TBT Committee Decision on Principles for the Development of International Standards. Despite the important role played by international standards in promoting international harmonisation of standards, the TBT Agreement does not define the scope of international standards. Nevertheless the TBT Committee Decision has enunciated six principles for the development of international standards: transparency, openness, impartiality and consensus, relevance and effectiveness, coherence and developing country interests.[174] Extraordinarily, the AB held in *US – Tuna II* that the TBT Committee Decision is a 'subsequent agreement'

[170] Note by the Secretariat, 'Twenty-Fifth Annual Review of the Implementation and Operation of the TBT Agreement', G/TBT/44 (19 February 2020) 20.

[171] WTO ISO Standards Information Gateway www.tbtcode.iso.org accessed 1 March 2020.

[172] ISO/IEC Guide 59:2019; FSC Principles and Criteria for Forest Stewardship (22 July 2015); ISEAL Code of Good Practice (December 2014).

[173] A Lang and J Scott, 'The Hidden World of WTO Governance' (2009) 20(3) *European Journal of International Law* 575, 597–598.

[174] Note by the WTO Secretariat, 'Decisions and Recommendations Adopted by the WTO Committee on Technical Barriers to Trade since 1 January 1995', G/TBT/1/Rev.14 (24 September 2019), Annex 2.

between the WTO Members within the meaning of Article 31(3)(a) of the VCLT. As such, a WTO panel is obliged to take it into account when interpreting whether a standard is an 'international standard' for the purpose of the TBT Agreement.[175] Subsequently, the TBT Committee Decision has been accepted and integrated into many ISBs' standardisation procedures.[176]

### *iii. The SPS Agreement*

A key element of Uruguay Round negotiations was liberalisation of trade in agriculture. This led some countries to fear that if an agreement was reached lowering agricultural tariffs, governments would resort to restrictive SPS measures to appease domestic producers in the politically sensitive agriculture sector.[177] At the same time, the US and the EC were engaged in a long-standing dispute over the EC's import restrictions on meat treated with hormones. The parties lacked confidence in the capacity of the GATT panel's ability to resolve a scientific dispute of this nature in the context of GATT 1947 and the provisions of the Standards Code.[178] The initial Uruguay Round negotiations were merely intended to add stronger disciplines on SPS measures to the Standards Code. But by 1988, a separate Working Party was created to draft the SPS Agreement, as negotiators had concluded that the SPS disciplines could not be conveniently incorporated into the TBT Agreement. The conclusion of the SPS Agreement was described as one of the most significant achievements of the Uruguay Round.[179] As an elaboration of the NT obligation, it provides additional criteria to distinguish whether a measure operates 'so as to afford protection' in the sense of Article III:1 of the GATT.[180] The term 'SPS measures' is defined in Annex A.1 of the SPS Agreement. Different from a technical regulation or standard which is defined by reference to product characteristics in the TBT Agreement, the SPS measures are defined by reference to their purpose and the location where the purpose is pursued, i.e., SPS measures are measures applied to protect human, animal and plant life or health within the territory of a WTO Member. In determining whether the SPS Agreement is applicable to a particular WTO dispute, a panel usually looks to the purpose of the measure and whether it matches one or more of the risk categories such as food, animal or plant risks as set out in

[175] Appellate Body Report, *US – Tuna II* (n 2) para 372.

[176] ISO (n 171).

[177] TE Josling, S Tangerman and TK Warley, *Agriculture in the GATT* (Macmillan, 1996) 10.

[178] T Christoforou, 'Settlement of Science-Based Trade Disputes in the WTO: A Critical Review of the Developing Case Law in the Face of Scientific Uncertainty' (2000) 8 *NY University Environmental Law Journal* 622, 625.

[179] S Charnovitz, 'Improving the Agreement on Sanitary and Phytosanitary Standards' in GP Sampson & WB Chambers (eds), *Trade, Environment and the Millennium* 2nd edn (United Nations University Press, 2001) 171.

[180] B Rigod, 'The Purpose of the WTO Agreement on the Application of Sanitary and Phytosanitary Measures (SPS)' (2013) 24 (2) *European Journal of International Law* 503, 525–8.

the Annex A.1. In *EC – Biotech Products*, whether the EC approval scheme of biotech products is an SPS measure was at issue. The panel held that regard must be had to such elements as to the purpose of the measure (protection of human, animal and plant life or health), its legal form (laws, decrees, regulations) and its nature (requirements and procedures including product criteria and PPMs etc).[181] Among the three elements, the purpose of a measure is central to the division of jurisdiction between the TBT and the SPS Agreement.[182]

WTO Members must comply with several basic obligations under the SPS Agreement. The first, and the most important, is that SPS measures must be based on scientific principles and are not to be maintained without scientific evidence (Article 2.2 and Article 5.1). Where scientific evidence is insufficient, WTO members may adopt emergency or precautionary SPS measures on a provisional basis but are required to obtain additional information for a more objective assessment of the risk and to review the measures within a reasonable period of time (Article 5.7). SPS measures are applied only to the extent necessary to protect human, animal or plant life or health, and they cannot be applied in a manner which would constitute a means of arbitrary or unjustifiable discrimination among members where the same conditions prevail or a disguised restriction on international trade (Articles 2.2 and 2.3). The SPS Agreement also promotes harmonisation by requiring SPS measures to be based on international standards (Article 3). Similar to the TBT Agreement, the SPS Committee has adopted decisions to further elaborate the substantive SPS obligations, one prominent example of which is the guideline to further the practical implementation of the Article 5.5 consistency requirement.[183]

## V. CONCLUSION

Chapter 1 provides an overview of product standards in international trade, including the definition, economic functions, trade impact, taxonomy as well as the GATT/WTO legal framework regulating product standards. The chapter starts by outlining the central research question to be systematically explored in the book: to what extent should WTO disciplines penetrate into the regulatory space of WTO Members, non-governmental bodies and other international standardising bodies (ISBs) in setting product standards based on their alleged trade concerns? Then the definitional scope of 'standard' in the WTO law is analysed, highlighting how its key components such as 'recognised bodies', 'PPMs' and 'voluntary' are interpreted, drawing on both the GATT/

[181] WTO Panel Report, *European Communities – Measures Affecting the Approval and Marketing of Biotech Products (EC – Biotech)*, WT/DS291/R, adopted 21 November 2006, paras 7.148–9.

[182] Marceau and Trachtman (n 144) at 418.

[183] Committee on Sanitary and Phytosanitary Measures, 'Guidelines to Further the Practical Implementation of Article 5.5', G/SPS/15 (18 July 2000).

WTO negotiating history and WTO dispute settlement practices. The analysis of the definition of 'standards' is followed by an examination of their functions, ambiguous trade effects and classification from trade law perspective. I proceed to trace the introduction and development of relevant rules on product standards in the GATT/WTO law from the Tokyo Round until present, showing the motivations and regulatory concerns of WTO Members underlining the relevant rules governing voluntary standards in international trade. Finally, a roadmap of relevant WTO rules regulating product standards is introduced. Whether these rules have struck a proper balance between trade liberalisation and legitimate regulatory space of standardising bodies and WTO Members will be critically examined in the following chapters.

# 3

# *The Basic WTO Obligations on Product Standards*

THE DEFINITION OF 'standards' in Annex 1.2 of the TBT Agreement is almost identical to that of technical regulation in Annex 1.1 except that the former are voluntary measures enacted by governmental and recognised non-governmental bodies while the latter are mandatory governmental measures. All public and private standards falling within the definition of Annex 1.2 are subject to the disciplines of the TBT Code of Good Practice (CGP) in Annex 3. The CGP is open to acceptance to all governmental, local and non-governmental standardising bodies which are active in the territory of a WTO Member.

Article 4 of the TBT Agreement has imposed different levels of legal obligations on WTO Members depending on the nature of standardising bodies. For central government standardising bodies, WTO Members are obliged to ensure that they accept and comply with the CGP. For local government and non-governmental standardising bodies, by contrast, WTO Members shall take 'reasonable measures' as may be available to them to ensure that they accept and comply with the CGP. Article 4 shows that the obligation for WTO Members to ensure compliance with the TBT CGP refers to standardising bodies, and not to the standards they draft. To stress that the obligations are imposed on WTO Members, and not on standardising bodies directly, Article 4.1 further provides that irrespective of whether or not a standardising body has accepted the CGP, the obligations of WTO Members with respect to compliance of standardising bodies with the provisions of the CGP always apply.

Neither Article 4 of the TBT Agreement nor the CGP has been tested before the WTO dispute settlement body. Nevertheless, there is no doubt that TBT Article 4 has imposed enforceable obligations on WTO Members.[1] Moreover, the purpose of the CGP is similar to the TBT Agreement in general, ie striking a delicate balance between allowing standardising bodies to adopt and

[1] A Davies, 'Technical Regulations and Standards under the WTO Agreement on Technical Barriers to Trade' (2014) 41(1) *Legal Issues of Economic Integration* 37, 43; Enrico Partiti, 'What Use is an Unloaded Gun? The Substantive Disciplines of the WTO TBT Code of Good Practice and its Application to Private Standards Pursuing Public Objectives' (2017) 20 (4) *Journal of International Economic Law* 829, 833.

apply standards necessary to achieve legitimate objectives and preventing such standards to be unjustified obstacles to international trade. For this purpose, WTO Members have committed to largely identical disciplines to reduce the negative impact of standards in the CGP as they have done with regard to technical regulations. These disciplines include, among others, most-favoured national treatment and national treatment (paragraph D), avoiding unnecessary obstacles to international trade (paragraph E), using relevant international standards as a basis (paragraphs F and G), avoiding duplicative and overlapping standards (paragraph H), preference of standards based on performance rather than design or descriptive characteristics (paragraph I), and transparency (paragraphs J-P). Given the similarities of trade law disciplines governing standards and technical regulations, it is reasonable to argue that the AB's extensive interpretative guidance over the substantive obligations on technical regulations is in principle transposable to standards in the CGP.[2]

This position seems to be justified by the negotiating history of the TBT Agreement. When standards were first identified as potential trade barriers, the GATT Contracting Parties imposed the same set of substantive obligations on both technical regulations and standards by central government standardising bodies in the Tokyo Round Standards Code. During the Uruguay Round negotiations, standards were removed from the coverage of TBT Article 2 which now applies only to technical regulations. However, this change was not motivated by any desire to dilute the TBT obligations to central government standards, but by the desire to strengthen the application of TBT obligations to non-governmental standardising bodies, while preserving the already strong coverage of central government standards.[3] Moreover, the AB has repeatedly emphasised the relevance of the GATT 1994 for the interpretation of the TBT Agreement. In *US – Tuna II (Article 21.5)*, the AB emphasised the important parallels between the non-discrimination provisions between two agreements and concluded that it may be reasonable for a panel to rely on any relevant findings it made under the TBT Agreement in assessing the legality of the measure under the GATT 1994.[4] Therefore, a full grasp of the substantive obligations embodied in the CGP requires a comprehensive and accurate understanding of the relevant provisions that apply to technical regulations in the TBT Agreement as well as those in the GATT 1994.

[2] P Van den Bossche and W Zdouc, *The Law and Policy of the World Trade Organization* 4th edn (Cambridge University Press, 2017) 900–901.

[3] Revised Proposal by the European Economic Community, 'Code of Good Practice for the Preparation, Adoption and Application of Standards', TBT/W/137 (15 February 1990); See Davies (n 1) 43–44.

[4] Appellate Body Report, *United States- Measures Concerning the Importation, Marketing and Sale of Tuna and Tuna Products (Recourse to Article 21.5 of the DSU by Mexico)* (20 November 2015) para 7.278.

## I. NATIONAL TREATMENT

It is a basic undertaking by WTO Members not to use internal fiscal and non-fiscal measures, such as product standards, in a protectionist fashion. This obligation is enshrined in, among other places, the national treatment (NT) provision in Article III:4 of the GATT 1994. The NT obligation not only plays a central role in regulating product standards in the GATT/WTO system, it has also appeared in nearly all other trade agreements. This is not surprising as whatever the perceived threat to health, safety or other consumer interests, there can be no basis for knowingly disregarding the same threats from domestic products.[5] Despite the important role played by the NT obligation in constraining national regulatory measures, the WTO Appellate Body has never formulated a clear and consistent criterion for its application.[6] As one prominent WTO scholar lamented: 'after all these years, we are still in the dark as to the precise ambit of what has been time and again described as the "cornerstone" of the GATT edifice'.[7]

### A. The National Treatment Obligation in GATT 1994

Although the GATT 1994 makes no specific reference to technical regulations or standards, product standards fall into the purview of Article III:4, which provides:

> The products of … any contracting party imported into … any other contracting party shall be accorded *treatment no less favorable than* that accorded to *like products* of national origin in respect of *all laws, regulations and requirements affecting* their internal sale, offering for sale, purchase, transportation, distribution or use.

The essence of Article III:4 is that imported products must be offered '*treatment no less favorable*' than that accorded to domestic *like products*. In addition, Article III:4 should be read in light of Article III:1, which serves as a guiding principle of the whole Article III.[8] Article III:1 reads:

> The Members recognise that … internal laws, regulations and requirements … should not be applied to imported or domestic products *so as to afford protection* to domestic production.

[5] AO Sykes, 'Regulatory Protectionism and the Law of International Trade' (1999) 66 *University of Chicago Law Review* 1, 16.

[6] NF Diebold, 'Standards of Non-Discrimination in International Economic Law' (2011) 60 (4) *International and Comparative Law Quarterly* 831, 832–833; S Lester, 'Finding the Boundaries of International Economic Law' (2014) 17 (1) *Journal of International Economic Law* 3, 9.

[7] PC Mavroidis, 'Come Together? Producer Welfare, Consumer Welfare, and WTO Rules', in E-U Petersmann (eds) *Reforming the World Trading System: Legitimacy, Efficiency, and Democratic Governance* 277 (Oxford University Press, 2005) 284.

[8] WTO Appellate Body Report, *European Communities – Measures Affecting Asbestos and Asbestos-Containing Products (EC – Asbestos)*, WT/DS135/AB/R, adopted 5 April 2001, para 93.

The original rationale of the NT obligation was to protect the value of tariff concessions, bound by Article II, from being undermined by internal taxes or other regulatory measures, so that Members would have an incentive to further exchange concessions and hence liberalise trade.[9] Over time, however, it has been established that it represents a general and autonomous obligation applicable to all imported products.[10]

The interpretation of Article III:4 hinges principally on three key terms. First, 'like products'; second, 'no less favourable treatment' and third, 'not applied so as to afford protection'. As will be discussed in detail below, the interpretation of these key terms is not an easy exercise.[11] In particular, what has persistently puzzled WTO lawyers is how exactly should Article III:1 inform the interpretation of 'like products' and 'treatment no less favourable' in Article III:4.[12]

### *i. 'Like Products'*

#### a. The Competition-based Approach

'Like products' is one of the most mysterious concepts in the GATT/WTO law.[13] In *Japan – Alcoholic Beverages II*, the AB famously compared the concept to an accordion, which stretches and squeezes in different provisions of the WTO Agreement.[14] The leading case explicating 'like products' in GATT Article III:4 is the landmark *EC – Asbestos* case in which the panel was called to decide whether chrysotile asbestos, a known deadly carcinogen, and PCG fibres, which are less risky to human health, are 'like products'.[15] The AB reasoned that a determination of 'like products' under Article III:4 was fundamentally a determination about the nature and extent of a competitive relationship between and among products.[16] Based on a widely accepted list of criteria originally proposed in the Report of the Working Party on Border Tax Adjustment in the 1970s, the AB held that four factors must be examined in assessing this competitive relationship. They are (i) the properties, nature and quality of products; (ii) the end-uses of the products, ie, the extent to which the products are capable of serving the same or similar uses; (iii) consumers' tastes and habits, ie, the extent to which consumers perceive and treat the products

[9] JH Jackson, *World Trade and the Law of GATT* (The Bobbs- Merrill Company, 1969) 276–8.

[10] WTO Appellate Body Report, *Japan – Taxes on Alcoholic Beverages*, WT/DS8/AB/R, WT/DS10/AB/R, adopted 1 November 1996, 16–17.

[11] N DiMascio and J Pauwelyn, 'Nondiscrimination in Trade and Investment Treaties: Worlds apart or Two Sides of the Same Coin' (2008) 102 *American Journal of International Law* 48, 62–66.

[12] W Zhou, 'The Role of Regulatory Purpose under Article III:2 and 4- Toward Consistency between Negotiating History and WTO Jurisprudence' (2012) 11 (1) *World Trade Review* 81, 84–87.

[13] W-Mog Choi, *'Like Products' in International Trade Law: Towards a Consistent GATT/WTO Jurisprudence* (Oxford University Press, 2003) 256.

[14] Appellate Body Report, *Japan – Alcoholic Beverages II* (n 10) 21.

[15] Appellate Body Report, *EC – Asbestos* (n 8) para 109.

[16] Ibid, para 99.

as alternative means of performing particular functions in order to satisfy a particular want or demand; and (iv) the international classification of the products for tariff purposes.[17] The AB also clarified that it was not a *closed* list of criteria. A panel should have examined the evidence relating to *each* of those four criteria and then, weighed all of that evidence, along with any other pertinent evidence, in making an overall determination of whether the products at issue could be characterised as 'like'.[18]

Applying this analytical framework, the AB in *EC – Asbestos* found that the panel erred by basing its findings of 'like products' on its assessment of the evidence relating to only one criterion, ie, end-uses, rather than considering each of the four criteria separately. Notably, the panel refused to consider the health risks posed by chrysotile fibres and contended that health risks should only be dealt with under GATT Article XX exceptions. The AB ruled that the panel erred by a priori excluding health risk evidence from a panel's examination of 'like products'. The AB then concluded that the carcinogenicity, a defining aspect of the physical properties of chrysotile asbestos, rendered chrysotile asbestos physically different from PCG fibres.[19]

Moreover, the analysis of each criterion should be comprehensive and specific. The panel in *EC – Asbestos* found 'a small number of applications' for which the asbestos and PCG fibres were substitutable and concluded that they had the same end-uses. The AB found this conclusion problematic because the panel had not considered the other, different end-uses for these products.[20] In *US – Clove Cigarettes*, the AB found that 'to be smoked' did not exhaustively describe the more specific functions of cigarettes such as 'satisfying an addiction to nicotine' and 'creating a pleasure experience', thus did not provide sufficient guidance to determine whether clove cigarettes and menthol cigarettes had the same end-use.[21] At the same time, the AB emphasised what mattered was that a product was *capable of* performing a specific end-use, not that such end-use represents the principal or the most common end-use of that product. Since both menthol cigarettes and clove cigarettes are capable of performing the functions identified in the dispute, they share the same end-uses.[22] The AB's reasoning seems to have a contradictory effect. On the one hand, the AB's support for more specific end-uses would increase the flexibility that Members have to distinguish between products. On the other hand, the capability test

[17] Ibid, para 101.

[18] Ibid, paras 102–103.

[19] Ibid, paras 113–114.

[20] Ibid, para 119.

[21] Appellate Body Report, *United States – Clove Cigarettes*, WT/DS406/AB/R, adopted 24 April 2012, para 130. Even though the 'like products' analysis in *US – Clove Cigarettes* relates to Art 2.1 of the TBT Agreement, the Appellate Body's holding in that case applies to 'like products' analysis in Art III:4 as well.

[22] Ibid, para 132.

for end-uses ultimately diminishes Members' flexibility because it necessarily expands the overlap between products.[23]

### b. Regulatory Purpose and 'Like Products': The Rise and Requiem of the Aims and Effects Test

Article III:1 seeks to prevent Members from applying internal regulations in a discriminatory manner so as to afford protection to domestic production.[24] In *Japan – Alcoholic Beverages II*, the AB held that Article III:1 informed the rest of Article III and acted as a guide to interpreting the specific obligations contained in other paragraphs of Article III.[25] Over the years, there has been much uncertainty on the role of Article III:1 in interpreting Article III:4.

As stated above, the AB has consistently taken a competition-based approach to like products analysis. However, this competition-based analysis has been heavily criticised for technical, structural and normative reasons. In *EC – Asbestos*, the AB pondered the technical interpretative difficulties in 'like products' under Article III:4:

> First, 'like products' does not indicate *which characteristics or qualities* are important in assessing the 'likeness' of products … since most products will have many qualities and characteristics … Second, it provides no guidance in determining *the degree or extent* to which products must share quality or characteristics …, as products may share only a few characteristics or qualities, or they may share many … Third, it does not indicate *from whose perspective* 'likeness' should be judged. Ultimate consumers may have a view about likeness of two products that is very different from that of producers of those products.[26] (emphasis added)

Because of these difficulties, the AB asserted that panels could only apply their best judgment and their determination will always involve an unavoidable element of individual, discretionary judgment.[27]

Structurally, if a domestic regulatory measure is found to discriminate against imports in violation of Article III:4, the regulating government can seek to justify that discrimination by invoking Article XX exceptions. But this is not a desirable route as Article XX was traditionally interpreted stringently.[28] In addition, Article XX provides a closed list of legitimate objectives for government intervention. This is incongruent to the rise of the

[23] T Broude and PI Levy, 'Do you Mind if I do not Smoke? Products, Purpose and Indeterminacy in US – Measures Affecting the Production and Sale of Clove Cigarettes' (2014) 13 (2) *World Trade Review* 357, 379.

[24] Commission Notice on the definition of relevant market for the purposes of Community competition law [1997] OJ C 372/5 (Commission Relevant Market Notice) para 98.

[25] Appellate Body Report, *Japan – Alcoholic Beverages II* (n 10) 18.

[26] Appellate Body Report, *EC – Asbestos* (n 8) para 92.

[27] Appellate Body Report, *Japan – Alcoholic Beverages II* (n 10) 20–21.

[28] D McRae, 'GATT Article XX and the WTO Appellate Body' in M Bronckers and R Quick (eds), *New Directions of International Economic Law* (Kluwer International, 2000) 226.

regulatory state.[29] Normatively, the traditional 'like products' test raises a deeper and troubling issue of the very symbolism of political identity and internal hierarchy of values. In this regard, a competition-based test establishes a normative hierarchy whereby the default norm is liberalised trade, and for competing values, such as human health and safety and protection of the environment, to prevail, they have to be justified.[30]

Because of such difficulties, an alternative approach in understanding the NT obligation, known as the 'aims and effects' test, was proposed in the GATT/WTO jurisprudence. Originated in the GATT *US – Malt Beverages* case partly in response to the public outcry against the ruling of *US – Tuna* case in early 1990s, the aims and effects test can be viewed as an effort to relax the stark dichotomy of Article III:4 and Article XX, especially with regard to origin-neutral regulatory measures. According to this test, 'like products' will not be defined by reference to prevailing perceptions about the pair of products in the marketplace, but by reference to an examination of the aims and effects of a particular measure:

> A measure could be said to have the aim of affording protection if an analysis of the circumstances demonstrated that a change in competitive opportunities in favor of domestic products was a *desired outcome* and not merely an incidental consequence of the pursuit of a legitimate policy goal. A measure could be said to have the effect of affording protection to domestic production if it accorded greater competitive opportunities to domestic products than to imported products.[31]

Compared with the competition-based approach to 'like products', the aims and effects test tends to give more respect to WTO Members' domestic policy options as it emphasizes the need to accommodate the regulatory purpose of WTO Members in the context of Article III itself, rather than remitting to stringently-interpreted Article XX exceptions.[32] However, the AB explicitly rejected the aims and effects test in *Japan – Alcoholic Beverages II* on the following grounds.[33] First, Article III:4 contains no textual reference to Article III:1. Second, regulatory measures often pursue a multiplicity of objectives. If a panel were to focus only on one of the multiple objectives, it may reach a somewhat arbitrary result.[34] Third, the concept of 'like products' serve to define the scope of products that should be compared to establish whether

[29] EL Glaeser and A Shleifer, 'The Rise of the Regulatory State', (2003) 41 XLI *Journal of Economic Literature* 401–25.

[30] H Horn and JHH Weiler, 'EC- Asbestos' in H Horn and PC Mavroidis (eds), *The WTO Case Law of 2001* (Cambridge University Press, 2003) 31.

[31] GATT Panel Report, *United States – Taxes on Automobiles (US – Taxes on Automobiles)*, DS31/R, 11 October 1994, unadopted, para 5.10.

[32] GATT Panel Report, *United States – Measures Affecting Alcoholic and Malt Beverages (US – Malt Beverages)*, DS23/R, adopted 19 June 1992, BISD 39S/206, para 5.72.

[33] WTO Panel Report, *Japan – Taxes on Alcoholic Beverages (Japan – Alcoholic Beverages)*, WT/DS8/R, adopted 1 November 1996, paras 6.16–6.18.

[34] Appellate Body Report, *US – Clove Cigarettes* (n 21) paras 113–115.

less favourable treatment is being accorded to imported products. If products in a sufficiently strong competitive relationship are excluded from the group of like products on the basis of a measure's regulatory purpose, this would inevitably marginalise the 'less favourable treatment' comparison at a later stage because any negative trade effects tend to be regarded as incidental and fortuitous, as long as the measure in question carries no protectionist intentions.[35] Finally, the aims and effects test may render Article XX virtually redundant.[36] After *Japan – Alcoholic Beverages II*, it has been firmly established in GATT/WTO law that the regulatory purpose in Article III:1 should *not* be considered as part of the 'like products' inquiry.

### *ii. 'Treatment No Less Favourable'*

#### a. The General Analytical Approach

The GATT panel in *US – Section 337 Tariff Act* stated that the term 'treatment no less favourable' does not require the identical treatment, but the effective equality of competitive conditions between imported and domestic like products.[37] In *Korea – Beef*, the panel wrongfully assumed that any regulatory differences based exclusively on the national origin of the products was inconsistent with Article III:4. The AB reversed the panel and made it clear that formal difference in treatment between like products was neither necessary, nor sufficient, to show a violation of NT principle. Rather, what is relevant is whether such regulatory differences modified the conditions of competition in the market place to the detriment of imported products.[38]

On how to evaluate the implications of the contested measures for the equality of competitive conditions between imported and like domestic products, the AB has provided guidance in *Thailand – Cigarettes*. First, such an analysis must begin with careful scrutiny of the measure, including consideration of the design, structure, and expected operation of the measure. Such an analysis may involve, but need not be based on, the actual trade effects of the contested measure, nor should the panel anchor the analysis in an assessment of the degree of likelihood that an adverse impact on competitive conditions will materialise.[39] Second, if the regulation at issue indicates an origin-based, de jure discrimination, there is a significant indication that imported products

[35] Ibid, para 116; S Cho, *Free Markets and Social Regulation: A Reform Agenda of the Global Trading System* (Kluwer Law International, 2003) 22.

[36] Panel Report, *Japan – Alcoholic Beverages* (n 33) paras 6.16–6.18.

[37] GATT Panel Report, *United States Section 337 of the Tariff Act of 1930*, L/6439, adopted 7 November 1989, BISD 36S/345, para 5.11.

[38] Appellate Body Report, *Korea – Measures Affecting Imports of Fresh, Chilled and Frozen Beef*, WT/DS161/AB/R, adopted 10 January 2001, paras 137–144.

[39] Appellate Body Report, *Thailand – Customs and Fiscal Measures on Cigarettes from the Philippines* (*Thailand – Cigarettes*), WT/DS371/AB/R, adopted 15 July 2011, para 130.

are accorded less favourable treatment.[40] In *Thailand – Cigarettes*, Thailand exempted three sets of VAT-related administrative requirements for resellers of domestic cigarettes, but imposed these administrative requirements on resellers of imported cigarettes. The AB therefore established less favourable treatment with little difficulty.[41] Third, there must be in every case *a genuine relationship* between the measure at issue and its adverse impact on competitive opportunities for imported like products.[42] To identify the existence of a genuine relationship, the relevant question is whether it is the contested governmental measure at issue that affects the competitive conditions within the importing Member's territory.[43] In other words, the detrimental impact on competitive opportunities must be *attributable* to the contested measure at issue. Finally, less favourable treatment must affect the *group* of imported products, as compared to *the group* of domestic products.[44] The NT principle is breached only if imported products from the complaining party, *on the whole*, are treated less favourably than domestic like products. It is not enough that some like imported products from the complaining party receive worse treatment than some like domestic goods.[45] The AB report in *US – Clove Cigarettes* provides the best illustration of this point.[46]

#### b. The Role of Regulatory Purpose in 'Treatment No Less Favourable' Analysis

Similar to the interpretation of 'like products', there has been a long-standing debate on whether the regulatory purpose in Article III:1 should be considered in the interpretation of 'treatment no less favourable' in Article III:4.[47] The critical question is whether a finding of detrimental impact on imported products vis-à-vis like domestic products, without more, is sufficient to find a violation of NT obligation under Article III:4.

The WTO case law on this critical question has oscillated over the years. In *EC – Bananas III*, the AB found that since Article III:4 does not specifically refer to Article III:1, the regulatory purpose is irrelevant to a determination of whether there has been a violation of Article III:4.[48] In *EC – Asbestos*, the AB

[40] Ibid, para 133.
[41] Ibid, paras 139–140.
[42] Ibid.
[43] WTO Appellate Body Report, *European Communities – Measures Prohibiting the Importation and Marketing of Seal Products (EC– Seal Products)*, WT/DS400/AB/R, adopted on 18 June 2014, para 5.105.
[44] Appellate Body Report, *EC – Asbestos* (n 8) para 100.
[45] L Ehring, 'De Facto Discrimination in World Trade Law: National and Most-Favored-Nation Treatment- or Equal Treatment?' (2002) 36 (5) *Journal of World Trade* 921, 944.
[46] Appellate Body Report, *United States – Clove Cigarettes* (n 21) paras 185–198.
[47] MM Du, 'The Rise of National Regulatory Autonomy in the GATT/WTO Regime' (2011) 14 (3) *Journal of International Economic Law* 639, 655–664.
[48] Appellate Body Report, *EC – Bananas III*, WT/DS27/AB/R, adopted 25 September 1997, para 216.

implicitly retreated from *EC – Bananas III* and reiterated its earlier holding in *Japan – Alcoholic Beverages II* that Article III:1 'informs' Article III and should act as a guide to interpreting the specific obligations contained in Article III. In particular, the AB mysteriously stated:

> A Member may draw distinctions between products which have been found to be 'like', without, for this reason alone, according to the group of like imported products less favorable treatment than that accorded to the group of like domestic products.[49]

This has given some speculation that regulatory purpose should be part of the 'treatment no less favourable' analysis and that a non-protectionist explanation could render an otherwise discriminatory measure consistent with Article III:4.[50] However, it was later clarified in *Thailand – Cigarettes* that what the AB meant is only to reiterate what it had stated in *Korea – Various Measures on Beef*, ie, a formal regulatory distinction itself is not conclusive evidence of less favourable treatment. The investigative focus should be on whether *competition conditions* between like products were distorted to the detriment of imported products.[51]

The 2005 AB report of *Dominican Republic – Cigarettes* caused even more confusion. In this case, the AB found that the detrimental effect of the Dominican Republic's uniform bond requirement on imported cigarettes was not enough to find a violation of national treatment obligation:

> [T]he existence of a detrimental effect on a given imported product resulting from a measure does not necessarily imply that this measure accords less favorable treatment to imports *if the detrimental effect is explained by factors or circumstances unrelated to the foreign origin of the product* ...[52] (emphasis added)

After *Dominican Republic – Cigarettes*, almost all subsequent panels held that other than a modification of the conditions of competition to the disadvantage of imported products, the complainant must also show that those adverse effects are related to the foreign origin of the products. In other words, a non-protectionist explanation may be evidence that there is no less favourable treatment to imported products.[53]

[49] Appellate Body Report, *EC – Asbestos* (n 8) para 100.

[50] DH Regan, 'Regulatory Purpose and "Like Products" in Article III:4 of the GATT' in GA Bermann and PC Mavroidis (eds), *Trade and Human Health and Safety* (Cambridge University Press, 2006) 214; H Horn and JHH Weiler, 'European Communities- Measuring Affecting Asbestos and Asbestos-Containing Products' (2004) 3(1) *World Trade Review* 129, 147; A Porges and JP Trachman, 'Robert Hudec and Domestic Regulation: The Resurrection of Aim and Effects' (2003) 37 (4) *Journal of World Trade* 783, 796–797.

[51] Appellate Body Report, *Thailand – Cigarettes* (n 39) para 128.

[52] WTO Appellate Body Report, *Dominican Republic – Measures Affecting the Importation and Internal Sale of Cigarettes (Dominican Republic – Import and Sale of Cigarettes)*, WT/DS302/AB/R, adopted 19 May 2005, para 96.

[53] WTO Panel Report, *European Communities – Measures Affecting the Approval and Marketing of Biotech Products*, WT/DS291/R, adopted 21 November 2006, para 7.2514; Appellate Body

In *US – Clove Cigarettes*, the AB clarified that there was no additional inquiry of whether the detrimental impact is related to the foreign origin of the products under Article III:4. The AB's intriguing statement in *Dominican Republic – Cigarettes* simply stresses that a panel must consider whether any alleged disparate impact is caused by the challenged measure.[54] In that case, for example, the discriminatory effect on imported cigarettes was *not attributable to* the specific bond measure at issue but was a function of sales volumes.[55] The attribution test was later called a 'genuine relationship' test in *Thailand – Cigarettes* in which the AB required that in every case a genuine relationship must exist between the measure at issue and the disparate impact.[56] If some other factors, rather than the disputed measure, are accountable to the disparate impact, then the measure in dispute has not modified conditions of competition, hence no less favourable treatment.

It was not until *EC – Seal Products* that the AB finally stated unequivocally that that there was no need to consider the regulatory purpose of the measure in the 'treatment no less favourable' analysis, and a finding of a detrimental impact, without more, will automatically send the measure to be justified under Article XX. The AB rejected the EU's argument that a finding that a measure has a detrimental impact on competitive opportunities for imported products, compared to like domestic products, is not dispositive and that a panel must conduct an additional inquiry into whether the detrimental impact stems exclusively from a legitimate regulatory distinction.[57] Since Article III:4 does not explicitly refer to Article III:1, the AB considered that this omission of a textual reference to Article III:1 must be given meaning.[58] Then the AB held that Article III:4 is itself an expression of the principle set forth in Article III:1. If there is less favourable treatment of like imported products, there is, conversely, protection of like domestic products.

Admittedly, the AB's interpretation of 'no less favourable treatment' in *EC – Seal Products* has the advantage of a clear division of labour between Article III:4 and Article XX. The AB made it clear that only the trade impact of the contested measure will be considered under Article III:4. Any possible policy justifications for the detrimental trade impact, which delineate the scope of a Member's right to regulate, will only be considered under Article XX. Indeed, one major difficulty with the EU's argument in *EC – Seal Products* is that it is likely to disrupt the delicate balance between Article III:4 and Article XX and risk rendering Article XX inutile. Given the contextual discrepancies between

Report, *United States – Measures Concerning the Importation, Marketing and Sale of Tuna and Tuna Products (US- Tuna II)*, WT/DS381/AB/R, adopted 13 June 2012, para 224.

[54] Appellate Body Report, *United States – Clove Cigarettes* (n 21) fn 372.

[55] Appellate Body Report, *Dominican Republic – Cigarettes* (n 52) para 96.

[56] Appellate Body Report, *Thailand – Cigarettes* (n 39) para 134.

[57] Appellate Body Report, *EC – Seal Products* (n 43) para 5.100.

[58] Ibid, para 5.115.

Article III:4 of the GATT 1994 and Article 2.1 of the TBT, it is challenging to introduce the concepts such as 'legitimate regulatory distinction' and 'even-handedness' in Article 2.1 of the TBT to Article III:4, nor is it possible to consider adequately all possible non-protectionist policy justifications under Article III:1.

However, the AB's interpretation of 'treatment no less favourable' in *EC – Seal Products* is not free from concerns.[59] First, it deprives Article III:1 of any meaning. It is not clear how Article III:1 can 'inform' Article III:4 as the AB stressed in *Japan – Alcoholic Beverages*. Second, it may cause inconsistent rulings between Article III:2, the second sentence and Article III:4, leading to a curious result of internal fiscal measure may enjoy wider policy space than internal non-fiscal measures under the NT obligation. In *Chile – Alcoholic Beverages*, the AB reasoned that since in Article III:2, the second sentence specially refers to Article III:1, a separate finding is required to determine whether Article III:1 is violated.[60] However, other than the absence of an explicit reference to Article III:1, there isn't a valid policy rationale to explain why the AB should reject any regulatory purpose analysis in Article III:4.

Third, the AB's interpretation may create inconsistent rulings on the NT obligation between the GATT 1994 and the TBT Agreement. Article XX provides a closed list of legitimate objectives for government intervention. By contrast, under Article 2.1 of the TBT Agreement, the list of possible legitimate regulatory objectives that may factor into the 'treatment no less favourable' analysis is open. Thus, a technical regulation that has a detrimental impact on imports would be permitted under the TBT Agreement if such detrimental impact stems from a legitimate regulatory distinction, while, under Article III:4 of the GATT 1994, the same technical regulation would be prohibited if the objective that it pursues does not fall within the subparagraphs of Article XX.[61] However, the AB did not share such concerns in *EC – Seal Products* and challenged the EU to point to any concrete examples of such scenarios.[62] As the defending party, the EU was understandably reluctant to point out any example because such a move would prevent itself from invoking Article XX in certain disputes in the future.[63] On the other hand, by challenging the EU to identify a concrete example, the AB seemed to hint that the scope of legitimate objectives under GATT Article XX is similar to that of the TBT Agreement. If this were true, then the AB would necessarily interpret Article XX more flexibly in future

[59] R Howse, J Langille and K Sykes, 'Sealing the Deal: the WTO Appellate Body's Report in *EC – Seal Products*', 18 (12) ASIL Insights, June 2014.

[60] WTO Appellate Body Report, *Chile – Taxes on Alcoholic Beverages (Chile –Alcoholic Beverages)*, WT/DS87/AB/R, adopted 12 January 2000, paras 71–72.

[61] Appellate Body Report, *EC – Seal Products* (n 43) para 5.118.

[62] Ibid, paras 5.128–5.129.

[63] R Howse, 'The WTO Appellate Body Ruling in Seals: National Treatment Article III:4' http://www.worldtradelaw.typepad.com/ielpblog/2014/05/the-wto-appellate-body-ruling-in-seals-national-treatment-article-iii4.html accessed 26 February 2020.

disputes. The AB's liberal interpretation of 'public morals' in Article XX:(a) in *EC – Seal Products* may have already pointed to this direction.[64]

Ultimately, the debate on the merit of the AB's interpretive approach in *EC – Seal Products* boils down to whether the regulatory purpose of the measure should be considered under the less favourable treatment analysis in Article III:4 itself or under Article XX. It is submitted that, with regard to the outcome of a dispute, there is not really much difference. This point could be illustrated by the AB's interpretation of the national treatment obligation in Article 2.1 of the TBT Agreement. The first step in the AB's 'treatment no less favourable' analysis is the same disparate impact test in Article III:4; and the second step of determining whether the detrimental impact stems exclusively from a legitimate regulatory distinction is very similar to the chapeau test of GATT Article XX.[65] Then, we may wonder what purpose does it really serve to transpose the essentially Article XX case law to the 'treatment no less favourable' analysis in Article III:4? The AB has good reasons to choose a bright line 'disparate impact' test for the 'treatment no less favourable' analysis. It has the benefits of a clear division of function between Article III and Article XX; acute awareness of the textural differences among WTO Agreements and the avoidance of depriving Article XX of *effect utile*.

### *iii. The Future of National Treatment Obligation under Article III:4*

The AB's ruling in *EC – Seal Products* shows that the AB attaches great importance to the *effects* of the measure and defined protectionism solely by disparate impact on imported products. As Howse pointed out, the AB seems to have imposed a 'strict liability' on importing countries and many legislative or regulatory distinctions between products would fail this test. The outcome seems extreme and hard to reconcile with the intent and text of Article III:4.[66] Despite the AB's stringent interpretation of the NT obligation, I submit that there are still a few possible buffers which allow more regulatory space than conventionally assumed for non-protectionist regulations.[67]

The first possible buffer is the AB's 'genuine relationship' requirement between the measure at issue and its adverse impact on competitive opportunities

[64] J Pauwelyn, 'The Public Morals Exception after Seals- How to Keep it under Check?' http://worldtradelaw.typepad.com/ielpblog/2014/05/the-public-morals-exception-after-seals-how-to-keep-it-in-check.html accessed 26 February 2020; R Howse, J Langille and K Sykes, 'Pluralism in Practice: Moral Legislation and the Law of the WTO after Seal Products' (2015) 48 *George Washington International Law Review* 81, 132.

[65] J Norpoth, 'Mysteries of the TBT Agreement Resolved? Lessons to Learn from Climate Policies and Developing Country Exporters from Recent TBT Disputes' (2013) 47(3) *Journal of World Trade* 575, 594.

[66] Howse, Langille and Sykes (n 59).

[67] M Du, 'Treatment No Less Favourable and the Future of National Treatment Obligation in Article III:4 of the GATT 1994 after EC-Seal Products' (2016) 15 (1) *World Trade Review* 139, 155–163.

between like products.[68] In future trade disputes, whether there is a genuine relationship between the measure at issue and its adverse impact on imported products will likely be a main battlefield for the defending WTO Member. The AB report of *Dominican Republic – Cigarette* shed some light on how to determine whether the causal link exists. In this case, the AB examined all possible contributing factors and in essence made the determination that market share, rather than the bond requirement as issue, was a closer cause. This is not to deny that the bond requirement might also be a causal factor, but its link to the detrimental impact on trade was not sufficient or as strong as the market share factor. Therefore, one plausible interpretation is that the AB has recognised that to ensure absolute equality of treatment in all circumstances was too costly. The uniform bond requirement had only incidental and unintended disparate impact on imported cigarettes. The evidence showed that the bond requirement represented a very small cost for the importer – equivalent to 0.2 per cent of the value of cigarette imports in 2003.[69] Such a small cost did not affect the exportation of cigarettes from Honduras to the Dominican Republic. Indeed, the exports from Honduras have increased significantly over the years since the measure was introduced.[70] Another causal factor having little or nothing to do with the governmental measure, different market shares, better explains the disparate impact.

The second potential buffer is the role of 'the design, structure and expected operations of the measure' in the NT analysis. In *EC – Seal Products*, the AB explicitly denied the relevance of Article III:1 in interpreting 'treatment no less favourable'. Even so, there is lingering doubt on whether the AB has *implicitly* considered the regulatory purpose of the contested measure. This point could be observed from the AB's emphasis on examining 'the design, structure and expected operations of the measure' when assessing 'treatment no less favourable' in *Thailand – Cigarettes*.[71] This is precisely the same approach that the AB has taken when assessing whether the dissimilar taxation of imported and domestic like directly competitive or substitutable products is applied 'so as to afford protection' in the second sentence of Article III:2.[72] The second sentence of Article III:2 specifically refers to Article III:1 'so as to afford protection'. On how to establish this element, the AB made it clear that this is not an issue of intent behind a measure, but how the measure in question is applied, which can most often be ascertained from the design, the architecture, and the revealing structure of a measure.[73] In *Chile – Alcoholic Beverages*, the AB found

[68] Appellate Body Report, *Thailand – Cigarettes* (n 39) para 134.
[69] Appellate Body Report, *Dominican Republic – Cigarettes* (n 52) para 97.
[70] Ibid, para 71.
[71] Appellate Body Report, *Thailand – Cigarettes* (n 39) paras 130 and 134.
[72] Appellate Body Report, *Japan – Alcoholic Beverages II* (n 10) 28–29; Appellate Body Report, *Philippines – Distilled Spirits*, WT/DS396/AB/R, adopted 21 December 2011, para 190.
[73] Ibid, at 29.

that the structure of the Chilean tax did not relate to the purposes stated by Chile and concluded that this lack of correlation confirmed its finding that the Chilean measure was applied 'so as to afford protection'.[74] In practice, WTO panels will instinctively want to know if a measure has a bona fide regulatory purpose and to what extent its market effects are protective when they are called to decide whether the measure in question is in violation of the NT obligation.[75] By examining the same elements in Article III:4 as the second sentence of Article III:2, the AB will be able to ascertain, even if implicitly, whether the measure in dispute is applied 'so as to afford protection' for domestic production.

The third potential buffer is how flexible the AB will use the different factors for the determination of 'like products'. In *EC – Asbestos*, the AB agreed non-economic interests and values, such as health, may be considered in the determination of 'like products'.[76] In *US – Clove Cigarettes*, the AB confirmed that the regulatory concerns may play a role in determining 'like products'.[77] A more flexible and imaginative use of 'like products' analysis is surely a promising path to open up more regulatory space for a regulating WTO Member. In particular, it has been frequently suggested that some criteria such as consumer tastes and habits may be used to distinguish between products that would otherwise be seen as like, for example, sustainable versus unsustainable, or carbon-intensive versus low-carbon goods.[78] However, there are some stumbling blocks on this path. In *US – Clove Cigarettes*, the AB emphasised that the regulatory concerns are relevant to 'like products' determination only to the extent that they are *reflected* in the competitive relationship between and among the products concerned.[79] In other words, it is one thing to argue that an increasing number of consumers are interested in, and sensitive to, the labour, environmental and other social concerns embodied in a product, it is quite another to *demonstrate* that such regulatory concerns truly shape consumer preferences and guide consumer choices in the market place. In reality, more often consumers are primarily guided by the price and quality of the products in their choice between products.[80] If so, it is unlikely to overturn the 'like products' determination between two otherwise identical products with only divergent environmental impact. In *US – Tuna II*, the preference by American consumers for dolphin-friendly

[74] Appellate Body Report, *Chile – Alcoholic Beverages* (n 60) para 71.

[75] RE Hudec, 'GATT/WTO Constraints on National Regulation: Requiem for an "Aim and Effects" Test' (1998) 32 *The International Lawyer* 619, 634–5.

[76] Appellate Body Report, *EC – Asbestos* (n 8) paras 114 and 122.

[77] Appellate Body Report, *US – Clove Cigarettes* (n 21) para 120.

[78] E Vranes, 'Climate Labelling and the WTO: The 2010 EU Ecolabelling Programme as a Test Case under WTO Law', in C Hermann and JP Terhechte (eds), *European Yearbook of International Economic Law* 205 (Springer-Verlag Berlin and Heidelberg GmbH & Co, 2011) 212–213.

[79] Ibid.

[80] Bossche and Zdouc (n 2) 393.

tuna is so intense that all major American retailers no longer sell tuna caught by setting on dolphins.[81] The panel's finding that dolphin-friendly tuna and dolphin-unfriendly tuna are 'like products' was not appealed. However, given the intense consumer preferences, it could be argued that they were not 'like products', so that a different regulatory regime for dolphin-unfriendly tuna would have been deemed legitimate.[82]

Another stumbling block is the relationship between the government regulation and consumer preferences. The WTO panels have repeatedly warned that while the subjective factor of consumer taste should not be left out of account, government regulation should not be allowed to 'crystallise' consumer preferences for traditional domestic products.[83] The underlying assumption that government regulation should not influence consumer preferences is not surprising, given the free market basis of the WTO.[84] However, when applying this logic to a public policy context, it has radical implications. Governments routinely make normative regulations such as sustainability criteria to affect consumer preference and influence consumers to adapt to shifting or emerging norms. These regulatory preferences likely reflect their national values and priorities. It is important that the WTO system not act as a braking mechanism for more progressive regulations that support emerging norms such as regulations that support environmental sustainability, or climate change mitigation.[85]

## B. General Exceptions in GATT Article XX

The GATT 1994 inherited a basic bifurcated structure of policing product standards from the GATT 1947. On the one hand, substantive WTO obligations, such as Article I (most favoured nation treatment) and Article III (national treatment), prohibit WTO Members from using product standards to result in overt and covert discrimination between imported and domestic 'like products'. On the other hand, Article XX on 'General Exceptions' contains provisions permitting deviation from trade liberalisation commitments under enumerated circumstances.[86] If Article III represents the WTO's free market

[81] Panel Report, *US – Tuna II*, WT/DS381/R, adopted 13 June 2012, as modified by Appellate Body Report WT/DS/381/R, para 7.352.

[82] E Partiti, 'The Appellate Body Report in *US- Tuna II* and Its Impact on Eco-Labelling and Standardization' (2013) 40 (1) *Legal Issues of Economic Integration* 73, 81.

[83] GATT Panel Report, *Japan – Customs Duties, Taxes and Labelling Practices on Imported Wines and Alcoholic Beverages*, adopted on 10 November 1987, L/6216–34S/83, para 5.7; Panel Report, *Canada – Periodicals*, WT/DS/31/R, adopted 30 July 1997, as modified by Appellate Body Report WT/DS31/AB/R, para 5.22.

[84] EB Lydgate, 'Consumer Preferences and the National Treatment Principle: Emerging Environmental Regulations Prompt a New Look at an Old Problem' (2011) 10 (2) *World Trade Review* 165, 185.

[85] Ibid, 186.

[86] WTO Appellate Body Report, *United States – Standards for Reformulated and Conventional Gasoline*, WT/DS2/AB/R, adopted 20 May 1996, 29–30.

ideology, then Article XX stands for WTO Members' right to regulate for non-trade purposes, although in a limited dimension.[87] Article XX consists of an introductory clause (the chapeau) and ten subsequent clauses.

> Subject to the requirement that such measures are not applied in a manner which would constitute a means of arbitrary or unjustifiable discrimination between countries where the same conditions prevail, or a disguised restriction on international trade, nothing in this Agreement shall be construed to prevent the adoption or enforcement by any contracting party of measures:
>
> a) necessary to protect public morals;
>
> b) *necessary* to protect human, animal or plant life or health;
>
> ...
>
> g) *relating to* the conservation of exhaustible natural resources if such measures are made effective in conjunction with restriction on domestic production or consumption; ...

The AB has established a two-tiered analysis to Article XX. A measure must first be provisionally justified under one of the legitimate objectives listed in subparagraphs of Article XX before it is further appraised under the chapeau.[88] The responding party invoking Article XX bears the burden in the first instance of showing that its measures comply with the terms of Article XX. If the responding party provides sufficient evidence to demonstrate a justification, the burden shifts to the complaining party to show that the measures are not justified.[89]

For a long time, Article XX and its early GATT/WTO jurisprudence were frequently accused of demonstrating a strong pro-trade bias at the expense of WTO Members' national regulatory autonomy.[90] To begin with, Article XX is structured as 'general exceptions'. It comes into play only *after* violations of trade- related obligations are found. This dichotomy between trade liberalisation obligations and exceptions, which in itself voices a pro-trade bias, reflects fundamental characteristics of the GATT.[91] Moreover, because Article XX is categorised as 'exceptions', several GATT panels held that it should be

[87] Cho (n 35) 17.

[88] Appellate Body Report, *US – Gasoline* (n 86) 22; WTO Appellate Body Report, *United States – Import Prohibition of Certain Shrimp and Shrimp Products (US – Shrimp)*, WT/DS58/AB/R, adopted 6 November 1998, para 119 and 120.

[89] Appellate Body Report, *China – Measures Related to the Exportation of Various Raw Materials (China-Raw Materials)*, WT/DS394/AB/R (30 January 2012), para 354; Appellate Body Report, *China – Measures Related to the Exportation of Rare Earths, Tungsten, and Molybdenum (China-Rare Earth)*, WT/DS431/AB/R (7 August 2014), para 5.86; *EC – Seal Products* (n 43) para 5.169.

[90] G Kapterian, 'A Critique of the WTO Jurisprudence on Necessary' (2010) 59 *International and Comparative Law Quarterly* 89, 91; J Neumann and E Turk, 'Necessity Revisited: Proportionality in World Trade Organization Law after *Korea – Beef, EC – Asbestos* and *EC – Sardines*' (2003) 37 *Journal of World Trade* 199, 199–233; McRae (n 28) 219–36; S Gaines, 'The WTO's Reading of the GATT Article XX Chapeau: A Disguised Restriction on Environmental Measures' (2001) 22 *University of Pennsylvania Journal of International Law* 739, 739–862.

[91] Cho (n 35) 34.

interpreted narrowly as a general principle of law. This again indicates a ranking of interests in favour of trade liberalisation at the WTO.[92] Consequently, only in one case did a respondent ever succeeded by invoking a general exception throughout the GATT/WTO history.[93] Finally, the list of general exceptions in Article XX is both exhaustive and obsolete. Drafted more than half a century ago, many of these exceptions reflect the regulatory sensitivities of the 1940s. It is difficult to imagine that contemporary social concerns could be fully addressed in a mere ten exceptions. More recently, the evolving jurisprudence developed by WTO tribunals has shown a more sophisticated approach towards domestic regulatory priorities, suggesting that a more nuanced understanding of the AB Article XX jurisprudence is required.[94]

### *i. Regulatory Objectives*

To render one of the Article XX exceptions applicable, the measure at issue must address the particular interest specified in that paragraph and that there must be a 'sufficient nexus' between the measure and the interest protected.[95] So the first issue is to determine whether the measures in question are genuinely designed to achieve a specific legitimate objective as specified in Article XX. In many cases, such a determination is relatively straightforward and the panels generally show a degree of deference to Members' self-claimed objectives.[96] However, the determination could not be established entirely by a WTO Member's own articulation. In *EC – Seal Products*, the AB outlined the analytical approach that a panel should adopt:

> A Panel should take into account the Member' articulation of the objective … but it is not bound by that Member's characterizations of such objective. Indeed, a Panel must take account of all evidence put before it in this regard, including *the texts*

[92] M Hilf, 'Power, Rules and Principles- Which Orientation for WTO/GATT Law?' (2001) 4 *Journal of International Economic Law* 111, 128.

[93] Appellate Body Report, *United States – Import Prohibition of Certain Shrimp and Shrimp Products – Recourse to Article 21.5 of the DSU by Malaysia*, WT/DS58/AB/RW, adopted on 21 November 2001, para 152. For an overview of Article XX jurisprudence, see N Moran, 'The First Twenty Cases under GATT Article XX: Tuna or Shrimp Dear' in G Adinolfi et al (eds), International Economic Law: Contemporary Issues (Springer, 2017) 3–15; R Howse, 'Managing the Interface between International Trade Law and the Regulatory State: What Lessens Should (and should not) Be Drawn from the Jurisprudence of the United States Dormant Commerce Clause' in T Cottier and PC Mavroidis (eds), *Regulatory Barriers and the Principle of Non-Discrimination in World Trade Law* (Michigan University Press, 2000) 142.

[94] M Du and K Qingjiang, 'EC – Seal Products: A New Baseline for Global Economic Governance and National Regulatory Autonomy Debate in the Multilateral Trading System' (2016) 13 (1) *Manchester Journal of International Economic Law* 2, 2–21.

[95] Appellate Body Report, *EC– Seal Products* (n 43) para 5.169; Appellate Body Report, *United States- Measures Affecting the Cross-Border Supply of Gambling and Betting Services* (*US – Gambling*), WT/DS285/AB/R, adopted on 7 April 2005, para 292.

[96] A Sykes, 'Economic "Necessity" in International Law' (2015) 109 (2) *American Journal of International Law* 296, 303–304.

> *of the statutes, legislative history, and other evidence regarding the structure and operation of the measure at issue.*[97]

In *China – Rare Earth*, China argued that its export quotas on rare earth and tungsten were for the purpose of conservation of natural resources. The panel however found that various references to conservation in the texts of China's export quota documents were inconclusive because these documents referred to multiple policy objectives such as industrial policy, in addition to conservation.[98] It is not clear why the fact that the Chinese legislation expressing other non-conservation goals would necessarily invalidate its claims of conservation purpose.[99] As the AB recognised in *EC – Seal Products*, it is normal for a regulation to pursue multiple legitimate, and even inherently conflicting, policy objectives.[100] Therefore it is imperative for the panel to examine whether a real and substantial relationship exists between export quotas and the conservation of exhaustible natural resources before concluding that industrial policy was China's primary legislative intent.

The AB performed this examination and rejected China's conservation arguments. Take the 'signaling' function of the export quotas as an example. China argued that export quotas contributed to the effectiveness of China's overall conservation policy by signaling to foreign consumers the need to diversify their sources of supply of rare earth. The AB rejected this argument because, while export quota might send a conservation-related signal to foreign users, it simultaneously sent a perverse signal to domestic consumers that they should increase their consumption because of low prices.[101] In this regard, the mere existence of China's domestic production quotas would not necessarily mitigate any perverse signals from China's export quotas because the effectiveness of domestic production quotas depends on the level at which each production quota was set and the way in which the export and production quotas interact. There was no mechanism to ensure that no perverse incentives will be sent to domestic consumers.[102]

One may wonder whether the AB hasn't second-guessed China's regulatory purpose too intrusively in *China – Rare Earth*. There is no legal basis for the AB to require that no perverse incentives be sent to domestic consumers. Rather, the real issue was whether, despite the alleged perverse incentive sent to domestic consumers, the export quotas and domestic production caps could nevertheless make a positive contribution to China's purpose of conversation. This is a factual matter. According to Bond and Trachtman, the design and structure of

[97] Appellate Body Report, *EC – Seal Products* (n 43) para 5.144.

[98] Panel Report, *China – Rare Earth* (n 89) paras 7.390–7.405.

[99] EW Bond and J Trachtman, 'China – Rare Earths: Export Restrictions and the Limits of Textual Interpretation' (2016) 15 (2) *World Trade Review* 189, 204.

[100] Appellate Body Report, *EC – Seal Products* (n 43) para 5.167.

[101] Appellate Body Report, *China – Rare Earth* (n 89) para 5.156.

[102] Ibid, para 5.159.

an export quota could result in a reduction of foreign consumption in an amount greater than the increase in domestic consumption. Moreover, there is no doubt that China's production quota, considered alone, has the effect of reducing overall output, and thus consumption.[103] But the AB dismissed the evaluation of the actual effects of China's measures on conservation as unnecessary.[104]

### *ii. The Chapeau and 'Arbitrary or Unjustifiable Discrimination'*

The measure at issue must not only fall within one of the exceptions, it also must satisfy the requirements in the chapeau. The purpose of the chapeau is to prevent the 'abuse' or misuse of a Member's right to invoke the exceptions.[105] As explained by the AB in *US – Shrimp*:

> [The chapeau] ... embodies the recognition ... of the need to maintain a *balance* of rights and obligations between the right of a Member to invoke one or another of the exceptions of Article XX, on the one hand, and the substantive rights of the other Members under the GATT 1994, on the other hand.[106]

To locate and mark out a line of equilibrium so that 'neither of the competing rights will cancel out the other' is a delicate task because it 'moves as the kind and shape of the measures at stake vary and as the facts making up specific cases differ'.[107] Another handhold to grasp the chapeau is that it is simply 'but one expression of the principle of good faith', a principle of international law asserting that rights must be exercised bona fide and reasonably.[108] The chapeau contains both substantive and procedural requirements.[109] The burden of demonstrating that a measure meets the chapeau requirements rests with the responding party.[110]

The AB previously emphasised that in contrast to the sub-paragraphs of Article XX, which address the design, content, and structure of the measure, the focus of the analysis under the chapeau is the manner in which the measure was *applied*.[111] But such a distinction is spurious as it is only one single measure to be examined under both the subparagraphs and the chapeau.[112] In any case, the AB has downplayed the significance of this distinction in more recent rulings.

[103] Bond and Trachtman (n 99) 204.
[104] Appellate Body Report, *China – Rare Earth* (n 89) para 5.152.
[105] Appellate Body Report, *US – Gasoline* (n 86) 22.
[106] Appellate Body Report, *US – Shrimp* (n 88) para 156.
[107] Ibid, para 159.
[108] Ibid, para 158.
[109] Ibid, para 160.
[110] Appellate Body Report, *US – Gasoline* (n 86) 22-3.
[111] Ibid, 22.
[112] L Bartels, 'The Chapeau of the General Exceptions in the WTO GATT and GATS Agreements: A Reconstruction' (2015) 109 *American Journal of International Law* 95, 101; A Davies, 'Interpreting the Chapeau of GATT Article XX in Light of the 'New' Approach in *Brazil- Tyres*' (2009) 43 *Journal of World Trade* 507, 529–530.

In *EC – Seal Products*, the AB noted that 'whether a measure is applied in a particular manner can most often be discerned from the design, architecture, and the revealing structure of a measure'.[113]

The essential requirement of the chapeau is that a measure provisionally justified under one of the subparagraphs of Article XX must not be applied in a manner that 'would constitute a means of arbitrary or unjustifiable discrimination between countries where the same conditions prevail'.[114] This requirement is in essence an anti-discrimination provision. To find a violation of this requirement, three elements must exist. First, the application of the measure must result in *discrimination*. Second, the discrimination must be '*arbitrary or unjustifiable*' in character. Third, this discrimination must occur 'between countries where the same conditions prevail'.

For the first element of 'discrimination', the early WTO jurisprudence stated that the nature and quality of discrimination in the chapeau must be different from the discrimination found to be inconsistent with one of the substantive obligations of the GATT 1994.[115] The AB has since abandoned this position. In *EC – Seal Products*, the AB observed that its earlier holding 'does not mean that the circumstances that bring about the discrimination that is to be examined under the chapeau *cannot be the same* as those that led to the finding of a violation of a substantive provision of the GATT 1994'.[116] Similar to Article III.4, discrimination under the chapeau is fundamentally an economic concept that is determined by comparing like products from different countries that are competing in the domestic marketplace.[117] Still, significant variations may exist between the discrimination analysis under the substantive GATT provisions and the chapeau. In particular, the AB may consider a wide range of the circumstances that bring out the discrimination under the chapeau, including, *but are not limited to*, the circumstances that led to the finding of a violation of a substantive GATT provision.[118] For example, in *EC – Seal Products*, the AB considered whether the measure had any discriminatory effects on different indigenous communities, an issue that had not been considered in the discrimination analysis under Article 1.1 of the GATT 1994.[119]

The second element is to examine whether the discrimination is 'arbitrary or unjustifiable'. With the exception of *US – Shrimp*, the AB has not drawn

[113] Appellate Body Report, *EC – Seal Products* (n 43) para 5.302.

[114] The chapeau also requires that the measure must not constitute 'a disguised restriction to international trade'. However, the AB has consistently held that it had the same meaning as 'arbitrary and unjustifiable discrimination'. See Appellate Body Report, *US – Gasoline* (n 86) 25; Appellate Body Report, *Brazil – Measures Affecting Imports of Retreaded Tyres* (*Brazil – Retreaded Tyres*), WT/DS332/AB/R, adopted 17 December 2007, para 238.

[115] Appellate Body Report, *US – Gasoline* (n 86) 23; see also Appellate Body Report, *US – Shrimp* (n 88) para 150.

[116] Appellate Body Report, *EC – Seal Products* (n 43) para 5.298.

[117] Ibid, para 5.130.

[118] Ibid, para 5.316.

[119] Ibid, para 5.333.

any significant distinction between 'arbitrary' and 'unjustifiable' discrimination to date, and usually treated them as one single unified concept. Despite its central position in the chapeau, the AB hadn't constructed any analytical points for finding arbitrary or unjustifiable discrimination until *Brazil – Retreaded Tyres*.[120] For example, in *US – Shrimp*, the AB effectively read into the chapeau a number of due process requirements of notice and opportunity for hearing for the benefit of foreign states and economic actors. In addition, the AB seemed to have imposed a general duty to negotiate with other WTO Members prior to taking unilateral trade measures. But neither conclusion can be derived from any textual analysis of the term 'arbitrary or unjustifiable discrimination' or in the broader context of GATT 1994.[121] Therefore, the AB's expansive reading of the chapeau was criticised of giving itself broad, if not limitless, room to locate the line of equilibrium between trade and non-trade concerns wherever it saw fit.[122]

In *Brazil – Retreated Tyres*, the AB held that such a determination is essentially an analysis that relates primarily to the *cause or the rationale* of the discrimination put forward to explain its existence.[123] In this case, Brazil defended its exemption of remoulded tyres originating from South Common Market (MERCOSUR) countries from the application of the import ban on the basis that a MERCOSUR tribunal found that Brazil's import ban was prohibited under MERCOSUR rules. The AB dismissed the argument because it borne no relationship to the asserted legitimate objective of protecting human health pursued by the import ban, and even went against this objective.[124] After *Brazil – Retreated Tyres*, it was established that the determination of arbitrary or unjustifiable discrimination is examined in the light of the policy goals with respect to which the measure has been provisionally justified under one of the subparagraphs.[125]

However, such an analytical framework turns out to be problematic in *EC – Seal Products*. Different from other trade disputes in which the defending party pursued only one legitimate regulatory objective, the EU pursued two legitimate, whilst inherently conflicting, objectives: protecting public morals against inhumane killing of seals and protecting the traditional lifestyle of indigenous peoples. Applying the analytical framework set out in *Brazil – Retreated Tyres*,

[120] Gaines (n 90) 775.

[121] McRae (n 28) 230-1; RB Stewart and MRS Badin, 'The World Trade Organization: Multiple Dimensions of Global Administrative Law' (2011) 9 *International Journal of Constitutional Law* 556, 571.

[122] JH Knox, 'The Judicial Resolution of Conflicts between Trade and the Environment' (2004) 28 *Harvard Environmental Law Review* 1, 56.

[123] Appellate Body Report, *Brazil – Retreaded Tyres* (n 114) paras 225–6.

[124] Ibid, 228.

[125] Davies (n 112) 519. This position marked a departure from the AB's earlier holding in *US – Shrimp*, see Appellate Body Report, *US – Shrimp* (n 88) para 149. On the most recent application of this analytical framework, see Panel Report, *Indonesia – Importation of Horicultural Products, Animals and Animal Products Licensing*, WT/DS477/R, adopted on 22 November 2017, para 7.824.

the existence of indigenous communities exception (IC exception), no matter how it is designed and implemented, would constitute arbitrary or unjustifiable discrimination under the chapeau. This is because permitting hunting and killing seals by indigenous people runs counter to the EU objective of protecting seal welfare.[126] On the other hand, there is wide consensus in international legal instruments, such as the United Nations (UN) Declaration on the Rights of Indigenous Peoples, on the recognised interest of Inuit and indigenous people in preserving their traditions and cultures.[127] To carve out an IC exception to mitigate the adverse effects resulting from the EU seal regime is apparently a legitimate purpose. Therefore, the analytical framework outlined in *Brazil – Retreated Tyres* is too narrow and inappropriate for regulations with multiple legitimate purposes.[128]

If the AB could explicitly accept that justification for discrimination under the chapeau may or may not be based on the policy objectives listed in Article XX(a) to (j), then the IC exception could be analysed on its own terms, for example, whether the design and implementation of the IC exception constitutes arbitrary or unjustifiable discrimination.[129] However, the AB did not choose this approach, arguably out of concerns that the protection of traditional lifestyle of indigenous peoples is not listed in Article XX as a legitimate objective and that the AB had not conducted a necessity test for the IC hunts exceptions under one of the subparagraphs. As a compromise, the AB modified its position in *Brazil – Retreated Tyres*, stating that:

> the relationship of the discrimination to the regulatory objective is only 'one of the most important factors, but not the sole test, that is relevant to the assessment of arbitrary or unjustifiable discrimination … there could be additional factors that may also be relevant to that overall assessment'.[130]

This statement is an implicit recognition that *the rationales behind the exceptions* could still provide justification to discrimination, even if they do not positively relate to the immediate policy objective of the measure at issue.[131] By doing so, the AB has opened the door for considering a broader scope of policy rationales under the chapeau, such as protection of traditional lifestyle of indigenous peoples, beyond the list of policy objectives specified in Article XX.[132]

[126] Panel Report, *EC – Seal Products* (n 43) para 7.275.

[127] Ibid, para 7.295; WJ Moon and AS Sweet, 'Consensus Analysis, State Practice, and Majoritarian Activism in the WTO', AJIL Unbound (25 June 2015).

[128] D Regan, 'Measures with Multiple Purposes: Puzzles from *EC – Seal Products*', AJIL Unbound (25 June 2015).

[129] G Shaffer and D Pabian, '*European Communities – Measures Prohibiting the Importation and Marketing of Seal Products*' (2015) 109 *American Journal of International Law* 154, 158.

[130] Appellate Body Report, *EC – Seal Products* (n 43) para 5.321.

[131] HH Jia, 'The Legitimacy of Exceptions Containing Exceptions in WTO Law: Some Thoughts on *EC – Seal Products*' (2015) 14 (2) *Chinese Journal of International Law* 411, 414.

[132] J Qin, 'Accommodating Divergent Policy Objectives under the WTO Law: Reflections on *EC – Seal Products*', in AJIL Unbound (25 June 2015).

The AB then proceeded to find that the IC exception constituted arbitrary or unjustifiable discrimination for three reasons. First, the manner in which the EU treats IC hunts as opposed to commercial hunts cannot be reconciled with the policy objective of addressing EU public moral concerns. Second, because of the vagueness of the IC requirements such as 'subsistence' and 'partial use', the IC exception could not safeguard against its potential abuse. Third, the IC exception affects Inuit communities in different countries unevenly because the EU treated Greenlandic Inuit better than it did to Canadian Inuit.[133]

There is some apparent contradiction in the AB's reasoning. On the one hand, following *Brazil – Retreated Tyres*, the AB continued to criticise the lack of rationality between the IC exception and the EU's objective of safeguarding seal welfare. On the other hand, the AB did not demand the removal of the IC exception, but questioned the EU why it couldn't 'do anything further' to ensure that the welfare of seals is addressed *in the context of IC hunts exception*, and in particular the design and implementation of the IC hunts. This apparent contradiction shows that the AB has implicitly accepted the legitimate purpose of the EU Seal Regime to safeguard Inuit traditions. Following the AB's ruling, an agreement was reached between Canada and the EU regarding access of seal products obtained from Inuit hunts to the EU market under the IC exception.[134]

The AB could have clarified that, under the chapeau, there is no 'arbitrary or unjustifiable' discrimination if the alleged discrimination reasonably reflects a legitimate regulatory objective, even if this policy objective goes beyond the exhaustive list of Article XX(a) to (j). As Qin points out, textually, there is no obstacle for taking this interpretative position, since the chapeau does not limit the scope of reasons that may be used to justify the discrimination.[135] This approach would have also brought the reasoning under the GATT chapeau and TBT Article 2.1 into closer alignment.[136] But this interpretation leaves open the question of how to identify the set of objectives that can justify discrimination under the chapeau. Should the legitimate objective be recognised in the WTO Agreements or other international instruments, or any objective considered to be legitimate by the regulating WTO Member will suffice? Clearly, it will be much less controversial to justify the former than the latter.

It is also well settled in the existing WTO jurisprudence that there can be arbitrary or unjustifiable discrimination if reasonably available alternative measures exist that would achieve the legitimate objective in a *less discriminatory* (not less trade restrictive) manner.[137] In *US – Gasoline*, the AB found

[133] Appellate Body Report, *EC – Seal Products* (n 43) paras 5.320–5.333.

[134] 'Canada, EU Strike Deal on Indigenous-hunted Seal Products', www.nunatsiaqonline.ca/stories/article/65674canada_eu_strike_deal_on_indigenous-hunted_seal_products/ (10 October 2014).

[135] Qin (n 132).

[136] See part I.C below.

[137] GM Duran, 'Measures with Multiple Competing Purposes after EC-Seal Products: Avoiding a Conflict between GATT Article XX-Chapeau and Article 2.1 TBT Agreement' (2016) 19 *Journal*

that the US could cooperate with foreign producers to avoid the discrimination resulting from the application of different baseline requirements.[138] Precisely because of the failure on the part of the US to seek a less discriminatory alternative measure, the AB ruled that the US measure constituted a means of arbitrary or unjustifiable discrimination. Similarly, in *EC – Seal Products*, the EU could have made comparable efforts to facilitate market access for seal products deriving from Canadian Inuit hunts and could have ensured that all seal products deriving from hunts properly characterised as 'commercial' were prohibited. Both amendments would have been less discriminatory than the measure actually adopted.[139] Some commentators were concerned about the overlapping between the chapeau and the individual paragraphs of Article XX. In particular, since the suitability and necessity of the measure has already been examined under the subparagraphs, the risk of double-testing may occur if the analysis under subparagraphs plays a role under the chapeau analysis as well.[140] After *EC – Seal Products*, it should be clear that these concerns are not warranted. There is a clear division of labour between the two. The analysis under the chapeau could go beyond the policy objectives contained in Article XX(a) to (j). Also, while the necessity test under the subparagraphs considers the *trade restrictiveness* of the measure, the *discriminatory effects* of the measure are considered under the chapeau. Even if the alternative less discriminatory measure may be more trade restrictive than the measure at issue, it does not affect the conclusion. For example, in *US – Gasoline*, the AB suggested that the US could have imposed 'higher statutory baseline without differentiation as between domestic and imported gasoline'.[141] In the same vein, in *EC – Seal Products*, the AB suggested that the EU could adopt tighter measures to prevent all commercial hunts.[142]

In summary, the determination of 'arbitrary and unjustifiable discrimination' is essentially an analysis to ascertain the cause or the rationale of the discrimination. To fulfil the chapeau requirements, the measure at issue must meet two essential criteria. First, it must be pursuing a legitimate regulatory objective. Importantly, this objective does not necessarily coincide with the policy objectives contained in Article XX(a) to (j). Second, the measure at issue must be 'necessary' in the sense that no reasonably available alternative measures exist that would achieve the legitimate objective in a *less discriminatory manner*. This implicit necessity test in the chapeau of GATT Article XX should

*of International Economic Law* 467, 481–482; W Zhou, '*US – Clove Cigarettes* and *US – Tuna II* (Mexico): Implications for the Role of Regulatory Purpose under Article III:4 of the GATT' (2012) 15 (4) *Journal of International Economic Law* 1075, 1120; E Vranes, *Trade and the Environment: Fundamental Issues in International Law, WTO Law, and Legal Theory* (Oxford University Press, 2009) 280.

[138] Appellate Body Report, *US – Gasoline* (n 86) 28–29.

[139] Bartels (n 112) 119–120.

[140] Vranes (n 137) 277–278.

[141] Appellate Body Report, *US – Gasoline* (n 86) 25.

[142] Appellate Body Report, *EC – Seal Products* (n 43) para 5.328.

be distinguished from the explicit necessity test in the subparagraphs, to be discussed in part III below.

For the last element, 'between countries where the same conditions prevail', the AB held that arbitrary or unjustifiable discrimination could occur not only between different exporting Members, but also between exporting and importing Members.[143] The term 'conditions' could potentially encompass a very wide range of different circumstances, such as different cultural, religious, geographical, political and economic conditions. However, the identification of the relevant conditions should be understood by reference to the relevant regulatory objectives of Article XX under which the measure was provisionally justified and the substantive obligations under the GATT 1994 with which a violation has been found.[144] The burden of proof falls on the respondent to show that the conditions prevailing in different countries are not 'the same'. It remains unclear how wide/narrow the concept of 'the same conditions prevail' is. To date, the AB has never found that 'conditions' were not the same in different countries. In *EC – Seal Products*, the AB held that the conditions were the same between Canada, Norway and Greenland because of the same animal welfare concerns from seal hunting.[145] While the EU has pointed to the different level of development in the organisation of the marketing structure achieved by the Inuit communities in Greenland as compared to the Canadian Inuit communities, the AB held that the EU failed to explain how these differences would render the conditions prevailing in Canada and Greenland different in a respect that would be relevant under the chapeau.[146] Nevertheless, it is clear that if the AB holds that 'conditions' in different countries are not the same, then some discrimination may be justified under the chapeau test. Going forward, how will the AB interpret 'the same conditions' may prove to be the key to open up more policy space for a regulating WTO Member.[147]

### a. An Evaluation of the Article XX Jurisprudence

While loosening the interpretative rigor of the subparagraphs, the AB has made an 'epochal and revolutionary' move by shifting its interpretative focus to the chapeau.[148] For a long time, the AB's interpretation of the chapeau was accused

[143] Appellate Body Report, *US – Shrimp* (n 88) para 150.

[144] Appellate Body Report, *EC – Seal Products* (n 43) paras 5.300–5.301; Bartels (n 112) 112.

[145] Ibid, para 5.317.

[146] Ibid.

[147] One view argues that the expression 'arbitrary or unjustifiable discrimination between countries where the same conditions prevail' should be examined as a whole. This means that the elements 'unjustifiable' and 'between countries where the same conditions prevail' can be scrapped, as the instances falling thereunder can be subsumed under the arbitrariness test. See C Riffel, 'The Chapeau: Stringent Threshold or Good Faith Requirement' (2018) 45 (2) *Legal Issues of Economic Integration* 141, 175.

[148] Cho (n 35) 47.

of imposing extraordinary preconditions on member governments, an approach that resulted in a very limited role for Article XX.[149] If these assertions are true, it means that even if the AB has loosened the previously stringent interpretation of the subparagraphs, the same stringency may now move to the chapeau.

Previous criticisms to the AB's interpretation of the chapeau mainly came from two fronts. The first criticism concerned the AB's general conception of the status of the chapeau in the WTO framework. In the case law, the AB highlighted that (1) the purpose and object of the chapeau is generally the prevention of 'abuse' of exceptions of Article XX;[150] (2) the actual process of applying the chapeau is a *balancing process* between the right to invoke an exception and the rights of other Members under varying substantive provisions; and (3) Article XX exceptions are 'limited and conditional'. The AB's treatment of the burden of proof under the chapeau is also revealing. In *US – Gasoline*, this burden was said to be 'of necessity' heavier than the burden of meeting the other requirements of Article XX.[151] Taken together, there was a strong indication that the AB viewed the exceptions in Article XX as measures that take away treaty rights, not as measures that are in themselves treaty rights. Provisions that take away treaty rights such as Article XX deserve to be interpreted stringently.[152] As Gaines criticised:

> [The AB] … only underscores the need for a clear analysis of when an environmentally-based trade measure can be said to cross the line between a valid invocation of the treaty-based Article XX right and an illegitimate abuse of that right, without discussing the risk that one Member could abuse its 'substantive rights' in a way that devalue the right of another Member to national action within the scope of Article XX.[153]

The second criticism was directed at the AB's interpretation of 'arbitrary or unjustifiable discrimination'. In *US – Shrimp*, the AB read the chapeau as giving it broad powers to strike a balance, or draw a 'line of equilibrium' between the legitimate public interests protected by the specific exceptions in Article XX and the trade interests furthered by what it called the 'substantive' provisions of GATT. However, the AB had failed to construct any analytical point for its findings of 'arbitrary or unjustifiable discrimination', and consistently imposed additional duties on WTO Members without textual support.[154]

To what extent are these criticisms still valid today? It is submitted that the AB has rectified most of the problems identified by earlier commentators. It is no

[149] McRae (n 28) 230; Gaines (n 90) 743.

[150] The doctrine of abuse of rights does not serve as an analytical basis for delimiting the chapeau from the subparagraphs of the general exceptions because it may well be argued that the conditions in the subparagraphs are also for the purpose of preventing abuse of rights. See Bartels (n 112) 102.

[151] Appellate Body Report, *US – Gasoline* (n 86) 23.

[152] McRae (n 28) 232.

[153] Gaines (n 90) 831.

[154] McRae (n 28) 230-1; Knox (n 122) 56.

longer justifiable to criticise the AB for not fully appreciating the value of non-trade interests. In *Brazil – Retreated Tyres*, the AB stressed that to determine the appropriate level of protection (ALOP) in a given context is *a fundamental principle* of the right that WTO Members have.[155] In addition, the AB clarified that an analysis of 'arbitrary or unjustifiable discrimination' is in essence an evaluation of whether the reasons given for the discrimination bear any rational connection to the purported regulatory objective. In other words, it is a test of rationality. More specifically, the AB has constructed essential reference points to analyse arbitrary or unjustifiable discrimination: the measure at issue must be both pursuing a legitimate regulatory objective and 'necessary' in the sense that no reasonably available alternative measures exist that would achieve the legitimate objective in a less discriminatory manner.

The least discriminatory requirement in the chapeau test is a stringent one. As the AB illustrated in *US – Gasoline*, *US – Shrimp* and *EC – Seal Products*, the AB may consider a wide range of circumstances that bring out the discrimination under the chapeau, including, but are not limited to, the circumstances that led to the finding of violation of a substantive provision.[156] Recall that the necessity test in the subparagraphs of Article XX has imposed a least trade restrictive requirement on the measure at issue, it may be argued that Article XX as a whole demands a regulation found to be inconsistent with a substantive obligation to be both least trade restrictive and least discriminatory to be justifiable. Undoubtedly, this is a high bar. On the other hand, in *EC – Seal Products*, the AB has opened the door for considering a broader scope of policy rationales under the chapeau, well beyond the list of policy objectives specified by the subparagraphs of Article XX. This has increased the policy space for a WTO Member to regulate for a legitimate purpose, although the outward boundary of legitimate purposes is still open to debate. In addition, different from the necessity test in the subparagraphs of Article XX, a violation of which may require a WTO Member to withdraw the measure at issue and adopt an alternative less trade restrictive measure, a violation of chapeau usually only requires a WTO Member to eliminate the discriminatory features of the measure at issue.

## C. The National Treatment Obligation in the TBT Agreement

One of the main purposes for negotiating the TBT Agreement was to prevent countries from protecting domestic industries by using technical regulations to discriminate against imported products. Article 2.1 provides:

> Members shall ensure that in respect of technical regulations, products imported from the territory of any Member shall be accorded treatment no less favourable

[155] Appellate Body Report, *Brazil – Retreaded Tyres* (n 114) para 210.
[156] Appellate Body Report, *EC – Seal Products* (n 43) para 5.316.

than that accorded to like products of national origin and to like products originating in any other country.

The NT obligation in TBT Article 2.1 is similar to Article III:4 of the GATT. But how closely should TBT Article 2.1 follow the jurisprudence of Article III:4 is a matter of debate.[157] The principal difference between GATT Article III:4 and TBT Article 2.1 is that the GATT provides affirmative defences for violations in Article XX exceptions. By contrast, the TBT Agreement does not contain any similar provisions. Without exception provisions, the AB faces the challenge of how to interpret Article 2.1 to achieve its purpose of protecting legitimate regulation while preventing trade discrimination.

According to the AB, for a violation of the NT obligation in Article 2.1 to be established, three elements must be satisfied: (i) the measure at issue must be a technical regulation; (ii) the imported and domestic products at issue must be 'like products'; and (iii) the treatment accorded to imported products must be less favourable than that accorded to like domestic products.[158] In recent TBT disputes, the AB has developed a consistent interpretation of the NT obligation in Article 2.1.

### *i. 'Like products'*

In *US – Clove Cigarettes*, the panel questioned the rationale of a competition-based approach in determining 'like products' in Article 2.1 of the TBT Agreement. Instead, the panel argued that such a determination should be influenced by the fact that the measure in question was a technical regulation having the immediate purpose of regulating cigarettes for public health reasons.[159] In essence, the panel attempted to revive at least part of the aims and effects test in determining like products under the TBT Agreement.[160] The AB firmly rejected such an attempt and held that the determination of 'like products' under TBT Article 2.1 should adopt the same competition-oriented approach as GATT Article III:4. It is a determination about the nature and extent of a competitive relationship between and among products at issue.[161]

Moreover, the AB drew a distinction between the regulatory *purpose* of the measures and the regulatory *concerns* underlying the measure. While the

[157] J Flett, 'WTO Space for National Regulation: Requiem for a Diagonal Vector Test' (2013) 16 (1) *Journal of International Economic Law* 37, 73; MA Crowley and R Howse, '*Tuna – Dolphin II*: A Legal and Economic Analysis of the Appellate Body Report' (2014) 13 *World Trade Review* 321, 332.

[158] Appellate Body Report, *US – Clove Cigarettes* (n 21) para 87.

[159] Ibid, para 107; G Marceau, 'The New TBT Jurisprudence in *US – Clove Cigarettes, US – II, and US – COOL*' (2014) 8 (1) *Asian Journal of WTO and International Health Law and Policy* 1, 7.

[160] J Meltzer and A Porges, 'Beyond Discrimination? The WTO Parses the TBT Agreement in US-Clove Cigarettes, US-Tuna II (Mexico) and US-Cool' (2013) 14 *Melbourne Journal of International Law* 1, 14.

[161] Appellate Body Report, *US – Clove Cigarettes* (n 21) para 120.

regulatory purpose should not be considered in determining 'like products', the regulatory concerns may play a role in the determination of like products to the extent that they are relevant to the examination of certain likeness criteria and are reflected in the competitive relationship between and among the products concerned.[162] In *EC – Asbestos*, for example, health risks associated with chrysotile asbestos were considered relevant in determining whether chrysotile asbestos and PCG fibres were like products. This is because health risks affect physical properties as well as consumer tastes and preferences.[163]

The AB also clarified that a panel should discount any distortive effects that the measure at issue may itself have on the competitive relationship, and reserve the consideration of such effects for the analysis of less favourable treatment.[164] Clearly, the requirement to consider the competitive relationship between the products *in isolation from* the measure at issue is based on the AB's appreciation that a regulation itself can inform consumers of product differences, which in turn affect consumer tastes and habits.[165] However, the AB's assumption that regulation can be separated out from the market disregards the extent to which regulation permeates modern economics and informs consumers' attitude. This will require a panel to base its decisions on hypothetical speculation about how consumers would behave absent the challenged measure. As Meltzer and Porges warned, a panel engaged in hypothetical inquiry of this sort may be pulled away from the objective facts of whether and how goods compete in the market, toward its own assessment of how consumers should view the products at issue.[166]

### *ii. 'Treatment No Less Favourable' and 'Legitimate Regulatory Distinction'*

The interpretation of 'treatment no less favourable' is a tricky one in the TBT Agreement. The TBT Agreement does not contain a general exceptions clause similar to GATT Article XX. If 'treatment no less favourable' were interpreted in the same way as Article III:4, then *any* technical regulation having a detrimental impact on the group of imported products vis-à-vis the group of domestic like products would violate Article 2.1. This will be the case even if the technical regulation in question has a legitimate regulatory objective and is executed even-handedly. Clearly, this is not an acceptable outcome, as it would prioritise trade liberalisation with no regard to other non-economic social values.

In *US – Clove Cigarettes*, referring to the sixth recital of the preamble of the TBT Agreement, which highlights that no countries should be prevented

162 Ibid, para 120.

163 Appellate Body Report, *EC – Asbestos* (n 8) paras 114 and 122.

164 Ibid, para 111.

165 MF Teisl, B Roe and RL Hicks, 'Can Eco-Labels Tune a Market? Evidence from Dolphin-Safe Labelling' (2002) 43 *Journal of Environmental Economics and Management* 339.

166 Meltzer and Porges (n 160), 15–16.

from taking measures necessary to pursue policy objectives, the AB first argued that the purpose of Article 2.1 was not to prohibit a priori any obstacles to international trade. Rather, a WTO Member has the right to pursue legitimate regulatory objectives.[167] The AB proceeded to reason that a finding of 'treatment no less favourable' under Article 2.1 requires a two-step analysis. First, a panel must find that the measure at issue modifies the conditions of competition in the relevant market to the detriment of like imported products. It is submitted that the first step mirrors much of GATT Article III:4. However, different from GATT Article III:4, the existence of such a detrimental effect, by itself, is not sufficient to demonstrate less favourable treatment in Article 2.1 of the TBT Agreement. In the second step, a panel must further analyse whether the detrimental impact on imports *stems exclusively from a legitimate regulatory distinction*.[168] Textually, the term 'legitimate regulatory distinction' can be taken to mean a measure which has the effect of differentiating between products in a fair and justifiable manner in pursuance of a reasonable and justifiable objective.[169] As a legal test constructed by the AB, the TBT Agreement does not provide much guidance on how to assess the legitimacy of the distinction that a measure draws. For this reason, the AB, informed by the sixth recital of the TBT Agreement, extrapolated the arbitrary and unjustifiable discrimination test from GATT Article XX chapeau test and has applied it in the context of TBT Article 2.1.[170] If a regulatory distinction is not designed and applied in an even-handed manner, then it constitutes a means of arbitrary or unjustifiable discrimination and the distinction cannot be considered 'legitimate'.[171] In assessing even-handedness, a panel must scrutinise the design, architecture, revealing structure, operation and application of the technical regulation at issue.[172]

In *US – Clove Cigarettes*, the panel found that clove cigarettes and menthol cigarettes were 'like products' and that clove cigarettes were banned whilst menthol cigarettes were permitted. Moreover, clove cigarettes sold in the US market were primarily imported from Indonesia. By contrast, the permitted menthol cigarettes were primarily produced in the US, accounting for about 26 per cent of the total US cigarette market.[173] Based on the evidence, there was

[167] Appellate Body Report, *US – Clove Cigarettes* (n 21) para 95.

[168] Ibid, para 182.

[169] JH McMillan, 'The Legitimate Regulatory Distinction Test: Incomplete and Inadequate for the Particular Purposes of the TBT Agreement' (2016) 15(4) *World Trade Review* 543, 553–554.

[170] F Valinaki, 'Repairing the Defects of Article 2.1 of the WTO Barriers to Trade Agreement: An Amendment Proposal' (2016) 43 (1) *Legal Issues of Economic Integration* 65, 80; Norpoth (n 65) 594; J Meltzer, 'The WTO Ruling on U.S. Country of Origin Labeling' ("COOL"), 16 (23) *ASIL Insight* (2012); Zhou (n 137) 1100.

[171] Appellate Body Report, *United States – Certain Country of Origin Labeling (COOL) Requirements (US – Cool)* WT/DS384/AB/R, adopted 29 June 2012, para 271; Appellate Body Report, *US – Cool (Recourse to Article 21.5 by Canada and Mexico)*, WT/DS384/AB/RW, adopted 29 May 2015, para 5.93.

[172] Appellate Body Report, *US – Clove Cigarettes* (n 21) para 182.

[173] Ibid, para 224.

little difficulty for the AB to conclude that such differential treatment was to the detriment of the imported clove cigarettes. In *US – Tuna II*, Mexico challenged the US labelling scheme that prohibited the use of the 'dolphin-safe' label on tuna marketed in the US in any instance where the tuna was caught by a method involving encircling or setting upon dolphins. Most tuna caught by Mexican vessels were not eligible for the label whilst most tuna caught by the US and other countries were eligible for a 'dolphin-safe' label. The 'dolphin-safe' label has significant commercial value since major US canners and distributors buy only tuna that carries the label. The AB found that the lack of access to the 'dolphin-safe' label had a detrimental impact on the competitive opportunities of Mexican tuna products in the US market.[174] In *US – Cool*, the US government imposed on retailers an obligation to provide country of origin labelling (COOL) information on a range of meat products. In order for retailers to comply with the COOL and affix an appropriate label, upstream meat producers segregated livestock according to origin to enable record-keeping regarding livestock origin although the COOL measure does not require it. Because imported livestock constitute a small percentage of the overall US market, the least costly way of complying with the COOL measure is to avoid segregation by relying exclusively on US livestock.[175] Citing *Korea – Beef*, the AB stated:

> Whenever the operation of a measure in the market creates incentives for private actors systematically to make choices in ways that benefit domestic products to the detriment of like imported products, then such a measure may be found to treat imported products less favourably.[176]

For the second step of ascertaining whether the detrimental impact on imported products stems exclusively from a legitimate regulatory distinction, the analytical approach of identifying the rational connection between the disputed measure and a legitimate regulatory objective outlined by the AB in *Brazil – Retreaded Tyres* has informed the recent TBT cases. This is not surprising given the similarity of the legitimate regulatory distinction test in TBT Article 2.1 and the chapeau test of GATT Article XX. In *US – Tuna II*, tuna harvested in the ETP may be labelled 'dolphin-safe' only if the captain and an observer certify that no dolphins were killed or seriously injured and that there was no setting on dolphins during the same fishing trip.[177] However, the US labelling requirement did not address at all mortality (observed or unobserved) arising from fishing methods *other than setting on dolphins outside the ETP*. As a result, tuna caught in a non-ETP fishery would be eligible for the label even if dolphins had in fact been killed or seriously injured during the fishing trip.[178] This regulatory

[174] Appellate Body Report, *US – Tuna II* (n 53) paras 235–240.
[175] Appellate Body Report, *US – Cool* (n 171) para 287.
[176] Ibid, para 289.
[177] Ibid, para 176.
[178] Appellate Body Report, *US – Tuna II* (n 53) para 251.

distinction clearly cannot be reconciled with the US regulatory objectives of dolphin conservation and provision of reliable information to consumers.

In *US – Cool*, the AB found that the recordkeeping and verification requirements in the COOL measure imposed a *disproportionate* burden on upstream producers and processors.[179] This disproportionality cannot be explained by the need to convey to consumers through labels information on country of origin because the COOL measure as applied was unlikely to be successful in conveying accurate information to consumers for a number of reasons. First, the level of information conveyed to consumers was far less detailed and accurate than the information required to be tracked and transmitted. As a result, consumers were not able to comprehend the meaning of the labels accurately. Second, some labels led to confusing or inaccurate origin information conveyed to consumers. Third, upstream producers may be subject to the COOL measure's onerous recordkeeping and verification requirements even when the meat was ultimately exempt from the labelling requirements altogether. This led the AB to conclude that no rational basis existed for the large amount of information that upstream producers were required to collect in contrast to the small amount of information conveyed to consumers via the labels. The AB then concluded that the regulatory distinctions imposed by the COOL measure were not applied in an even-handed manner.[180]

Similar to the chapeau test in GATT Article XX, the detrimental impact under Article 2.1 of the TBT Agreement is not restrained by a rigid rational connection requirement. If a disputed measure pursues multiple competing objectives, it may also be justified by reference to reasons other than the main objective of the measure.[181] In *US – Clove Cigarettes*, for example, having found that the regulatory distinction between prohibited clove cigarettes and permitted menthol cigarettes could not be explained by the principal objective of the measure to reduce youth smoking, the AB went on to consider whether other unrelated reasons put forward by the US could nonetheless justify the regulatory distinction. The US argued that the exemption of menthol cigarettes from the ban was legitimate because of the severe potential impact of a menthol ban on US health care system such as withdrawal treatment and the potential development of a black market for cigarettes. However, the AB found that the evidence was not clear that these risks would materialise if menthol cigarettes were to be banned, insofar as regular cigarettes would remain in the market.[182] In fact, an advisory committee to the US Food and Drug Administration concluded in 2011 that removal of menthol cigarettes from the marketplace would benefit public health in the US.[183] Ultimately, the lack of legitimate regulatory distinction was

[179] Appellate Body Report, *US – Cool* (n 171) para 349.
[180] Ibid, paras 341–347.
[181] Duran (n 137) 484.
[182] Appellate Body Report, *US – Clove Cigarettes* (n 21) para 225.
[183] T Voon, 'Flexibilities in WTO Law to Support Tobacco Control Regulation' (2013) 39 *American Journal of Law & Medicine* 199, 203.

based on the finding that the rationale offered by the US to justify the distinction was not supported, or even contradicted by the available evidence.[184]

It can be seen that the analytical approach adopted by the AB necessitates the identification of legitimate regulatory objectives in TBT Article 2.1. Then, what regulatory objectives may be considered 'legitimate' under Article 2.1? Given that the text of Article 2.1 leaves this issue entirely open, it is likely that a panel will normally defer to a WTO Member's chosen regulatory objective as a policy matter because of the limited mandate of the WTO.[185] In particular, TBT Article 2.2, the fifth recital of the preamble and other WTO Agreements have been recognised as the relevant context for assessing the legitimacy of the invoked objectives. If a given objective falls within the listed objectives in one of the WTO Agreements, then its validity may be presumed.[186] If an objective is not listed, then a panel will conduct an independent inquiry of its legitimacy. On the other hand, not all regulatory objectives will be considered legitimate. In *US – Cool* (Article 21.5), the AB held that the cost saving enjoyed by US entities through the exemptions in the amended COOL measure could not justify the detrimental impact on imported livestock.[187] Finally, as the scope of legitimate objectives in Article 2.1 is open-ended, some suggested that a wider range of policy objectives may be permitted under TBT Article 2.1 than under GATT Article XX.[188] However, in *EC – Seal Products*, the AB challenged this notion and hinted that it would interpret the closed list of legitimate objectives in GATT Article XX more liberally so that there would not be asymmetry between the two provisions.[189]

The 'legitimate regulatory distinction' test in TBT Article 2.1 not only requires a rational connection between ends and means, but also *no less discriminatory* alternative measure is available that would be at least equally effective in fulfilling the objective pursued by the disputed measure.[190] In *US – Tuna II*, not convinced by the US argument that imposing a similar requirement outside the ETP would have significant monetary and infrastructure implications, the AB concluded that the US labelling requirements were not *proportionately calibrated* to the risks to dolphins arising from different fishing methods in different areas of the ocean, and thus they were not even-handed.[191] In *US – Cool*, the reason why the AB faulted the US measures was the fact that 'the informational

[184] Appellate Body Report, *US – Clove Cigarettes* (n 21) para 225.

[185] MM Du, 'From Non – Discrimination to Harmonization, Autonomy under the TBT Agreement' (2007) 6 *Chinese Journal of International Law* 269, 296.

[186] Appellate Body Report, *US – Tuna II* (n 53) para 313; Appellate Body Report, *US – Cool* (n 171) para 370; Appellate Body Report, *EC – Seal Products* (n 43) para 7.416.

[187] Appellate Body Report, *US – Cool* (Art 21.5) (n 171) paras 5.110–5.113.

[188] PI Levy and DH Regan, 'EC – Seal Products: Seals and Sensibilities' (TBT Aspects of the Panel and Appellate Body Reports) (2015) 14 (2) *World Trade Review* 337, 362.

[189] Appellate Body Report, *EC – Seal Products* (n 43) para 5.128.

[190] Duran (n 137) 487–488. PC Mavroidis, 'Last Mile for Tuna (to a Safe Harbour): What is the TBT Agreement All About?' (2019) 30 (1) *European Journal of International Law* 279, 294.

[191] Ibid, paras 293–297.

requirements imposed on upstream producers under the COOL measure were *disproportionate* as compared to the level of information communicated to consumers through the mandatory retail labels'.[192] However, proportionality is traditionally used to determine if a measure is necessary.[193] The AB's finding of disproportionality was not really a matter of discrimination between like products but a question of necessity of the measure as a whole.[194] It must be emphasised that what matters under Article 2.1 is whether a given legitimate objective can be achieved in a less discriminatory manner, even if not necessarily a less trade restrictive one, which is required by TBT Article 2.2.[195] In *US – Tuna II*, for example, in order to comply with the WTO ruling, the U.S. was obliged to address adverse effects on dolphins outside the ETP, even though the modified measure is more restrictive of trade in tuna products.[196]

Though a line could be drawn between Article 2.1 and 2.2 of the TBT Agreement as described above, the WTO case law in GATT Article XX shows that there are no facts that are per se excluded from the assessment of whether or not a measure is applied in an even-handed manner. Such facts may include the objective of the measure, whether the objective is legitimate, how is the measure applied, the extent to which the measure contributes to the objective at the chosen level, the existence of less trade discriminatory alternatives, whether the restrictiveness of the measure is somewhat disproportionate, and even the consistent treatment of similar situations.[197] Therefore, intentionally or unintentionally, the AB may examine under Article 2.1 what it is supposed to do under Article 2.2.[198] Under GATT Article XX, this problem does not exist because the order of analysis starts from the sub-paragraphs, and the necessity issue has already been dealt with *before* the chapeau test. In TBT Article 2.1, however, a necessary assumption of the AB's approach in *US – Cool* is that a less trade restrictive alternative exists that would require producers to keep track of less information. But without a full necessity analysis, it is unclear that the hypothetical alternative measure requiring less information from producers would be effective in fulfilling the US regulatory objective and would be reasonably available for implementation.[199] In addition, the determination of 'arbitrary or unjustifiable discrimination' in GATT Article XX is often examined in the

[192] Appellate Body Report, *US – Cool* (n 171) para 347.

[193] M Andenas and S Zlepting, 'Proportionality: WTO Law in Comparative Perspective' (2007) 42 *Texas Journal of International Law* 371, 407–8.

[194] J Pauwelyn, 'Cool … but what is Left now for TBT Art. 2.2?', http://worldtradelaw.typepad.com/ielpblog/2012/07/cool-but-what-is-left-now-of-tbt-art-22.html (3 July 2012).

[195] Bartels (n 112) 109.

[196] Appellate Body Report, *US – Tuna II* (Mexico) (*Article 21.5 Second Recourse*), WT/DS381/AB/RW2, adopted 14 December 2018, para 7.2.

[197] Flett (n 157) 63; B McGrady, *Trade and Public Health: The WTO, Tobacco, Alcohol, and Diet* (Cambridge University Press, 2011) 167; Zhou (n 137) 1120.

[198] Pauwelyn (n 194).

[199] J Carlone, 'An Added Exception to the TBT Agreement after Clove, II and Cool' (2014) 37 *Boston College International & Comparative Law Review* 103, 136.

light of regulatory objectives.[200] Again, the regulatory objectives have already been confirmed in the necessity analysis before the chapeau test under GATT Article XX. By contrast, the identification of regulatory objectives and the assessment of whether such regulatory objectives are 'legitimate' take place in Article 2.2 in the TBT Agreement. Therefore, it would be more logical for the AB to start the analysis from Article 2.2 before proceeding to Article 2.1.[201]

## II. THE MOST FAVOURED NATION TREATMENT

### A. Article I.1 of the GATT 1994

Different from the NT obligation which prohibits a WTO Member from favouring its domestic products over foreign like products, an MFN treatment obligation prohibits a WTO Member from favouring products from another WTO Member without extending the same favour to like products from any other WTO Members. Found directly and indirectly in a number of GATT provisions, it is considered as the cornerstone of GATT 1994 and one of the pillars of the WTO trading system.[202] Article I:1 of the GATT 1994 provides: '… any advantage … granted by any contracting party to any product originating in or destined for any other country shall be accorded immediately and unconditionally to the like product originating in or destined for the territories of all other contracting parties.' The object and purpose of the MFN treatment obligation is to ensure all WTO Members equality of competitive opportunities to import from, or export to, all other WTO Members, with the effect that like imported products from all WTO members are treated equally.[203] Similar to the NT obligation, the MFN obligation prohibits both de jure and de facto discrimination.[204] In *EC – Seal Products*, although the EC seal regime appeared neutral on its place, virtually all seal products originating in Greenland were likely to qualify under the IC exception for access to the EU market while the vast majority of seal products from Canada and Norway did not meet the IC requirement. The panel concluded that the EC measure was de facto inconsistent with Article I:1.[205]

To determine whether or not there is a violation of the MFN obligation of GATT Article 1:1, three questions must be answered: whether the measure at issue

[200] Appellate Body Report, *Brazil – Retreated Tyres* (n 114) paras 225–6; Davies (n 112) 519.

[201] PC Mavroidis, 'Driftin' too far from Shore- Why the Test for Compliance with the TBT Agreement Developed by the WTO Appellate Body is Wrong, and What Should the AB have Done Instead' (2013) 12 (3) *World Trade Review* 509, 524.

[202] Appellate Body Report, *European Communities – Conditions for the Granting of Tariff Preferences to Developing Countries*, WT/DS246/AB/R (7 April 2004), para 101.

[203] Appellate Body Report, *EC-Seal Products* (n 43) para 5.87; Appellate Body Report, *EC-Bananas III* (n 48) para 190.

[204] Appellate Body Report, *Canada- Certain Measures Affecting the Automotive Industry* (*Canada-Autos*), WT/DS139/AB/R (31 May 2000), para 78.

[205] Appellate Body Report, *EC-Seal Products* (n 43) para 5.95.

grants a trade advantage; whether the products concerned are 'like products'; and whether the advantage at issue is granted immediately and 'unconditionally' to all like products concerned. For the first question, the AB has given a broad definition to the term 'advantage', including any more favourable competitive opportunities or commercial relationships between like products of different origins.[206] For the second question, what has never been solved is the extent to which the term 'like product' under Article I:1 should be given the same meaning as the term 'like product' in GATT Article III as the case law on Article I:1 is very limited. Even though one should be cautious to transpose case law on 'like products' under Article III:4 to Article I:1 when non-tariff measures are involved, it is reasonable to expect that the objective factors that are taken into account in determining 'like products' under GATT Article III will inform the interpretation of the concept 'like products' in Article I:1.[207] This observation is based on the AB's interpretation of the purpose of the two provisions. In *EC-Seal Products*, the AB observed that, notwithstanding their textual differences, both provisions are concerned with prohibiting discriminatory measures and ensuring equality of competitive opportunities between products that are in a competitive relationship.[208]

For the third question on the meaning of 'unconditionally', the GATT/WTO has evolved over the years. From *Belgium-Family allowance* to *Indonesia – Auto*, most GATT/WTO panels interpreted the term as outlawing any conditions attached to the advantage accorded to all WTO Members. In *Indonesia – Autos*, the WTO panel took the view that duty and sales tax exemptions made conditional on local content requirements was inconsistent with the MFN 'unconditional' requirement because the right of Members cannot be made conditional on any contractual obligation.[209] From *Canada – Autos*, however, a second strand of cases took a different approach. This approach took the view that the term 'unconditionally' does not mean that a WTO Member is prohibited from attaching any conditions to the granting of an advantage within the meaning of Article I:1. Instead, it inquires whether an advantage, once it has been granted to the product of any country, is accorded 'unconditionally' to the like products of all other Members.[210] It prohibits only those conditions that have a detrimental impact on the competitive opportunities for like imported products from any Member.[211] The WTO AB has explicitly endorsed this new strand of jurisprudence in its recent rulings.[212]

[206] Panel Report, *United States- Certain Measures Affecting Imports of Poultry from China (US-Poultry)* (29 September 2010), para 7.415.

[207] D McRae, 'MFN in the GATT and the WTO' (2012) 7(1) *Asian Journal of WTO and International Health Law and Policy* 1, 13–14.

[208] Appellate Body Report, *EC – Seal Products* (n 43) para 5.82.

[209] WTO Panel Report, *Indonesia – Autos*, paras 14.143–14.146.

[210] WTO Panel Report, *Canada- Autos*, WT/DS139/R (11 February 2000), paras 10.22–10.24.

[211] Appellate Body Report, *EC – Seal Products* (n 43) para 5.88.

[212] Appellate Body Report, *EC – Tariff Preferences* (n 202) para 190; Art 21.5 Appellate Body Report, *US – Tuna II* (n 4) para 7.338.

### B. MFN in the TBT Agreement

Article 2.1 of the TBT Agreement provides that in respect of technical regulations, products imported from any WTO Member shall be accorded treatment *no less favourable than* that accorded to like products originating in any other country. Paragraph D of the CGP provides exactly the same MFN obligation, which stipulates that with respect to standards, the standardising body shall accord no less favourable treatment to all like products. The content of the MFN obligation in the TBT Agreement is clearly different from GATT Article I.1. To begin with, the test is no longer whether an advantage is accorded to 'like products' of all WTO Members unconditionally. Rather, it is whether imported products are receiving 'treatment no less favourable' than all other like imported products, similar to the NT obligation in GATT Article III:4 and the TBT Article 2.1. Moreover, GATT Article I:1 is tempered by GATT Article XX general exceptions, whilst the MFN treatment obligation in the TBT Agreement does not have a general exception provision of its own.

As the AB found in *US – Tuna II*, Article 2.1 sets out a largely similar three-tier test of consistency with the MFN treatment obligation as the national treatment obligation: (1) the measure at issue must be a technical regulation/standard; (ii) the imported products from other WTO Members are 'like products' and (iii) the imported products are accorded 'treatment no less favourable' than like products from any other WTO Members.[213] In view of the similarities of MFN treatment obligation and NT obligation under Article 2.1 of the TBT Agreement, all the analysis relating to 'like products' and 'treatment no less favourable' in part I.C.ii above is relevant to MFN treatment obligation as well. Specifically, for a finding of less favourable treatment, a panel must not only find that the technical regulation at issue modifies the conditions of competition in the relevant market to the detriment of imported products vis-à-vis like products originating in any other country, but also that the detrimental impact on imports does not stem exclusively from a legitimate regulatory distinction but reflects discrimination against imported products.[214]

In *US – Tuna II*, as the US applied different requirements to tuna caught by setting on dolphins inside the ETP and tuna caught by other fishing methods outside the ETP for access to the 'dolphin-safe' label even though the latter presented comparably high risks to dolphins, the AB found that the US measure was not calibrated to the risks to dolphins arising from different fishing methods in different areas of the ocean and therefore reflected a lack of even-handedness. The AB concluded that the US labelling scheme accorded less favourable treatment to Mexican tuna products than that accorded to tuna products originating in other countries.[215] After losing the case, the US amended tuna measures in

[213] Appellate Body Report, *US – Clove Cigarettes* (n 21) para 87.
[214] Appellate Body Report, *US – Tuna II* (n 53) para 215.
[215] Ibid, paras 293–297.

2013 to enhance the dolphin-safe requirement of tuna caught outside the ETP in an effort to comply with the ruling. The AB nevertheless found that the amended measures were still not calibrated to, or commensurate with, the risks to dolphins arising from different fishing methods in different areas of the oceans.[216] The US further amended tuna measures in 2016 to place three types of conditions on the use of the dolphin-safe label targeting different fishing methods and different areas. The AB finally upheld that the US 2016 tuna measures accord to Mexican tuna products treatment no less favourable than that accorded to like products from the US and other countries.[217]

In *EC – Seal Products*, the EU argued that the legal standard for the MFN treatment obligation under Article 2.1 of the TBT Agreement applies equally to Article I:1 of the GATT 1994. Give the structural difference between the GATT 1994 and the TBT Agreement, the AB rejected the EU's wholesale transplantation argument between the two provisions.[218] Nevertheless, the AB agreed that in assessing whether the measure affects competitive conditions under Article I:1, it may be reasonable to rely on any relevant findings it made in examining that measure's detrimental impact under Article 2.1 of the TBT Agreement.[219]

## III. UNNECESSARY OBSTACLES TO INTERNATIONAL TRADE

At first glance, there does not exist one uniform necessity test in the WTO law.[220] For example, the necessity test under GATT Article XX is to justify a measure found to be inconsistent with the GATT substantive obligations, whilst the necessity test under the TBT Agreement is an independent obligation applicable to all TBT measures.[221] One may also point to the seemingly more relaxed necessity test under the SPS Agreement as it requires the alternative measure not only feasible, but also *significantly* less trade restrictive. Nevertheless, beyond technicalities, the essence of the necessity test in WTO law is the same. The key question is whether there is an alternative measure not only less trade restrictive, but also reasonably available and able to achieve the regulatory objective pursued by the regulating WTO Member. The weighing and balancing test first outlined in *Korea – Beef* was precisely designed to perform this essential inquiry in a reasonable and transparent manner. As will be explored

[216] Art 21.5 Appellate Body Report, *US – Tuna II* (n 4) para 7.266.

[217] Appellate Body Report, *US – Tuna II* (Second Recourse to Art 21.5), WT/DS381/AB/RW2 (14 December 2018), paras 7.2–7.11.

[218] Appellate Body Report, *EC – Seal Products* (n 43) para 5.94.

[219] Art 21.5 Appellate Body Report, *US – Tuna II* (n 4) para 7.278.

[220] K Dawar and E Ronen, 'How "Necessary"? A Comparison of legal and Economic Assessments -GATT Disputes Settlements under Article XX (B), TBT 2.2 and SPS 5.6' (2016) 8 (1) *Trade, Law and Development* 1, 27–28.

[221] Du (n 185) 280.

in detail below, the necessity test across the WTO Agreements considers identical elements and follows the same line of inquiry. Despite their textual and structural differences, the AB has successfully pushed for a broad convergence in necessity tests across WTO Agreements.[222] The necessity test has been heavily criticised over the years. These criticisms centre around two issues. First, the legal standard that the AB formulated to evaluate 'necessity' was ambiguous, illogical, arbitrary and unpredictable.[223] The opaque legal standard has in turn led to the second problem of the expansion of the jurisdiction of WTO panels, demonstrating a disconcerting dependence on their discretion for the survival of domestic regulatory choices.[224] However, these oft-repeated criticisms are no longer justifiable in light of the recent developments in WTO case law. The AB has provided clear instructions on how to examine each element of the necessity test, how different elements interact and how to draw a conclusion after weighing and balancing these elements. Furthermore, the AB has substantially relaxed the necessity test over the past decade. This is particularly the case when the values or interests pursued by the disputed measures are important, such as human life or safety.[225]

### A. The Evolution of the Necessity Test under GATT Article XX

The term 'necessary' in Article XX was first interpreted in *US – Section 337* case, where the panel stated:

> [A] contracting party cannot justify a measure … as 'necessary' if an alternative measure which it could reasonably be expected to employ and which is not inconsistent with other GATT provision is available to it … [I]n cases where a measure consistent with other GATT provisions is not reasonably available, a contracting party is bound to use, among the measures reasonably available to it, that which entails the *least degree of inconsistency* with other GATT provisions.[226]

[222] M Du, 'The Necessity Test in WTO Law: What Now?' (2016) 15 (4) *Chinese Journal of International Law* 817, 846–7.

[223] DH Regan, 'The Meaning of 'Necessary' in GATT Article XX and GATS Article XIV: The Myth of Cost- Benefit Balancing' (2007) 6 *World Trade Review* 347, 348; CP Bown and JP Tratchman, '*Brazil – Measures Affecting Imports of Retreated Tyres*: A Balancing Act' (2009) 8 *World Trade Review* 85, 129–131.

[224] F Fontanelli, 'Necessity Killed the GATT Article XX and the Misleading Rhetoric about 'Weighing and Balancing' (2012) 4(2) *European Journal of Legal Studies* 39, 65–68; Kapterian (n 90) 91; B McGrady, 'Necessity Exceptions in WTO Law: Retreaded Tyres, Regulatory Purpose and Cumulative Regulatory Measures' (2008) 12 *Journal of International Economic Law* 153, 162–163.

[225] Du (n 222) 838–842; CI Nagy, 'Clash of Trade and National Public Interest in WTO Law: The Illusion of "Weighing and Balancing" and the Theory of Reservation' (2020) 23 (1) *Journal of International Economic Law* 143, 150–160.

[226] GATT Panel Report, *United States – Section 337* (n 37) para 5.26. The requirement for parties to use the 'least inconsistent' measure reasonably available is just a linguistic variant of a least restrictive means test. See AO Sykes, 'The Least Restrictive Means' (2003) 70 *University of Chicago Law Review* 403, 406.

For good reason, the early GATT jurisprudence was criticised as odd and demonstrating a strong 'pro-trade' bias.[227] To begin with, a textual reading of GATT Article XX shows that the task of a WTO panel is to address whether a measure found to be inconsistent with substantive GATT obligations is nevertheless 'necessary' for a legitimate regulatory objective. However, the GATT panels frequently inquired whether *the extent of inconsistency* between the measure and the WTO obligations was necessary.[228] As Schoenbaum criticised: 'necessary no longer relates to the protection of living things, but to whether or not the measure is a necessary departure from the trade Agreement'.[229] Second, although GATT panels stressed that they respect a contracting party's desired level of enforcement of the law, in practice they seemed to be bent on finding a hypothetically available alternative measure with less adverse trade effects, while neglecting the regulatory prerogatives of the defending GATT contracting parties.[230] Finally, GATT panels were largely insensitive to the practical regulatory experiences of national governments and little consideration was given to whether the proposed alternative measures were feasible in light of a Member's particular social, political and economic conditions.[231] Starting from *Korea – Beef*, the WTO jurisprudence on 'necessary' has begun its slow evolution from the least trade restrictive test. In *Korea – Beef*, the AB explained that the determination of whether a measure is 'necessary' requires a 'process of weighing and balancing' a series of factors.[232] In *US – Gambling*, the AB laid out the procedural steps to conduct the process:

> [It] *begins with* 'an assessment of the 'relative importance' of the interests or values furthered by the challenged measure ... a panel should *then* turn to the other factors ... one factor is the contribution of the measure to the realization of the ends pursued by it; the other factor is the restrictive impact of the measure on international commerce.[233]

If the first step of the analysis yields a preliminary conclusion that the measure is 'necessary', it must be confirmed in the second step by comparing the measure with possible alternative measures, which may be less trade restrictive while providing an equivalent contribution to the achievement of the

[227] R Howse, 'Human Rights in the WTO: Whose Rights? What Humanity? Comments on Petersmann' (2002) 13 *European Journal of International Law* 651, 657.

[228] *US – Section 337* (n 37), para 5.27; See also *EC – Seal Products* (n 43), para 5.185.

[229] T Schoenbaum, 'International Trade and Protection of the Environment: the Continuing Search for Reconciliation' (1997) 91 *American Journal of International Law* 268, 269.

[230] Kapterian (n 90) 103.

[231] GATT Panel Report, *Thailand – Restrictions on Importation of and Internal Taxes on Cigarettes (Thailand – Cigarettes)*, DS10/R, adopted 7 November 1990, BISD 37S/200, paras 27, 51; DA Osiro, 'GATT/WTO Necessity Analysis: Evolutionary Interpretation and Its Impact on the Autonomy of Domestic Regulation' (2002) 29 *Legal Issues of Economic Integration* 123, 127–28.

[232] Appellate Body Report, *Korea – Beef* (n 38) para 164.

[233] Appellate Body Report, *US – Gambling* (n 95) para 306.

objective pursued.[234] This comparison should be carried out in the light of the importance of the interests or values at stake.[235] The more vital or important those common interests or values are, the greater the contribution to the realisation of the end pursued; the less trade-restrictive impact on imports, the easier a measure would be accepted as 'necessary'.[236]

At best a crude cost-benefit analysis, the weighing and balancing test was criticised as being ambiguous. First, the AB has only outlined a range of variables that should be taken into account, but never clearly illustrated how to weigh and balance these variables and in particular, how the variables would interact in making the final determination. As Bown and Trachtman criticised, it enables the AB to keep maximum adjudicatory flexibility but it leaves Member States uncertain of the legality of their measures.[237] Second, there is an inherent tension between the fundamental principle of WTO Members enjoying an autonomous right in setting their own ALOP and a multi-factor weighing and balancing test.[238] If the AB, as it has repeatedly insisted, respects the ALOP set by a Member, then the only question to be asked is whether the measure adopted to achieve that level is the least restrictive in its trade effects. By contrast, the weighing and balancing test may prompt a panel to balance the benefits obtained by the measure, the trade loss associated to the measure, and to strike down the measure if the cost-benefit analysis is disproportionate. In doing this, a WTO panel will be substituting its value judgment for that of the Member in determining the level of acceptable risk.[239]

More recently, the AB has clarified much of the confusion and developed a more clearly structured weighing and balancing test. The AB reversed its previous holding that the two-step sequence analysis must be strictly followed and instead held that a preliminary conclusion was not considered a requisite aspect of the order of analysis.[240] More important, the AB has provided clear instructions on how to examine each element of the weighing and balancing test and what constitutes a 'reasonably available' alternative measure, the key issues of the necessity analysis.

The first element is the relative importance of the values furthered by the challenged measure. The WTO case law shows that this element has played an important role in ascertaining the efficacy of proposed alternative measures in achieving a Member's regulatory objective. If the value at stake is high, for example, human health and safety, the AB tends to respect the Member's regulatory choice and considers 'necessary' very strict enforcement measures

[234] Appellate Body Report, *Brazil – Retreaded Tyres* (n 114) para 156.

[235] Appellate Body Report, *US – Gambling* (n 95) para 304.

[236] Appellate Body Report, *Korea – Beef* (n 38) para 162–3.

[237] Bown and Trachtman (n 223) 88.

[238] JHH Weiler, 'Comment on *Brazil – Retreaded Tyres*' (2009) 8 *World Trade Review* 137, 141.

[239] MM Du, 'Autonomy in Setting Appropriate Level of Protection: Rhetoric or Reality?' (2010) 13 *Journal of International Economic Law* 1077, 1096.

[240] Appellate Body Report, *EC – Seal Products* (n 43), fn 1299 to para 5.215.

aimed at even zero risk, even if that meant a very heavy burden on imports. *EC – Asbestos, US – Gambling* and *Brazil – Retreated Tyres* are typical examples in which important values were at stake. By contrast, where the interests and values furthered by the disputed measure are perceived as relatively less important, the AB tends to condemn the challenged regulation even when the efficacy of the proposed alternative may be less than that of the challenged regulation.[241] *Korea – Beef* and *Dominican Republic – Cigarettes* fall into this category.[242] In *EC – Seal Products*, Canada raised an interesting question of how to assess the importance of public moral concerns over the seal welfare. The AB dodged the question but insisted that a panel has authority to assess the importance of the value.[243]

The second element is the contribution of the measure to the realisation of the regulatory objective. In *Brazil – Retreated Tyres*, the AB found such a contribution exists when there is *a genuine relationship of ends and means* between the objective pursued and the measure at issue.[244] The AB then concluded that the prohibition on the importation of retreaded tyres was *capable of making a contribution* to the objective pursued by Brazil. When the EC argued that the panel should have sought to establish the '*actual contribution*' of the measure to its stated goal, the AB rejected the EC's argument and held that the assessment of the contribution could be performed either quantitatively or qualitatively.[245] Moreover, the AB indicated that the extent of the contribution required depends on the trade restrictiveness of the measure at issue. If the measure is as restrictive as a ban, then it must be apt to make a material contribution to the achievement of its objective.[246]

Almost immediately after *Brazil – Retreated Tyres*, the AB retreated from its position. In *China – Audiovisual Products*, the AB explicitly required that a panel should always perform the 'actual contribution' analysis.[247] In this case, the AB found it problematic that the panel report contained no quantitative projections nor qualitative reasoning discussing how or to what extent that Chinese State plan requirement can or does make a material contribution to the protection of public morals in China.[248] Similarly, in *EC – Seal Products*, the panel examined only the design, structure, and expected operation of the EU Seal Regime. The AB found that this finding 'was not very detailed, nor provided much information as to *the precise degree or extent of*

[241] Sykes (n 226) 416.
[242] Du (n 239) 1095–1096.
[243] Appellate Body Report, *EC – Seal Products* (n 43), para 5.202.
[244] Appellate Body Report, *Brazil – Retreated Tyres* (n 114) para 145.
[245] Ibid, paras 146–47.
[246] Ibid, para 150.
[247] Appellate Body Report, *China – Measures Affecting Trading Rights and Distribution Services for Certain Publications and Audiovisual Entertainment Products* (*China – Audiovisual Products*), WT/DS363/AB/R (21 December 2009) para 252.
[248] Ibid, para 294.

*the contribution*'.[249] The explicit requirement to consider the actual contribution that the disputed measure makes to the regulatory objective facilitates the later analysis of whether an alternative measure will be as effective as the disputed measure in achieving the ALOP desired by the responding party.

In *EC – Seal Products*, the AB has made some further clarifications of the contribution analysis. First, there is no pre-determined threshold in the contribution analysis, even if the measure at issue is highly trade restrictive. This is because a measure's contribution to its regulatory objective is only one component of the necessity calculus under Article XX.[250] Second, despite the AB's requirement for the 'actual contribution' analysis, there is still an important role for the '*capable of* making a contribution' or '*apt to* make a material contribution' test to play in the contribution analysis under certain circumstances. For example, in *Brazil – Retreated Tyres*, the Brazilian import ban formed part of a comprehensive policy designed and implemented to deal with the public health and environmental consequences of waste tyres. This has caused some practical difficulty of 'isolating the contribution to public health of one specific measure from those contributing to other measures that are part of the same comprehensive policy'.[251] Moreover, the impact of the Brazilian measure was not yet realised, but it was apt to induce changes over time in the behaviour and practices of commercial actors in a manner contributing to the regulatory objective. Such changes were not immediately observable at the time of the WTO legal proceeding and 'can only be evaluated with the benefit of time'. In such circumstances, it is appropriate for the panel to 'projec*t* what contribution will be brought about by the measure'[252]

The third element to be weighted and balanced is the restrictive impact of the disputed measure on international trade. In *China – Audiovisual Products*, the AB stated that the meaning of trade restrictiveness should be understood in light of the substantive GATT obligations being violated, and that the assessment may extend beyond the restrictive effects on imported products.[253] In that case, China submitted evidence showing that despite the Chinese measures in dispute, the number of titles of newspapers and publications imported into China had increased from 2002 to 2006. However, the panel found that this increase did not necessarily indicate that China's measures had no trade restrictive effects because the statistics did not indicate what import levels might have been if the measures had not been imposed.[254]

The last step of the weighing and balancing test contemplates a determination as to whether a WTO-consistent, or a less WTO-inconsistent measure

[249] Appellate Body Report, *EC – Seal Products* (n 43) para 5.228.

[250] Ibid, para 5.213–5.216.

[251] Appellate Body Report, *Brazil – Retreated Tyres* (n 114) para 151; Appellate Body Report, *EC – Seal Products* (n 43) para 5.224.

[252] Ibid.

[253] Appellate Body Report, *China – Audiovisual Products* (n 247) para 306.

[254] Ibid, para 300.

is reasonably available.[255] A 'reasonably available' alternative must meet four conditions. First, it must be less trade restrictive than the measure at issue.[256] Second, it must preserve for the responding Member its right to achieve its desired ALOP. Third, it is not merely theoretical in nature. The responding Member must be capable of taking it, and the measure will not impose an undue burden *on that Member*, such as prohibitive costs or substantial technical difficulties[257] Finally, the alternative measure must be consistent or less inconsistent with the WTO.[258] In *China – Audiovisual Products*, the AB clarified that the identification of a reasonably available alternative measure is usually done by the panel assessing the contribution that the alternative measure would make to the protection of the legitimate interests, and its restrictive impact, and then compare them to the panel's previous analysis of these same factors in the first step of the weighing and balancing test.[259]

In practice, a complainant's assertion that a proposed alternative measure is less trade restrictive and that it is consistent or less inconsistent with the WTO Agreements has rarely been challenged.[260] Most controversy centers on the extent to which a proposed alternative measure could achieve the responding Member's desired ALOP and/or whether it is practically feasible for a responding Member to adopt it. In *EC – Seal Products*, instead of a ban, the proposed alternative measure consisted of market access for seal products that would be conditioned on compliance with EU animal welfare standards, certification and labelling requirements.[261] The AB found that even the most stringent certification system would be difficult to implement and enforce, and would lead to increased numbers of inhumanly killed seals.[262] The AB further found that making the certification and labeling requirements more lenient would make the alternative measure more reasonably available but would not meaningfully contribute to addressing EU public moral concerns regarding seal welfare.[263] On this basis, the AB held that the alternative measure was not reasonably available to the EU.

Whether a proposed alternative measure is 'reasonably available' may be considered either from a WTO Member's or the affected industry's perspective.

[255] Appellate Body Report, *EC – Seal Products* (n 43) para 5.261; Appellate Body Report, *Korea – Beef* (n 38) para 166.

[256] Appellate Body Report, *Brazil – Retreated Tyres* (n 114) para 156; Appellate Body Report, *EC – Seal Products* (n 43) para 5.261.

[257] Appellate Body Report, *Brazil – Retreated Tyres* (n 114) para 156. Also see Appellate Body Report, *US – Gambling* (n 95) para 308.

[258] Appellate Body Report, *EC – Seal Products* (n 43) para 5.261; Appellate Body Report, *Korea – Beef* (n 38) para 166.

[259] Appellate Body Report, *China – Audiovisual Products* (n 247) para 324.

[260] T Voon, 'Exploring the Meaning of Trade-Restrictiveness in the WTO', 14 (3) *World Trade Review* (2015) 451, 468.

[261] Appellate Body Report, *EC – Seal Products* (n 43) para 5.262.

[262] Ibid, para 5.279.

[263] Ibid.

In *EC – Seal Products*, the AB held that an alternative measure may be deemed not reasonably available due to significant costs or difficulties faced by the *affected industry*, in particular where such costs or difficulties could affect the ability or willingness of the industry to comply with the requirements of that measure.[264]

A reasonably available alternative cannot be determined by reference to the efforts undertaken by a Member to *negotiate an alternative measure.* In *US – Gambling*, the AB rejected Antigua's contention that its engagement in consultations with the US *with a view to* arriving at a negotiated settlement that achieves the same objective, was a reasonably available alternative because consultations are a process, the results of which are uncertain and therefore not capable of comparison with the measure at issue.[265] Necessity must be a property of the measure itself.

A complementary measure in a broader regulatory scheme is not a reasonably available alternative measure. Frequently, two or more measures may *each* be necessary to achieve a particular regulatory goal. They have different effects and work cumulatively, rather than interchangeably, towards a broader regulatory scheme. In this sense, the necessity of one measure is not undermined by the availability of another measure that will advance the same regulatory goal.[266] In *Brazil – Retreated Tyres*, the EC proposed a series of alternative measures such as a better implementation of existing collection and disposal schemes instead of an import ban. The AB considered that these measures constituted mutually supportive elements of a comprehensive policy to deal with waste tyres so that they could not be considered real alternative to the import ban.[267]

## B. Article 2.2 of the TBT Agreement

### *i. The Analytical Approach*

Article 2.2 of the TBT Agreement provides that technical regulations shall not be 'more trade-restrictive than necessary' to fulfil a legitimate objective, taking account of the risks non-fulfilment would create. In contrast to the necessity test embodied in GATT Article XX, Article 2.2 of the TBT Agreement is independent of any substantive TBT obligations. For example, even if a technical regulation does not discriminate against imported like products, it could still violate Article 2.2 if it is found 'more trade restrictive than unnecessary'.[268] Similar to GATT Article XX, Article 2.2 recognises a wide spectrum of

[264] Appellate Body Report, *EC – Seal Products* (n 43) para 5.277.
[265] Appellate Body Report, *US – Gambling* (n 95) paras 316–317.
[266] McGrady (n 197) 166-68.
[267] Appellate Body Report, *Brazil – Retreaded Tyres* (n 114) para 211.
[268] Du (n 185) 280.

legitimate values from human health and safety to the prevention of deceptive practices.

Similar to TBT Article 2.2, paragraph E of the CGP provides: 'The standardising body shall ensure that standards are not prepared, adopted or applied with a view to, or with the effect of, creating unnecessary obstacles to international trade'. Compared to Article 2.2 of the TBT Agreement, it does not require standards being 'no more restrictive then necessary to fulfill a legitimate objective, taking account of the risks non-fulfillment would create.' Nor does it offer an indicative list of legitimate objectives. However, the textual difference does not seem to affect the interpretation of paragraph E.[269]

To find a violation of Article 2.2, a panel usually follows four steps. The first step is to identify the objectives of the measure at issue. In *US – Cool*, the AB stresses that it is important to identify the objective pursued by a Member with sufficient clarity and consistency.[270] When identifying the objective, a panel should take into account a Member's articulation of what objectives it pursues, but is not bound by it. Instead the panel must independently and objectively assess the objectives. For this purpose, a panel must take into account all the evidence before it, including the texts of statutes, legislative history, and other evidence regarding the structure and operation of the measure.[271]

The second step is to determine whether the objectives pursued through the measure are legitimate.[272] An objective is of course legitimate if it is among those explicitly listed in Article 2.2.[273] However, the use of the words '*inter alia*' in Article 2.2 suggests that the provision does not set out a closed list of legitimate objectives.[274] In practice, panels have generally adopted a deferential approach when it comes to reviewing the legitimacy of a regulatory objective.[275] In *US – Cool*, at issue was whether the provision of consumer information on origin of meat could be considered 'legitimate'. The AB observed that the objective of the COOL measure bears some relation to the objective of preventing deceptive practices reflected in both Article 2.2 itself and GATT Article XX(d).[276] The AB ultimately held that the U.S. objective was legitimate on the grounds that the complainants had failed to rebut that this was not the case.[277]

The third step is to evaluate the degree to which the measure 'fulfills' a legitimate objective. In *US – Cool*, the AB emphasised that a panel must seek to

[269] Davies (n 1) 43.
[270] Appellate Body Report, *US – Cool* (n 171) para 387.
[271] Ibid, para 314.
[272] Ibid, para 313.
[273] Ibid, para 372.
[274] Ibid, para 444.
[275] Petros C. Mavroidis and Kamal Saggi, 'What is not so Cool about *US–Cool Regulations?* A Critical Analysis of the Appellate Body's Ruling on *US–Cool*' (2014) 13(2) *World Trade Review* 299, 305.
[276] Appellate Body Report, *US – Cool* (n 171) para 445.
[277] Ibid, para 453.

ascertain to what degree, if at all, the challenged technical regulation *actually contributes* to the achievement of the legitimate objective.[278] This is because there is no requirement in Article 2.2 that the measure at issue must fulfil the objectives completely or satisfy some minimum level of fulfilment of that objective.[279]

The last step is for the panel to determine whether the challenged measure is 'more trade-restrictive than necessary' to fulfil the legitimate objective, taking account of the risks that non-fulfilment would create. The AB observed in *US – Tuna II* that such an assessment involves a 'relational analysis' of the following factors: the trade-restrictiveness of the technical regulation; the degree of contribution that it makes towards the achievement of a legitimate objective; and the risks non-fulfilment would create.[280] In summary, the AB explained the analytical framework under Article 2.2 as follows:

> [A] panel should begin by considering factors that include: (i) the degree of contribution made by the measures to the legitimate objective at issue; (ii) the trade-restrictiveness of the measure; and (iii) the nature of the risks at issue and the gravity of consequences that would arise from non-fulfillment of the objectives pursued by the Member through the measure. In most cases, a comparison of the challenged measure and possible alternative measures should be undertaken. In particular, it may be relevant for the purpose of this comparison to consider whether the proposed alternative is less trade restrictive, whether it would make an equivalent contribution to the relevant legitimate objective, taking account of the risks non-fulfillment would create, and whether it is reasonably available.[281]

Under Article 2.2, the complainant must make a prima facie case to establish that the challenged measure is more trade restrictive than necessary to achieve the contribution it makes to the legitimate objective. A complainant also needs to identify a possible alternative measure that is less trade restrictive, makes an equivalent contribution to the relevant objective, and is reasonably available. It is then for the respondent to rebut the complainant's prima facie case.[282]

The AB's interpretation of Article 2.2 of the TBT Agreement is very similar to its GATT Article XX jurisprudence.[283] The analysis under both provisions considers almost the identical factors. The only difference may be that Article 2.2 explicitly requires consideration of the risks of non-fulfilment of the regulatory objective, but this factor is akin to making an assessment of the relative importance of interests pursued under GATT Article XX. Similar to the AB's approach to contribution analysis in *US – Cool*, the AB has recently

[278] Appellate Body Report, *US – Tuna II* (n 53) para. 317.
[279] Appellate Body Report, *US- Cool* (n 171) para 468.
[280] Appellate Body Report, *US – Tuna II* (n 53) para 318.
[281] Ibid, para 322.
[282] Ibid, para 323.
[283] Panel Report, *US – Clove Cigarettes* (n 21) paras 7.368–7.369; Panel Report, *US – Cool*, WT/DS384/R (18 November 2011) para 7.670; Voon (n 260) 458.

clarified in *EC – Seal Products* that there is no generally applicable standard requiring the use of a pre-determined threshold of contribution, and that the panel must seek to ascertain to what extent the challenged measure actually contributes to the legitimate objective in analysing the necessity of a measure under GATT Article XX.[284] In the same vein, similar to the necessity test under GATT Article XX, the AB in *US – Cool* Article 21.5 proceedings stated that the particular manner of sequencing the steps of the necessity analysis in Article 2.2 of the TBT Agreement is adaptable, and may be tailored to the specific claims, measures, facts, and arguments at issue in a given case.[285]

### *ii. The Limited Role of Article 2.2*

Although many scholars expressed concerns about the potential of Article 2.2 to be interpreted as severely constraining WTO Members' right to regulate, such concerns have not materialised. To begin with, in TBT cases, the AB appeared to accord national regulators considerable discretion to set their own policy objectives.[286] This is consistent with prior GATT practice. Moreover, the AB has clarified in *US – Cool* that a panel's assessment under Article 2.2 should focus on ascertaining the *actual* degree of contribution achieved by the measure, rather than on answering the questions of whether the measure fulfills the objectives completely or satisfies some minimum level of fulfilment of that objective.[287] In this regard, the AB did not impose any particular standards in terms of the quantity or clarity of information the label needs to convey to consumers so long as it has made *some* contribution. This leaves WTO Members with significant flexibility when designing labeling schemes.[288] Finally, the AB has demonstrated great sensitivity when evaluating whether proposed alternative measures are able to achieve the WTO Members' regulatory objectives. This is the case even when the values or interests pursued by the challenged measure are not particularly important. In *US – Cool*, Mexico proposed voluntary origin labeling as a less trade restrictive alternative. The AB noted the unwillingness of US consumers to pay for origin information and low participation in voluntary labeling programs in the past, and expressed doubts on the effectiveness of a voluntary labeling scheme to achieve the US objective.[289] With regard to a mandatory labeling scheme based on the country of substantial transformation, the AB observed

[284] Appellate Body Report, *EC – Seal Products* (n 43) para 5.213; Appellate Body Report, *US – Tuna II* (n 53) para 317.

[285] Appellate Body Report, *US – Cool* (Recourse to Art 21.5 of the DSU by Canada and Mexico), WT/DS384/AB/RW (18 May 2015) para 5.205.

[286] G Marceau, 'The New TBT Jurisprudence in *US – Clove Cigarettes, US – Tuna II, and US – COOL*' (2014) 8 (1) *Asian Journal of WTO and International Health Law and Policy* 1, 15.

[287] Appellate Body Report, *US – Cool* (n 171) para 468.

[288] J Meltzer, 'The WTO Ruling on U.S. Country of Origin Labeling' ("COOL") (2012) 16 (23) *American Society of International Law* Insight.

[289] Appellate Body Report, *US- Cool* (n 171) para 483.

that this could only partially contribute to the US objective of providing information to consumers and ruled out its availability.[290]

In *US – Tuna II*, the US regulatory objectives were (1) ensuring that consumers are not misled or deceived about dolphin safety and (2) contributing to the protection of dolphins.[291] The panel found that Mexico's proposal of coexistence of the US 'dolphin-safe' label and the AIDCP label provided a less trade-restrictive means of achieving the US objectives.[292] The co-existence of both labels arguably better suits the need of consumers since about 90 per cent of US consumers are only concerned about dolphin mortality but do not care about the additional 'unobserved harm' to dolphins from setting upon them.[293] However, allowing the existence of AIDCP would not make an equivalent contribution to the achievement of the US dolphin protection objective. The AB's ultimate rejection of the co-existence of two labels supports the argument that a WTO Member is entitled to achieve all of the legitimate objectives it pursues. A WTO Member cannot be required to accept a trade-off between the fulfillments of two different objectives that the Member itself has not chosen.[294]

For all the decisions under the TBT Agreement up to date, the AB found that the defending party had not violated Article 2.2. In a general sense, one might conclude that the AB is likely to grant more leeway to Members in determining what is necessary to achieve a legitimate policy goal.[295] This is consistent with the loosening of the necessity test under GATT Article XX as discussed in part II.A above.

## C. Article 5.6 of the SPS Agreement

Article 5.6 of the SPS Agreement provides that, when establishing or maintaining SPS measures to achieve the appropriate level of protection, Members shall ensure that such measures are not more trade-restrictive than required to achieve the ALOP, taking into account technical and economic feasibility. The footnote to Article 5.6 clarifies that a measure is not more trade-restrictive than required if a complaining WTO Member could identify an alternative measure that (1) is 'reasonably available', taking into account technical and economic feasibility; (2) achieves the Member's ALOP; and (3) is significantly

[290] Ibid, para 485.

[291] Ibid, para 302.

[292] Ibid, para 324.

[293] MJ Robertson, 'The Fairy Tale of US 'Dolphin Safe' Labelling: False Claims, Unintended Consequences' (2012) 6(1) BIORES 14, 16.

[294] Crowley and Howse (n 157) 337.

[295] T Voon, A Mitchell and C Gascoigne, 'Consumer Information, Consumer Preferences and Product Labels under the TBT Agreement', in T Epps and M Trebilcock (n 70) 473.

less restrictive to trade.[296] Article 5.6 should be read in context in light of Article 2.2 of the SPS Agreement, which provides that 'Members shall ensure that any sanitary measure is applied only to the extent necessary to protect human, animal or plant life or health'. In *EC – Biotech Products*, the panel states that Article 5.6 is a more specific expression of the general obligation found in Article 2.2, a measure that is found to be in violation of Article 5.6 must also be presumed to violate Article 2.2.[297]

It is usually easy to identify an alternative SPS measure that is reasonably available and significantly less restrictive to trade, the first and third limb of the necessity test in the SPS Agreement. The most controversial aspect, as the *Australia – Salmon* Article 21.5 panel recognised, is how to determine with confidence whether the less trade restrictive alternative measure would meet a WTO Member's predetermined ALOP.[298] Part of the difficulty arises from the fact that the Member's ALOP is usually expressed in vague terms.[299] The ALOP does not need to be determined in quantitative terms, the panel however noted parenthetically that a more explicit and in particular a quantitative expression of a Member's ALOP would greatly facilitate the consideration of compliance with the necessity test in Article 5.6 of the SPS Agreement.[300] Although the specification of the ALOP is a prerogative of a WTO Member, the AB made it clear in *India – Agricultural Products* that it does not mean that a panel must defer completely to a respondent's characterisation of its own ALOP. Rather, a panel is required to ascertain the respondent's ALOP on the basis of the totality of the arguments and evidence on the record.[301] This ruling runs the risk of acting as a double-edged sword. On the one hand, it deals effectively with the problem of a WTO Member specifying its ALOP in an insufficiently precise way or asserting an unfounded ALOP. On the other hand, it potentially enables the panel to second-guess and re-characterise a WTO Member's ALOP, a prerogative right of a WTO Member. It is thus strongly suggested that a WTO panel exercise this power cautiously with deference to the WTO Member.

[296] Appellate Body Report, *Australia – Measures Affecting Importation of Salmon* (*Australia – Salmon*) WT/DS18/AB/R, adopted 20 October 1998, para 194.

[297] WTO Panel Report, *European Communities – Measures Affecting the Approval and Marketing of Biotech Products (EC – Biotech)*, WT/DS291/R, adopted 21 November 2006, para 7.3374.

[298] Panel Report, *Australia – Measures Affecting Importation of Salmon – Recourse to Article 21.5 of the DSU by Canada*, WT/DS18/RW (Feb. 18, 2000), paras 7.128–7.131. H Schebesta and D Sinopoli, 'The Potency of the SPS Agreement's Excessivity Test: The Impact of Article 5.6 on Trade Liberalization and the Regulatory Power of WTO Members to Take Sanitary and Phytosanitary Measures' (2018) 21 *Journal of International Economic Law* 123, 131–141.

[299] In most SPS disputes, the ALOP was only vaguely defined and the panel had to induce the ALOP. The only exception is Panel Report, *Japan – Measures Affecting Agricultural Products (Japan – Agricultural Products II)* WT/DS76//R, adopted 27 October 1998.

[300] Art 21.5 Panel Report, *Australia- Salmon* (n 298) para 7.128.

[301] Appellate Body Report, *India – Measures Concerning the Importation of Certain Agricultural Products*, WT/DS430/AB/R, adopted 15 June 2015, para 5.221.

As it is a 'prerogative right' for a WTO Member to set its preferred ALOP, no trade-off is demanded between trade restrictiveness of an SPS measure and the achievement of a Member's ALOP. In the shadow of this 'prerogative' right, the panel examines whether the measures adopted are more trade restrictive than necessary to reach the ALOP.[302] In *Australia – Salmon*, the AB refused to accept Canada's argument that an alternative measure was available on the basis that its ability to achieve Australia's ALOP had not been scientifically established.[303] In *Japan – Agricultural Products II*, the panel rejected the test by products as a viable alternative to test by varieties as the scientific experts it consulted could not state with an appropriate level of certainty that the alternative measure would be able to achieve Japan's ALOP.[304] In *Australia – Salmon* 21.5 Panel Report, the panel found that, based on the evidence submitted by the parties and scientific experts' testimony, other alternative protective measures, without imposing consumer-ready requirements, would reduce risk significantly and may achieve Australia's ALOP. Even so, the panel remained reluctant to hold out no consumer-ready requirement as a viable alternative and did not reach any definitive conclusion.[305]

Although early SPS jurisprudence demonstrated deference to a WTO Member's choice of measures in achieving its ALOP, a phase of stricter application has begun after 2012 in which in all cases Article 5.6 violations were found.[306] In *US – Animals*, the US argued that the OIE's Terrestrial Code would not meet its ALOP in preventing the introduction of foot and mouth disease into the US territory. The panel evaluated Argentina's proposed alternative to apply the US law on protocols of beef from Uruguay to Northern Argentina and found that it would meet the U.S. requirement.[307] In *India- Agricultural Products*, though the panel concluded that India's ALOP was very high or very conservative, the OIE's Terrestrial Code would meet this ALOP. Consequently, the challenged measure was found to be inconsistent with Article 5.6.[308] Similarly, the panel held that the provisions of the OIE's Terrestrial Code would meet Russia's ALOP in *Russia – Pigs*.[309] It is important to note that the relevant international standards, if they exist after all, are the most likely alternative measure fulfilling a

[302] J Scott, *The WTO Agreement on Sanitary and Phytosanitary Measures: A Commentary* (Oxford University Press, 2007), at 157.

[303] Appellate Body Report, *Australia – Salmon* (n 296) paras 210–213.

[304] WTO Appellate Body Report, *Japan – Measures Affecting Agricultural Products (Japan – Agricultural Products II*) WT/DS76/AB/R, adopted 19 March 1999, paras 8.83–4.

[305] Panel Report, *Australia – Salmon 21.5 Panel Report* (n 298) paras 7.132–7.137.

[306] Schebesta and D Sinopoli (n 298) 148.

[307] Panel Report, *United States – Measures Affecting the Importation of Animals, Meats and Other Animal Products from Argentina* (*US – Animals*), WT/DS447/R, adopted 24 July 2015, para 7.511.

[308] Panel Report, *India – Agricultural Products* (n 300) para 7.585–7.597.

[309] Panel Report, *Russian Federation- Measures on the Importation of Live Pigs, Pork and Other Pig Products from the European Union* (*Russia – Pigs*), WT/DS495/R, adopted 19 August 2016, para 7.827–7.834.

WTO Member's ALOP. In addition, in all SPS cases, the panels relied heavily on scientific experts in determining whether the alternative measures were able to achieve the defending party's ALOP. If scientific experts were highly confident of the effectiveness of the alternative less trade restrictive measure in achieving the defending party's ALOP, the panel was more likely to endorse the alternative measure. Although there are good reasons to challenge whether science is indeed able to provide definitive answers to regulatory choices,[310] the heavy reliance on science does show that the panel in general respects the Member's ALOP and choice of means to achieve it.

Compared to the necessity test in the GATT and the TBT Agreement, Article 5.6 of the SPS Agreement and its related footnote are more specific. Indeed, at least from its wording, Article 5.6 of the SPS Agreement may be said to be more protective of domestic regulatory autonomy compared to the necessity test in GATT Article XX because it explicitly eliminates any possibility of balancing the purported regulatory objective of the measure against its trade restrictive effects.[311] Nevertheless, empirical analysis of the SPS case law does not show significant divergence from the other two Agreements. If anything, it may be argued that the necessity test under the SPS Agreement seems to be even more stringent than that of the GATT 1994 and the TBT Agreement. This observation must be understood in its proper context. The SPS Agreement regulates specific categories of risks and explicitly designates relevant international standards. In other words, the regulatory scope of the SPS Agreement is much narrower and normative reference points are much clearer compared to the TBT Agreement. For most recent SPS disputes, there was little controversy about either the relevant international standard or scientific evidence. Thus the panel was more confident about supporting the less trade restrictive measure.

## IV. TRANSPARENCY

The Associate Justice of US Supreme Court Louis Brandeis famously used the metaphor of sunlight to describe the benefits of transparency when he wrote in 1914: 'publicity is justly commended as a remedy for social and industrial diseases. Sunlight is said to be the best of disinfectants …'.[312] In the WTO context, transparency is defined as 'the degree to which trade policies and practices, and the process by which they are established, are open and predictable'.

[310] VR Walker, 'The Myth of Science As a "Neutral Arbiter" For Triggering Precautions' (2003) 26 *Boston College International and Comparative Law Review* 197, 204–12.

[311] Neumann and Turk (n 90) 221–222; FJ Garcia, 'The Salmon Case: Evolution of Balancing Mechanisms for Non-Trade Values in WTO', in Bermann and Mavroidis (n 50) 134.

[312] LD Brandeis, *Other People's Money and How the Bankers Use it* (Frederick A Stokes Company, 1914) 92.

As one of the fundamental norms of the WTO trading system, transparency is said to be the most important work of the WTO, more so than conducting formal rounds of negotiations and settling trade disputes.[313]

With the rise of product standards in international trade, transparency has been playing a key role by reducing information asymmetry and enhances the effectiveness of the WTO Agreements. To begin with, they make 'behind the border' and frequently ambiguous technical regulations and standards known and publicly available. Advance notification enables exporting Members to be informed of proposed new or amended TBT measures. This gives Members the opportunity to make comments regarding these proposals at an early stage and to have these comments taken into account in the regulatory process.[314] The prompt publication requirement for adopted TBT measures greatly reduces the cost and difficulty of obtaining information from their trading partners. The provision of a reasonable period before the entry into force of a published measure enables exporters to adjust to new requirements.[315] The obligation to provide justification supplements other transparency obligations by enabling WTO Members to obtain information beyond the existence and content of technical regulations, such as its legitimate objective and the reasons for its deviation of international standards.[316] By doing so, these transparency provisions enhance the consultation processes domestically, allow other Members, in particular developing countries, to adapt to newly adopted standards, and help to avoid conflict and prevent disputes.

Transparency at the WTO has undergone substantial transformations through three generations. The first-generation transparency refers to the original GATT policies on information from 1947 as elaborated over the years. It is mainly concerned with the obligation of publication of all proposed and adopted measures. The second generation refers to the monitoring and surveillance mechanisms. It is implemented through notification as well as regulatory dialogues among WTO Members, such as raising specific trade concerns (STCs) at the TBT and SPS Committees. The third-generation transparency focuses on efficiency of procuring information by the public. The major tools provided by the WTO are the requirements to establish enquiry points and the use of new technologies.[317]

[313] PC Mavroidis and R Wolfe, 'From Sunshine to a Common Agent: The Evolving Understanding of Transparency in the WTO' (2015) 21(2) *Brown Journal of World Affairs* 117, 117–118.

[314] H Horn, PC Mavroidis and EN Wijkstrom, 'In the Shadow of the DSU: Addressing Specific Trade Concerns in the WTO SPS and TBT Committees' (2013) 47 (4) *Journal of World Trade* 729, 733.

[315] Appellate Body Report, *US – Clove Cigarettes* (n 21) para 272.

[316] D Prevost, 'Transparency Obligations under the TBT Agreement', in Epps and Trebilcock (n 70) 162.

[317] R Wolfe, 'Letting the Sunshine in at the WTO: How Transparency Brings the Trading System to Life', WTO Staff Working Paper ERSD-2013-03, 7–14.

## A. The Trigger of Transparency Obligation

The most significant WTO transparency obligations apply to proposed regulations, rather than adopted measures. Article 2.9 and 5.6 of the TBT Agreement and Annex B of the SPS Agreement lay down similar transparency obligations for WTO Members, including publication of a notice, notifications, provision of copies and reasonable time between notification and implementation for comments. WTO Members are obligated to comply with these obligations whenever they plan to adopt a measure that is 'not in accordance with the technical contents of relevant international standards' (or whenever a relevant international standard does not exist) and if it may 'have a significant effect on trade'.

First, transparency obligations apply mainly to *proposed* regulations, including all proposed technical regulations, CAPs and SPS measures. Second, TBT and SPS measures based on international standards are presumed not to create unnecessary barriers to international trade. Therefore the transparency obligations apply only when international standards are not followed. Nevertheless, both the TBT and SPS Committee have encouraged Members to notify measures even when they do comply with international standards as long as they have a significant effect on trade. This is an useful practice because WTO Members may not have shared understanding of what the relevant international standard is, and even TBT and SPS measures based on international standards may entail adaptation costs for traders.[318] Third, only TBT and SPS measures that may have significant trade effects should be notified. It may be difficult for a WTO Member to determine whether a measure may have significant effect on trade and the TBT Committee encourages Members to notify measures if they are not sure of their trade effects.[319] Moreover, both the TBT and SPS Committee have noted that both import-enhancing and import-reducing effects on the trade of other WTO members are covered by the provision.[320] If an SPS measure is 'trade-facilitating', the SPS Committee allows Members not to open the 60-day period for comment before its adoption.[321]

All adopted measures must be published promptly. This publication requirement is not dependent on the conditions of deviation from an international standard and significant trade effects. Also, they do not need to be notified to other WTO members through the centralised notification systems.[322]

[318] Scott (n 302) 194.

[319] TBT Committee, 'Sixth Triennial Review of the Operation and Implementation of the Agreement on Technical Barriers to Trade under Article 15.4', G/TBT/32 (29 November 2012) para 12.

[320] Note by the Secretariat, 'Decisions and Recommendations Adopted by the WTO Committee on Technical Barriers to Trade Since 1 January 1995', G/TBT/1/Rev.14, para 4.3.1.1; G/SPS/7/Rev.3, para 10. SPS Committee, 'Recommended Procedures for Implementing the Transparency Obligations of the SPS Agreement (Article 7)', G/SPS/7/Rev.4 (4 June 2018) para 10.

[321] SPS Committee, ibid, para 2.8.

[322] MB Karttunen, *Transparency and Dispute Settlement: Complements or Substitutes* (EUI PhD Thesis, 2016) 61.

## B. The Content of Transparency Obligation

The WTO Secretariat has described transparency obligations under the TBT Agreement to be divided into three pillars: publication, notification and responding to inquiries.[323]

### *i. Publication*

There are two publication requirements in the TBT and SPS Agreements. The first requirement is to publish a notice in a publication at an early appropriate stage that a particular technical regulation, CAP or SPS measure will be introduced.[324] The publication notice is designed to encourage Members to engage in a cooperative dialogue even before the drafting of a measure has started. As there is no uniformity between Members as to how this notice is to be published, the TBT Committee requires Members to specify the names of the publications used to make the notice.[325] However, despite the WTO Secretariat's efforts to centralise the information on publications, a large number of WTO Members either have not published a notice or failed to provide websites for others to access such information.[326] The second requirement is the prompt publication of all adopted technical regulations, CAPs and SPS measures to enable interested parties in other Members to become acquainted with them.[327] WTO Members are also required to leave a reasonable interval of normally six months between the publication of the adopted measure and its entry into force.[328]

### *ii. Notification and Comment*

Both the TBT and SPS Agreements require Members to notify draft regulations with significant effect trade when relevant international standards are absent. For example, Article 2.9.2 of the TBT Agreement requires WTO Members to notify other Members through the WTO Secretariat of the product coverage, the objective and the rationale of their proposed technical regulations, at an early appropriate stage.[329] The fulfilment of publication obligation does not waive a WTO Member's notification obligation even though the publication has made all the information publicly available.[330] The TBT and SPS Committees

[323] TBT Committee, 'Minutes of the Meeting Held on 29 June 2001', G/TBT/M/24 (14 August 2001) Annex 1.

[324] Art. 2.9.1 and 5.6.1 of the TBT Agreement; para 5 of SPS Agreement.

[325] Note by the Secretariat (n 308) 18.

[326] MB Karttunen (n 322) 71.

[327] Art. 2.11 and 5.8 of the TBT Agreement; para 1 of the SPS Agreement.

[328] Art. 2.12 and 5.9 of the TBT Agreement, Annex B & 2 of SPS Agreement.

[329] Art. 2.9.2 and 5.6.5 of the TBT Agreement; para 5(b) of Annex B of the SPS Agreement.

[330] Panel Report, *US – Clove Cigarettes* (n 21) para 7.541.

have further issued model notification format to provide more specific guidance on what information should be covered in the notifications.[331]

First, the WTO notification mechanism is centralised. The notification must be done through the WTO Secretariat, who shares it with all other Members and interested international standardising bodies, as well as flags the draft regulations that may particularly affect the interest of developing countries. For SPS measures, the SPS Committee encourages Members to identify and alert the countries that may be particularly affected by the draft SPS measure.[332] Second, the notification does not include the actual content of the regulations. If a Member is concerned about the effects of draft regulations, it may make inquiry for further information from WTO Members. WTO Members are required to provide other Members particulars or copies of the notified regulation and respond to all reasonable questions.[333] Third, the timing of notification should be appropriate in light of the specific national legislative procedures. The very purpose of the notification is to provide opportunity for comment before the proposed measure enters into force, when there is time for changes to be made before it is too late.[334] Both the TBT and SPS Agreements require that WTO Members 'allow reasonable time for other Members to make comments in writing, discuss these comments upon request, and take written comments and the results of discussions into account'.[335] The TBT and SPS Committees have suggested a minimum of 60 days for comments while more days for comments such as 90 days are encouraged. Comments to notifications are a remarkable transparency tool as they allow a WTO Member to influence final requirements of other Members, enhance domestic consultation process, and enhance harmonisation as well as lead to transfer of technology. Empirically, the number of TBT and SPS notifications has grown significantly over the past 20 years.[336] This shows an overall better availability of information on draft standard measures. Nevertheless, due to resource constraints, reluctance to disclose sensitive information and other factors, there remains information gaps from notifications and a significant number of measures were not notified.[337]

With the development of electronic tools, the sharing of information such as the notification of standards has become more efficient. For example, the WTO, United Nations and International Trade Centre have jointly launched a new database 'ePing'. This new system allows access to WTO Members' notifications of TBT and SPS measures. It also facilitates dialogue among the public and

[331] Note by the Secretariat (n 320) 51–54.
[332] SPS Committee (n 320) 11.
[333] Art. 2.9.3 and 5.6.3 of the TBT Agreement; para (5)(c) of Annex B of the SPS Agreement.
[334] Panel Report, *US – Clove Cigarettes* (n 21) para 7.536.
[335] Art 2.9.4 of the TBT Agreement; para 5(d) of Annex B of the SPS Agreement.
[336] TBT Committee, 'Eighth Triennial Review of the Operation and Implementation of the Agreement on Technical Barriers to Trade under Article 15.4', G/TBT/41 (19 November 2018) 16.
[337] Wolfe (n 317) 16–19.

private sector in addressing potential trade problems at an early stage. Users of ePing will be able to easily keep up-to-date with notifications affecting foreign markets and products of particular interest to them.[338]

Notification is one leg of second-generation transparency obligations, the other being the establishment of monitoring and surveillance mechanisms such as raising STCs at the TBT and SPS Committees. WTO Members have the opportunity to flag issues at committee meetings calling for an exchange of views with the Member adopting a new regulation, and are required to notify the status of their STCs, whether it has been resolved or partially resolved.

#### *iii. Enquiry Points*

Article 10.1 of the TBT Agreement provides that each member shall ensure that an enquiry point exists which is able to answer all reasonable inquiries from other Members and interested parties in other Members. The obligation to establish enquiry points offers a remarkable tool to ensure efficient access to information relating to other Members' product standards. By using enquiry points, private traders do not have to depend on their home governments and they are able to get information directly from foreign governments beyond what is covered in notification obligations.[339] This help reduces information costs of traders.

### C. Transparency of Standard-Setting

Similar to technical regulations and CAPs, paragraphs J to Q of the CGP have prescribed extensive publication and notification requirements for standardising bodies. To begin with, at least every six months, the standardising body shall publish in a national or regional publication a work program containing the standards it is currently preparing and the standards which it has adopted in the preceding period (paragraph J). Second, the CGP establishes the centralisation of information on standards. No later than the time of publication of its work program, the standardising body shall notify the existence thereof to the ISO/IEC Information Centre in Geneva. This is because the standards are not developed by WTO members but by standardising bodies (paragraph J). Third, before adopting a standard, the standardising body shall publish a notice announcing the comment period in the same publication where the work program is published. The notice shall include information on whether the draft standard deviates from relevant international standards. The standardising body shall allow a period of at least 60 days for the submission

[338] WTO, 'New Global Trade Alert System Launched to Boost Market Access for Developing Countries' (8 November 2016).

[339] Mavroidis and Wolfe (n 313) 3.

of comments on the draft standard by interested parties (paragraph L). At the request of any interested party, the standardising body shall provide a copy of the draft standard on which it seeks comments (paragraph M). The standardising body shall take into account and reply to the comments received (paragraph N). Finally, once a standard has been adopted, it shall be promptly published (paragraph O).

At the TBT Committee, WTO Members noted that while the notification requirements for technical regulations and CAPs had functioned very well, in general less information about standards was available. They attributed this information deficiency to the difference between notification requirements for technical regulations and those for standards. To address the problem, the TBT Committee encourages the standardising bodies that have accepted the CGP to publish their work programs on their website and notify the specific website addresses where the work programs are published to the ISO/IEC Information Centre, and to share information about the publication of notice announcing the period for commenting on a draft standard (eg, title and volume of publication and website address).[340] In November 2016, the WTO-ISO Standards Information Gateway was launched to replace the ISO/IEC Information Centre. This website provides information about standardising bodies that have accepted or withdrawn from the CGP; the work programmes these bodies must publish at least every six months; and the templates for notification of this information.[341]

## V. SCIENTIFIC EVIDENCE

Before the establishment of the WTO in 1995, the GATT panels made only little use of science in settling trade disputes. In *Thailand – Cigarettes*, Thailand banned the importation and sale of US cigarettes on the basis that US cigarettes were more harmful to human health than Thai cigarettes due to the presence of chemicals and other additives and specific production processes.[342] Any finding in this respect by the panel was clearly very important because it could influence the assessment of whether the Thai measure was 'necessary' to protect human health and safety at the level pursued by the Thai Government. However, the panel did not address this key question.

For the first time in the GATT/WTO history, the negotiators explicitly brought science to the WTO regime during the Uruguay Round and elevated it to become an independent benchmark in assessing the legality of SPS measures.[343]

340 TBT Committee, 'Minutes of the Meeting of 10-11 November 2016', G/TBT/M/70 (17 February 2017) 76–77.

341 TBT Committee (n 336) 15–16.

342 GATT Panel Report, *Thailand – Cigarettes* (n 231) para 28.

343 DA Wirth, *The Role of Science in the Uruguay Round and NAFTA Trade Disciplines* (1994) 27 *Cornell International Law Journal* 817, 825.

Moreover, even though the role of science is not explicitly addressed in the TBT Agreement and GATT 1994, it is now widely used in those agreements to ascertain whether two competing products are 'like products' and whether the measures are 'more trade restrictive than necessary', albeit in a less demanding manner.[344] The wide employment of science is unsurprising in view of the increasingly complex and politically contentious trade disputes. Long characterised as an objective and value-free yardstick, science helps to resolve competing claims in a neutral manner, evade normative judgments with their distributional implications, and legitimise legal decisions through the authority of science. The legitimising nature of science is particularly useful for a relatively new international organisation with powerful dispute settlement mechanisms such as the WTO.[345]

The CGP does not specifically prescribe that voluntary product standards must be based on scientific evidence. Nevertheless, it is an explicit requirement for many national and international standards. For example, Principle 3 of ISO 14020: 2001 Environmental Labels and Declarations: General Principles states that 'environmental labels and declarations shall be based on scientific methodology that is sufficiently thorough and comprehensive to support the claim and that produces results that are accurate and reproducible'. The EU Ecolabel regulation also requires that all ecolabel criteria must be determined on a scientific basis considering the whole life cycle of products, taking into consideration the latest technological developments.[346] It is thus useful to explore the role of scientific evidence in designing and implementing standards schemes.

## A. The Role of Science in the SPS Agreement

At the heart of the SPS Agreement is its apparent addition to the traditional 'discrimination' or 'protectionism' rationale of GATT disciplines of a second 'unjustified obstacles' rationale that goes beyond the NT requirement.[347] Among the most contentious SPS disputes, such as *EC – Hormones* and *EC – Biotech Products*, the real issue was not that science has wrongfully weeded out

[344] L Gruszczynski, 'Science and the Settlement of Trade Disputes in the World Trade Organization', in B Mercurio and K-J Ni, *Science and Technology in International Economic Law: Balancing Competing Interests* 11 (Routledge, 2014) 29.

[345] G Shaffer, 'Risk, Science, and Law in the WTO: The Centrality of Institutional Choice', America Society of International Law Proceedings 2010, at 19.

[346] Recital 5, Regulation (EC) No 66/2010 of the European Parliament and of the Council of 25 November 2009 on the EC Ecolabel.

[347] JO McGinnis and ML Movsesian, 'The World Trade Constitution' (2000) 114 *Harvard Law Review* 511, 550; J Bohanes, 'Risk Regulation in WTO Law: A Procedure-Based Approach to the Precautionary Principle' (2002) 40 *Columbia Journal of Transnational Law* 323, 326–327; R Hudec, 'Science and "Post-Discriminatory" WTO Law' (2003) 26 *Boston College International and Comparative Law Review* 185, 187.

protectionist regulations that discriminated against foreign products. The AB explicitly stated in *EC – Hormones* that the EC measures were implemented in response to widespread public concerns and consumer anxieties in Europe.[348] Nevertheless, the AB struck down the EC import ban simply because it was not scientifically warranted by the results of risk assessment. In other words, science, by itself, has become the benchmark in deciding whether SPS measures should be maintained.[349] Elevating science as the ultimate arbiter of trade disputes in the SPS Agreement has raised difficult issues as to how far a WTO panel can go toward invoking the epistemic authority of sound science to overcome claims based on national political authority. At stake in the answers to these questions are the very parameters of state self-determination to pursue its regulatory objectives in the WTO regime.[350]

The SPS Agreement requires that all SPS measures be based on scientific principles and cannot be maintained without sufficient evidence (Articles 3.3 and 2.2). This obligation is operationalised through Article 5.1, which requires that all SPS measures must be based on a risk assessment. As the key term underpinning the science-based disciplines in the SPS Agreement, the WTO case law has proven that the risk assessment requirement presents a formidable hurdle for WTO Members. Indeed, in the entire history of WTO dispute settlement, all risk assessments in SPS disputes were found deficient in some ways by WTO panels.[351] This leads to the question of what constitutes a proper risk assessment under the SPS Agreement.

First, risk assessment must be sufficiently *specific* to the risk at issue. In *EC – Hormones*, although the EC could point to studies showing the carcinogenic potential of growth hormones in general, the AB found that the scientific studies submitted were not sufficiently specific to the case at hand, because they were:

> general studies which do indeed show the existence of a general risk of cancer; but they do not focus on and do not address the particular kind of risk here at stake- the carcinogenic or genotoxic potential of the residues of those hormones found in meat

[348] WTO Appellate Body Report, *European Communities – Measures Concerning Meat and Meat Products* (*EC – Hormones*), WT/DS48/AB/R (16 Jan. 1998), para 245; WTO Panel Report, *European Communities – Measures Affecting the Approval and Marketing of Biotech Products* (*EC – Biotech Products*), WT/DS291/R (29 Sept. 2006).

[349] VR Walker, 'Keeping the WTO from Becoming the "World Trans-Science Organization: Scientific Uncertainty, Science Policy, and Fact-Finding in the Growth Hormones Dispute' (1998) 31 *Cornell International Law Journal* 251, 253.

[350] D Winickoff et al, 'Adjudicating the GM Food Wars: Science, Risk and Democracy in World Trade Law' (2005) 30 *Yale Journal of International Law* 81, 84.

[351] In *US – Continued Suspension*, the panel found that EC risk assessment was deficient. The AB reversed some of the panel's legal reasoning but could not reach conclusion due to insufficient facts before the AB. See Appellate Body Report, *United States – Continued Suspension of Obligations in the EC – Hormones Dispute* (*US-Continued Suspension*), WT/DS320/AB/R (Oct. 16, 2008), para 735.

> derived from cattle to which the hormones had been administered for growth promotion purposes.[352]

In *Japan – Apples*, Japan's risk assessment report studied several possible hosts of fire blight. Recognising that the risk of transmission of fire blight could vary significantly from plant to plant, the AB found that the risk assessment was not sufficiently specific because 'the conclusion of the risk assessment did not purport to relate exclusively to the introduction of the disease through apple fruit, but rather more generally through any susceptible host'.[353]

Second, risk assessment must be *sufficient*. In *Australia – Salmon*, the AB highlighted that the risk assessment report 'only evaluates elements of probability for *some* of the disease of concern', 'addresses *some* elements of both probability and possibility' and 'provides *some* evaluation of the extent to which alternative risk reduction means could reduce risk'. The AB emphasised that 'some' evaluation of the likelihood of the potential risk was not enough.[354] Similarly, in *Japan – Apples*, the AB held that Japan's 'considerably less substantial' risk assessment was not proper.[355]

Third, risk assessment must meet a certain level of *objectivity*. In *Australia – Salmon* 21.5 proceedings, the panel identified the possibility that some risk assessment studies might be flawed or biased to such extent that they couldn't be said to meet any standard of objectivity. If so, such studies could not be a proper risk assessment under the SPS Agreement.[356] On the other hand, the panel found it difficult to read into the definition of risk assessment specific requirements such that 'minor flaws or misconceptions at a detailed level would preclude a study from falling within the SPS definition of risk assessment … as risk assessment, in particular a qualitative risk assessment, invariably includes subjective elements …'.[357]

In *EC – Hormones*, the AB held that the term 'based on' requires that the result of the risk assessment must reasonably support the SPS measure at stake.[358] It does not mean that SPS measures have to *conform to* the risk assessment. There is a certain margin of discretion in favour of WTO Members. As a risk assessment does not necessarily lead to a monolithic scientific conclusion, a WTO Member is entitled to base its SPS measures on a divergent minority scientific opinion. This is because a divergent opinion does not necessarily signal the absence of a reasonable relationship between the SPS measure and the risk assessment, 'especially where the risk involved is life-threatening in character

[352] Appellate Body Report, *EC – Hormones* (note 348) para 200.
[353] Appellate Body Report, *Japan – Measures Affecting the Importation of Apples* (*Japan – Apples*), WT/DS245/AB/R (Nov. 26, 2003) para 191.
[354] Appellate Body Report, *Australia – Salmon* (n 296) paras 127–135,
[355] Appellate Body Report, *Japan – Apples* (n 353) para 194.
[356] *Australia –Salmon* Article 21.5 Panel Report (n 298) para 7.47.
[357] Ibid, para 7.57.
[358] Appellate Body Report, *EC – Hormones* (n 348) para. 193.

and is perceived to constitute a clear and imminent threat to public health and safety'.[359]

Where 'relevant scientific evidence is insufficient', Article 5.7 permits WTO Members to take provisional measures on the basis of available pertinent information. In *Japan – Apples*, the AB concluded that 'insufficient scientific evidence' referred to the situation in which 'the body of available scientific evidence does not allow, in quantitative or qualitative terms, the performance of an adequate assessment of risks as required under Article 5.1'.[360] As the AB stressed, Article 5.7 is not triggered by scientific uncertainty, but rather by the insufficiency of scientific evidence. These two concepts are not interchangeable because scientific uncertainty does not necessarily prevent a risk assessment from being performed.[361] Furthermore, 'insufficient scientific evidence' is a relative concept, whether the available information is sufficient to perform a risk assessment itself may be highly contested. A WTO Member could rely on a divergent or minority opinion in settling the controversy.[362] Importantly, the availability of a prior risk assessment does not a priori exclude the application of Article 5.7. The AB in *US – Continued Suspension* clarified that whether scientific evidence is insufficient or not should be evaluated in the light of the WTO Member's chosen level of protection and the ever-evolving nature of science. It is possible that evidence sufficient to perform a risk assessment when a low level of protection is set becomes insufficient when the Member aims at a higher level of protection.[363] Similarly, WTO Members are permitted to take provisional measures 'where new evidence from a qualified and respected source puts into question the relationship between the preexisting body of scientific evidence and the conclusions regarding the risks'.[364]

On the other hand, the AB held that national SPS measures in response to fear of risk, if not substantiated by any reliable scientific evidence, were inconsistent with the SPS Agreement. In *EC – Hormones*, though there was ample evidence showing that European consumers were intensely anxious about the safety of beef treated with hormones, the AB held that consumer anxieties unsupported by a proper risk assessment could not justify a risk regulation under the SPS Agreement. According a more expansive role to the precautionary principle, the AB reasoned, would largely eviscerate the SPS Agreement; at least if the principle was understood as justifying a regulatory action purely on the basis of entirely unsubstantiated conjectures about future safety risks.[365]

[359] Ibid, para 194.
[360] Appellate Body Report, *Japan – Apples* (n 353) para 179.
[361] Ibid, para 184.
[362] Appellate Body Report, *US – Continued Suspension* (n 351) para 677.
[363] Ibid, paras 688–698.
[364] Ibid, para 703.
[365] Appellate Body Report, *EC – Hormones* (n 348) para 124.

## B. The Role of Science in the TBT Agreement and GATT 1994

Standard setting is largely a technical process and the confidence in the technical content of the standard is crucial for its legitimacy and widespread use. A good standard will reflect state-of-the-art scientific and technological information.[366] The TBT Agreement explicitly refers to the role of science in complying with the TBT disciplines. To begin with, Article 2.2 requires that technical regulations shall not be more trade-restrictive than necessary to fulfil a legitimate objective, taking account of the risks non-fulfilment would create. When assessing the risks of non-fulfilment, WTO Members are expected to consider, among other things, available scientific and technical information. Accordingly, science plays an important role in determining the necessity of the disputed measure in the TBT Agreement, in particular whether there is a genuine risk to be addressed, the nature of such risk, the extent of contribution of a measure to the achievement of the regulatory objective, and the feasibility of alternative less trade restrictive measures.[367] Furthermore, Article 14.2 confirms the right of a panel to consult experts on questions of a technical nature. Finally, at the TBT Committee, WTO Members have stressed the importance of international standardising bodies taking into account science and technology developments in the elaboration of international standards to ensure their effectiveness and relevance.[368]

In *US – Clove Cigarettes*, the panel referred to scientific evidence to establish that clove and menthol cigarettes were 'like products'.[369] In addition, the panel was confronted with the question of the effectiveness of the US ban on flavoured cigarettes in order to reduce youth smoking. The panel conducted a careful analysis of the relevant scientific evidence and ultimately supported the US assertion on this point. In the context of its analysis, the panel also recognised that quality minority scientific opinion could constitute a sufficient basis for TBT measures.[370] In *US – Tuna II*, the panel was faced with the questions of whether the US 'Dolphin Safe' label fulfilled its stated objectives and whether there were other less trade-restrictive alternatives. To answer these questions, the panel analysed a large amount of scientific data on the impact of purse seine operations on the health of dolphins, dolphin mortality rates associated with fishing techniques other than 'setting on' dolphins and risks of dolphin morality outside of the Eastern Tropical Pacific Region.[371]

[366] E Wijkstrom and D McDaniels, 'Improving Regulatory Governance: International Standards and the WTO TBT Agreement' (2013) 47(5) *Journal of World Trade* 1013, 1036–1037.

[367] Gruszczynski (n 344) 29.

[368] TBT Committee, 'Second Triennial Review of the Operation and Implementation of the Agreement on Technical Barriers to Trade', G/TBT/9 (13 November 2000).

[369] Panel Report, *US – Clove Cigarettes* (n 21) para 7.229.

[370] Ibid, para 7.401.

[371] Panel Report, *US – Tuna II*, WT/DS381/R (15 September 2011) para 7.529.

Turning to the GATT 1994. Although at first the AB followed the previous approach under the GATT 1947 of making little use of science in GATT 1994, it changed the approach with the landmark *EC – Asbestos* case. Indeed, the approach to science adopted in *EC – Asbestos* shares considerable similarities to that of the SPS Agreement. To begin with, the panel consulted with experts on a number of scientific issues, such as the existence of risk from exposure to asbestos and the efficacy of alternative measures in achieving the French health objectives. When the relevant scientific evidence showed that asbestos may potentially cause cancer, the AB concluded that carcinogenicity constituted one of the defining elements of the physical properties of the products in determining 'like products'.[372] Similarly, based on available scientific evidence, the AB rejected Canada's argument that 'controlled use' would be an alternative measure that would achieve the regulatory objective sought by France.[373] Furthermore, the AB recognised that risk could be measured in either qualitative or quantitative terms; that the disputed measure could be supported by minority views from qualified and respected resources, and that the role of the panel was not to act as an arbiter of the opinions expressed by the scientific community.[374]

The subsequent WTO case law relating to health and environmental measures has followed the precedent established in *EC – Asbestos*. In *Brazil – Retreated Tyres*, the panel examined whether the accumulation of used tyres may constitute a risk to human health. Although the panel did not consult experts, it frequently referred to scientific evidence in its analysis. Moreover, scientific analysis played a dominant role in analysing the necessity of the Brazilian ban, including the extent of the contribution of the ban to the reduction of risks and the availability of alternative measures.[375]

Even though the AB has assigned a role to science in both the TBT and the GATT case law, it must be stressed that the AB has not sought to extend the principles of the SPS Agreement to the other two agreements. It makes sense as the SPS Agreement contains more detailed provisions than other WTO Agreements with respect to the scientific justification of a measure. For example, different from the SPS Agreement, WTO Members have no obligation to base their TBT or GATT measures on a rigorous risk assessment. In *Brazil- Retreated Tyres*, the panel was satisfied with the evidence of only general nature, such as international instruments and practices in other countries, which suggested a correlation between the spread of diseases and the accumulation of used tyres. The panel did not require any specific evaluation or actual negative health effects of such risks as in the SPS Agreement.[376]

[372] Appellate Body Report, *EC – Asbestos* (n 8) para 128.
[373] Ibid, para 174.
[374] Ibid, para 167–178; Panel Report, *EC – Asbestos* (n 8) para 8.181.
[375] Appellate Body, *Brazil – Retreated Tyres* (n 114) paras 134–183.
[376] Panel Report, *Brazil-Retreated Tyres* (n 114) paras 7.61, 7.68 and 7.77.

Even though the CGP does not specifically refer to science, a strong argument can be made that science plays an important role both in standard setting and dispute settlement involving standards in view of the close resemblance of substantive disciplines in the CGP and the TBT Agreement. In particular, it is expected that relevant scientific evidence may contribute to the determination of 'like products' and whether the standard in question is an 'unnecessary obstacle to international trade'.

## VI. CONCLUSION

All public and private standards falling within the definition of Annex 1.2 are subject to the disciplines of the CGP in Annex 3 of the TBT Agreement. Article 4 of the TBT Agreement has imposed different levels of legal obligations on WTO Members depending on the nature of standardising bodies. For central government standardising bodies, WTO Members are obliged to ensure that they accept and comply with the CGP. For local government and non-governmental standardising bodies, by contrast, WTO Members shall take 'reasonable measures' as may be available to them to ensure that they accept and comply with the CGP. Neither Article 4 of the TBT Agreement nor the CGP have been tested before the WTO dispute settlement body. Nevertheless, WTO Members have committed to largely identical disciplines to reduce the negative impact of standards in the CGP as they have done with regard to technical regulations. Given the similarities of trade law disciplines governing standards and technical regulations, it is reasonable to argue that the AB's extensive interpretative guidance over the substantive obligations on technical regulations is in principle transposable to standards in the CGP. This is in particular true for standards adopted by central government standardising bodies.[377] Accordingly, Chapter 3 has provided an up-to-date analysis of the basic WTO disciplines on standards, including standardising bodies must offer national treatment and MFN to all like products; standards cannot constitute unnecessary restriction on international trade; standards must be transparent and that standards must be based on scientific evidence. Drawing on the rich case law the WTO panels and the AB has developed on technical regulations, the scope and nuances of these obligations in the CGP are outlined.

[377] For additional considerations when applying the same reasoning to private standards, please refer to ch 5.

# 4

# *International Regulatory Cooperation in Product Standards*

## I. THE CONCEPT OF INTERNATIONAL REGULATORY COOPERATION

As demonstrated in Chapter 3, to a large extent, the WTO has retained the traditional GATT-style negative integration approach to reduce unnecessary regulatory diversity. WTO Members are free to pursue their legitimate policy objectives, but are prohibited from adopting discriminatory and unnecessary standards so as to reduce adverse trade effects to the minimum. At the same time, the WTO has evolved from negative integration to positive integration in the form of regulatory cooperation.[1] The Organisation for Economic Cooperation and Development (OECD) defines international regulatory cooperation as 'any agreement or organisational agreement, formal or informal, between countries to promote some form of cooperation in the design, monitoring, enforcement, or ex-post management of regulation, with a view to support the converging and consistency of rules across borders'.[2] The increase in regulatory cooperation in global trade governance is only natural because, despite historical, cultural, political and legal differences, states frequently face similar challenges to their welfare. They can improve their domestic regulatory process by learning from each other's regulatory choices, being more aware of likely effects of their domestic regulations on parties outside their jurisdictions and developing common standards and frameworks to similar risks. Therefore, regulatory cooperation has potential to transfer good regulatory practices, to level the playing field, to reduce costs, and to contribute to the reduction of unnecessary barriers to trade as well as mitigate the economic impact of necessary trade barriers.[3]

[1] R Basedow, 'The WTO and the Rise of Plurilateralism – What Lessons can we Learn from European Union's Experience with Differentiated Integration?' (2018) 21(2) *Journal of International Economic Law* 411, 414; ME Footer, *An Institutional and Normative Analysis of the World Trade Organisation* (Martinus Nijhoff Publishers, 2006) 335.

[2] OECD, *International Regulatory Cooperation: Addressing Global Challenges* (OECD Publishing, 2013) 19.

[3] MB Karttunen, *Transparency and Dispute Settlements: A Study of the Agreements on Sanitary and Phytosanitary Measures and Technical Barriers to Trade* (EUI PhD Thesis, 2016) 107.

Regulatory cooperation can take various forms. From the least to the most legally binding, they include dialogue/exchange of information; recognition and incorporation of international standards; transgovernmental networks of regulators; mutual recognition; trade agreements with regulatory provisions; joint rule-making through intergovernmental organisations; regulatory cooperation partnerships; specific negotiated agreements; and regulatory harmonisation through supranational institutions.[4] Almost all these cooperation forms are adopted in modern trade agreements. In the WTO context, the TBT and SPS Agreements contain substantive provisions on harmonisation through international standards, and mutual and unilateral recognition of foreign standards. In addition, the adoption of good regulatory practices has been regularly discussed at the TBT Committee. The analysis below focuses on these international regulatory cooperation tools in the WTO and selected mega-regional trade agreements

## II. THE ROLE OF INTERNATIONAL STANDARDS IN THE WTO

### A. The Economics of Harmonisation

Harmonisation involves the adoption of the identical standards by two or more jurisdictions.[5] Until the 1980s, setting product standards had been primarily an internal matter for firms or the domain of private sector technical bodies at the national level. International standards were few and far between.[6] However, with the rise of heterogeneous product standards and their associated economic loss, harmonisation through international standards has increasingly served as instruments of trade liberalisation. Harmonisation has the potential to facilitate trade across borders by creating economies of scale and allowing more efficient allocation of resources. First, the use of identical standards leads to products manufactured in different countries more homogeneous and therefore better substitutes for both producers and consumers. Second, the adoption of common standards acts as a quality signal to improve consumer confidence in importing countries about the quality of the goods produced abroad. Third, identical standards will enhance compatibility between imported and domestic products, allowing network externalities to more readily spill over internationally. Fourth, the adoption of identical standards eliminates the need for firms to comply with different set of regulations, and the associated costs. Finally, to the extent that different standards have

[4] OECD (n 2) 22–25.

[5] B Hoekman, 'Trade Agreements and International Regulatory Cooperation in a Supply Chain World', (EUI Robert Schuman Centre for Advanced Studies 2015/04) 4.

[6] W Mattli and T Buthe, 'Setting International Standards: Technological Rationality or Primacy of Power?' (2003) 56 *World Politics* 1, 1–2.

artificially segmented the domestic from foreign markets, harmonisation will enhance competition.[7]

The empirical literature provides robust evidence on the positive impact of harmonisation in increasing international trade flows. Moenius studied data covering 471 industries in 12 Western European countries and found that shared standards have a positive and significant effect on bilateral trade. He estimated that a 10 per cent increase in the number of shared standards enhances bilateral trade by about 3 per cent.[8] Focusing on trade within the EU, Vancauteren and Weiserbs found that harmonisation has a significant effect on trade within the EU.[9] Similarly, focusing on the electronics sector, Reys examined the response of US firms to the harmonisation of EU standards with IEC standards. His study found that increasing harmonisation increases US exports to the EU. In particular, the increase was due to more new US small- and medium-sized firms entering into the EU market.[10]

There is also evidence showing that developing countries may benefit from harmonisation of product standards in international trade. Using a gravity model of trade for the period 1995–2002, Clougherty and Grajek found that conformity with ISO 9000 in developing countries appears to enhance exports to developed countries.[11] Focusing on the exports of textiles, clothing and footwear, Shepherd found that a 10 per cent increase in the total number of non-harmonised EU Standards led to a 6 per cent decrease in product variety from trading partners. By contrast, a 10 per cent increase in the proportion of EU standards harmonised with ISO standards led to an increase of 0.2 per cent in the variety of imports to the EU, mainly from low-income countries.[12] This shows that harmonisation has a positive effect on the diversification of export varieties.

On the other hand, there are potential negative effects of harmonisation on trade. To begin with, harmonisation imposes a cost in terms of reduced product variety. Although this cost is small in the presence of network externalities, it may be significant in other cases. For example, to the extent that demand for foreign goods is driven by love of variety, the harmonisation would then reduce trade. Furthermore, the gains from harmonisation are not distributed evenly among countries since not all of them possess expertise or bargaining power to enable them to take full part in international standards-setting activities.

[7] World Trade Report, *Exploring the Links between Trade, Standards and the WTO* (2005) 54.

[8] J Moenius, 'Information versus Product Adaptation: The Role of Standards in Trade' (February 2004) 15–17 https://ssrn.com/abstraact=608022 Accessed 1 March 2020.

[9] M Vancauteren and D Weiserbs, 'Intra-European Trade of Manufacturing Goods: An Extension of the Gravity Model', ECON Discussion Papers (2005) 22.

[10] J-D Reyes, 'International Harmonisation of Product Standards and Firm Heterogeneity in International Trade', The World Bank Policy Research Paper 5677 (2011) 18–19.

[11] JA Clougherty and M Grajek, 'The Impact of ISO 9000 Diffusion on Trade and FDI: A New Institutional Analysis' (2008) 39(4) *Journal of International Business Studies* 613, 629–630.

[12] B Shepherd, 'Product Standards, Harmonisation, and Trade: Evidence from the Extensive Margin' (2007) World Bank Policy Research Working Paper 4390, at 23.

Consequently, harmonisation may generate asymmetric compliance costs for different countries.[13] Moreover, international standards are likely to be more rigid than national standards. Once put in place, they are less likely to adapt to new information and changes in technology simply because the consensus required to create them may not exist to change them.[14] Next, there are natural limits as to how far harmonisation could go to reduce regulatory heterogeneity. It is often socially productive to respect differences in national preferences where those preferences reflect legitimate differences such as risk tolerance, levels of development, geography, cultures and values. Finally, harmonisation is a slow process and it usually takes many years of work to introduce an international standard to the market.[15]

Harmonisation can be pursued at both international and regional levels. For example, international harmonisation involves the alignment of national standards with international standards issued by international standardising bodies such as the Codex Alimentarius Commission (Codex) or the International Organization for Standardization (ISO).[16] Alternatively, regional harmonisation entails the adoption of standards issued by regional bodies such as European Committee for Standardization and the ASEAN Consultative Committee for Standards and Quality (ACCSQ). Harmonisation in the WTO realm is circumscribed to the international level. Nevertheless, harmonisation is now common in free trade agreements as well. When occurring at regional level, harmonisation might have different implications for trade with countries outside of the free trade agreements (FTAs). Chen and Mattoo found that harmonisation agreements in FTAs can increase trade between participating countries but will not necessarily increase trade with other countries. In particular, they found that harmonisation increased exports from developed countries outside the FTAs but it reduced exports from developing countries outside the FTAs.[17] In short, regional integration of product standards has trade-diverting effects, especially to the detriment of developing countries.

### B. International Standards as Global Public Goods and Global Administrative Law

The concept of public goods has traditionally been discussed within the framework of the nation-state, and only recently has the discourse on public goods

[13] WTO Trade Report 2005 (n 7) 54.

[14] AO Sykes, 'The (limited) Role of Harmonisation in International Goods and Services Market' (1999) 2 *Journal of International Economic Law* 49, 51–52.

[15] RE Baldwin, 'Regulatory Protectionism, Developing Nations, and a Two-Tier World Trade System' (2000) Brookings Trade Forum 237, 264–265.

[16] HZ Schroder, *Harmonisation, Equivalence and Mutual Recognition of Standards in WTO Law* (Wolters Kluwer, 2011) 22.

[17] MX Chen and A Mattoo, 'Regionalism in Standards: Good or Bad for Trade?' (2008) 41 (3) *Canadian Journal of Economics* 838, 860–861; S Baller, 'Trade Effects of Regional Standards: A Heterogeneous Firms Approach', World Bank Policy Research Working Paper 4124 (2007) 26.

been extended to the global sphere.[18] In economic theory, a public good, in contrast to a private good, is defined by two characteristics: non-rivalry and non-excludability. Firstly, there is no rivalry between potential users of a public good: one person can use it without diminishing its availability to others. Secondly, it is non-excludable because no one can be excluded from the consumption of a public good, even if he does not contribute to its production. A frequently used example of public good is clean air. Our breathing does not deplete it, and it cannot be appropriated by a few.[19]

Global public goods come in different varieties. The economists usually classify global public goods into three varieties: single-best-effort goods, aggregate-effort goods and weakest-link goods.[20] A single actor or group of actors can provide the single-best-effort goods. For example, if an asteroid about to pulverise the earth has been deflected away by an interceptor missile launched by one state, then a global public good-safety in this case is provided.[21] Aggregate-effort goods refer to global public goods that can only be produced through the aggregate efforts of multiple countries. For example, climate change mitigation is a function of the total level of greenhouse gas emission reduction achieved by all of the countries in the world. Although individual countries can make efforts to contribute to the goal of climate change mitigation, their efforts will not be able to solve the problem if other major emitting countries are not required to reduce their emission reductions.[22] Weakest-link goods, often encountered in relation to safety and security issues such as eliminating infectious diseases and curtailing the proliferation of weapons of mass destruction, require action by all, including those least willing or lack capacity to do so. Otherwise a single actor that fails to do its part can undo the efforts of the vast majority of actors.[23]

Different varieties of public goods entail different governance challenges to international law. Weakest-link goods involve a holdout problem, whether the holdout is an unwilling one or an unable one.[24] That of aggregate-effort goods involves collective action and free riding problems. Nation states and other actors will not invest in global public goods if their independent action

[18] N Krisch, 'The Decay of Consent: International Law in an Age of Global Public Goods' (2014) 108 *American Journal of International Law* 1, 3.

[19] I Kaul, I Grunberg and MA Stern, 'Defining Global Public Goods', in I Kaul, I Grunberg and MA Stern (eds), *Global Public Goods: International Cooperation in the 21st Century* (Oxford University Press, 1999) 3–4.

[20] For an overview of such classification, see S Barrett, *Why Cooperate? The Incentive to Supply Global Public Goods* (Oxford University Press, 2007).

[21] Ibid, 22–37.

[22] Ibid, 74–102; See also S Barrett, 'Rethinking Climate Change Governance and Its Relationship to the World Trading System' (2011)34 World Economy 1863, 1878.

[23] DG Arce M and T Sandler, 'Transnational Public Goods: Strategies and Institutions' (2001) 17 (3) *European Journal of Political Economy* 493, 496–497.

[24] G Shaffer, 'International Law and Global Public Goods in a Legal Pluralist World', 23 *European Journal of International Law* 669, 679.

will have no impact, or if they can free ride on the investment of others.[25] And that of single-best-effort goods involves the problem of unilateralism. Since not all global public goods are normatively desirable, a unilateral action to provide global public goods is not free from risks and legitimacy inquiries.[26] One major contribution of global public goods discourse to international law is that different varieties of global public goods call for different institutional responses and that international law plays a variable role in their production.[27] For aggregate-effort public goods, for example, there is a greater need for centralised institutions to produce them and international law can play an important role in their provision. International institutions can provide a forum for negotiations and thereby help to reduce transaction costs. They can also promote a learning process, through which countries change their evaluation of the costs and benefits of providing the global public good. International law may also change the incentive structure that states face by lowering the costs of participating in an agreement and raising the costs of staying out; and help to legitimise action by those who have an interest in producing a public good to put pressure on others to participate in supplying that good.[28] That being said, the production of aggregate-effort goods presents the severest challenge to global governance today. The cooperation of at least the most influential players is essential to its provision and international law has had only intermittent success in providing aggregate-effort public goods.[29]

It is submitted that international standards, referring to standards adopted by International Standardising Bodies (ISBs), should be viewed in global public goods terms.[30] Similar to other international institutions that are designed to address global concerns, a wide range of ISBs have been set up to harmonise heterogeneous product standards and increase global economic efficiency. The most prominent examples include the ISO, the International Electrotechnical Commission (IEC), and the International Telecommunication Union (ITU). Take ISO as an example. ISO has so far developed over 23,147 international standards on a variety of subjects, covering almost all aspects of technology and manufacturing.[31] International standards are both non-rivalrous and non-excludable global public goods because they are available to all and no state can monopolise their use. Indeed, the very purpose of international standards is inclusive: the more often they are used in a global scale, the better.

[25] I Kaul, 'Global Public Goods: Explaining Their Underprovision' (2012) 15 (3) *Journal of International Economic Law* 729, 737–738.

[26] D Bodansky, 'What is in a Concept? Global Public Goods, International Law and Legitimacy' (2012) 23 *European Journal of International Law* 651, 664.

[27] Shaffer (n 24) 679–680.

[28] Ibid, at 659–660.

[29] Krisch (n 18) 4.

[30] J Wieland, *Governance Ethics: Global Value Creation, Economic Organisation and Normativity* (Springer, 2014) 61–72.

[31] Available at www.iso.org/iso/home/about.htm, accessed on 20 April 2020.

Specifically, international standards are aggregate-effort goods in the sense that they can only be produced through the aggregate efforts of multiple stakeholders.

Even if all states agree that a global public good should be provided, they may hold different opinions on whether a global public good is normatively good or bad. This is so because global public goods may have a different impact on different actors and states may have different tastes and value choices.[32] In other words, the recognition of the virtues of global public goods has not solved the issue of how they should be produced and whether the production mechanism is legitimate. As a result, attempting to invest an international organisation with authority to make decisions regarding the provision of global public goods would raise some difficult questions. For example, what should be the composition of the decision-making body? Should institutions producing global public goods be open to all states, reflecting the global nature of the public goods or should they have more limited membership to promote more efficient decision-making? What is the appropriate decision-making rule? Should consensus be required, which has proved problematic in the UN climate change regime or should institutions be able to make decisions by qualified majority vote?[33]

These are precisely the issues that international standards bring to the world trading system. Even though there exists a general consensus on the positive role of international standards in reducing non-tariff trade barriers, what constitutes an international standard has emerged as a key issue in trade disputes. In *US – Tuna II*, the Appellate Body (AB) refused to recognise AIDCP as a relevant international standard because it was not automatically open to all interested parties. In *EC – Sardines*, it was not entirely clear whether the relevant international standard, Codex Stan 94, was adopted by consensus.[34] In *EC – Hormones*, the Codex standard that was key to the ruling against the EC was adopted by a secret vote of 33-29 with 7 abstentions.[35] In both *EC – Sardines* and *EC – Hormones*, the EC was practically bound by international standards that it has never consented to in the first place, not to mention that the close vote strongly indicated how controversial those international standards were when being adopted. Unsurprisingly, a number of important questions need to be answered. Is universal participation of all interested parties an essential procedural condition for all international standards? Must all international standards be adopted by consensus? Can standards adopted by non-governmental organisations (NGOs) and industry groups be recognised as international standards for the purpose of the TBT Agreement?

[32] Bodansky (n 26) 655–656.

[33] Ibid, 667.

[34] WTO Appellate Body Report, *European Communities – Trade Description of Sardines* (*EC – Sardines*), WT/DS231/AB/R, adopted 23 October 2002, para 226.

[35] Codex Alimentarius Commission, *Report of the 21st Session*, ALINORM 95/37 (July 8, 1995).

Who has the power to decide whether or not an international standard should be recognised?

The controversy on the attributes of international standards is unsurprising. Before the TBT and SPS Agreements came into effect in the 1990s, many international standards rarely received significant attention outside of scientific circles and they had no international legal consequences for states. A state could simply refuse to accept an international standard and then ignore it.[36] The unbinding nature of international standards and voluntary acceptance procedure gave states maximum control over which standards they would adopt, avoiding potential conflicts. However, the incorporation of international standards into the TBT and SPS Agreements has changed the nature of these previously voluntary standards. Since the outcome of a major trade dispute may hinge on what the relevant international standard is, WTO Members now have strong incentives to ensure that international standards meet certain criteria before they are willing to afford them normative force.

This leads to the issue of how we can hold the producers of international standards accountable for their decision-making, so that international standards, both procedurally and substantively, not only meet the functional needs of the world trading system, but also are perceived as legitimate for their newly found normative force in the TBT Agreement. We argue that the accountability mechanisms highlighted by the global administrative law project are particularly relevant to address the concerns raised here. The global administrative law provides practical tools drawn from domestic administrative law for enhancing the accountability of decision-making in the production of global public goods at the international level. As outlined by the leading proponents of the project, these tools include both procedural and substantive requirements such as procedural participation, transparency and access to information, reasoned decisions, monitoring, inspection, reporting, notice and comment procedures, mechanism of review by a court or other independent tribunal, proportionality, means-ends rationality, avoidance of unnecessarily restrictive means and meeting legitimate expectations.[37] These accountability mechanisms may be developed through international treaties, internal mechanism adopted by international institutions, or international judicial decisions.[38]

But how far global administrative law tools and principles have been accepted across international institutions remain unresolved, at least they have not been

[36] DG Victor, 'The Sanitary and Phytosanitary Agreement of the World Trade Organisation: An Assessment after Five Years' (2000) 32 *New York University Journal of International Law and Politics* 865, 891.

[37] B Kingsbury, N Krisch and RB Stewart, 'The Emergence of Global Administrative Law' (2005) 68 *Law and Contemporary Problems* 15, 37–41; DC Esty, 'Good Governance at the Supranational Level: Globalizing Administrative Law' (2006) 115 *Yale Law Journal* 1490, 1527–1536; C Harlow, 'Global Administrative Law: The Quest for Principles and Values' (2006) 17 *European Journal of international Law* 187, 189–207.

[38] Kingsbury at al., ibid, at 31–37.

instituted across different governance areas despite strong calls for effective accountability mechanisms at international level.[39] In the next section, I will critically review how WTO administrative and judicial bodies deal with international standards. Special emphasis is placed on the role of global administrative law tools and the role of the WTO judicial body as a gatekeeper to filter out transnational standards that are not international standards for the purpose of the TBT Agreement.

## C. Basic WTO Rules on International Standards

The preamble of the TBT Agreement captures the important role of international standards in improving production efficiency and facilitating international trade. Article 2.4 of the TBT Agreement provides that WTO Members are obliged to use relevant existing or imminent international standards 'as a basis' for technical regulations unless they are ineffective or inappropriate to achieve their regulatory objectives. Similarly, paragraph F of the Code of Good Practice (CGP) provides that international standards should be used 'as a basis for' standards. Article 2.5 of the TBT Agreement further provides that technical regulations adopted in accordance with international standards are afforded the rebuttable presumption of not creating unnecessary obstacles to international trade. In addition, Article 2.9 imposes additional notification requirements in case relevant international standards are not used. These requirements have created strong incentives for WTO Members to make domestic technical regulations consistent with relevant international standards. An OECD empirical study confirmed that WTO Members have implemented Article 2.4 of the TBT Agreement in various ways.[40]

Similarly, Article 3.1 of the SPS Agreement requires that SPS measures be based on international standard where they exist. In contrast to the TBT Agreement, international standards in the SPS Agreement are currently limited to standards established by Codex and those developed under the auspices of the International Office of Epizootics (OIE) or the International Plant Protection Convention (IPPC).[41] Annex A(3)(d) to the SPS Agreement provides the possibility that the SPS Committee may decide to recognise other international standards. Nevertheless, the SPS Committee has not identified any other relevant international organisations to date.[42]

[39] Sabino Cassese, 'Administrative Law without the State? The Challenge of Global Regulation' (2005) 37 *New York University Journal of International Law and Politics* 663, 692.

[40] B Fliess et al., 'The Use of International Standards in Technical Regulation', OECD Trade Policy Papers No 102 (OECD Publishing, 2010) 32.

[41] Annex A to the SPS Agreement.

[42] S Bernstein and E Hannah, 'Non-State Global Standard Setting and the WTO: Legitimacy and the Need for Regulatory Space' (2008) 11 *Journal of International Economic Law* 575, 594.

### *i. International Standards 'As a Basis' for Domestic Standards*

Both Article 2.4 of the TBT Agreement and paragraph F of the CGP provide that international standards should be used 'as a basis for' technical regulations or standards. The AB concluded that 'as a basis for' requires that the relevant international standard serve as a 'principal constituent' or 'fundamental principle' of a TBT measure. More than 'a rational relationship', it implies 'a very strong and very close relationship'.[43] At a minimum no such relationship can exist where there is a contradiction between an international standard and a technical standard.[44] In *EC – Sardines*, since the EC regulation on the definition of 'preserved sardines' contradicts the relevant international standard Codex Stan 94, it cannot be said to serve 'as a basis for' the EC regulation.[45]

Similarly, Article 3.1 of the SPS Agreement requires that SPS measures be 'based on' international standards where they exist. In *EC – Hormones*, the panel erroneously equated 'based on' with 'conform to'.[46] The AB reversed the panel and stated that 'based on' means that the SPS measure 'stands' or is 'founded' or 'built' upon or 'is supported by' the international standard. By contrast, to 'conform to' an international standard would mean that the SPS measure embodies the international standard completely and, for practical purposes, coverts it into a municipal standard.[47] As the harmonisation of heterogeneous SPS measures on the basis of international standards was only projected an aspirational objective, yet to be realised in the future, it is wrong to transform international standards to legally binding norms to be complied with here and now.[48] Furthermore, the term 'based on' does not imply a procedural interpretation.[49] WTO Members have no obligation actually to deliberate upon international standards in the process of setting domestic standards. Instead, what is required is substantive consistency between SPS measures and the relevant international standards in question. The AB confirmed that its clarifications of 'based on' in the SPS Agreement are relevant to the interpretation of 'as a basis for' in the TBT Agreement.[50]

In *EC – Sardines*, the EC argued that its regulation was in essence based on international standards Codex Stan 94 and requested the panel to consult with the Codex to clarify the true meaning of Codex Stan 94. The panel declined the request.[51] Relying on Article 13.2 of the WTO Dispute Settlement

[43] Appellate Body Report, *EC – Sardines* (n 34) para 243–245.
[44] Ibid, para 248.
[45] Ibid, para 249.
[46] WTO Panel Report, *EC Measures Concerning Meat and Meat Products (Hormones), Complaint by the United States*, WT/DS26/R/USA, adopted 13 February 1998, para 8.76.
[47] WTO Appellate Body Report, *EC Measures Concerning Meat and Meat Products (Hormones)*, WT/DS26/AB/R, adopted 13 February 1998, para 170.
[48] Ibid, para 165.
[49] Ibid, para 189.
[50] Ibid, para 244.
[51] Panel Report, *EC– Sardines* (n 34) para 6.8.

Understanding, the AB upheld the panel's full discretion in deciding whether to seek external advice.[52] It is submitted that the panel's stance should not be a role model for other panels to follow in more complex cases in which international standards can be highly complex and technical. The WTO panel may simply lack technical expertise to interpret the international standard at issue. That would create unnecessary anger and mistrust towards the WTO, not to mention natural suspicion of the legitimacy and correctness of the interpretation. The ISB which adopted the relevant international standard clearly possesses better expertise to state authoritatively what Members have agreed upon when the standards were approved. It is therefore suggested that consultation with relevant ISBs be a regular feature in the dispute settlement process when the meaning of an international standard is in doubt.

A technical regulation adopted in accordance with international standards is afforded the presumption of not creating unnecessary obstacles to international trade.[53] The rationale behind the favourable presumption is economic efficiency: regulations based on widely agreed international standards are less likely to cover a state policy aimed at externalising the cost of compliance by shifting it onto foreign players.[54] However, it remains an open question whether the technical regulation concerned is consistent with other provisions of the TBT Agreement and the GATT. This is in contrast to the much wider presumption in the SPS Agreement. Article 3.2 of the SPS Agreement provides that SPS measures, which conform to international standards, shall be presumed to be consistent with the relevant provisions of the SPS Agreement as well as the GATT. It should be noted that only SPS measures that '*conform to*' international standards enjoy the benefits of this rebuttable presumption. The AB held that this practically means that a Member fully endorses international standard as a domestic standard with no deviation.[55] By contrast, if a Member chooses only to use the international standard as a basis, the SPS measure will not benefit from the presumption of consistency. This raises the question of what a Member has to gain from basing its SPS measures on (but not conforming to) international standards.[56]

### *ii. Ineffective and Inappropriate International Standards*

The purpose of international standards is to promote the harmonisation of national product standards on as wide a basis as possible.[57] Conceptually, if

[52] Appellate Body Report, *EC – Sardines* (n 34) para 302.

[53] Art 2.5 of the TBT Agreement, Art 3.2 of the SPS Agreement.

[54] F Fontanelli, 'ISO and Codex Standards and International Trade Law: What Gets Said is not What's Heard' (2011) 60 (4) *International and Comparative Law Quarterly* 895, 915.

[55] AB Report, *EC – Hormones* (n 47) para 163.

[56] D Hurst, 'Hormones: European Communities- Measures Affecting Meat and Meat Products' (1998) 9 *European Journal of International Law* 182, 183.

[57] *EC – Hormones* (n 47) para 177.

a relevant international standard exists, a WTO Member has four possible choices. First, it may choose to convert the international standard into the domestic technical regulation and enjoy the rebuttable presumption of not creating unnecessary barriers to international trade. Second, it may use the international standard as a basis for (but not conform to) the technical regulation. Such a technical regulation is still subject to the full scrutiny of the WTO panel on its consistency with all TBT disciplines. Third, a Member may set its technical regulation with a lower protection level than that of an international standard. Finally, under Article 2.4 of the TBT, a WTO Member may choose to deviate from the relevant international standard because it is inappropriate or ineffective to achieve its regulatory objective. For example, a WTO Member may have set a level of protection higher than would be achieved by a relevant international standard. In other words, international standards are *not* the 'ceiling' standard for WTO Members.

The AB noted that the words 'ineffective' and 'inappropriate' refer to two different scenarios. An 'ineffective' means is a means which does not have the function of accomplishing the legitimate objective pursued, whereas 'inappropriate' means is a means which is not suitable for the fulfilment of the legitimate objective pursued. The question of effectiveness bears upon the *results* of the means employed, whereas the question of appropriateness relates more to the *nature* of the means employed.[58] Whether the relevant international standard is 'ineffective' or 'inappropriate' must be assessed in light of the legitimate objectives pursued by a WTO Member. Under the TBT Agreement, a WTO Member has a wide discretion in pursing regulatory objectives that it deems legitimate. However, a WTO panel retains the power to examine the legitimacy of the purported regulatory objectives.[59] Nevertheless, it is difficult to imagine that a WTO panel will easily dismiss a purported objective as illegitimate or not worth pursuing.

In *EC – Sardines*, the stated objectives of the EC regulation were market transparency, consumer protection and fair competition. The AB accepted these were legitimate regulatory objectives. The real issue then was whether the relevant international standard in question, Codex Stan 94, was both 'effective' and 'appropriate' to achieve the regulatory objectives. The AB finally ruled against the EU on two factual findings. First, contrary to the EC argument, the EC had not established that consumers in *most member states* always associate the common sardines with *sardina pilchardus*. So there was no firm basis for the alleged consumer confusion in the EU. Second, since Codex Stan 94 contains labelling regulations to ensure market transparency and reduce consumer confusion in a manner not to mislead consumers, the EC's regulation was superfluous and too restrictive.[60] But why must consumers in most members of the EU be

[58] *EC – Sardines* (n 34) para 285.
[59] Ibid, para 286.
[60] *EC – Sardines* (n 34) para 290.

adversely affected for the EC regulation to be legal? Why is it not enough to prove that *some* consumers in *some* European countries have developed such a habit of exclusive association? By holding such an assumption, the AB has implicitly put a ceiling on how far a Member can go to achieve its regulatory objective, in contrast to the premise of the TBT Agreement that it does not compromise the autonomy of a Member to determine the acceptable degree of risk.[61]

In *US – COOL*, the panel found that the relevant Codex standard did not have the function or capacity of accomplishing the legitimate objective sought by the measure – it was thus neither effective nor appropriate.[62] This was because the Codex standard in question confers origin according to the concept of substantial transformation (thus, an animal's origin is determined exclusively by where it was slaughtered), and therefore could not achieve the US objective of providing information to consumers about the countries in which an animal was born, raised and slaughtered.[63] Similarly, in *US – Tuna II*, the panel was of the view that while the AIDCP standard did contribute to the objective sought by the US, it failed to do so in some respects – for example, it failed to address unobserved adverse effects on dolphins by using the method of setting on dolphins.[64] Mexico had thus failed to show that it was an effective and appropriate means to fulfil the US objectives.

### *iii. The Allocation of Burden of Proof in Article 2.4*

There are strong conceptual similarities between Article 2.4 of the TBT Agreement on the one hand, and Article 3.1 and Article 3.3 of the SPS Agreement on the other hand.[65] In *EC – Hormones*, the panel allocated the burden of proof on the party who deviates from the international standard. One main reason for such allocation was that the panel perceived the relationship between Article 3.1 and Article 3.3 of the SPS Agreement as a 'general rule-exception'. Whilst Article 3.1 imposes an obligation on all Members to base their domestic SPS measures on international standards, Article 3.3 permits a Member to depart from an international standard if the Member seeks a level of protection higher than would be achieved by the international standard with sound scientific justification. The panel thereby suggested by implication that when a measure is not so based, the burden is on the respondent to show that the measure is scientifically

[61] J Scott, *The WTO Agreement on Sanitary and Phytosanitary Measures: A Commentary* (Oxford University Press, 2007) 329.

[62] Panel Report, *United States – Certain Country of Origin Labelling (Cool) Requirements*, WT/DS384/R (18 November 2011), paras 7.734–7.735.

[63] Ibid, para 7.734.

[64] Panel Report, *United States- Measures Concerning the Importation, Marketing and Sale of Tuna and Tuna Products (US-Tuna II)*, WT/DS381/R (15 September 2011), para 7.738.

[65] AB Report, *EC – Sardines* (n 34) para 274.

justified under Article 3.3.[66] The AB reversed such a characterisation and stated that Article 3.1 merely excludes from its scope of application the kinds of situations covered by Article 3.3. Article 3.3 recognises that the WTO Members have an 'autonomous right' to establish a level of protection higher than would be achieved by international standards.[67] Exercising such an autonomous right does not impose a special burden of proof upon the Member who has decided to deviate from the international standard. The complaining party therefore needs to prove a prima facie case that the respondent has breached Article 3.3, ie, there isn't scientific justification for the responding party's deviation from the relevant international standard.[68]

The AB has applied the same reasoning to the TBT Article 2.4. There is no 'general rule-exception' relationship between the first and the second parts of Article 2.4. To challenge a WTO Member's technical regulation or standard on the grounds that it is inconsistent with Article 2.4 or paragraph F of the CGP, the allocation of the burden of proof does not shift to the defending Member deviating from the relevant international standard. The *complainant* has to bear the burden of establishing that the relevant international standard has not been used 'as a basis for' the technical regulation, *as well as* that the international standard is both 'effective' and 'appropriate' to fulfil the legitimate objectives pursued by the Member through the technical regulation.[69] The AB justified its approach on the elaborate transparency obligations embedded in the TBT Agreement. A complaining party will not be disadvantaged because these transparency provisions will enable it to get acquaintance with the measures and explain why, in their view, notified measures have violated Article 2.4.[70] The AB's rejection of a general rule-exception relationship in respect of international standards has transformed Article 2.4 into a positive requirement for the complainant to prove that international standards would function as an effective and appropriate alternative to the disputed TBT measure.[71] This interpretation has apparently accorded a greater degree of deference to sovereign policy choices. It has made it easier for WTO Members to adopt TBT measures with a higher level of protection.[72]

The AB's rationale for this ruling is not convincing. Textually, there is a clear legislative mandate stating that international standards must be given priority, except when they are ineffective or inappropriate to serve as a basis. The term 'except' can only be understood as referring to an 'exception'. If this is

[66] AB Report, *EC – Hormones* (n 47) para 103.

[67] Ibid, para 104.

[68] Ibid, paras 101–102.

[69] AB Report, *EC – Sardines* (n 34) para 275.

[70] Ibid, para 285.

[71] E Vranes, *Trade and the Environment: Fundamental Issues in International Law, WTO Law, and Legal Theory* (Oxford University Press, 2009) 313.

[72] J McDonald, 'Domestic Regulation, International Standards, and Technical Barriers to Trade' (2005) 4 *World Trade Review* 249, 264.

the case, then it seems reasonable for the party who deviates from the default obligation to assume the burden of proof, as the GATT Article XX case law shows. This interpretation is also consistent with one of the key objectives of the TBT Agreement – harmonisation. Second, as a practical matter, relying on transparency provisions in the TBT Agreement may put a complaining party at a disadvantage. Take *EC – Sardines* as an example. What if the EU had withheld information from its WTO partners and the TBT Committee? What if the notification or rationale provided by a notifying member is inadequate? How then can the transparency obligations be of much help to Peru?[73] That being said, the significance of this shift of burden of proof should not be overstressed. As a practical matter, the defending party will ultimately need to demonstrate that the international standard is either inappropriate or ineffective for the fulfilment of the legitimate objectives pursued.[74] In *EC – Sardines*, Peru won the Article 2.4 claim before the AB by providing the same quantum of evidence it had already argued before the panel, despite the AB ruling that it should assume the burden of proof itself.

## D. What Constitutes a Relevant International Standard?

Article 2.4 of the TBT Agreement represents an extraordinary mechanism for the creation of new international legal norms. As Howse points out, by virtue of Article 2.4 of the TBT Agreement, a very broad range of normative materials, which are mostly of a voluntary nature, may be converted or transformed into international legal obligation.[75] Precisely because international standards have normative value in designing and implementing national product standards, what constitutes a relevant international standard is an important threshold question. Different from the SPS Agreement, the TBT Agreement does not explicitly name any ISB as a 'relevant' body for the purposes of implementing Article 2.4. This leaves flexibility to WTO Members to decide which international standard, if any, may be relevant in a given situation.[76] This flexibility, however, has caused much complexity in WTO dispute settlement processes.

[73] PC Mavroidis, 'Last Mile for Tuna (to a Safe Harbour): What is the TBT Agreement All About?' (2019) 30 (1) *European Journal of International Law* 279, 294–295.

[74] J Pauwelyn, 'Does the WTO Stand for 'Deference to' or 'Interference with' National Health Authorities When Applying the SPS Agreement'? in T Cottier and PC Mavroidis (eds), *The Role of Judge in International Trade Regulation* (The University of Michigan Press, 2003) 178.

[75] R Howse, 'A New Device for Creating International Legal Normativity: The WTO Technical Barriers to Trade Agreement and 'International Standards' in C Joerges and E-U Petersmann (eds), *Constitutionalism, Multilevel Trade Governance and Social Regulation* (Hart Publishing, 2006) 393.

[76] E Wijkstrom and D McDaniels, 'Improving Regulatory Governance: International Standards and the WTO TBT Agreement' (2013) 47(5) *Journal of World Trade* 1013, 1015.

### *i. A Critique of the AB's Hands-off Approach in EC – Sardines*

In *EC – Sardines*, the EC challenged the panel's finding that Codex Stan 94 was a relevant international standard on the basis that only standards that were adopted *by consensus* could be qualified as international standards for the purpose of Article 2.4 of the TBT Agreement.[77] On this issue, the TBT Committee Decision adopted on the second Triennial Review of the TBT Agreement in 2000 explicitly provides that when developing international standards, consensus procedures should be established that seek to take into account the views of all parties concerned and to reconcile any conflicting arguments.[78] Nevertheless, the panel in *EC – Sardines* delegated the TBT Committee Decision as a mere 'policy statement of preference' and not the controlling provision in interpreting Article 2.4.[79] The panel further found that *Codex Rules of Procedure* permit measures to be adopted by means of a formal vote.[80] The panel then quoted the explanatory note to Annex 1.2 (defining the term 'standard') of the TBT Agreement, which states: '... standards prepared by the international standardisation community are based on consensus. This Agreement covers also documents that are not based on consensus.' The panel explained the above two sentences of the Explanatory Note as follows:

> [T]he first sentence reiterates the norm of international standardisation community that standards are prepared on the basis of consensus. The following sentence, however, acknowledges that consensus may not always be achieved and that international standards that were not adopted by consensus are within the scope of TBT Agreement. This provision therefore confirms that even if not adopted by consensus, an international standard can constitute a relevant international standard.

The AB then upheld the panel's interpretation that a standard could constitute a relevant international standard even if it was not adopted by consensus, viewing the omission of a consensus requirement as a deliberate choice on the part of the drafters of the TBT Agreement.[81]

It is submitted that the AB' s interpretation was flawed. To begin with, it is a controversial interpretative technique to construct the meaning of international standards by using elements from the generic definition of standard enshrined in Annex 1.2 and its Explanatory Note. A careful reading of the Explanatory Note allows two different interpretations, which seem to be equally plausible.[82]

[77] AB Report, *EC – Sardines* (n 34) para 219.

[78] WTO, Second Triennial Review of the Operation and Implementation of the Agreement on Technical Barriers to Trade, WTO Doc. G/TBT/9 (13 November 2000), Annex 4, para 8.

[79] WTO Panel Report, *European Communities – Trade Description of Sardines* (*EC– Sardines*), WT/DS231/R, adopted 23 October 2002, as modified by Appellate Body Report WT/DS231/AB/R, para 7.91.

[80] Appellate Body Report, *EC – Sardines* (n 34) para 226.

[81] Ibid, para 227.

[82] Howse (n 75) 390; H Horn & JHH Weiler, '*European Communities – Trade Description of Sardines*: Textualism and its Discontent', in H Horn and PC. Mavroidis (eds), *The WTO Case Law*

The AB found that the word 'also' in the last sentence of the Explanatory Note makes it clear that the word 'documents' in the same sentence can only refer to 'standards prepared by the international standardising community'. However, it is entirely equally possible that 'documents' refer to standards in the generic sense. Not all standards are international standards. The Explanatory Note to a generic definition of standard naturally covers other standards (municipal or transnational) that may not qualify as international standards, for example, they do not require consensus to be adopted, but are still subject to the TBT disciplines.

Moreover, as an extension of viewing the TBT Committee Decision as having no legal binding force, the AB in *EC – Sardines* took a hands-off approach when it came to controlling or double-checking the legitimacy of international standards.[83] It announced that how international standards were set outside the WTO was 'not for us to decide'.[84] It is clear that the AB turned a blind eye to *who* set international standards and *how* international standards were developed in international standardisation bodies. The normative force of international standards was rendered automatically in the sense that the AB took international standards as mere facts, whilst declining to consider the origin, nature, scientific quality, legitimacy and accountability of the standards in question. Consequently, international standards that were never conceded to by the disputing parties and were merely voluntary in nature were given teeth in the settlement of global trade disputes. This is all the more striking if we consider the nature, composition and working processes of some international standardisation bodies.

### a. The Capture of International Standardising Bodies

Governance arrangements for international standards are complex, involving a range of actors (eg governments, national standardising bodies, private sector) and settings (eg dedicated international standard setting organisations, private sector consortia, or the marketplace).[85] Indeed, the vast majority of international standards emanate from private sector standards developing organisations or private/public partnerships in which non-state actors,

*of 2002* (Cambridge University Press, 2005) 254–256; P Delimatsis, ' "Relevant International Standards" and "Recognised Standardisation Bodies" under the TBT Agreement', in P Delimatsis (eds), *The Law, Economics and Politics of International Standardisation* (Cambridge University Press, 2015) 104.

[83] J Pauwelyn, 'Rule-Based Trade 2.0? The Rise of Informal Rules and International Standards and How They May Outcompete WTO Treaties' (2014) 17 *Journal of International Economic Law* 739, 749.

[84] Appellate Body Report, *EC – Sardines* (n 34) para 227.

[85] KW Abbot and D Snidal, 'International 'Standards' and International Governance' (2001) 8 *European Public Policy Journal* 345, 361–367.

including business associations and NGOs, are the driving force.[86] For example, the ISO and the IEC are largely private sector organisations in which states and governments cannot be members and the primary stakeholder is the industry sector.[87]

Whereas technological rationality is an important factor in standardisation activities, international standardisation remains a highly politicised process.[88] For instance, national standardising bodies, along with private sector stakeholders, are arguably most concerned with minimising their domestic switching costs as a result of standardisation. The more important standardisation becomes, the fiercer is the competition for increased influence in international standard-setting bodies. Moreover, international standard setting can also be captured by the industries involved. Since industries organised themselves more efficiently than consumers, there is a risk of bias in international standard setting towards industry interests rather than interests of consumers and the general public.[89] For example, evidence shows that much of the work within technical committees in the ISO is largely dominated by industry- driven interests.[90]

### b. Competing International Standards

Since the TBT Agreement does not contain a list of international standardising organisations, each WTO Member enjoys the flexibility to select an international standard that it deems relevant in a given situation.[91] This is problematic because in the real world multiple international standardising bodies co-exist and they sometimes create duplicative and possibly contradictory international standards. For example, the global standard setting in the information and communication technology (ICT) industry was descried as a 'balkanised paradigm'.[92] Driven by government policy, technological advance, business strategy, regional integration and changed ideology among scientists and engineers, numerous industry consortia have emerged and in some way to compete

[86] D Wirth, 'The International Organisation for Standardisation: Private Voluntary Standards as Swords and Shields' (2009) 36 *Boston College Environmental Affairs Law Review* 79, 87.

[87] Mattli and Buthe (n 6) 4.

[88] J Swinnen and T Vandemoortele, 'Trade and Political Economy of Standards' (2012) 11(3) *World Trade Review* 390, 392–395.

[89] J Alvarez, *International Organisations as Law-makers* (Oxford University Press, 2005) 221; MA Livermore, 'Authority and Legitimacy in Global Governance: Deliberation, Institutional Differentiation, and the Codex Alimentarius' (2006) 81 *New York University Law Review* 766, 785.

[90] NR Arriaza, 'Soft Law in a Hybrid Organisation: The International Organisation for Standardisation', in DL Shelton (ed), *Commitment and Compliance- The Role of Non-binding Norms in the International Legal System* (Oxford University Press, 2000) 263.

[91] M Trebilcock, R Howse and A Eliason, *The Regulation of International Trade* 4th edn (Routledge, 2012) 318.

[92] H-W Liu, 'International Standards in Flux: A Balkanised ICT Standards-Setting Paradigm and its Implications for the WTO' (2014) 17 (3) *Journal of International Economic Law* 551, 553–558.

with the traditional international standardising bodies like the ISO and IEC. In practice, WTO Members frequently have different opinions as to what the relevant international standard is, and they tend to disagree on which international standardising bodies are relevant to the purpose the TBT Agreement.

### c. Developing Countries' Concerns

Significant economic resources and technical expertise are prerequisites for active participation in international standardisation. Different resources, size of economies, level of private sector development and involvement, and scientific and technological capacity have structurally disadvantaged small developing countries in the international standard setting process.[93] As a result, the resulting standards may not reflect their needs and concerns. Evidence suggests that power politics and regulatory capture by the big developed states may be endemic in international standard setting.[94] In short, the decision-making process in international standardising bodies may suffer 'democratic deficit' and is unduly shaped by powerful countries and actors, thus unfit to settle politically sensitive trade disputes.[95]

A related issue is that the development of international standards within international standardising bodies is time-consuming, with an average development period of five years or more. Consequently, international standards adopted by international standardising bodies may not necessarily reflect the status of existing technologies, but are obsolete, scientifically or technically flawed and not relevant to the global market.[96] Once put in place, international standards are likely to resist adapting to new information and technologies simply because the consensus required in creating them may not exist to change them. There is a danger of perpetuating an international standard that may later be revealed by subsequent developments as out-dated.[97] The concerns of international standardisation processes has been a central issue in the non-agricultural market access (NAMA) negotiations within the WTO.[98]

[93] G Mayeda, 'Developing Disharmony? The SPS and TBT Agreement and the Impact of Harmonisation on Developing Countries' (2004) 7 (4) *Journal of International Economic Law* 737, 746–749.

[94] DW Drezner, *All Politics is Global: Explaining International Regulatory Regimes* (Princeton University Press, 2007).

[95] NR Arriaza, 'Shifting the Point of Regulation: The International Organisation for Standardisation and Global Law Making on Trade and the Environment' (1995) 22 *Ecology Law Quarterly* 479, 522–529.

[96] US Paper on the First TBT Triennial Review, G/TBT/W/40 (25 April 1997); Submission from Japan, 'Issues Concerning International Standards and International Standardisation Bodies', G/TBT/W/113 (15 June 1999).

[97] Sykes (n 14) 69.

[98] WTO Negotiating Group on Market Access, 'Market Access for Non-Agricultural Products-International Standards in Support of Trade and Economic Development: Strengthening the Contribution of the Committee Decision', TN/MA/W/141 (March 29, 2011).

Moreover, from 1995 to 2018, WTO Members have raised 228 specific trade concerns (STCs) on international standards, accounting for more than one third of all STCs registered at the TBT Committee.[99] The raised STCs have shown that the concerns outlined above are major causes of many trade issues.[100] For example, a number of WTO Members, including China and the European Union, challenged a restrictive US regulation for the transportation of lithium batteries by air, which went beyond those laid out in international standards set by the International Civil Aviation Organisation (ICAO). However, the US argued that the ICAO standard-setting process was procedurally flawed, since it did not take account of all relevant scientific information, and thus led to a standard that was deficient from a technical perspective.[101] Similarly, the US challenged the EU olive oil grading for its deviation from the relevant Codex standard. The US argued that the EU measure was following the International Oliver Council (IOC) standards, which it did not consider to be an internationally recognised ISB since its standards reflected input exclusively from its members in European and Mediterranean countries.[102]

These STCs testify that the deferential approach taken by the AB to international standardising bodies in *EC – Sardines* was untenable. The objective of the TBT Agreement could fail if institutions to which the TBT has delegated standard-setting functions failed to deliver high quality and widely recognised standards. On the other hand, these challenges in no way mean that it is inappropriate for WTO Members to delegate quasi-legislative authority to international standardising bodies. The WTO does not by itself develop international standards, nor does it coordinate the harmonisation of different standards across international standardising bodies. Allowing 'legislative acts' on internationals standards to take place outside the WTO provides enormous benefits to the WTO regime. This structure allows subject-matter specialists, as opposed to trade specialists, to take a leading role in formulating the standards.[103] The only issue is that international standards should not be taken as mere facts. Their suitability as a normative benchmark for standard setting should be critically evaluated, rather than being taken for granted.

### *ii. Evaluating the Appellate Body's Intrusive Approach in US – Tuna II*

The WTO obligation to use relevant international standards as a basis for domestic technical regulations is a continuous one, in the sense that WTO

[99] Note by the Secretariat, 'Twenty-Fourth Annual Review of the Implementation and Operation of the TBT Agreement', G/TBT/42 (25 February 2019) 27.

[100] Wijkstrom and McDaniels (n 76) 1021–1023.

[101] Minutes of the Meeting of 15–16 June 2011, G/TBT/M/54 (20 September 2011) paras 198–204.

[102] WTO, *United States – Olive Oil*, G/TBT/N/USA/395 (6 April 2008); *EC – Marketing Standards for Olive Oil*, G/TBT/N/EEC/226 (22 October 2008).

[103] G Marceau and JP Trachtman, 'A Map of the World Trade Organisation Law of Domestic Regulation of Goods: The Technical Barriers to Trade Agreement, the Sanitary and Phytosanitary

Members have an ongoing obligation to reassess existing technical regulations in light of new or revised international standards.[104] Despite the fact that different approaches and procedures are adopted by ISBs in their standardisation activities, the obligation for WTO Members to use relevant international standards is the same.[105] Because international standards have normative value in designing and implementing municipal standards, what constitutes an international standard has become an important threshold question in TBT-related disputes.

Although the TBT Agreement provides definitions to 'standard' in Annex 1.2 and 'international body' in Annex 1.4, there is no explicit definition of 'international standard' in the TBT Agreement. In *US – Tuna II*, the AB has for the first time outlined some signposts to determine whether a standard at issue is an 'international standard' for the purpose of the TBT Agreement. The introductory clause of Annex 1 provides that, unless they are given definitions in the TBT Agreement, the terms shall have the same meaning as given in the ISO/IEC Guide 2:1991 (the 'Guide'). Thus, the Guide constitutes important context for dispute settlement purposes by directing the WTO judiciary to have recourse to a non-WTO document to clarify certain TBT terms.[106] The term 'international standard' is defined in the Guide as 'a standard that is adopted by an international standardizing/standards organisation and made available to the public'. Since Annex 1.2 of the TBT Agreement stipulates that a 'standard' is to be approved by a 'body', not 'organisation' as used in the Guide, and that a specific definition in the TBT Agreement prevails upon the Guide, the AB concluded that an international standard is '*a standard adopted by an international standardizing body*'.[107] This definition suggests that it is primarily the characteristics of the ISB that lends a standard its international character.[108] Then, what is an ISB? The Guide defines a standardising body as 'a body that has recognised activities in standardisation'. In addition, Annex 1.4 to the TBT Agreement defines 'international body' as a 'body whose membership is open to the relevant bodies of at least all Members'. Reading these definitions together, the AB held that, for the purpose of the TBT Agreement, an ISB must have *recognised activities* in standardisation and whose membership is open to the *relevant bodies* of at least all WTO Members.[109]

At least three questions emerge from this definition. First, *who* must recognise an entity's activities in standardisation? Second, *how* to determine whether or not an entity has 'recognised activities' in standardisation? Third, is it possible

Measures Agreement, and the General Agreement on Tariffs and Trade' (2014) 48 (2) *Journal of World Trade* 351, 389.

[104] Appellate Body Report, *EC– Sardines* (n 34) para 216.

[105] WTO (n 78) para 19.

[106] Delimatsis (n 82) 125.

[107] Appellate Body Report, *US – Tuna II* (n 64) para 356.

[108] Ibid, para 353.

[109] Ibid, para 359.

for standards adopted by a non-governmental body, such as a non-governmental organisation or industrial consortium, to be recognised as international standards? With respect to the first question, the AB clarified that evidence of recognition by either WTO Members or national standardising bodies would be relevant.[110] Thus, the high level of acceptance and market technology of the standard, ie, the recognition of the standard by the market and industry, is not enough.[111]

With regard to the second question of what constitutes 'recognised activities', the AB concluded that the term 'recognise' falls along a spectrum that ranges from a factual end (acknowledgement of the existence of something) to a normative end (acknowledgement of the validity or legality of something). The 'factual' and 'normative' recognition constitute cumulative requirements.[112] The factual dimension of the concept 'recognition' would appear to require, at a minimum, that WTO Members are aware, or have reason to expect, that the international body in question is engaged in standardisation activities.[113] For the normative dimension of the concept, the AB provided a number of signposts on what 'recognition' might entail. To begin with, WTO Members' participation in an ISB's standardising activities could constitute evidence suggesting that the international body is engaged in 'recognised activities'. However, the recognition of those who participated in the development of a standard would not necessarily be sufficient to find that a body has recognised activities in standardisation. This is because international standards apply to all WTO Members, not merely those who participated in the development of the respective standard. Nevertheless, the AB stated that the larger the number of countries that participated in the development of a standard, the more likely it might be said that the respective body's activities in standardisation are 'recognised'.[114] Furthermore, the recognition of a body's standardisation activities may be inferred from the recognition of the resulting standard, ie, when its existence, legality and validity have been acknowledged. This, however, does not mean that only a body whose standards are widely used can have recognised activities in standardisation.[115] Moreover, an international body that develops a single standard could have 'recognised activities in standardisation' if other evidence suggests that the body's standardisation activities are recognised. It is not necessary that the preparation and adoption of standards is a principal function of the body in question.[116]

Extraordinarily, the AB held that the TBT Committee Decision is a 'subsequent agreement' between the WTO Members within the meaning of

[110] Ibid, para 363.

[111] HZ Schroder, 'Definition of the Concept 'International Standard' in the TBT Agreement' (2009) 43(6) *Journal of World Trade* 1223, 1254.

[112] E Partiti, 'The Appellate Body Report in *US – Tuna II* and Its Impact on Eco-Labelling and Standardisation' (2013) 40 (1) *Legal Issues of Economic Integration* 73, 90.

[113] Appellate Body Report, *US – Tuna II* (n 64) para 362.

[114] Ibid, para 390.

[115] Ibid, para 392.

[116] Ibid, para 394.

Article 31(3)(a) of the Vienna Convention on the Law of Treaties ('VCLT'). As such, a WTO panel is obliged under Article 3.2 of the WTO Dispute Settlement Understanding to take it into account when interpreting specific TBT provisions.[117] The TBT Committee Decision has enunciated six principles for the development of international standards:

> [T]here was a need to develop principles concerning *transparency, openness, impartiality and consensus, relevance and effectiveness, coherence and developing country interests* that would clarify and strengthen the concept of international standards under the Agreement.[118]

The AB held that the TBT Committee Decision bears specifically on the interpretation and application of the concept of 'recognised activities in standardisation'.[119] From a factual perspective, the standardising activities of a body that disseminates information about its standardisation activities, as envisaged by the transparency procedures of the TBT Committee Decision, would presumably be acknowledged to exist, accorded notice or attention, and treated worthy of consideration by all WTO Members that make a good faith effort to follow international standardisation activities. From a normative perspective, it would be easier for an international standardising body to be 'recognised' to the extent that it has complied with the principles and procedures of the TBT Committee Decision which WTO Members have decided 'should be observed' in the development of international standards.[120]

In *US – Tuna II*, at issue was whether or not the AIDCP constituted an international standard. The AIDCP is a legally binding multilateral agreement which entered into force in February 1999 and both Mexico and the US are parties to the AIDCP.[121] Any state or regional economic integration organisation can be invited to accede to the AIDCP on the basis of a decision by the parties. The US argued that becoming a party to the AIDCP was not an option available to at least all WTO Members because it was available only to those Members invited. Mexico responded that being invited to accede was only a formality and 'no additional countries or regional economic integration organisations have expressed interests in joining the AIDCP'.[122] The AB held that the TBT Committee Decision bears specifically on the interpretation of the term 'open' and referred to the relevant part of it, which states:

> Membership of an international standardizing body should be open on a non-discriminatory basis to relevant bodies of at least all WTO members. This would

[117] Appellate Body Report, *United States – Measures Affecting the Production and Sale of Clove Cigarettes* (*US – Cloves*), WT/DS406/AB/R, adopted 24 April 2012, para 258.

[118] WTO (n 78) para 20.

[119] Appellate Body Report, *US – Tuna II* (n 64) para 372.

[120] Ibid, para 376.

[121] WTO Panel Report, *US – Tuna II*, WT/DS381/R, adopted 13 June 2012, as modified by Appellate Body Report, WT/DS381/AB/R, para 2.35.

[122] Appellate Body Report, *US – Tuna II* (n 64) paras 398 and 399.

include openness without discrimination with respect to the participation at the policy development level and at every stage of standards development.

Thus, in order for a standardising body to be considered 'international', the body must be open to the relevant bodies of at least all WTO Members on a non-discriminatory basis. Any de jure or de facto disadvantage of accession tends to indicate that a body is not an international standardising body.[123] In addition, the body must be open 'at every stage of standards development'. It is not sufficient for the body to be open at a particular point of time.[124] Applying the test to the AIDCP, the AB ruled that if the invitation occurred automatically once a Member or its relevant body had expressed interest in joining a standardising body, an invitation might indeed be a formality. However, the parties to the AIDCP had to take the decisions to issue an invitation by consensus. Therefore, the AIDCP was not an international standardising body and the AIDCP dolphin-safe definition was not an international standard for the purpose of Article 2.4 of the TBT Agreement.[125]

On the last question, a number of WTO scholars argued that standards adopted at both international governmental and non-governmental bodies could be recognised as international standards.[126] Granted, it cannot be excluded that, under specific circumstances, Member States might be required to use as a basis standards that were created by the private sector. This is the case, for example, when a non-governmental body's standardisation activities comply with the TBT Committee Decision and are recognised, both in terms of the factual dimension and the normative dimension, by WTO Members. What I would like to emphasise, however, is that for non-governmental bodies, the recognition of the standards adopted by a considerably large number of governments or national standardising bodies is essential. From a legal perspective, it does not really help if one argues that the standard is of high quality and reflects the market needs, or that the six principles listed in the TBT Committee Decision are followed. In *US – Tuna II*, the AB has made it crystal clear that only evidence of recognition by *WTO Members* as well as evidence of recognition by *national standardising bodies* would be relevant.[127] In other words, the link of WTO Members' official recognition is critical in the determination of whether a non-governmental standard-setting organisation can meet the criteria. This is of course not to say that all WTO Members must recognise the non-governmental bodies' standardisation activities. The AB left open the possibility that support from a large number of WTO Members may be sufficient, so long as the standardising body is open to all WTO Members.[128]

[123] Ibid, para 375.
[124] Ibid, para 374.
[125] Ibid, para 398.
[126] Pauwelyn (n 83) 750; Partiti (n 112) 91–93.
[127] Appellate Body Report, *US – Tuna II* (n 64) para 363.
[128] Ibid, para 390.

## E. An Analysis of the TBT Committee Decision on Principles for the Development of International Standards

### i. The Scope and Nature of the TBT Committee Decision

The AB's approach to the TBT Committee Decision in *US – Tuna II* was radically different from its previous position in *EC – Sardines*. For a long time, it was unclear of the legal implication of decisions, principles and recommendations developed in the WTO special committees.[129] The panel in *EC – Sardines* considered the TBT Committee Decision as a mere 'policy statement of preference' and not the controlling provision in interpreting Article 2.4.[130] By contrast, in *US – Tuna II*, the AB treated the TBT Committee Decision as a 'subsequent agreement' within the meaning of Article 31(3)(a) of the VCLT binding all WTO Members and enforced it strictly. Although the TBT committee does not have a role in monitoring adherence of ISBs to the Six Principles, ISBs have unilaterally claimed adherence to them as they all have an interest in making their standards recognised as 'international standards' in the WTO.[131] Moreover, one quarter of existing FTAs has sharpened the TBT Committee's decision by making it binding on the parties of FTAs.[132] It is safe to conclude that the Six principles play a key role in assessing whether or not the standard at issue constitutes an international standard in TBT disputes.

The TBT Committee Decision contains six principles that are directed specifically to ISBs, not to WTO members. The principle of transparency states that all essential information regarding standards development should be easily accessible to all WTO Members and that transparency procedures should be established to operationalise information sharing. The principle of openness requires both de facto and de jure nondiscriminatory participatory opportunities of all WTO Members at all stages of standards development. The principle of impartiality and consensus principle requires that the standards development process will not give privilege to, or favour the interest of, a particular supplier, country or region. All relevant parties of WTO Members should be provided with meaningful opportunities to contribute to the elaboration of an international standard. Consensus procedures should be established that seek to take into account the views of all parties concerned and to reconcile any conflicting arguments. The principle of effectiveness and relevance is essentially about standards being fit for purpose, including reflecting state of the art science,

[129] PC Mavroidis, 'No Outsourcing of Law? WTO Law as Practiced by WTO Courts' (2008) 102 *American Journal of International Law* 421, 430–434.

[130] Panel Report, *EC– Sardines* (n 79) para 7.91.

[131] ISO/IEC Guide 59:2019; ISEAL Alliance, Setting Social and Environmental Standards: ISEAL Code of Good Practice Version 6.0 (December 2014).

[132] D McDaniels, AC Molina and EN Wijkstrom, 'A Closer Look at WTO's Third Pillar: How WTO Committees Influence Regional Trade Agreements' (2018) 21 *Journal of International Economic Law* 815, 823–825.

prioritisation of performance-based standards and a requirement not to give preference to the needs or interests of particular counties and regions. The principle of coherence is designed to promote cooperation and coordination among relevant international standardisation bodies so as to avoid duplication. The last principle, the development dimension, requires facilitation of meaningful participation of developing countries as they face particular constrains when it comes to participation in setting international standards.[133]

In *US – Tuna II*, the AB gave transparency and openness particular normative weight in international standard setting. The AB found that transparency procedures through which a body disseminates information about its standardisation activities were an element of the factual dimension of the concept of 'recognition'.[134] The AB interpreted the openness requirement expansively: the ISB must be open to all WTO Members on a non-discriminatory basis at every stage of standard development. Thus an international organisation whose membership is restricted by geographical factors or development level like the OECD should not be considered an ISB under the TBT Agreement.[135] Moreover, the AB indicated that representative participation is also part of the openness requirement. The US pointed out that although all states whose vessels fish for tuna in the relevant area were eligible under the AIDCP, WTO Members with an interest other than fishing, such as consumer or conservation interests, were ineligible to become parties. The AB agreed with the US that an ISB must not privilege any particular interests in the development of international standards and highlighted the imperative that ISBs ensure representative participation and transparency in the development of international standards.[136]

As discussed in part II:B of this chapter, transparency and participation/openness are important global administrative law tools to enhance accountability of international institutions when they produce global public goods. Besides transparency and participation, other principles listed in the TBT Committee Decision such as impartiality and consensus, relevance and effectiveness, coherence and addressing the concerns of developing countries should also be viewed as global administrative law tools because they all contribute to the quality and legitimacy of international standards in the world trading system. In view of their global public goods nature and the quasi-legislative force, it is necessary that international standards meet these substantive and procedural requirements. That being said, the AB's ruling in *US – Tuna II* has left some uncertainties regarding the role of the principles set out in the TBT Committee Decision in future trade disputes. In *US – Tuna II*, except for the requirement of openness, the AB did not elaborate on how other principles

[133] WTO (n 78) para 20 and Annex 4.

[134] Appellate Body Report, *US – Tuna II* (n 64) para 376.

[135] AB Villarreal, *International Standardisation and the Agreement on Technical Barriers to Trade* (Cambridge University Press, 2018) 170.

[136] Appellate Body Report, *US-Tuna II* (n 64) paras 379 and 385.

listed in the TBT Committee Decision will be interpreted and enforced. How far will a WTO panel go in scrutinising the international standard at issue in light of all the principles outlined in the TBT Committee Decision? What standard of review will a WTO panel exercise in reviewing the international standardising bodies' compliance with the TBT Committee Decision? To what extent should a WTO panel show institutional sensitivity to other international standardising bodies?

As we will demonstrate below, though some principles listed in the TBT Committee Decision have created specific norms that ISBs must observe, such as transparency and open membership, and violation of which will lead to a denial of international standards status, other principles do not appear to create specific criterion and some may even be merely 'best efforts' obligations. It is therefore important to read the TBT Committee Decision closely to distinguish these two types of norms, and to explore how these principles may be implemented in practice.

Take consensus requirement as an example. Consensus is of course the desired way by which decisions are adopted in ISBs. But it is not the only mechanism. If efforts to develop consensus fail, a voting procedure is usually available. In Codex, for example, decisions are taken through voting and a draft standard is adopted if a majority of members vote in favour of it.[137] If a standard was adopted by voting at an ISB, will it be recognised as an international standard? In *EC – Sardines*, the AB has given a positive answer because the AB viewed the omission of a consensus requirement in the Explanatory Note to Annex 1.2 as a deliberate choice on the part of the drafters.[138] However, as discussed in Part II.D(i) above, the AB's interpretative technique on this issue was highly controversial. Moreover, the precedential value of the AB's ruling in *EC – Sardines* was also called into question in light of the AB's elevation of the TBT Committee Decision in *US – Tuna II* as a 'subsequent agreement' rather than a 'policy statement of preference' as the panel conceptualised in *EC – Sardines*. Unfortunately, in *US – Tuna II*, the AB avoided revisiting the consensus requirement and preferred to leave it to future cases.[139]

After *US – Tuna II*, there has been speculation on whether an international standard must be adopted by consensus to be recognised by the WTO.[140] This is of course a reasonable inference from the AB's ruling in *US – Tuna II*. If a violation of openness requirement will render an otherwise international standard disqualified, there is no good reason why a deviation from consensus requirement will not lead to the same result since both principles are clearly set out in the TBT Committee Decision. The uncertainty on this issue has already emerged

[137] Eg, Codex Alimentarius Commission, Procedural Manual (17th edn), Rule XII.2.
[138] Appellate Body Report, *EC – Sardines* (n 34) para 227.
[139] Appellate Body Report, *US – Tuna II* (n 64) para 353.
[140] G Marceau, 'The New TBT Jurisprudence in US– *Clove Cigarettes, US – Tuna II* and *US – Cool*' (2013) 8 *Asian Journal of WTO and International Health Law & Policy* 1, 26.

within the TBT Committee.[141] However, it is submitted that it is not necessary for a standard to be adopted by consensus in order to be recognised as an international standard. In *US – Tuna II*, the AB stressed that the extent to which the TBT Committee Decision will inform the interpretation of international standards depends on the degree to which it 'bears specifically on the interpretation and application of the respective term or provision'.[142] The relevant part of the TBT Committee Decision on consensus reads:

> All relevant bodies of WTO Members should be provided with meaningful opportunities to contribute to the elaboration of an international standard so that the standard development process will not give privilege to, or favour the interests of, a particular supplier/s, country/ies or region/s. *Consensus procedures should be established that seek to take into account the views of all parties concerned and to reconcile any conflicting arguments.*

It could be seen that what the TBT Committee Decision requires is only that consensus-building procedures are established to take into account the views of all parties and no particular interests should be favoured. There is nothing in the TBT Committee Decision requiring that international standards must be adopted by consensus.[143] In other words, the consensus principle is only a 'best effort' obligation. The same characterisation can also be said in respect of the requirement in the TBT Committee Decision to address developing country concerns.[144] WTO Members are charged with the responsibility of 'taking into consideration' that developing countries face to effectively participate in standards development and of 'seeking tangible ways of facilitating their participation'. However, it is not clear what specific obligations are owed to developing countries; who owes such obligations; or what real and effective programs should be implemented for this purpose.

Indeed, the suggestion that international standards must be adopted by consensus is likely to cause several difficulties. Firstly, the requirement seems to be too harsh because many standards adopted by ISBs will be disqualified as international standards simply because they were not adopted by consensus. Given that non-consensual procedures are explicitly permitted in ISBs, the denial of their international standards status by the WTO judicial body not only raises the issue of institutional sensitivity, but also opens a back door allowing non-cooperating countries to get a second bite of the apple in international standard setting. Secondly, as Article 3.1 of the SPS Agreement specifies that

[141] WTO Doc. Minutes of the Meeting of 15–16 June 2011 (20 September 2011), G/TBT/M/54, paras 198–204.

[142] Appellate Body Report, *US – Tuna II* (n 64) para 372.

[143] J Pauwelyn, RA Wessel and J Wouters, 'When Structures Become Shackles: Stagnation and Dynamics in International Lawmaking' (2014) 25 (3) *European Journal of International Law* 733, 754–755.

[144] R Howse, 'Regulatory Cooperation, Regulatory Trade Agreements, and World Trade Law: Conflict or Complementarity' (2015) 78 (4) *Law and Contemporary Problems* 137, 147–148.

all standards adopted by Codex, OIE and IPPC are automatically accepted as international standards, the legitimacy of these international standards will not be second-guessed in WTO dispute settlement processes. Significantly, all three ISBs designated in the SPS Agreement allow adopting international standards by voting in case efforts to reach consensus fail.[145] The SPS Agreement addresses the most sensitive trade disputes (relating to human health and safety) and it is long believed to impose more stringent obligations than the companion TBT Agreement. It is therefore difficult to pin down any policy reasons why consensus is required for international standards in the TBT Agreement, but not in the SPS Agreement.

Thirdly, it has long been criticised that the consent-based structure of international law presents a structural bias against effective action on global public goods, especially given the large number of sovereign states today. What is needed is a turn to nonconsensual lawmaking mechanisms, especially through powerful international institutions with majoritarian voting rules.[146] If this is true, then a rigorous emphasis on consensus will likely exacerbate the already severe collective action problem in producing international standards and reverse an emerging trend of loosening the consent element in international lawmaking process in order to provide more effectively global public goods.[147] Finally, an inflexible consensus requirement will not promote international standard and the function of international standards envisioned by TBT drafters will not be achieved. Because the TBT Agreement has raised the power and profile of ISBs, WTO Members have strong incentive to see that international standards adopted at international level conform to domestic standards to gain competitive advantage as well as avoid potential trade disputes. As a result, the international standard setting process is more politically charged and controversial than before. Evidence shows that voting has been used more frequently to adopt international standards in Codex since the adoption of the TBT Agreement, despite a strong preference for reaching decisions by consensus.[148] Thus, a mandatory consensus requirement at the WTO will only intensify the controversy or even paralyse the international standard setting process when stakes are high enough.

By contrast, there are a number of advantages to accept that adoption by consensus is not a condition to recognise an international standard. Firstly, the AB would avoid a sudden U-turn from its earlier ruling in *EC – Sardines*. Secondly, the exact meaning of consensus is not clear. In the context of the

[145] International Trade Centre UNCTAD/WTO and Commonwealth Secretariat, *Influencing and Meeting International Standards: Challenges for Developing Countries* (Geneva, 2003) 40.

[146] LR Helfer, 'Nonconsensual International Lawmaking', (2008) *University of Illinois Law Review* 71, 75; AT Guzman, 'Against Consent' (2012) 52 *Virginia Journal of International Law* 747, 781.

[147] Krisch (n 18) 12–25.

[148] F Veggland and SO Borgen, 'Changing the Codex: The Role of International Institutions', Norwegian Agricultural Economics Research Institute Working Paper 2002–16, at 25.

WTO, consensus is reached if no Member present at the meeting when the decision is taken formally objects to the proposed decision.[149] However, the ISO defines 'consensus' as 'a general agreement, characterised by the absence of *sustained opposition* to *substantial issues* by any *important part of the concerned interests* and by a process that involves seeking to take into account the view of all parties concerned and to reconcile any conflicting arguments. Consensus need not imply unanimity.'[150] Clearly, the definition of consensus in the ISO is quite vague. What are 'substantial issues'? What is 'an important part of the concerned interests'? What does 'the absence of sustained opposition' mean? The ISO has provided no guidance to these concepts and different interpretations have been proposed.[151] It is very likely that the AB will defer to the judgment of the ISO rather than making its own. Except for some highly unusual scenarios, a WTO panel will not set aside easily an international standard on the basis that it was not adopted by consensus but a voting. This argument is consistent with the observation that tribunals that are located within a global regime, such as WTO panels and the AB, are generally reluctant for prudential reasons to review closely the decisions of other bodies within the regime, or to rock the boat and disturb reciprocity by reviewing decisions of other regimes.[152] Nevertheless, reluctance cannot be equated to inattention or inaction. It must be stressed that the WTO tribunal retains a critical judicial role to intervene if the consensus-building procedures were grossly violated.

Lastly, empirical evidence shows that consensus is a main feature of the international standard setting process and voting takes place only on rare occasions.[153] Even if some international standards were not adopted by consensus, it should not cause much concern because WTO Members have the autonomous right to deviate from international standards that are not effective or appropriate to achieve their regulatory objectives. In *US – Tuna II and US – COOL*, for instances, the AB supported the claim that the relevant international standards did not have the function or capacity to fulfil the US objectives.

### *ii. The TBT Committee Decision and Competing Approaches to International Standard-Setting*

The debate on the flexibility of 'relevant international standard' in the TBT Agreement has also permeated into WTO trade negotiations. Under the

[149] Marrakesh Agreement Establishing the WTO, Art IX:1, fn 1.

[150] ISO/IEC Directives, Part 1, Edition 10.0, 2013-10, clause 2.5.6; ISO, *Engaging Stakeholders and Building Consensus* (2010) 11, available at www.iso.org/iso/guidance_nsb.pdf (last accessed 20 April 2020).

[151] Schroder (n 16) 231.

[152] RB Stewart and MRS Badin, 'The World Trade Organisation: Multiple Dimensions of Global Administrative Law' (2011) 9 *International Journal of Constitutional Law* 556, 583.

[153] Inter-American Institute of Cooperation on Agriculture, *Handbook of Good Practices for Participation in Codex Alimentarius Meetings* (IICA, 2009) 41.

Non-Agricultural Market Access discussions of non-tariff barriers during the Doha Round, WTO Members hold diametrically different views on how the status quo may be improved. One group of Members led by the EU supports a 'centralised approach', arguing that relevant ISBs should be explicitly named and only standards adopted or approved by such bodies can be recognised as international standards for the purpose of the TBT Agreement.[154] They argue this approach will incentivise a broad participation by stakeholders, in particular industry, thus ensuring market relevance, reflecting technological developments, and facilitating regulatory convergence. They also view the existence and competition between multiple standard-setting organisations as an impediment to the TBT's goal of promoting harmonisation, leading to fragmentation of markets, unnecessary compliance costs and even capture of regulators by protectionist interests.[155]

Another group of Members led by the US argues the exact opposite 'decentralised approach'. In this view, ISBs should not be confined to certain institutions because whether a standard is relevant and effective for the purpose of the TBT Agreement depends on the standard itself, not on the body that developed it. It is also argued that a limited number of designated bodies cannot produce the breath and diversity of standards needed to fulfil all of the regulatory and market needs that are the purview of the TBT Agreement. As a practical matter, many standard-setting bodies are setting standards and it is the diversity of bodies that will promote innovation and help ensure that standards are of high quality.[156] Furthermore, they suggest that the EU's centralised approach would run counter to the TBT Committee Decision because it would essentially endorse all standards that such designated bodies produce without reviewing their content, even if in cases where the standards might not reflect the interests of all Members, or, disproportionately reflects those of only a few.[157]

The divergence of approaches towards international standard setting between the EU and the US is a reflection of different institutional endowments and local political and economic cultures.[158] The standardisation in the US is characterised by fragmentation and contestation: multiple private standard-setters seek dominance through extensive market competition. There is little government oversight of the process or public financial support. By contrast, the EU standardisation system is characterised by a high degree of coordination under the umbrella of a single domestic institution with a hieratical structure,

[154] Communication from the European Union, TN/MA/W/129/Rev.1 (23 June 2010).

[155] Market Access for Non-Agricultural Products, International Standards Communication from the Delegation of the European Union, India, Malaysia, Norway, the Philippines, Switzerland and Thailand, Negotiating Group on Market Access, JOB/MA/81 (19 January 2011).

[156] WTO Negotiating Group on Market Access, 'Communication from the United States: International Standards', TN/MA/W/138 (28 June 2010).

[157] Ibid.

[158] JK Winn, 'Governance of Global Mobile Money Networks: the Role of Technical Standards' (2013) 8 *Washington Journal of Law, Technology and Art* 197, 203–204.

supplemented by private-sector organisations that reinforce these structures. Both systems have served their respective domestic economies well by generally producing high-quality standards. However, they differ in how well they serve the interests of domestic stakeholders now that the main and locus of standardisation has shifted to the global level, as domestic structures influence the positioning of particular national interests within ISBs.[159] For example, it is frequently asserted that the EU's centralised approach allows its Member States to speak with one voice and enables it to have a greater influence over the traditional ISBs such as ISO and IEC.[160]

The TBT Committee Decision does little to clarify the WTO's position on the competing approaches to international standards setting.[161] On the one hand, it doesn't name any specific ISBs and leaves open the possibility that standards developed by private organisations may be recognised as international standards. The WTO retains a judicial role in determining whether a standard at issue is an international standard on a case-by-case basis. On the other hand, the 'openness' requirement seems to put emphasis on the formal structure and membership of an organisation. It may in practice put voluntary consensus standards organisation at a disadvantage.

### *iii. A Distinctive Pathway for the Development of Global Administrative Law*

The AB's new approach to international standards in *US – Tuna II* marks a distinctive pathway for the development of global administrative law. This approach is also consistent with contemporary demands for more transparency and due process within global governance institutions and openness in international standard setting in particular.[162] The TBT Agreement does not contain a list of ISBs that qualify to promulgate international standards, nor does it provide any definition of international standards within the meaning of Article 2.4. The TBT Committee, a WTO administrative organ at probably the lowest level, has adopted a decision setting out a number of principles and procedures that ISBs are expected to comply with. Although several panels were reluctant to recognise the legal value of WTO committee decisions,[163] the AB interpreted the TBT Committee Decision as a 'subsequent agreement' between

[159] T Buthe and W Mattli, *The New Global Rulers: The Privatisation of Regulation in the World Economy* (Princeton University Press, 2011) 148–159.

[160] Communication from the United States (n 156) 4.

[161] H Schepel, 'The Empire's Drains: Sources of Legal Recognition of Private Standardisation under the TBT Agreement, in C Joerges and E-U Petersmann (eds), *Constitutionalism, Multilevel Trade Governance and Social Regulation* (Hart Publishing, 2006) 406.

[162] A von Bogdandy, 'The European Lesson for International Democracy: The Significance of Articles 9–12 EU Treaty for International Organisations' (2012) 23 *European Journal of International Law* 315, 331.

[163] Panel Report, *EC – Sardines* (n 79) para 7.91; See also Panel Report, *United States – Certain Measures Affecting Imports of Poultry from China*, WT/DS392/R, adopted on 29 September 2010, para 7.136.

WTO Members within the meaning of Article 31(3)(a) of the VCLT. The concept of subsequent agreement is an ambiguous one as there is no specific guidance in the VCLT on the issue of what constitutes a subsequent agreement. Other than a temporal requirement that the agreement must be adopted subsequently to the relevant treaty, nothing is said in the VCLT about the form which a subsequent agreement between the parties should take.

In *US – Clove Cigarettes*, the AB has offered some broad guidance to the meaning of subsequent agreement in the VCLT. According to the AB, the term 'agreement' in Article 31(3)(a) of the VCLT refers, fundamentally, to substance rather than to form.[164] Citing *EC – Bananas III*, the AB stated that a subsequent agreement is one that 'bears specifically upon the interpretation' of a treaty provision.[165] This would seem to involve specific reference to provisions in the WTO Agreements, or at least the express intention of affecting WTO law.[166] In addition, a subsequent agreement must 'clearly express a common understanding, and an acceptance of that understanding among Members' with regard to a specific provision of the WTO Agreements.[167] Applying these criteria to the TBT Committee Decision in *US – Tuna II*, the AB noted that the TBT Committee Decision was adopted subsequent to the conclusion of the TBT Agreement. Moreover, the membership of the TBT Committee comprises all WTO Members and that the TBT Committee Decision was adopted by consensus.[168] Finally, the content of the TBT Committee Decision expresses an agreement between Members on the interpretation or application of international standards and it bears directly on the interpretation of the term 'open' in Annex 1.4 to the TBT Agreement, as well as on the interpretation and application of the concept of 'recognised activities in standardisation'.[169] Therefore, the TBT Committee Decision can be considered as a subsequent agreement within the meaning of Article 31(3)(a) of the VCLT.

The AB's interpretation of the TBT Committee Decision is a major step in expanding the scope of multilateral legislation.[170] Different from other WTO decision-making bodies, such as the Ministerial Conference, which clearly have authority to make binding decisions on WTO Members, the TBT Committee, like other 20 committees of its kind, meets monthly and is attended by government representatives with no formal decision-making powers. If a TBT Committee decision qualifies as a subsequent agreement, so do all decisions made by consensus by organs and bodies whose membership comprises all WTO

[164] Appellate Body Report, *US – Clove Cigarettes* (n 117) para 267.

[165] Ibid, para 265.

[166] G Vidigal, 'From Bilateral to Multilateral Law-making: Legislation, Practice, Evolution and the Future of Inter Se Agreements in the WTO' (2013) 24 (4) *European Journal of International Law* 1027, 1034.

[167] Appellate Body Report, *US – Clove Cigarettes* (n 117) para 267.

[168] Appellate Body Report, *US – Tuna II* (n 64) para 371.

[169] Ibid, para 372.

[170] Vidigal (n 166) 1034.

Members, regardless of hierarchical level.[171] Even so, the understanding of the term 'subsequent agreement' which is not limited to subsequent international treaty and extends to less formal or even informal arrangements is compatible with the practice of other international courts.[172] Nevertheless, it must be emphasised that the reason why the TBT Committee Decisions could be taken into account in *US – Tuna II* was because it *bears directly on* the interpretation of certain terms and provisions in the TBT Agreement. If not, it would not be regarded as a subsequent agreement among WTO Members.

By recognising the TBT Committee Decision as a subsequent agreement, the AB has in effect transformed what would be at best the 'soft law' of the TBT Committee Decision into a code of administrative procedure and practice for international standardisation.[173] The scrutiny from the WTO panels helps ensure that only standards that are impartial, effective, well reasoned, and generated through transparent and open procedures are given legal effect. These procedural and substantive requirements, also known as global administrative law tools, would help ensure that the resulting standards embody a fair consideration of affected interests, and thereby would reduce the risk of suppressing local regulatory autonomy through invocation of international standards that may lack public legitimacy.

Moreover, the AB's ruling has transformed ISBs, formerly forums for discussion, deliberation and dissemination of scientific knowledge, into sites of negotiation for quasi-binding standards. WTO Members could no longer pick and choose international standards they prefer without proper justifications. The raise of power and profile has created a new set of challenges for ISBs. Since WTO Members have strong incentive to see that the new international standards conform to possible future national TBT measures, consensus on new international standards can no longer be assumed.[174] Such a trend will likely damage the credibility of relevant ISBs.

Against this backdrop, the AB's confirmation of the TBT Committee Decision as a key element that shall be taken into account in interpreting international standards practically force ISBs to review the integrity and effectiveness of their international standards setting process if they still want to be relevant in the standardisation business. The price of not complying with the TBT Committee Decision, a set of global administrative principles, is simply too high to ignore. Indeed, key ISBs have announced their support of the TBT

[171] Ibid.

[172] L Gruszczynski, 'Re-Tuning Tuna? Appellate Body Report in *US –Tuna II*' (2012) 3 *European Journal of Risk Regulation* 430, 435.

[173] MA Crowley and R Howse, 'Tuna – Dolphin II: A Legal and Economic Analysis of the Appellate Body Report' (2014) 13 (2) *World Trade Review* 321, 342.

[174] TP Stewart and DS Johanson, 'The SPS Agreement of the World Trade Organisation and International Organisations: The Roles of the Codex Alimentarius Commission, the International Plant Protection Convention, and the International Office of Epizootics' (1998) 26 *Syracuse Journal of International Law and Commerce* 27, 34.

Committee Decision and they have taken various initiatives to improve their internal standards-setting processes in light of the TBT Committee Decision.[175] This move in turn provides international standards promulgated by these ISBs with additional legitimacy as global public goods.

Although the AB's handling of the TBT Committee Decision should be much praised, it is doubtful whether all the concerns presented by the incorporation of previously voluntary standards into a binding international trade regime have been effectively dealt with. For example, it is argued that the principles set out in the TBT Committee Decision are not sufficiently inclusive and additional criteria would need to be developed. One example is impact assessment. Like domestic regulations, the impact of international standards should be periodically reviewed and the assessment process should lead to the amendment of the standard if necessary. So far the impact assessment procedure does not exist in the TBT Agreement.[176] Another example is that it is not clear to what extent non-economic interests such as environmental sustainability should be considered in the international standard-setting process.[177] Other concerns include the missing of important principles such as accountability and balance of interests.[178] On the other hand, some initiatives taken at ISBs are quite controversial. For example, struggling to be relevant in the fast-changing ICT global standards-setting scene, ISO and IEC seek to spend up their standard-setting process by borrowing the standards of other new standardising actors. This strategy may undercut ISO and IEC's legitimacy because these ISBs have shifted from pure standard development to the inclusion of formalisation of external standards, and their 'democratic ideals have been slightly adapted to cater to economic demands for timely standards'.[179]

## III. MUTUAL RECOGNITION AND EQUIVALENCE

### A. The Economics of MRAs and Equivalence

Despite many benefits of harmonisation as described in part I, there are natural limits on the extent of harmonisation to reduce regulatory heterogeneity.

[175] See, eg, Statement of The IEEE Standards Association Board of Governors, An International Standards Developer: IEEE Adheres to the WTO Principles for International Standardisation (12 December 2011).

[176] Delimatsis (n 82) 134–135; Communication from India, G/TBT/WT/345 (10 November 2011).

[177] In *US – Tuna II*, the Appellate Body pointed out that an international standardising body must not privilege any particular interests in the development of international standards. However, it is unclear how this statement will impact the standard setting in practice. Environmental sustainability, for example, is not mentioned in the TBT Committee Decision.

[178] Villarreal (n 135) 184.

[179] TM Egyedi, 'Institutional Dilemma in ICT Standardisation: Coordinating the Diffusion of Technology', in K Jakobs (ed), *Information Technology Standards and Standardisation: A Global Perspective* (IGI Global Book, 2000) 56.

Normatively it is questionable international harmonisation is always the best policy option to address regulatory heterogeneity.[180] As a positive matter, harmonisation is not often successfully pursued at the global level due to limits to the resources, the time-lag between the identification of need for an international standard and the agreed outcome, and the difficulty in achieving consensus on an international standard.[181] To facilitate trade in cases in which harmonisation is either undesirable or unfeasible, the WTO legal regime has provided two additional tools: equivalence and mutual recognition agreements (MRAs). Whilst equivalence is unilateral recognition of exporting Member's standards, an MRA is an agreement in which two or more members recognise the equivalence of each other's standards, technical regulations or conformity assessment procedures (CAPs). Article 6.3 of the TBT Agreement restricts the use of MRA to where WTO Members recognise the results of each other's CAPs as equivalent, while the unilateral recognition of equivalence and other MRAs are called 'equivalence agreement'. Nevertheless, equivalence and MRAs are similar both in design and essence. They allow importing countries to accept certain products that meet the applicable technical requirements of the exporting country, as if they met their own applicable requirements.[182]

MRAs and equivalence are highly desirable policy tools in international trade because they bring many economic benefits. These include the increase of trade flows through greater administrative efficiency, such as the elimination of extra fees and delays associated with additional approval in the country of destination. The reduction of transaction costs in turn leads to the reduction in consumer prices of final goods.[183] MRAs are particularly useful to developing countries looking for new export markets. Wilson shows that developing countries are likely to secure a 52.3 per cent increase in exports if there is in place an MRA. The positive effects are even more significant in the agricultural sector.[184] Moreover, even though harmonisation is in general expected to boost trade more than mutual recognition, some economists consider that mutual recognition can avoid the negative impact on trade brought by harmonisation because it allows a country to choose one standard and sell products meeting that standard to its trading partners. A foreign firm can freely access its partner's markets without

[180] Sykes (n 14) 66–67.

[181] Note from New Zealand, 'Equivalency of Standards: An Interim Measure to Facilitate Trade in the Absence of Relevant International Standards', G/TBT/W/88 (15 September 1998) para 5.

[182] Communication from the European Union, 'A Policy Framework for the Facilitation of Trade in the Fields of Standardisation and Conformity Assessment: A Toolbox of Instruments', WTO Doc. G/TBT/W/173/Add.1 (19 April 2002), para 53.

[183] AC de Brito, C Kauffmann, J Pelkmans, 'The Contribution of Mutual Recognition to International Regulatory Co-operation', OECD Regulatory Policy Working Papers No 2 (OECD Publishing, 2016), 54–56. SM Stephenson, 'Mutual Recognition and Its Role in Trade Facilitation' (1999) 33 *Journal of World Trade* 141, 142.

[184] HZ Schroder, *Harmonisation, Equivalence and Mutual Recognition of Standards in WTO Law* (Wolters Kluwer, 2011) 135.

the additional cost of harmonising its standards. Therefore, when love for variety is important for trade or when costs of adaptation to a new harmonised technology are high, mutual recognition should be expected to boost trade more than harmonisation.[185]

However, there are practical difficulties for WTO Members to make full use of these tools. To begin with, the evaluation of equivalence for technical measures usually involves a complicated process of identifying legitimate objectives and parameters that can be used for comparison.[186] Given the thematically diverse and wide range of technical standards, the equivalence assessment has to be carried out sector-by-sector, or even product-by-product. If there is any change in the relevant standard of one of the parties to a MRA, a new evaluation of equivalence may be required. Therefore it is very costly to negotiate a MRA in practice.[187] Moreover, since standards are assumed to be equivalent in achieving a certain policy objective under MRAs, MRAs require a certain degree of trust among countries regarding their respective ability to adequately monitor the validity of testing abroad. Therefore MRAs are more likely to occur in regional trade agreement among developed countries than at the multilateral level, excluding developing countries.[188] Since 1995, 149 MRAs have been notified to the TBT Committee and OECD countries initiate most of them.[189] Next, the practical gains that can be derived from technically very complex and time-consuming equivalence negotiations may be too small and domestic stakeholders may not accept the equivalence agreements.[190] In practice, certain developed countries demand 'sameness' rather than 'equivalence' of measures.[191] Consequently, these policy tools have only achieved limited success so far.[192] Finally, when occurring at regional level, MRAs have different implications for trade with countries outside of the FTA. Chen and Mattoo found that MRAs tend to increase trade within the region. Outside the region, whether MRAs can maximise economic welfare will depend on how they are designed. If rules of origin are contained in an MRA, trade with countries outside the region is negatively affected, especially exports from developing countries.[193]

[185] WTO Trade Report, *Trade and Public Policy: A Closer Look at Non-Tariff Measures in the 21st Century* (2012) 150.
[186] F Veggeland, 'Trade Facilitation through Equivalence and Mutual Recognition: The EU Model', Norwegian Agricultural Economics Research Institute Report 2006-3, at 31.
[187] Communication from the European Union (n 182) para 51.
[188] WTO Trade Report 2005 (n 7) 55.
[189] Note by the Secretariat, 'Twenty-Fourth Annual Review of the Implementation and Operation of the TBT Agreement', G/TBT/42 (25 February 2019) 19.
[190] Submission from the US, 'Equivalence', G/SPS/GEN/212 (7 November 2000) 15–16.
[191] Statement by Egypt at the Meeting of 7–8 July 1999, G/SPS/GEN/128, para 2.
[192] Ministry of Business, Innovation & Employment of New Zealand, 'Evaluation of Conformity Assessment Mutual Recognition Agreements and Arrangements' (April, 2018) 11.
[193] Chen and Mattoo (n 17) 860–861.

## B. The WTO Legal Framework of Mutual Recognition and Equivalence

Mutual recognition and equivalence can be applied to both technical regulations (2.7) and conformity assessment procedures in relation to technical regulations and standards (6.1 and 6.3 of the TBT). Similar provision in the SPS Agreement on equivalence is Article 4.

### *i. Equivalence of Technical Regulations and Standards*

Article 2.7 of the TBT Agreement imposes a legal obligation on WTO Members to 'give positive consideration to accepting as equivalent technical regulations of other Members, even if these regulations differ from their own, provided they are satisfied that these regulations adequately fulfill the objectives of their own regulations'. Article 2.7 appears to impose on WTO Members only a 'best efforts' obligation because the nature of the obligation is only to 'give positive consideration' to an equivalence recognition request. Moreover, even this obligation of positive consideration is conditional upon a subjective criterion that this WTO Member is satisfied with the effectiveness of a foreign technical regulation.[194] This is in contrast to Article 4.1 of the SPS Agreement, which provides that Members *shall accept* the SPS measures of other Members as equivalent if the exporting Member *objectively demonstrates* to the importing Member that its measures achieve the importing Member's appropriate level of protection (ALOP).

Even if Article 2.7 only considers unilateral recognition of equivalence, the equivalence system is technically feasible and politically acceptable only on a bilateral, country-by-country basis.[195] Neither does Article 2.7 give any guidance on how Article 2.7 is implemented in practice. By contrast, the SPS Committee has adopted one decision on the implementation of equivalence.[196] The decision has clarified the obligations of both importing and exporting Members in equivalence determinations. First, the burden of proving equivalence rests with the exporting country. It shall provide appropriate science-based and technical information to support its objective demonstration that its measure achieves the ALOP pursued by the importing country as well as provide reasonable access to the importing Member for inspection, testing and other procedures. Second, the importing Member shall explain the objective and rationale of the SPS measure and identify clearly the risks that the relevant measures intend to address

[194] L Tamiotti, 'Article 2 TBT', in R Wolfrum, P-T Stoll and A Seibert-Fohr (eds), *WTO, Technical Barriers to Trade and SPS Measures* (Nijhoff, 2007) 226.

[195] AB Zampetti, 'Mutual Recognition in the Transatlantic Context: Some Reflections on Future Negotiations', in T Cottier and PC Mavroidis (eds), *Regulatory Barriers and the Principle of Non-Discrimination in World Trade Law* (University of Michigan Press, 2000) 318.

[196] SPS Committee, 'Decision on the Implementation of Article 4 of the Agreement on the Application of Sanitary and Phytosanitary Measures', G/SPS/19/Rev.2 (23 July 2004).

are supported by a risk assessment report; to indicate the ALOP which its SPS measures is designed to achieve; and to give full consideration of the exporting Member's request for the recognition of equivalence in a timely manner. Third, the decision formally encourages Codex, OIE and IPPC to complete work on equivalence and encourages WTO Members to actively participate their work. Accordingly, all three organisations have adopted guidelines on equivalence that will assist WTO members in implementing Article 4.[197]

The TBT CGP does not impose any similar requirements on bodies developing voluntary standards. New Zealand recommended inclusion in the CGP of a provision similar to Article 2.7, requiring a standardising body to consider accepting as equivalent standards originating from other WTO Members.[198] The TBT Committee did not endorse the recommendation, but noted that some WTO Members had chosen to do so and considered that WTO Members may find it useful to further explore equivalence of standards as an interim measure to facilitate trade in the absence of relevant international standards.[199]

### *ii. Equivalence and Mutual Recognition of Conformity Assessment Procedures*

Article 6.1 of the TBT Agreement concerns the unilateral recognition of equivalence of CAP, which provides: '… Members shall ensure, whenever possible, that results of CAP in other Members are accepted … provided that they are satisfied that those procedures offer an assurance of conformity with applicable technical regulations or standards equivalent to their own procedures'. Similar to Article 2.7, Article 6.1 leaves unilateral recognition of CAP to the goodwill of the importing WTO Member because the importing Member must be satisfied with the foreign CAP.[200] When assessing the technical competence of the relevant conformity assessment bodies in the exporting Member, Article 6.1.1 provides that the importing Member shall take into account whether relevant guides of international standardising bodies are complied with. Other than this, Article 6.1 does not specify the procedures on how to recognise and accept foreign CAP results. In practice International guidelines dealing with recognition and acceptance of CAP results, such as ISO/IEC Guide 68:2002 and the Codex 2003, are frequently referred to by WTO Members. In contrast to Article 6.1, Article 6.3 of the TBT Agreement concerns the mutual recognition and acceptance of the results of each other's CAPs. A MRA on CAPs authorises the conformity assessment bodies of one party to certify products' conformity with the technical regulations or standards of another party (and vice versa),

[197] Schroder (n 16) 113–117.

[198] Note from New Zealand (n 181) para 24.

[199] TBT Committee, 'Second Triennial Review of the Operation and Implementation of the Agreement on Technical Barriers to Trade', G/TBT/9 (13 November 2000) para 23.

[200] R Munoz, 'Article 6 TBT' in Wolfrum, Stoll and Seibert-Fohr (n 194) 285.

so the products may be offered for sale in the market of the second party without undergoing its CAPs. Article 6.3 provides:

> Members are encouraged, at the request of other Members, to be willing to enter into … mutual recognition of results of each others [CAPs]. Members may require that such agreements fulfill the criteria of paragraph [6.1] and give mutual satisfaction regarding their potential for facilitating trade in the products concerned.

By referring to Article 6.1, Article 6.3 makes it clear that a WTO Member is entitled to demand equivalence of CAPs as a precondition for the conclusion of a MRA if it chooses to do so. Also relevant to the consideration are the verified compliance with the guidelines and recommendations issued by ISBs (Article 6.1.1) and the limitation of the acceptance of CAP results to those produced by designated bodies in the exporting Member (Article 6.1.2). This shows that mutual recognition and equivalence are usually interlinked. On the other hand, MRAs do not necessarily presuppose equivalence of standards or technical regulations. It is possible that products can be manufactured according to the standards of the importing country and then approved before export in the country of production. Indeed, an analysis of the MRAs notified to the WTO shows that they do not depend on any previous process of harmonisation and equivalence of standards for their negotiation.[201]

## C. Mutual Recognition and the MFN Obligation

A bilateral or regional MRA is a challenge to the MFN non-discriminatory structure of the WTO.[202] The legal issue for WTO Members entering a MRA is to what extent may a third WTO Member claim that, based on the MFN clause embodied in Article 2.1 and Article 5.1.1 of the TBT Agreement, the rights and advantages in the MRA should be extended to this third Member. In particular this third Member may claim that its technical regulations or CAPs are equal to what the MRA has recognised or that it has already entered a similar MRA with one of the Members.[203] The consensus appears to be that a WTO Member can legally limit the extension of bilateral MRAs to other Members and their products. First, whether the third Member is afforded 'less favourable treatment' under TBT Article 2.1 depends on whether its technical regulations are genuinely equivalent to the Members of the MRA. If this third Member is unable or unwilling to meet the criteria stipulated in the MRA, there is no violation of the MFN obligation and other WTO Members are entitled to make a legitimate

[201] Schroder (n 16) 131–133.

[202] JP Trachtman. 'Embedded Mutual Recognition at the WTO' (2007) 14 (5) *Journal of European Public Policy* 780, 790–791.

[203] JA Zell, 'Just Between You and Me: Mutual Recognition Agreements and the Most-Favored Nation Principle' (2016) 15(1) *World Trade Review* 3, 5.

regulatory distinction in disfavour of the third Member's products.[204] Second, and more importantly, Article 2.7 assumes that the recognition of the equivalence of technical regulation by an importing WTO Member depends upon whether those technical regulations can fulfil that Member's regulatory objectives. An importing Member is under no obligation to recognise as equivalent any technical regulations that it considers unsuitable.[205] Moreover, the use of the words 'giving positive consideration' indicates that the importing Member enjoys much leeway in making a subjective decision on the request for recognition of equivalence. It is difficult to pin down any substantive obligations on an importing Member other than considering the request from another WTO Member. Finally, Article 10.7 'encourages' WTO Members to extend most favoured national treatment to other WTO Members with respect to their MRAs. It implies that the parties to MRAs are under no obligation to accord an unconditional MFN to other WTO Members. Following the same logic, Article 5.1.1 does not require parties to MRAs to extend an unconditional MFN relating to CAPs to other WTO Members. In conclusion, as long as a MRA is not an entirely closed recognition system and open to request for recognition of equivalence, the parties to a MRA will face little WTO legal risk.[206]

## IV. REGULATORY COOPERATION IN FREE TRADE AGREEMENTS (FTAS)

As discussed in this chapter, the TBT and SPS Agreements have employed a myriad of tools to promote international regulatory cooperation between the WTO Members.[207] The two Agreements provide a multilateral transparency framework requiring notification of proposed regulatory measures with potentially significant trade effects. They encourage WTO Members to use relevant international standards as the basis for their national standards. In addition, disciplines on mutual recognition and equivalence of foreign technical regulations and CAPs help ensure that traders do not face duplicative requirements or procedures when regulations differ across markets. To support implementation and operation of these disciplines, the TBT and SPS Committees provide a forum for countries to learn about each other's regulatory systems, to discuss drafts and implemented regulations affecting international trade, to raise STCs, and to adopt decisions and recommendations to help Members better and more

[204] Ibid, at 22.

[205] L Bartels, 'The Legality of the EU Mutual Recognition Clause under the WTO Law' (2005) 8 (3) *Journal of International Economic Law* 691, 703.

[206] B Rigod, 'TBT-Plus Rules in Preferential Trade Agreements' (2013) 40(3) *Legal Issues of Economic Integration* 247, 266–267.

[207] WTO & OECD, *Facilitating Trade through Regulatory Cooperation: The Case of the WTO's TBT and SPS Agreements and Committees* (2019) 4–5.

efficiently implement specific provisions of the TBT and SPS Agreements.[208] All these disciplines encourage the reduction of regulatory heterogeneity and associated trade costs.

Nevertheless, it is frequently argued that although these disciplines have given Members a launch pad for international regulatory cooperation, additional tools, mechanisms and institutional support going beyond current WTO rules are needed. First, there is little evidence that the TBT provisions have convinced countries not to adopt unilateral non-discriminatory regulatory measures that are nevertheless duplicative, unnecessarily divergent, or inefficient.[209] The TBT and SPS Agreements include provisions encouraging MRAs and equivalence arrangements to help address the problem, but they are limited to best endeavours and do not provide the framework needed for engaging regulatory authorities on adopting regulatory cooperation arrangements.[210] Second, the current WTO rules focus mainly on 'regulatory outputs' with little attention to 'regulatory inputs' in the domestic rule-making process.[211] WTO Members officially placed on the agenda of the TBT Committee the notion of good regulatory practices for domestic regulations, encouraging the exchange of information and implementation experiences.[212] However, without a greater mandate and more institutional support, these efforts seem more likely to serve as guidelines for unilateral actions by Members, rather than the first step towards establishing a forum for cooperation between WTO Members.[213]

In view of the failed Doha Round and the current stagnation of WTO negotiations, the focus of attention on reducing unnecessary, duplicative and cumbersome regulations has moved away from the WTO and towards FTAs. Consequently, new or additional requirements and mechanisms on regulatory cooperation have emerged as one of the unique features of recent FTAs.[214]

## A. General Trends of Regulatory Cooperation in FTAs

With the increasing importance of TBT and SPS measures in international trade, they have been systematically included in FTAs since 2010 and their

[208] EN Wijkstrom, 'The Third Pillar: Behind the Scenes, WTO Committee Work Delivers', E15 Task Force on Regulatory Systems Coherence Think Piece (August 2015), 2–5.

[209] RW Stiger and AO Sykes, 'International Trade, National Treatment and Domestic Regulation' (2011) 40 *Journal of Legal Studies* 149.

[210] TJ Bollyky and PC Mavroidis, 'Trade, Social Preferences and Regulatory Cooperation: The New WTO-Think' (2017) 20 (1) *Journal of International Economic Law* 1, 12–13.

[211] S Lester and I Manak, 'Addressing Regulatory Trade Barriers in Mega-Regional Trade Agreements', in T Rensmann (ed), *Mega-Regional Trade Agreements* 337 (Springer, 2017) 347–348.

[212] TBT Committee, 'Eighth Triennial Review of the Operation and Implementation of the Agreement on Technical Barriers to Trade', G/TBT/41 (19 November 2018).

[213] Bollyky and Mavroidis (n 210) 15.

[214] B Hoekman and PC Mavroidis, 'Regulatory Spillovers and the Trading System: From Coherence to Cooperation', E15 Task Force on Regulatory Systems Coherence Overview Paper (April 2015).

scope has evolved to cover *inter alia* standards, technical regulations, CAPs, regulatory cooperation, and transparency. Molina and Khoroshavina found that 72 per cent of 238 FTAs notified to the WTO before 2015 contains TBT provisions.[215] According to a recent WTO assessment, those FTAs that commit to deep integration on TBT measures have lasting and significant benefits for production networks, increasing trade between member countries by almost 8 per cent.[216]

The TBT provisions contained in FTAs have demonstrated some unique features. First, although language may differ and provisions may be more detailed than those in the TBT Agreement, these FTAs rarely go beyond the TBT Agreement and to a large extent merely replicate or mirror the WTO TBT obligations. The TBT provision with the highest frequency in these FTAs (85%) is the explicit reference to the TBT agreement to affirm their rights and obligations under the TBT Agreement, to incorporate all or part of the TBT Agreement into the FTA, or to specify that the TBT Agreement governs any issues between the parties, even if the FTA involves non-WTO Members.[217]

Second, some innovations emerged in a limited number of FTAs in recent years with more stringent commitments that go beyond the WTO TBT Agreement. To begin with, in terms of coverage, other than technical regulations, standards and CAPs, some FTAs concluded by Latin American countries, the US and the EU also cover metrology, authorisation procedures to sell a product in a market, and public procurement.[218] Furthermore, compared to the WTO TBT provisions in respect to harmonisation (Article 2.4) and equivalence (Article 2.7) of technical regulations, commitments embodied in FTAs go beyond the TBT Agreement by requiring parties to harmonise their technical regulations through *specified* international standards, regional technical regulations or in certain cases using the respective technical regulation of one of the parties *within a specified time period*, and to accept *unconditionally* as equivalent the technical regulations of the other parties when the same policy objectives are met.[219] In particular, some FTAs include a unique feature of containing detailed sector-specific harmonisation and equivalence commitments. In *EU-Republic of Korea* FTA, for example, in the case of consumer electronics, the parties agreed to harmonise their domestic regulations on the basis of international standards established by the ISO, IEC and the ITU. The parties also agreed to accept as

[215] AC Molina and V Khoroshavina, 'Technical Barriers to Trade Provisions in Regional Trade Agreements: To What Extent do They Go beyond the WTO TBT Agreement?', in R Acharya (ed), *Regional Trade Agreements and the Multilateral Trading System* 371 (Cambridge University Press, 2016) 373.

[216] WTO, *The WTO and Preferential Trade Agreements: From Co-existence to Coherence* (2011) 145–6.

[217] Molina and Khoroshavina (n 215) 377–379.

[218] S Alshareef, 'Technical Standards Liberalisation in FTAs of the United States, the European Union and China' (2019) 53(3) *Journal of World Trade* 433, 438.

[219] Molina and Khoroshavina (n 215) 382–383.

equivalent within a period of five years the vehicles and its parts that comply with the United Nations Economic Commission for Europe (UNECE) standards.[220] Another example is Article 8.5.2 in the TBT chapter of the Comprehensive and Progressive Trans-Pacific Partnership (CPTPP), which draws on the WTO dispute settlement practice and explicitly obliges each party to apply the TBT Committee Decision when determining whether an international standard should be used as a basis for technical regulation or standard.[221] Finally, some FTAs go further than the TBT Agreement to establish robust institutional mechanisms to foster regulatory cooperation, harmonisation and mutual recognition of product standards.[222]

Similarly, compared to the relevant WTO TBT provisions in the area of CAPs, some FTAs has strengthened the disciplines by requiring the parties to harmonise their respective CAPs with one of the parties (in particular FTAs concluded between the EU and the candidates or potential candidates for accession to the EU), to accept as equivalent unconditionally CPA results of other parties, and to conclude MRAs. The importing country must explain, upon request, the reasons for not accepting as equivalent the results of a CAP conducted in the territory of the other party.[223]

Third, there appears to be an overall tendency for FTAs to favour harmonisation over mutual recognition of product standards.[224] Equivalence and mutual recognition appear to be the preferred options only to deal with CAPs. But harmonisation of certification standards is often still a precondition for considering mutual recognition of CAPs. Finally, it is questionable whether all the commitments that go beyond the TBT Agreement are enforceable binding legal obligations. Puig and Dalke find that nearly half of the TBT and SPS provisions in Canada's FTAs are unenforceable either because the language is too imprecise for enforcement or they do not allow access to dispute settlement mechanisms.[225] By contrast, most of the FTAs concluded by the EU and the US are highly enforceable. It also seems that the US and the EU have taken different approaches to regulatory cooperation in their FTAs. The US prefers the equivalent approach to technical regulations and CAPs, and tends to establish special institutions charged with the administration of the FTAs and the resolution of

[220] EU-Korea FTA, Annex 2-B, Art 2(2); Appendices 2-C-2 and 2-C-3.

[221] Global Agenda Council on Trade & FDI, 'Will the Trans-Pacific Partnership Agreement Reshape the Global Trade and Investment System?' (July 2016) 13.

[222] DP Stegar, 'Institutions for Regulatory Cooperation in "New Generation" Economic and Trade Agreements' (2012) 39(1) *Legal Issues of Economic Integration* 109, 126.

[223] Molina and Khoroshavina (n 215) 387.

[224] R Piermartini and M Budetta, 'A Mapping of Regional Rules on Technical Barriers to Trade', in A Estevadeordal, K Suominen and R Teh (eds), *Regional Rules in the Global Trading System* 250 (Cambridge University Press, 2009) 291.

[225] GV Puig and ED Dalke, 'Nature and Enforceability of WTO-Plus SPS and TBT Provisions in Canada's PTAs: From NAFTA to CETA' (2016) 15(1) *World Trade Review* 51, 70–77.

disputes. By contrast, the EU prefers to harmonise technical regulations based on EU standards in its FTAs (hegemonic harmonisation).[226]

Similar to the TBT provisions, overall only few SPS provisions in FTAs go beyond the SPS Agreement.[227] Some SPS chapters in FTAs do include more detailed or demanding rules, such as moving from *ex post facto* administrative action to preventive measures and improving coordination and communication between domestic regulatory agencies.[228] However, genuine improvements over the SPS Agreement largely occur only on procedural matters such as transparency and information sharing on SPS measures.[229]

### *i. Case Study: The CETA*

The EU-Canada Comprehensive Economic and Trade Agreement (CETA) entered into force on 21 September 2017. The CETA breaks new ground for FTAs in the sense that it includes a separate chapter on regulatory cooperation, in addition to the TBT and SPS Agreements which are covered in chapter 4 and 5 of the CETA respectively.[230] The chapter applies to the development, review and methodological aspects of a wide range of regulatory measures, including the TBT and SPS measures.[231]

The overarching goal of the regulatory cooperation chapter is to address regulatory trade barriers, including regulatory protectionism (unnecessary barriers to trade), regulatory divergence (regulatory compatibility, recognition of equivalence, and convergence), and regulatory effectiveness (good regulatory practices).[232] This is clearly set out in Article 21.2 and Article 21.3 as principles and objectives of the CETA. Article 21.4 provides a detailed list of 19 suggested regulatory cooperation activities with 17 sub-items further elaborated, ranging from bilateral discussions on regulatory governance and exchanging information to providing texts of proposed regulations or greater convergence in sectors identified by parties. In addition, the CETA encourages cooperation by calling for consideration of regulatory measures by the other party on similar issues and provides opportunities for stakeholders and interested parties to engage in regulatory cooperation activities.[233] These provisions give a clear picture of

[226] Alshareef (n 218) 448.

[227] LA Jackson and H Vitikala, 'Cross-cutting Issues in Regional Trade Agreements: Sanitary and Phytosanitary Measures', in Acharya (ed) (n 215) 362.

[228] C-F Lin, 'SPS-Plus and Bilateral Treaty Network: A 'Global' Solution to the Global Food Safety Problem?' (2012) 29 *Wisconsin International Law Journal* 694, 715.

[229] M Wagner, 'The Future of Sanitary and Phytosanitary Governance: SPS-Plus or SPS-Minus' (2017) 51(3) *Journal of World Trade* 445, 451.

[230] RP Lazo and P Sauve, 'The Treatment of Regulatory Convergence in Preferential Trade Agreements' (2018) 17(4) *World Trade Review* 575, 590.

[231] Art 21.1 of CETA.

[232] S Lester and I Manak, 'Addressing Regulatory Trade Barriers in Mega-Regional Trade Agreements', in T Rensmann (ed), *Mega-Regional Trade Agreements* 337 (Springer, 2017) 359.

[233] Art. 21.5 and 21.8 of the CETA.

what specific activities are expected in regulatory cooperation, and emphasise sustained interaction between regulatory agencies so as to prevent unnecessary barriers from arising in the first place, while also seeking opportunities to bridge the gap in pre-existing regulatory divergence.

The CETA also establishes the Regulatory Cooperation Forum (RCF), a specialised committee as well as a new institutional forum chaired by senior representatives from both parties, to facilitate and promote regulatory cooperation. The functions of the RCF include providing a forum to discuss regulatory policy issues; assisting individual regulators to identify potential partners for cooperation activities; reviewing regulatory initiatives; and encouraging the development of bilateral cooperation activities.[234] However, the RCF has no direct power to adopt legally binding decisions. As such, it is no supervisor or even censor for the regulatory work of the parties. However, since the RCF may submit draft decisions to the CETA Joint Committee for adaptation and such drafts are usually highly technical in nature, it is possible that the discussions at the RCF have a determining effect on the Joint Committee's decision-making and shape the regulatory agenda of the parties to some extent.[235] In many ways, the functions of the RCF mirror that of the Regulatory Cooperation Council created in 2011 with a mandate to identify and recommend opportunities to enhance regulatory cooperation between the US and Canada.[236]

In general, the CETA sets out ambitious obligations and establishes a new and comprehensive institutional framework for regulatory cooperation and the reduction of regulatory divergence between Canada and the EU. However, it is important to highlight the voluntary, procedural and open-ended nature of regulatory cooperation between the parties. In many cases, neither specific form of regulatory cooperation nor specific outcome is required.[237] As the CETA does not set detailed and binding obligations, the parties generally retain wide discretion on whether and how to conduct regulatory cooperation. To reinforce the voluntary nature of the CETA, Article 21.2.6 specifies that 'regulatory cooperation on any specific matter is voluntary. Parties are not obligated to engage in any particular regulatory cooperation activity. They only have the obligation to provide reasons when they are not willing to participate in a new initiative or withdraw from ongoing initiatives of regulatory cooperation'. As if these provisions were not clear enough, Canada and the EU signed a Joint Interpretative Instrument in October 2016, reiterating that regulatory authorities do not have an obligation to engage in cooperation, or to apply the outcome of their cooperation. This has led some commentators to argue that regulatory cooperation

[234] Art 21.6 of CETA.

[235] N Meyer-Ohlendorf, C Gerstetter and I Bach, 'Regulatory Cooperation under CETA: Implications for Environmental Policies' (The Ecologic Institute, 1 November 2016) 18.

[236] S Lester and I Barbee, 'The Challenge of Cooperation: Regulatory Trade Barriers in the TTIP' (2013) 16 *Journal of International Economic Law* 847, 860–863.

[237] See, eg, Art. 21.4, 21.5 and 21.7 of the CETA.

under the CETA is to some extent 'a journey with no clear destination'.[238] Others pointed out that successful regulatory cooperation relies on clear and precise rules and joint institutions to implement such rules.[239] A Joint Study commissioned by the EU and Canada prior to the commencement of the CETA negotiations also recognised the need of additional binding rules for effective regulatory cooperation.[240] Nevertheless, the final regulatory cooperation chapter in the CETA seems to fall short of the original ambition.

### B. Regulatory Coherence in FTAs

The idea of regulatory coherence originated in US administrative law and then further evolved in the OECD and the Asia Pacific Economic Cooperation (APEC) before it has been exported to regional and international economic fora. Originally designed to limit the scope of discretion enjoyed by administrative bodies, regulatory coherence is concerned about the use of good regulatory practices to ensure rationality, democratic accountability and the rule of law in domestic regulatory process. Key elements of regulatory coherence include transparency and public consultation, regulatory impact analysis in particular cost-benefit analysis, interagency coordination and compatibility, and administrative and judicial review.[241] In return, regulatory coherence promises to reduce the adverse effects of domestic regulations on international trade. By contrast, regulatory cooperation is the process of interaction or closer partnership between national regulators, aimed at reducing regulatory divergence and enhancing regulatory interoperability.[242] The term 'regulatory cooperation' covers a wide scope of cooperative mechanisms, ranging from dialogue and an agreement to notify and consult on a new or proposed regulatory measure to an obligation to adopt international standards or to recognise or harmonise with another nation's laws.[243]

While regulatory coherence and regulatory cooperation can be conceptually separated, they are by no means practically insulated and mutually exclusive.[244] Regulatory cooperation among national regulators is an effective means of peer learning and of disseminating good regulatory practices. Effective regulatory

[238] Meyer-Ohlendorf et al (n 235) 4.

[239] Steger (n 222) 124–126.

[240] Global Affairs Canada, 'Canada-European Union Joint Report: Towards a Comprehensive Economic Agreement' (5 March 2009) para 3.9.

[241] C-F Lin and HW Liu, 'Regulatory Rationalisation Clauses in FTAs: A Complete Survey of the US, EU and China' (2018) 19 (1) *Melbourne Journal of International Law* 149, 150–151.

[242] The US Chamber of Commerce, 'Regulatory Coherence & Cooperation in the TTIP' (17 February 2015) 1–2.

[243] OECD (n 2) 22–25.

[244] H-W Liu and C-F Lin, 'The Emergence of Global Regulatory Coherence: A Thorny Embrace for China?' (2018) 40 (1) *University of Pennsylvania Journal of International Law* 133, 151.

cooperation often requires good regulatory practices such as transparency and consultation throughout the regulatory development process and exploring alternative approaches to regulation. Likewise, the application of good regulatory practices can support the development of compatible regulatory approaches among the parties, and reduce or eliminate unnecessarily burdensome, duplicative, or divergent regulatory requirements. Good regulatory practices are also fundamental to effective regulatory cooperation.[245]

More recently, the term 'regulatory coherence' appears to be used in an expansive manner to incorporate regulatory cooperation in mega-regional FTAs in which the US has played a leading role. For example, Article 25.1 of the CPTPP defines regulatory coherence as 'the use of good regulatory practices in the process of planning, designing, issuing, implementing and reviewing regulatory measures in order to facilitate achievement of domestic policy objectives, and *in efforts across governments to enhance regulatory cooperation* in order to further those objectives and promote international trade and investment, economic growth and employment'. Regulatory cooperation clauses are also included as part of the good regulatory practices chapter of United States-Mexico-Canada Agreement (USMCA).[246] In the same vein, the regulatory cooperation chapter of some recent FTAs, such as the CETA, seems to cover the idea of regulatory coherence as well. For example, one of the objectives of the regulatory cooperation chapter in the CETA is to 'improve the planning and development of regulatory proposals, promote transparency and predictability in the development and establishment of regulations, enhance the efficacy of regulations, identify alternative instruments, recognise the associated impact of regulations …'[247] Some of the illustrative regulatory cooperation activities are in essence similar to good regulatory practices encouraged in the CPTPP to be discussed below.[248] The lack of strict separation of the two closely related terms in treaty design has led scholars to use them interchangeably.[249]

### *i. CPTPP*

Starting from a modest free trade agreement (FTA), originally known as the Trans-Pacific Strategic Economic Partnership Agreement (P-4 Agreement) among Brunei, Chile, New Zealand, and Singapore, the Trans-Pacific Partnership (TPP) Agreement quickly rose to prominence since the US joined the negotiations in 2008. The Obama Administration continued the talks and framed the TPP as

[245] Art 21.4 of CETA and Art 28.12 of USMCA.

[246] Art 28.17 of USMCA.

[247] Art 21.3(b) of CETA.

[248] Art 21.4 of CETA.

[249] E Sheregold and AD Mitchell, 'The TPP and Good Regulatory Practices: An Opportunity for Regulatory Coherence to Promote Regulatory Autonomy?' (2016) 15(4) *World Trade Review* 587, 590–593.

the centrepiece of the US' strategic pivot to the Asia-Pacific region.[250] After 19 rounds of negotiations, the 12 member countries (US, Canada, Japan, Mexico, Chile, Peru, Australia, New Zealand, Vietnam, Singapore, Malaysia, and Brunei) signed the TPP pact in early 2016. However, the deal was never ratified by the US congress and President Trump formally withdrew from the TPP on his first day in office in January 2017. The remaining TPP countries have forged ahead with a new version of the pact, known as the CPTPP, keeping most of the original treaty intact.[251]

One of the most innovative parts of the CPTPP is the chapter on regulatory coherence. It marks the ground-breaking first step in codifying as a global norm that countries should establish central coordination and review mechanisms for regulation, and follow good regulatory practices (GRPs), in particular regulatory impact assessment (RIA), to help achieve domestic policy objectives and promote regulatory cooperation.[252] Each CPTPP party retains the flexibility to determine the scope of measures that are subject to the regulatory coherence obligations, with the proviso that 'each Party should aim to achieve significant coverage'.[253]

To begin with, the chapter encourages each member to consider establishing a central coordinating body to facilitate the effective interagency coordination and review of proposed regulatory measures. The objectives of the review are to determine whether the measures were developed using GRPs, to strengthen interagency consultation and coordination among domestic agencies to help avoid potential overlap, duplication and inconsistency; and to develop recommendations for systemic improvement with respect to regulation.[254]

Moreover, the regulatory coherence chapter encourages CPTPP countries to follow GRPs when developing regulatory measures that are covered by the chapter. These GRPs mainly focus on the conduct of regulatory impact assessment procedures, including assessing the need for a regulatory proposal, examining feasible alternatives, explaining the grounds for selecting a particular alternative, and relying on the best relevant scientific, technical, economic or other information.[255] On the specific methodology for RIA, the CPTPP highlights the relevance of the cost-benefit analysis in examining feasible alternative regulatory measures and explaining why a particular alternative is selected. While

[250] M Du, 'Explaining China's Tripartite Strategy towards the TPP' (2015) 18 (2) *Journal of International Economic Law* 407, 411–414.

[251] J McBride and A Chatzky, 'What is the Trans-Pacific Partnership (TPP)?', Council on Foreign Relations Backgrounder (4 January 2019).

[252] J Weiss, 'The Regulatory Coherence Chapter of the Trans-Pacific Partnership Agreement: Making the Link between Adherence to Good Regulatory Practice Principles and Promoting International Trade and Regulatory Cooperation', Notice and Comment, Yale Journal of Regulation (11 February 2016) www.yalejreg.com/nc/the-regulatory-coherence-chapter-of-the-trans-pacific-partnership-agreement-making-the-link-between/ Accessed 11 March 2020.

[253] Art 25.3 of CPTPP.

[254] Art 25.4 of CPTPP.

[255] Art 25.5(2) of CPTTP.

recognising that quantification and monetisation of some costs and benefits may be difficult, the CPTPP requires parties to consider the costs and benefits of alternative regulations 'to the extent feasible'. This is consistent with the OECD and APEC documents which suggest that cost–benefit analysis is the preferable tool for evaluating a regulation and its alternatives in an RIA.[256] Other GRPs include ensuring that regulations are plainly written; taking into account the potential impact of proposed regulations on small- and medium-sized enterprises; making information on new measures publicly available, reviewing measures at regular intervals to determine whether they should be revised or repealed etc.

Recognising that differences in the parties' institutional, social, cultural, legal and developmental circumstances may result in specific regulatory approaches, the CPTPP is quick to affirm each party's sovereign right to identify its regulatory priorities and establish and implement regulatory measures to address these priorities at the level that the party considers appropriate.[257] This is an open recognition that some regulatory diversity is inevitable and not necessarily inappropriate. Nothing in the CPTPP requires a member to use another country's regulatory measure as a basis of its own regulation.[258]

To further dispel concerns that the inclusion of a regulatory coherence chapter may unnecessarily constrain a party's regulatory autonomy, the CPTPP makes it clear it is not subject to dispute settlement mechanisms under the agreement.[259] Arguably this exclusion is necessary to encourage greater participation by states in view of the mixed level of development among the CPTPP parties, and the inclusion of a broad range of domestic regulatory measures within the scope of the regulatory coherence chapter.[260]

### *ii. USMCA*

The US, Canada and Mexico signed the USMCA in November 2018 to modernise and replace the 1994 North American Free Trade Agreement (NAFTA). The new agreement is the first major trade treaty negotiated by the Trump Administration and it is widely seen as indicative of how the US will engage in future international trade negotiations.[261] The USMCA and CPTPP share a lot of similarities. First, the scope of the chapter on GRPs seems very similar to the

[256] Sheregold and Mitchell (n 249) 599.

[257] Art 25.2(2) of CPTTP.

[258] TJ Bollyky, 'Regulatory Coherence in the TPP Talks', in CL Lim, DK Elms, and P Low (eds), *The Trans-Pacific Partnership: A Quest for a Twenty-first Century Trade Agreement* 171 (Cambridge University Press, 2012) 182.

[259] Art 25.11 of CPTTP.

[260] Sheregold and Mitchell (n 249) 600.

[261] MA Villarreal and IF Fergusson, 'NAFTA Renegotiation and the Proposed United States-Mexico- Canada Agreement (USMCA)', Congressional Research Service R44981 (26 February 2019) 1–2.

regulatory coherence chapter of the CPTPP as it intends to 'set forth specific obligations with respect to good regulatory practices, including practices relating to the planning, design, issuance, implementation, and review of the Parties' respective regulations'.[262] Second, similar to the CPTPP, the USMCA stressed the role of central regulatory coordinating bodies in promoting GRPs, performing key advisory, coordination and review functions to improve the quality of regulations, and developing improvements to their regulatory system.[263] Finally, the USMCA also stresses the value of using RIAs when developing proposed regulations.[264]

Still, the USMCA has taken the regulatory coherence agenda to a new level with commitments that are more detailed and prescriptive.[265] First, while the CPTPP allows each party to determine the scope of regulatory measures that would be covered by the relevant disciplines, the USMCA places all regulatory measures within its ambit. Second, compared to the CPTPP, the USMCA contains more detailed provisions on transparency. For example, there are 'early planning' provisions in the USMCA that resemble an 'early warning system' for new regulations, so that parties have enough time to provide feedback on proposed measures. Each party shall publish annually a list of regulations that it reasonably expects within the following 12 months to adopt. Each regulation identified should be accompanied by a description of the proposed regulation, a timetable, a point of contact and an indication of sectors to be affected and its impact on trade.[266] The provision on transparent development of regulation further imposes specific requirements on the publication of draft regulations and collection of comments.[267] Compared to the WTO notification requirements, the USMCA transparency provisions clearly go into great details and lay out more specific obligations.[268] Granted, as a core component of GRP, regulatory transparency is dealt with extensively in other CPTPP chapters such as Transparency and Anti-Corruption (chapter 26), TBT (chapter 8) and SPS measures (chapter 7). This may explain why it is not specifically addressed in the regulatory coherence chapter of the CPTPP.

Along the same vein, the third innovation is that the USMCA has further developed the content of GRPs in preparing and implementing regulations, such as the best practice in the use of reliable and high quality information and expert advice.[269] Finally, different from the CPTPP, the GRPs chapter is subject

[262] Art 28.2(2) of USMCA.
[263] Art 28.3 of USMCA.
[264] Art 28.11 of USMCA.
[265] R Labonte et al, 'USMCA (NAFTA 2.0): Tightening the Constraints on the Right to Regulate for Public Health' (2019) 15 Global Health 1, 7.
[266] Art 28.6 of USMCA.
[267] Art. 28.9 and 28.15 of USMCA.
[268] I Manak, 'Regulatory Issues in the New NAFTA', in International Economic Law and Policy Blog (10 October 2018).
[269] Art. 28.5 and 28.10 of USMCA.

to the dispute settlement processes under the USMCA if there is 'a sustained and recurring course of action or inaction that is inconsistent with a provision of this chapter'.[270] This inclusion may reflect the closer economic integration and the learning experience gained from the NAFTA era in the USMCA. By contrast, there are quite a few developing countries with relatively underdeveloped regulatory regimes in the CPTTP. To subject the chapter to dispute settlement procedures would aggravate their concerns that the GRPs would erode their regulatory autonomy and impose regulatory convergence.[271]

## V. CONCLUSION

Regulatory cooperation has the potential to transfer good regulatory practices, to level the playing field, to reduce costs, and to contribute to the reduction of unnecessary barriers to trade as well as mitigate the economic impact of necessary trade barriers.[272] In the WTO context, the TBT and SPS Agreements contain substantive provisions on harmonisation of product standards through international standards, and mutual or unilateral recognition of foreign standards. In addition, new developments have emerged in recent years. For instance, the topic of GRPs have been regularly discussed at the TBT Committee. Moreover, TBT and SPS disciplines in FTAs have gone beyond the relevant WTO disciplines and embody much more stringent commitments. This chapter provides a detailed review of these international regulatory cooperation tools.

Since international standards assume special legal significance under the TBT Agreement, what standards may be recognised as international standards have become an important threshold question. This chapter conceptualises international standards as global public goods and argues that following the global administrative law principles provides ISBs with additional legitimacy as producers of global public goods. I traced how the WTO AB has changed its original hands-off approach in *EC – Sardines* to a more intrusive approach in *US – Tuna II*, applying global administrative law principles embodied in the TBT Committee Decision to vet international standards before they are afforded quasi-legislative status. It is submitted that the AB's new approach to international standards marks a distinctive pathway for the development of global administrative law in producing global public goods. The elevation of international standards to 'first preference' status in the TBT Agreement involves a delegation of regulatory power from the WTO to ISBs.[273] Such a delegation

[270] Art 28.20 of USMCA.

[271] S Trew, 'International Regulation and the Public Good' (Canadian Centre for Policy Alternative, 2019) 32–34.

[272] Karttunen (n 3) 107.

[273] T Buthe, 'The Globalisation of Health and Safety Standards: Delegation of Regulatory Authority in the SPS Agreement of the 1994 Agreement Establishing the World Trade Organisation' (2008) 71 *Law and Contemporary Problem* 219, 227–230.

creates potential agency problems over whether these 'agents' are faithful to the WTO's objectives.[274] The WTO judicial review provides an important external check on international standards that are truly appropriate for the purpose of the TBT Agreement. I have also argued that there is a need to distinguish two types of obligations embodied in the TBT Committee Decision. Some principles in the TBT Committee Decision have created specific norms that ISBs must observe, such as transparency and open membership, and violation of which may lead to a denial of international standard status. By contrast, other principles such as consensus and addressing developing countries' concerns are merely procedural requirements and they may only represent 'best efforts' obligations. At any rate, the inconsistency with one of the principles of the TBT Committee Decision will not automatically lead to the rejection of the standard in question as an international standard. The AB will make the decision on a case-by-case basis.

Other than the use of international standards, MRAs and equivalence are also highly desirable policy tools in the WTO law. However, there are practical difficulties for WTO Members to make full use of these two tools. As a result, these two policy tools have only achieved limited success in the multilateral trading system. In view of the failed Doha Round and the current stagnation of WTO negotiations, new additional requirements and mechanisms on regulatory cooperation have emerged as one of the unique features of recent FTAs.

[274] J Trachtman, 'Addressing Regulatory Divergence through International Standards' in A Mattoo and P Sauve (eds), *Domestic Regulation and Service Trade Liberalisation* (World Bank/Oxford University Press, 2003) 27–31.

# 5

# *The Regulation of Private Standards in the WTO*

SINCE PRIVATE STANDARDS were raised for the first time as a specific trade concern in 2005 regarding EurepGAP (now GlobalGAP) standards for bananas destined for sale in UK supermarkets, they have been a recurrent issue of discussion at the WTO SPS and TBT Committees.[1] Private standards are set by non-governmental entities without regulatory authority. Voluntary by definition, private standards include individual firm schemes (eg, Tesco Nature's Choice, Carrrefour Filière Qualité) drafted to structure relations within their value chain and deliver products in line with consumers' preferences,[2] collective national schemes (eg, British Retail Consortium (BRC) Global Standard, Assured Food Standards) and collective international schemes (eg, GlobalGAP, ISO 22000, Global Food Safety Initiative).[3] Private standards may cover any and all stages of production, from processing to distribution, including packaging, certification and/or labelling schemes. They may address a variety of consumer interests including quality assurance, food safety, environment, social or labour conditions, corporate responsibility and even carbon footprint.[4] Being market-driven, private standards are more economically efficient, take less time to develop and offer more flexibility in implementation. The United Nations Conference on Trade And Development (UNCTAD) estimated in 2007 the number of private schemes at 400 and rising.[5] The belief that private standards are playing, and will continue to play, a key role in determining the nature and terms of international trade has taken root in the international trade community.[6]

[1] Note by the Secretariat, 'Possible Actions for the SPS Committee Regarding SPS-Related private Standards', G/SPS/W/247/Rev.3 (11 October 2010) para 1; Committee on Technical Barriers to Trade, 'Fifth Triennial Review of the Operation and Implementation of the Agreement on Technical Barriers to Trade under Article 15.4', G/TBT/26 (13 November 2009) para 26.

[2] MP Vandenbergh, 'The New Wal-Mart Effect: The Role of Private Contracting in Global Governance' (2007) 54(4) *UCLA Law Review* 913.

[3] Note by the Secretariat, 'Private Standards and the SPS Agreement', G/SPS/GEN/746 (24 January 2007) paras 5–6.

[4] L Fulponi, 'Private Voluntary Standards in the Food System: The Perspective of Major Food Retailers in OECD Countries' (2006) 31 (1) *Food Policy* 6–8.

[5] WTO Secretariat (n 3) para 3.

[6] Submission by Switzerland, 'Voluntary Standards' (20 October 2009), G/SPS/GEN/967, para 3.

In principle, WTO Agreements, as an international treaty, only apply to its Member States, and not directly to private bodies.[7] When the adverse trade impact of EurepGAP was raised in the SPS Committee, the EC responded that EurepGAP was not an official EC body and that any EurepGAP standard could not be seen as an EC requirement. The EC's response simply reflected a widely-held view that exclusive private actions independent of government intervention do not fall within the scope of WTO rules.[8] However, following the proliferation of private standards in international commerce in recent decades, it has become clear that private standards can have adverse effects on international trade and world welfare in the same way that government-imposed mandatory regulations do.[9] In many instances, private standards are de facto mandatory either because they have become an industry norm or when compliance with a private standard is a requirement for suppliers to access the proprietary value chain of transnational corporations and large retailers.[10] Moreover, as most of the initiatives to adopt private standards have emerged in developed countries and have considerably affected exports of developing countries, a large number of their governments have criticised private standards as new trade barriers that reduce their export opportunities and undermine their rights to development.[11]

Both the TBT Agreement and the SPS Agreement make some inroads into regulating private standards. Article 13 of the SPS Agreement obliges WTO Members to take 'such reasonable measures' as may be available to them to ensure that non-governmental bodies within their territories comply with the relevant provisions of the SPS Agreement. There is a similar provision in Article 4.1 of the TBT Agreement to the same effect. However, the scope of Article 13 of the SPS Agreement has long been criticised for being vague and open to divergent interpretations.[12] In order to deal with the adverse effects of private standards, developing countries have repeatedly called for the WTO to put private standards within its normative regulatory framework.[13] Despite intense negotiations on the issue in the WTO SPS Committee, little progress has

[7] Communication from Canada on Eco- Labeling, G/TBT/W/9 (5 July 1995) 2; RJ Zadalis, 'When Do the Activities of Private Parties Trigger WTO Rules?' (2007) 10 (2) *Journal of International Economic Law* 337–338.

[8] Submission by Switzerland (n 6) paras 7–8; D Prevost, 'Private Sector Food- Safety Standards and the SPS Agreement: Challenges and Possibilities' (2008) 33 *South African Yearbook of International Law* 6.

[9] World Trade Report 2012, *Trade and Public Policies: A Close Look at Non-Tariff Measures in the 21st Century* 167.

[10] G Smith, 'Interaction of Public and Private Standards in the Food Chain' (2009) OECD Food, Agriculture and Fisheries Working Paper No 15, 15.

[11] M Maertens and J Swinnen, 'Private Standards, Global Food Supply Chains and the Implications for Developing Countries' in A Marx, M Maerrtens, J Swinnen and J Wouters (eds), *Private Standards and Global Governance: Economic, Legal and Political Perspectives* 153 (Edward Elgar, 2012) 153–154.

[12] T Wlostowski, 'Selected Observations on the Regulation of Private Standards by the WTO' (2010) 30 *Polish Yearbook of International Law* 229.

[13] Communication from Nigeria, 'Private Standards', G/SPS/GEN/1398 (16 March 2015); Communication from Belise, 'Belise's Comments on Private Standards', G/SPS/W/288 (14 July 2015).

been made because of divergent views on private standards between developing and developed countries.[14]

This chapter starts from the premise that the debate on the proper role of the WTO in regulating private standards should move beyond the search for a reasonable interpretation of Article 13 of the SPS Agreement and Article 4.1 of the TBT Agreement and start to engage with fundamental normative questions concerning the legitimacy and accountability of private standards in international trade and the potential role of the WTO in regulating transnational private regulations. In particular, what justifies a role for the WTO, a multilateral intergovernmental organisation, in regulating private behaviour? If such a role is justifiable, how could the regulatory mechanism be designed and implemented in practice? The rest of the chapter proceeds as follows. Part II clarifies several definitional puzzles of private standards in the WTO discourse. Part III explains the drivers behind the rise of private standards as well as the pros and cons of private standards from an international trade perspective. Part IV provides a detailed legal analysis of the current WTO legal framework governing private standards. Part V inquires into whether the WTO is normatively justified to exercise oversight on private standards and critically engages with the concerns of WTO Members about private standards. Part VI concludes the article.

## I. THE DEFINITIONAL CHALLENGE OF 'PRIVATE STANDARDS'

### A. Defining SPS-Related Private Standards in the SPS Committee

Despite its common employment at WTO negotiation forums and policy discourse, there is no consensus on the definition of 'private standards' in the WTO context. In response to concerns raised by some WTO Members regarding the function of private standards in international trade, the SPS Committee adopted a decision to develop a working definition of SPS-related private standards in March 2011.[15] Since then, the SPS Committee's work on private standards has focused on reaching a consensus on a definition of these standards.[16]

The SPS Committee initially discussed a working definition on the basis of draft definitions prepared by the WTO Secretariat in October 2012.[17] As no consensus emerged from these discussions, WTO Members agreed to set up an 'electronic working group' (e-WG) to move forward the consultation process.

[14] Note by the WTO Secretariat, 'Summary of the SPS Committee Meeting of 22–23 March 2017', G/SPS/R/86 (1 June 2017) 33.

[15] SPS Committee, 'Decision of the Committee: Actions Regarding SPS-Related Private Standards', G/SPS/55 (6 April 2011).

[16] SPS Committee, 'Review of the Operation and Implementation of the SPS Committee- Draft Report of the Committee', G/SPS/W/280/Rev.2 (6 November 2014), para 14.2.

[17] Note by the Secretariat, 'Proposed Working Definition of SPS-Related Private Standards', G/SPS/W/265/Rev.2 (28 September 2012).

After many rounds of consultation, the e-WG proposed a compromise working definition in September 2014 as follows:

> An SPS-related private standard is a *written requirement* or condition, or a set of written requirements or conditions, related to food safety, or animal or plant life or health that may be used in commercial transactions and that is *applied* by *a non-governmental entity* that is not exercising governmental authority.[18]

There has been general agreement among WTO Members on the co-Stewards' proposed text for a working definition apart from the EU and US who remain concerned about the use of the terms 'non-governmental entity' and 'requirement' in the working definition.[19] The EU suggested replacing 'non-governmental entity' with 'private entity' and deleting the term 'requirement'. However, the co-Stewards considered it necessary and appropriate to maintain these two terms in the working definition, pointing out that they were used in the SPS Committee Decision from which the mandate of the SPS Committee to develop a working definition of SPS-related private standards originated and that these two terms are generic and not specific to the SPS Agreement. Consequently, the SPS Committee could not reach a consensus on a working definition of SPS-related private standards and so agreed to a proposal from the co-Stewards of the e-WG for a 'cooling off' period to reflect on how to overcome the impasse. The failure to build a consensus on the definition had led to a stalemate in the SPS Committee from October 2014 over the adoption of the Fourth Review Report of the SPS Agreement. WTO Members finally reached a compromise in July 2017 by introducing wording which suggested that WTO Members were unable to agree on a working definition of SPS-related private standards.[20]

The standoff in the negotiation at the SPS Committee seems implausible. Although the terms 'non-governmental entity' and 'requirements' are the elements of the definition about which the most diverse views were expressed, as China and New Zealand argued, these two terms are widely used by international standardising bodies such as the Codex Alimentarius Commission (Codex) and the World Organization for Animal Health (OIE) in their definitions of private standards and they had never before met any objections. As the chairman of the SPS Committee correctly pointed out, the disagreement on the definition was not a drafting issue but reflected a fundamental divergence of views regarding private standards. Developed countries have held the strong view that private standards fall outside the scope of the SPS Agreement, and hence should have no

[18] SPS Committee, 'Second Report of the Co-Stewards of the Private Standards E-Working Group on Action 1 (G/SPS/55)', G/SPS/W/281 (30 September 2014) para 15.

[19] SPS Committee, 'Report of the Co-Stewards of the Private Standards E-Working Group to the March 2015 Meeting of the SPS Committee on Action 1 (G/SPS/55)', G/SPS/W/283 (17 March 2015) para 22.

[20] WTO, 'WTO Members Adopt Report on Food Safety Agreement' (14 July 2017) www.wto.org/english/news_e/news17_e/sps_13jul17_e.htm Accessed on 2 March 2020.

definition at all, or have an innocuous definition that would not be perceived as acceptance that they should come under the aegis of the WTO.[21] This position at least partly reflects the fact that most private standards originate from and are applied in developed countries. Most producers and retailers in developed countries benefit from the widespread adoption of private standards whilst the cost of complying with private standards mainly falls on exporters from developing countries.[22] Moreover, the adoption of private standards is considered normal market behaviour of private economic actors which a government has little control over in domestic law. Therefore, developed countries do not have much incentive to impose additional disciplines on private standards. As the use of the term 'non-governmental entities' in the draft definition echoes the language of Article 13 of the SPS Agreement, some developed countries are worried that to accept that term would imply that the private standards fall within the regulatory scope of the SPS Agreement.

In considering a working definition of SPS-related private standards, the WTO Secretariat prepared a useful summary of existing definitions of 'private standards' that are used by various international organisations.[23] Based on the existing definitions, it is possible to summarise the core features defining 'private standards'. First, private standards are established by non-governmental/private entities, ie any entity that does not possess, exercise or is not vested with governmental authority. There are myriad differences among categories of private standards schemes in terms of scope, objective, content and characteristics.[24] Second, private standards are by definition voluntary in nature in the sense that exporters are not legally required to comply with private standards. Nevertheless, some private standards may be de facto mandatory for access to important markets because of the market power of the non-governmental entities that adopted them. On the other hand, some non-governmental standardising bodies may enjoy a government franchise/mandate to coordinate standards in their respective countries. The standards adopted by these national non-governmental bodies are not private standards.[25] For example, the private sector American National Standards Institute (ANSI) has the responsibility to coordinate national standardisation activities and to represent the US at the ISO and IEC. American national standards accredited by ANSI are therefore not private standards.

[21] PC Mavroidis and R Wolfe, 'Private Standards and the WTO: Reclusive No More' (2017) 16 (1) *World Trade Report* 13.

[22] P Liu, 'Private Standards in International Trade: Issues and Opportunities' (WTO Workshop on Environment-related Private Standards, Certification and Labeling Requirements, Geneva, 9 July 2009) 16–17.

[23] Note by the Secretariat, 'Existing Definitions of Private Standards in other International Organizations', G/SPS/GEN/1334/Rev.1 (5 August 2014).

[24] K Purnhagen, 'Mapping Private Regulation- Classification, Market Access and Market Closure Policy and Law's Response' (2015) *Journal of World Trade* 309, 313–315.

[25] WTO Secretariat (n 17).

Third, private standards may address any aspects of product characteristics but they predominantly focus on production and process methods. Indeed, one of the defining characteristics of private standards is an increasing focus on the processes by which products are produced.[26] Fourth, private standards pursue a wide range of objectives, such as environmental conservation, ensuring food safety and protection of social and human rights, as well as promoting good agricultural and manufacturing practices, sanitary safety and animal welfare issues. Finally, unlike international standards such as Codex and ISO, private standards are not primarily aimed at harmonising heterogeneous national standards.[27] Non-governmental entities tend to prefer to keep their own brands original and different from others. This is because one important objective of private standards is to provide product differentiation, mainly to support claims about credence characteristics.

### B. Private Standards and 'International Standards'

One particularly confusing element in the definition of private standards is the term 'non-governmental entities'. As a generic term, it makes no distinction between non-governmental standardising bodies *recognised* by WTO Members at either national or international level and other non-governmental organisations not so recognised. This conceptual differentiation is not an issue in the context of the SPS Agreement because it explicitly names three international standardising bodies regarding food safety, animal health and plant health. However, this conceptual differentiation is of utmost importance in the TBT Agreement because not all technical standards created by non-governmental entities are equal. In the TBT Agreement, for example, an 'international standard' is defined as a standard adopted by an international standardising body. In order to qualify as an international standardising body, the entity in question must have *recognised* activities in standardisation and its membership must be open to the relevant bodies of at least all WTO Members.[28] Significantly, standards developed by non-governmental bodies may be recognised as 'international standards' in the TBT Agreement if certain conditions are fulfilled.[29] The ISO, for instance, is a non-governmental standardising body whose standards are

[26] S Henson and J Humphrey, 'The Impacts of Private Food Safety Standards on the Food Chain and on Public Standard-Setting Processes' (2009) Paper Prepared for FAO/WHO 14.

[27] J Nakagawa, 'Private Standards and Global Governance: Prospects and Challenges' (2017) ISS Research Series No 62, 8.

[28] WTO Appellate Body Report, *United States – Measures Concerning the Importation, Marketing and Sale of Tuna and Tuna Products (US – Tuna II)*, WT/DS381/AB/R (13 June 2012) para 359.

[29] J Pauwelyn, 'Rule-Based Trade 2.0? The Rise of Informal Rules and International Standards and How They may Outperform WTO Treaties' (2014) 17 *Journal of International Economic Law* 749; HW Liu, 'International Standards in Flux: A Balkanised ICT Standard-Setting Paradigm and its Implications for the WTO' (2014) 17 *Journal of International Economic Law* 586.

most likely to be recognised as international standards.[30] In *US – Tuna II*, the US also argued that certain non-governmental standard-setting organisations, such as the Institute of Electrical and Electronics Engineers, could qualify as an international standardising body for the purpose of the TBT Agreement.[31] As an important condition to be recognised as an international standardising body, an international non-governmental standard-setting organisation must adhere to the core WTO TBT principles of transparency, openness, impartiality and consensus, effectiveness and relevance, coherence, and address the concerns of developing countries.[32] These principles are further complemented by compliance with the disciplines of Annex 3 of the WTO TBT Agreement Code of Good Practice (CGP) for the preparation, adoption and application of standards.

International standards have assumed special legal significance under both the TBT and the SPS Agreement. WTO Members are obliged to use relevant international standards as a basis for their domestic technical regulations/standards, and domestic standards based on international standards are effectively immunised from challenges in the WTO dispute settlement system. If standards developed by non-governmental entities are endorsed as 'international standards', they should no longer be regarded as private standards in view of their special legal status under WTO law. By contrast, some non-governmental entities either do not follow the TBT principles and the CGP in developing voluntary standards, or they are simply not recognised as international standardising bodies by WTO Members. In both cases, the standards they adopt are properly called private standards.

## C. Are Private Standards and Public Regulations Two Separate Worlds?

It must be emphasised that the distinction between private and public regulations has become increasingly blurred in the context of profound changes in the role of government in market regulation. As a good governance strategy, modern governments have actively engaged the private sector to achieve certain policy goals, and product standardisation is no exception.[33] Many standards are developed to support governmental regulatory needs. There are diverse ways through which public regulations and private standards may interact. For example, many private standards originate from national or international legislation and then

[30] ISO, 'International Standards and Private Standards' (2010) www.probus-sigma.com/wp-content/uploads/downloads/2014/02/International-standards-and-private-standards.pdf accessed on 2 March 2020.

[31] WTO Panel report, *US – Tuna II*, WT/DS381/R (15 September 2011) para 7.655.

[32] M Du and F Deng, 'International Standards as Global Public Goods in the World Trading System' (2016) 43 (2) *Legal Issues of Economic Integration* 127–132.

[33] S Henson and J Humphrey, 'Understanding the Complexity of Private Standards in Global Agri-Food Chains as They Impact Developing Countries' (2010) 46 (9) *The Journal of Development Studies* 1641.

get further specified through a process of private decision-making. In this way, government or intergovernmental regulation forms the framework within which the private standard-setting process takes place. Firms are able to undertake conformity assessment of their own to comply with public regulations. What emerges is not so much a difference between public and private but a standard-setting process in which private actors further operationalise and refine public standards.[34]

Similarly, referencing standards in regulation is a general practice and many public regulations rely on technical specifications and initiatives by private standard-setting organisations.[35] Governments may delegate certain tasks to non-governmental entities, and public regulations may incorporate, by reference or verbatim, the contents of a private standard for all or some of the details, thereby making compliance with the private standard a part of, or a presumption of, compliance with a public regulation. For example, EU directives covering CE marking for telecommunications and electronic products refer to the voluntary ISO 9000 as a benchmark. The UK Food Standards Agency has instructed enforcement authorities to take account of membership of 'recognised' private farm assurance schemes, such as Assured Food Standards and Global Food Safety Initiative (GFSI), in determining the frequency of inspection of product facilities.[36] More recently, private standards are increasingly integrated in sustainable public procurement policies.[37] In *European Commission v Kingdom of Netherlands*, the province of Noord Holland in the Netherlands internalised the private standards EKO label (on organic agricultural production) and the Max Havelaar label (on fair trade) in a public tender and the compliance with these two private standards was regarded as proof of compliance in the public tender. The ECJ's ruling confirmed that fair-trade principles and a reference to labels developed by private entities can be included in public tenders as award criteria.[38] In short, the boundary between 'public' and 'private' is becoming increasingly blurred and it is better to view the sharp dichotomy as opposing ends on a continuum.[39] In any event, public standards and private standards are not two separate worlds.

[34] A Marx, 'The Public-Private Distinction in Global Governance: How Relevant is it in the Case of Voluntary Sustainability Standards?' (2017) 3 *The Chinese Journal of Global Governance* 14.

[35] Committee on Technical Barriers to Trade, 'Eighth Triennial Review of the Operation and Implementation of the Agreement on Technical Barriers to Trade under Article 15.4', G/TBT/41 (19 November 2018) 14.

[36] T Havinga and F Waarden, 'Enforcing Compliance with Food Regulation: Modalities in the Relationship between Public Enforcement Agencies and Private Parties' (ECPR General Conference, September 2013) 12.

[37] MA Corvaglia, 'Public Procurement and Private Standards: Ensuring Sustainability under the WTO Agreement on Government Procurement' (2016) 19 *Journal of International Economic Law* 608.

[38] ECJ, Judgment of the Court (Third Chamber), *European Commission v Kingdom of the Netherlands*, Case C-368/10 (10 May 2012).

[39] D Vogel, 'Private Global Business Regulation' (2008) 11 *Annual Review of Political Science* 265.

## II. THE PROLIFERATION OF PRIVATE STANDARDS AND THEIR TRADE IMPLICATIONS

### A. Explaining the Rise of Private Standards in International Trade

While private standards initially emerged in the area of food safety, they now encompass environmental protection, ethical trading, animal welfare, organic production and so on. It has also become standard practice for an individual food safety standard to govern a wide array of product attributes. It is therefore increasingly difficult to make a distinction between food safety standards, environmental standards and social or ethical standards.[40] Since food standards are predominantly private, and formal negotiations on private standards have mainly taken place in the SPS Committee, this part will take private food standards as an example but the same logic applies to private standards in other areas as well.

The proliferation of private food standards in international trade is closely linked to the economic environment as well as institutional and legal frameworks in which the firms operate in the global markets. The first factor is the structural and institutional transformation of global agricultural and food markets. Thanks to rapid progress in information and communication technology and a favourable policy environment that encourages more liberal international trade, the supply chain for agricultural and food products has extended beyond national borders. Global sourcing reduces food costs and supplies new food to consumers but also creates new risks as food is increasingly subject to greater transformation and transportation and supply chains are fragmented across multiple enterprises. Private standards are therefore a useful tool for multinational enterprises to coordinate their supply chain through standardisation of product and process requirements on an international level.[41] Moreover, the expansion of supermarkets in food retailing, both nationally and internationally, has increased retailer market concentration and market power. The OECD estimates that in Europe the five largest retailers accounted for more than half of all food sales.[42] This structural shift has given food retailers greater bargaining power vis-à-vis other businesses in the supply chain, enabling them to impose private standards on their suppliers.

Second, high profile food scandals, such as the infamous bovine spongiform encephalopathy (BSE) incident in a number of developed countries, have fuelled consumer concerns over food safety risks and eroded consumer confidence in prevailing mechanisms of food safety control which focused predominantly

[40] Henson and Humphrey (n 33) 1633.

[41] S Henson and T Reardon, 'Private Agri- Food Standards: Implications for Food Policy and the Agri- Food System' (2005) 30 *Food Policy* 241.

[42] L Fulponi, 'Final Report on Private Standards and the Shaping of the Agro- Food System' (2006) OECD Doc AGR/CA/APM (2006)9/Final 10–11.

on public regulation.[43] Some advances in food technology, such as genetically modified food, have generated further concerns among consumers in the form of so-called 'technological risks'.[44] In order to counter food scares and offer confidence, firms sign up to voluntary private standards or develop their own. Private standards help differentiate their products and protect or even enhance their market share in national and international markets which are increasingly driven by quality-based competition.[45]

Third, broader demographic and social trends have altered the expectations and demands of consumers with respect to food safety and quality. Nowadays many of the quality attributes expected by consumers go beyond the physical traits of food and include process and production aspects such as animal welfare, environment, labour conditions and health.[46] Civil society and consumer advocacy groups have also influenced the agendas of private companies by targeting their procurement policies through a variety of media strategies, including media campaigns, organised boycotts or protests against certain retailers, and league tables announcing the most ethical supermarkets.[47] By implementing private standards in this context, firms can supply blends of product and process attributes and communicate them to consumers which set them apart from their competitors. Hence, the adoption of private standards can be an important mechanism to minimise reputation risks, to earn and maintain customer loyalty and to enhance the overall quality image of a firm's brand.

Finally, the legal requirements on companies to demonstrate due diligence in the prevention of food safety risks are also a driving force behind the adoption of private standards. For example, in the wake of a number of food scares the UK passed the Food Safety Act in 1990 under which any supplier of a branded product is responsible for the safety of that product. Accordingly, enforcement action could be taken against a wholesaler or a retailer even if the offence was committed by other parties in the food chain (eg, overseas exporters and food importers) unless the retailer could provide due diligence demonstrating that he has been proactive in ensuring that food from suppliers conforms to legal food safety standards.[48] Major food retailers in the UK then responded to the new law by developing private food safety protocols for their suppliers that were enforced through third-party audits. This due diligence requirement

[43] G Chia- Hui Lee Stagiaire, 'Private Food Standards and Their Impacts on Developing Countries' (2006) www.trade.ec.europa.eu/doclib/docs/2006/november/tradoc_127969.pdf accessed on 2 March 2020, at 8.

[44] S Henson, 'The Role of Public and Private Standards in Regulating International Food Markets' (2008) 4 *Journal of International Agricultural Trade and Development* 67.

[45] Fulponi (n 42) 9.

[46] Ibid, 10.

[47] S Washington and L Ababouch, 'Private Standards and Certification in Fisheries and Aquaculture: Current Practice and Emerging Issues' (2011) FAO Fisheries and Aquaculture Technical Paper 553, 19.

[48] C Scott, 'Continuity and Change in British Food Law' (1990) 56 *Modern Law Report* 792–794.

was later adopted in the EU Food Law Regulation of 2002 and most recently in the US Food Safety Modernization Act in 2011.[49] More broadly, in recognising the limits of the traditional command-and-control approach in the global food supply era, governments in OECD countries have been increasingly engaging the private sector in the implementation of good practices to ensure product safety and quality. This partial and progressive shift of responsibility from public authority to the private sector has prompted business to develop internal food safety management systems and reduced the reliance on government inspection services. In this context, private standards may be seen as a reflection of private firms assuming and extending this responsibility.[50]

In summary, private food standards are institutionalised market instruments to address food chain governance challenges. They appear to be simultaneously a useful tool for the private sector to regulate supply chains, a substitute for inadequate public regulation, a response to increasingly stringent government regulation and potential litigation, and a means of exceeding public regulations to provide credible product differentiation.

## B. The Effects of Private Standards on International Trade

### *i. Negative Effects of Private Standards on International Trade*

Private standards can be significant trade barriers, especially for small-scale producers or exporters in developing countries.[51] The trade-impeding effects of private standards may arise from either the content of private standards or the ability of exporters to comply with them. To begin with, some private standards are de facto compulsory in the international market. This is especially the case where a few supermarket chains control the greatest share of the market, making compliance with their private standards a prerequisite for exporting to many developed country markets.[52] Furthermore, some private standards exceed not only those of the relevant international standards but also official national regulations of importing Members which are themselves at times more restrictive than the relevant international standards for the same products.[53] For example, many retailers require significantly lower maximum residue limits (MRLs) for pesticides than those of Codex. Some major German retailers have even insisted that MRLs should be limited to no more than one third of the EU

[49] J Humphrey, 'Food Safety, Private Standards Schemes and Trade: The Implications of the FDA Food Safety Modernization Act' (2012) IDS Working Paper No 403, 39.

[50] Washington and Ababouch (n 47) 18.

[51] Note by the Secretariat, 'Effects of SPS- Related Private Standards- Compilation of Replies', G/SPS/GEN/932/Rev.1 (10 December 2009) 2.

[52] T Havinga, 'Private Regulation of Food Safety by Supermarkets' (2006) 28 (4) *Law and Policy* 522–523.

[53] T Vandemoortele and K Deconinck, 'When are Private Standards More Stringent than Public Standards?' (2014) 96 (1) *American Journal of Agricultural Economics* 154–155.

official requirement.[54] This has resulted in the exclusion of certain producers from the market even though they meet official national standards or international standards.[55]

These highly restrictive private standards lead to high compliance costs. It is estimated that the average annual certification fee ranges between US$2,000 and US$8,000 for a private standard.[56] As the costs of compliance are always borne entirely by suppliers (farmers, processors and exporters), large numbers of small suppliers who cannot afford such costs are excluded from high value market segments.[57] To make the situation worse, regardless of the investments needed to obtain certification, compliance with private standards does not necessarily deliver a price premium. Even if there is one, only a small percentage accrues to the producers and most of it is captured by downstream operators, in particular the retailers.[58]

Moreover, the development process of many private standards is neither participatory nor transparent. Exporters and other stakeholders who are potentially affected by the private standard developed are either excluded from the standard-setting process entirely or only given a consultative role.[59] The standard-setting process is opaque and information provision is voluntary, selective and based on self-reports. There are no appeal procedures to correct any defects.[60] Clearly, an inclusive and transparent process involving other stakeholders such as suppliers and independent experts when developing a standard would make the compliance with private standards less costly and less complicated.[61]

Next, private labelling schemes often lack neutrality and frequently serve local commercial and protectionist interests.[62] For example, the methodology used by some private climate change labelling schemes to calculate food miles, such as Bio Suisse standards in Swiss, fails to take into consideration the full array of greenhouse gases from European producers such as carbon emissions coming from tractors, truck transport and hothouse heating systems. As a result, local Swiss farmers stand to benefit most from these standards.[63] Similarly, comparing

[54] Stagiaire (n 43) 27.

[55] SPS Committee, 'Actions Regarding SPS-Related Private Standards- Communication from Belise', G/SPS/GEN/1374 (23 October 2014).

[56] DH Schepers, 'Challenges to Legitimacy at the Forest Stewardship Council' (2010) 92 (2) *Journal of Business Ethics* 287.

[57] Liu (n 22) 16.

[58] P Liu, 'Certification in the Value Chain for Fresh Fruits: The Example of Banana Industry' (2009) FAO Commodity Studies No 4, 71–85.

[59] D Fuchs, A Kalfagianni and T Havinga, 'Actors in Private Food Governance: the Legitimacy of Retail Standards and Multistakeholder Initiatives with Civil Society Participation' (2011) 28 *Agriculture and Human Values* 362.

[60] WTO Secretariat (n 51) paras 27–37.

[61] Liu (n 22) 15.

[62] AE Appleton, 'Private Climate Change Standards and Labelling Schemes under the WTO Agreement on Technical Barriers to Trade' in T Cottier, O Nartova and SZ Bigdeli (eds) *International Trade Regulation and the Mitigation of Climate Change* (Cambridge University Press, 2009) 131, 132.

[63] J Clayton, 'Organic Farmers Face Ruin as Rich Nations Agonise over Food Miles, *The Times* (1 August 2007).

carbon emissions from cut roses produced in Kenya and the Netherlands for the British market, one recent study showed that emissions released in conjunction with the sale of Kenyan flowers (including air freight emissions) are 5.8 times lower than those of Dutch hothouse flowers, based on a life cycle analysis considering more than 500 inputs rather than a single issue of food miles.[64]

Finally, and in sharp contrast to the use of harmonised international standards, as foreseen in the SPS and TBT Agreements, producers and exporters have to comply with different and potentially conflicting private standards in order to sell to different supply chains. The multiplicity of private standards and the lack of harmonisation among them increase the complexity of requirements applicable in a certain sector as well as the compliance and certification costs.[65]

### *ii. Positive Effects of Private Standards on International Trade*

The predominant discourse on the trade effects of private standards has focused on how they may act as trade barriers. However, it is also widely recognised that private standards, alongside the regulatory requirements of export markets, can claim credit for facilitating international trade.[66] Similar to public regulations, private standards are viewed, at least in part, as a necessary bridge between increasingly demanding consumer requirements and the participation of international suppliers. Private standards provide a common language in supply chains, reducing transaction costs, satisfying evolving consumer demands and promoting consumer confidence in the safety and quality of traded products even if there is no price premium, without which the market for certain products could not be enhanced.[67] Moreover, compared to government programmes, private standards can be more effective in improving hygiene and safety for farmers and processors in developing countries. Private standards normally provide detailed requirements for every step of the production and processing chain and a direct incentive to meet these requirements. They reach down to the level of each individual producer or processing plant, avoiding some of the delays and problems of more general national or regional programmes.[68] As a result, private standards lead to more standardised farming, processing, and packaging activities, promoting productivity and predictability, and facilitating compliance with international standards.[69]

[64] A Williams, 'Comparative Study of Cut Roses for the British Market Produced in Kenya and the Netherlands', Precis Report for World Flowers (12 February 2007).

[65] GH Stanton, 'Food Safety-related Private Standards: The WTO Perspective', in A Marx et al (n 11) 242.

[66] S Jaffe, 'Food Safety and Agricultural Health Standards: Challenges and Opportunities for Developing Country Exports' (2005) World Bank Report No 31207, XI–XII.

[67] S Henson and S Jaffee, 'Understanding Developing Country Strategic Responses to the Enhancement of Food Safety Standards' (2008) 31 (4) *The World Economy* 552.

[68] Stanton (n 65) 242.

[69] WTO Secretariat (n 51) para 39.

More significantly, some developing countries could utilise the potential opportunities offered by the rise of private standards to their competitive advantage. In the real world where private standards predominate, the key issue for any exporter is to gain access to a given buyer's supply chain. If exporters do gain access to these supply chains, the benefits in terms of long-term trade relations through systems of 'preferred suppliers', including better relationships with buyers, marketing guarantees, enhanced quality and increased yields, technical support and training, as well as increased access to credit, can be significant and even outweigh the direct financial impact of private standards.[70] From this perspective, the challenges associated with compliance to strict private standards can be fundamental catalysts for developing countries to upgrade infrastructure and facilities, build capacity and modernise export supply chains, which in turn provide opportunities to position themselves strategically in key export markets.[71] Empirical evidence confirms that farmers/producers who manage to comply with private standards maintain a stable presence in a number of major export markets and possibly expand their market share, while those who cannot are displaced.[72] For example, it is well documented in the literature that Kenya has positioned itself as a globally competitive exporter of fresh and processed vegetables through concerted efforts to upgrade its food safety capacity in line with GlobalGAP.[73]

Further, some empirical studies show that through increased attention to the spread and adoption of good practices in the supply of products to export markets, there may be spillover effects into the domestic market, including better wages and employment opportunities in the agro-industry, to the benefit of the local population and domestic producers. Thus, the associated costs of compliance with private standards may be at least partially offset by an array of benefits, both foreseen and unforeseen, from this enhancement of private standards.[74]

It must be highlighted that since existing empirical studies have applied different theoretical approaches and diverse methodologies to very different commodities and geographic contexts, great caution has to be taken when drawing any macro-level conclusions.[75] The point here is only that there is evidence supporting the argument that private standards do indeed result in a positive

[70] International Trade Centre, 'The Impact of Private Standards on Producers in Developing Countries: Literature Review Series on the Impacts of Private Standards – Part II' (2011) 23– 24.

[71] C Dolan and J Humphrey, 'Governance and Trade in Fresh Vegetables: The Impact of UK Supermarkets on the African Horticulture Industry' (2000) 37 (2) *Journal of Development Studies* 169.

[72] S Jaffee and S Henson, 'Standards and Agri- food Exports from Developing Countries: Rebalancing the Debate' (2004) World Bank Policy Research Working Paper No 3348, 37–38.

[73] S Jaffee, 'From Challenges to Opportunities: Transforming Kenya's Fresh Vegetables Trade in the Context of Emerging Food Safety and Other Standards in Europe' (2003) World Bank Agriculture and Rural Development Discussion Paper No 2, 59.

[74] Maertens and Swinnen (n 11) 153–169.

[75] N Grijp, T Marsden and J Cavalcanti, "European Retailers as Agents of Change towards Sustainability: The Case of Fruit Protection in Brazil' (2005) 2 (4) *Environmental Sciences* 445–460.

social, economic and environmental impact and a better livelihood for producers and their surrounding community. Therefore, observing the issue merely from a trade and development perspective may lead to an incomplete conclusion about the costs and benefits of private standards as a mode of governance.[76]

## III. PRIVATE STANDARDS IN THE UNITED STATES, EUROPEAN UNION AND CHINA: A COMPARATIVE ANALYSIS

### A. The Standardisation System in the United States

Voluntary consensus standards serve as the cornerstone of the US standardisation system and foundation of the US economy. While most other countries adhere to a 'top-down' approach to standardisation where the government serves as the standards setter or mandates what standards will be developed, the US standardisation system is characterised by its high degree of decentralisation.[77] The US standardisation community is comprised of hundreds of non-governmental standards developing organisations (SDOs) that are based on industrial sectors.[78] This voluntary fragmented standardisation system is strongly driven by market demand in the sense that standards are created in response to specific concerns and needs expressed by industry, government and consumers. This unique structure reflects a strong cultural and political bias that society will benefit and innovation and creativity will flourish in a system that is in favour of market solutions.[79]

The American National Standards Institute (ANSI) is a private, not-for-profit organisation responsible for coordinating the US voluntary standardisation and conformity assessment system. It receives negligible financial support from the government and funding from companies, organisations, sale of publications and membership fees account for the most part of ANSI revenue. It does not develop standards itself, limiting itself to accrediting SDOs and approving their standards as American National Standards (ANS). The accreditation is open to any SDO whose procedures meet the requirements for due process and criteria for approval and withdrawal of ANS, as described in the *ANSI Essential Requirements: Due Process Requirements for American National Standards*. By August 2019, the ANSI has accredited 240 SDOs and approved 13136 American national standards.[80] The ANSI serves as the US member of international

[76] CF Lin, 'Public-Private Interaction in Global Food Safety Governance' (2014) 69 (2) *Food and Drug Law Journal* 159.

[77] H Schepel, *The Constitution of Private Governance: Product Standards in the Regulation of Integrating Markets* (Hart Publishing, 2005) 145.

[78] ANSI, *Overview of the U.S. Standardization System* 3rd edn (2010) 4–5.

[79] S Krislov, *How Nations Choose Standards and How Standards Change Nations* (University of Pittsburg Press, 1997) 114.

[80] ANSI, '2018–2019 Annual Report: Expanding to New Horizons' (31 August 2019) 30.

standards bodies such as the ISO and IEC, and co-ordinates American participation in international technical committees. But the US standardisation system remains characterised by contestation and fragmentation. The status of the ANSI has not been fully accepted by major players in the American standards community and a few key organisations keep acting independently of the ANSI.[81]

Whatever the specific mechanism used by varieties of accredited SDOs for the development of ANS, the ANSI requires that they must adhere to a set of essential due process requirements. First, participation shall be open to all persons who are directly and materially affected by the activity in question and there shall be no undue financial barriers to participation. Voting membership on the consensus body shall not be conditional upon membership in any organisation, nor unreasonably restricted on the basis of technical qualifications or other such requirements. Second, standards development should be transparent. Notification of standards activity shall be announced in suitable media as appropriate. Written procedures shall govern the methods used for standards development and shall be available to any interested person. Third, the standards development process should have a balance of interests from at least producer, user (including consumer, industrial user, government and labour) and general interest, and shall not be dominated by any single interest category, individual or organisation. Fourth, standards are to be adopted by consensus. Prompt consideration shall be given to the written views and objections of all participants. Fifth, good faith efforts shall be made to resolve potential conflicts between and among existing ANS and candidate ANS. Sixth, an identifiable, realistic and readily available appeals mechanism for the impartial handling of procedural appeals should be instituted.[82] As a result of, American national standards tend to arise from an open process, a vigorous discussion of all viewpoints, and agreement among a diverse range of stakeholders representing the viewpoints of industry, consumer and labour organisations, and government agencies.

These characteristics of ANS developed by SDOs distinguish them from other private standards such as some consortia standards, de facto standards or private retail standards.[83] Consortia standards are often developed by a group of companies in areas of rapidly developing technologies. They are usually developed under an accelerated timeframe, and participation in the development process may be limited to members of consortia and tied to a substantial financial contribution. De facto standards are developed outside the traditional framework and appeal to a more narrow market than standards written by SDOs. These standards do not feature the broad and open participation, due

[81] T Buthe and W Mattli, *The new Global Rulers: The Privatization of Regulation in the World Economy* (Princeton University Press, 2011) 150–151.

[82] ANSI, 'ANSI Essential Requirements: Due Process Requirements for American National Standards' (January 2019) 4–10.

[83] ANSI, 'European Questions about the U.S. Standardization System' (July 2018) 5.

process or consensus-based approval.[84] Private retail standards refer to standards internal to the company and might simply reflect product and process specifications required of suppliers or requirements for certification to any independent third-party certification scheme. These categories of private standards are developed without following the rigorous procedures stipulated by the ANSI. Consequently, they cannot be approved as ANSI, nor can they be recognised as international standards.

According to Article 4.1 of the TBT Agreement, the US is obliged to take such reasonable measures as may be available to it to ensure that non-governmental standardising bodies within their territories accept and comply with the CGP. The ANSI and ANSI-accredited SDOs clearly fall within the definition of 'non-governmental standardising bodies'. The ANSI accepted the CGP in 1997. The updated United States Standards Strategy in 2015 published under the ANSI auspices highlights the trade implications of standards and emphasises the US commitment to WTO-endorsed principles for standards development as reflected in the WTO TBT Agreement and the Decision on Principles for the Development of International Standards adopted by the WTO TBT Committee. In addition, the US is committed to processes that are flexible, timely and balanced.[85] Though ANSI-accredited SDOs have not accepted the CGP up to date and it is not clear what 'reasonable measures' the US government may take to ensure they accept and comply with the CGP, one may argue that the WTO principles are reflected in the *ANSI Essential Requirements: Due Process Requirements for American National Standards* that SDOs must meet in order to be accredited by the ANSI.

The decentralised, flexible, sector-based, and market-driven US standards system is undeniably extremely responsive to changing US domestic market demands.[86] However, the shift of standard making to the international level may question the effectiveness of this fragmented system in representing the US interests in international standardising organisations such as the ISO. The ISO is best described as a centrally coordinated global network comprising hundreds of technical committees spread all over the world, involving tens of thousands of experts representing industry and other groups. The decentralised nature of ISO standard setting suggests that early and direct involvement in the right working groups and technical committees is crucial for stakeholders to influence the content of international standards. However, effective participation at the international level requires not only that stakeholders receive early and good information, but also effective domestic mechanisms enabling domestic standards bodies to speak with a single national voice. In this respect, the institutional complementarity between the fragmented US domestic system featured by multiple competing SDOs and the ISO is low. The institutional

[84] ANSI (n 78) 6.
[85] ANSI, *United States Standards Strategy* (2 December, 2015) 7.
[86] ANSI (n 78) 10.

fragmentation in the US impedes efficient information flows between domestic SDOs and makes the aggregation of technical preferences at the national level more difficult. Consequently, it is alleged that the US standardisation system may be at a disadvantage in positioning their domestic firms for exerting influence in global standard-setting.[87]

## B. The European System of Standardisation

In contrast to the American standardisation system, the European standardisation system is hierarchical, centralised, closely tied to the public authorities, and relatively well endowed with resources. What is more, standards systems are converging towards what could be termed a 'European Model' featuring centralised private associations enjoying public recognition and monopoly power, elaborating and promulgating standards according to a rather homogenous set of procedures built on the core principles of consensus, openness, and transparency.[88]

At the national level, most European countries have one recognised central national standard-setting body that adopts technical specifications and represents national interest at the regional and international levels, such as the British Standards Institution (BSI), the German Institute for Standardization (DIN) and the Swedish Standards Institute (SIS). The national standards bodies may be either public or private sector organisations or combinations of the two.[89] They not only enjoy a monopoly in the mobilisation and coordination of national interests at the domestic level, but also establish close relationships with national governments either by regulation or contract. In recognition of the public policy interest in standardisation, they receive part of their funding from the government, but are also required to involve representatives of a broad range of societal interests and to comply with comprehensive rules on public enquiries and publication.[90]

The non-binding nature of standards does not bar the application of Article 28 EC, which prohibits 'quantitative restrictions on imports and all measures having equivalent effect', as even non-binding standards may effectively close off markets to those products which do not comply with them.[91] However, the European Court of Justice has consistently held that Article 28 concerns only 'public measures and not the conduct of undertakings'.[92] As a

[87] Buthe and Mattli (n 81) 147.
[88] Schepel (n 77) 145.
[89] F Cafaggi, Scuola Nazionale Dell'Amministrazione and HMW Elgar (eds), *The Regulatory Function of European Private Law* (Edward Elgar, 2009) 37.
[90] Buthe and Walter Mattli (n 81) 154.
[91] Case 325/00 *Commission v Germany* [1982] ECR I-9977, para 24.
[92] Case 311/85 *Vlaamse Reisbureaus* [1987] ECR3801, para 30.

result national standards emanating from private standards bodies may escape the reach of Article 28 in EU law. The EU legislators then sought to eliminate obstacles created by divergent national standards by encouraging the drafting and use of European standards.

European standardisation has played an enabling role in European integration. The traditional approach to technical harmonisation in the EU consisted of a programmed patchwork of Directives establishing product-by-product and hazard-by-hazard regulation. This approach was extremely time-consuming. It was hard to find consensus on sensitive issues of health and safety regulations and the Directives contained complicated technical details and specifications. Consequently, it frequently took so long to adopt that these regulations were outdated long before they actually came into force.[93] In 1985, the 'new approach' to technical harmonisation was introduced in which harmonisation legislation was limited to 'essential requirements' with which products placed on the market must conform. Voluntary technical standards that provide solutions for compliance with the essential requirements are to be developed by the recognised European standards organisations (ESOs). Products manufactured in conformity to these harmonised standards are presumed to comply with the essential requirements and certified products can circulate freely throughout the internal market.[94] However, compliance with the harmonised standards remains voluntary and it is possible for product manufacturers to demonstrate compliance with the legislative requirements by other means. Once adopted, European standards would become national standards and existing national standards inconsistent with the European standards would have to be withdrawn.[95] The most obvious consequence of the rapid development of European standardisation is the decrease in importance of national standardisation.[96]

The new approach has effectively given ESOs a monopoly in European standards work. Article 2 of Regulation (EU) 1025/2012 recognises the European Committee for Standardization (CEN), the European Committee for Electrotechnical Standardization (CENELEC), and the European Telecommunication Standards Institute (ETSI) as ESOs. The CEN is responsible for standardisation activities in all fields, except for electrotechnology standards, which are developed by the CENELEC and telecommunication standards, which are developed by the ETSI. The CEN and CENELEC are private 'intergovernmental' associations of 34 national standards bodies of EU Member States, the

[93] R van Gestel and HW Micklitz, 'European Integration through Harmonization: How Judicial Review is Breaking down the Club House of Private Standardization Bodies' (2013) 50 *Common Market Law Review* 145 (2013) 156.

[94] Council Resolution of 7 May 1985 on a new approach to technical harmonization and standards [1985] OJ C136/1.

[95] CEN, 'European Standardization', www.cen.eu/you/europeanstandardization/pages/default.aspx accessed on 20 April 2020.

[96] R Schutze, *European Union Law* (Cambridge University Press, 2018) 549.

same domestic level standards bodies that represent European countries in the ISO and IEC. In the case of the ETSI, industry and other stakeholders are the direct members.[97]

European standards are developed through a process of collaboration between experts nominated by business and industry, research institutes, consumer and environmental organisations and other stakeholders.[98] The Commission subsidises the work of ESOs and regularly requests the ESOs to develop European standards for products and services to support the EU legislation and policies.[99] A standardisation request sets requirements for harmonised standards and the requirements must be adhered to during the drafting process. In this respect, ESOs may be considered as semi-private bodies, tied to industry but still co-operating closely with the EU institutions. The ESOs can also develop standards at the initiative of the industry users. Non-mandated standards constitute more than 70 per cent of ESOs' work.[100]

One distinguishing feature of the EU standardisation system is the close cooperation between ESOs and international standardisation bodies such as the ISO. For example, as soon as the CEN Technical Board established the need for a new work item, the CEN is bound by the so-called Vienna agreement of 1991 with the ISO to consider existing ISO standards or working drafts, or, if no such document is available, to offer the work to the ISO to develop, with a given time, a standard that is mutually acceptable.[101] Compared to the decentralised and uncoordinated standards system in the US, the hierarchical European standards system has strong institutionalised lines of communication between the different levels of the hierarchy and are geared towards preference aggregation since they exist to produce a single set of standards. As a result, the organisational structure of the European standardisation system may be more effective in representing the European firms' interest in international standardising organisations.[102]

## C. The Chinese System of Standardisation

The Chinese standardisation system has undergone profound transformations over the past 30 years. Prior to the 2017 amendment of the Standardisation Law,

[97] European Commission, *Independent Review of the European Standardization System Final Report* (March 2015) 6.

[98] CEN, CENELEC and EFSI, 'Questions and Answers Regarding the European Standardization System' (July 2019).

[99] Art 22 of Regulation (EU) 1025/2012 of the European Parliament and of the Council of 25 October 2012 on European Standardization.

[100] P Delimatsis, 'Standardization in Services- European Ambitions and Sectoral Realities' (2016) 41(4) *European Law Review* 513, 523.

[101] ISO/CEN, 'Guidelines for the Implementation of the Agreement on Technical Cooperation between ISO and CEN' (the Vienna Agreement) 7th edn (2016).

[102] Buthe and Walter Mattli (n 81) 160.

which was originally adopted in 1988, it was a top-down, government-led standardisation system, which was formed during the planned economy period and deeply rooted in the Chinese tradition and culture.[103] Under Article 5 of the 1988 Standardisation Law, the government, specifically the central government, played a leading role with the Standardization Administration of China ('SAC'), a body under the State Council responsible for the unified administration of standardisation. The SAC authorises its subordinate technical committees to set standards for different fields. Relevant bodies under different governmental ministries and provincial government were also assigned responsibility for standardisation within their various jurisdictions, whether industrial or geographic. Trade associations and scientific research institutions should be involved in the formulation of standards but their role was largely consultative. Article 12 also mandated that a governmental department engaged in the formulation of a standard shall organise a committee on standardisation and the committee was responsible for drafting and examining the standard. These articles codified the government leadership in standardisation.[104]

Article 6 of the 1988 Standardisation Law recognised four types of technology standard: national standard, industry standard adopted by industrial ministries, regional standard adopted by government at provincial level and enterprise standard. The adoption of a national standard would supersede any overlapping industry standard and similarly, once adopted, an industry standard would override an existing duplicate regional standard. Enterprise standards may be developed where no national standard or ministerial standard exists. Enterprises were also encouraged to set standards more stringent than national or ministerial standards if they exist. Standards could be either mandatory or voluntary. Those standards for safeguarding human health and ensuring personal and property safety and those standards for compulsory implementation as prescribed by law or administrative regulations shall be mandatory, and others shall be voluntary.[105] Therefore, national, industry and local standards could be classified as either mandatory or voluntary, and enterprise standards only as voluntary standards.[106]

The government-led standardisation system played a positive role at the preliminary stage of Chinese economic reform. In particular, standardization

[103] P Wang and Z Liang, 'Beyond Government Control of China's Standardization System- History, Current Status and Reform Suggestions' in D Ernst and MG Plummer (eds), *Megaregionalism 2.0- Trade and Innovation within Global Networks* 311 (World Scientific, 2018) 312–313.

[104] D Breznitz and M Murphree, 'The Rise of China in Technology Standards: New Norms in Old Institutions', Research Report Prepared on Behalf of the U.S. – China Economic and Security Review Commission (January 16, 2013) 15–17.

[105] Art 7 of 1988 Standardization Law.

[106] Studio Legal Stefanelli and Stefanelli, 'New China's Standardization Law: An Overdue Reform' (30 January 2018) www.lexology.com/library/detail.aspx?g=dc14088b-9061-48d6-9ee4-0be8bd610e3dAccessed 1 March 2020.

became an effective channel for advanced western technology to be transferred to China rapidly. For example, as an important component of China's technology catching-up strategy, the former State Bureau of Technical Supervision began to promote a 'dual-adoption' policy in standardisation. International standards (such as ISO, IEC and ITU standards) and foreign advanced standards (such as IEEE and DIN standards) should be adopted when preparing Chinese national and industry standards.[107] This policy has given full play to the technology diffusion function of standard.

Though the top-down standardisation system was instrumental for China to capture the technology spillover effect in the course of international trade, it was plagued with some weaknesses that had to change as China's economy became more internationally integrated. First, the Chinese standardisation system was characterised by institutional fragmentation and multiple decision-making bodies. While the Ministry of Industry and Information Technology and the Ministry of Science and Technology remain the most active ministries in standardisation, standards organisations under other ministries, local governments and industry may adopt competing standards. The lack of coordination led to a confused standardisation environment.[108] In electric vehicles, for example, different local governments have established their own regional standards for charging stations, thus making equipment from different regions incompatible.[109] Second, the strong role for the Chinese Government in standard setting has the benefit of marshaling resources and directing industry to invest in standards development. At the same time it requires intimate familiarity with technology and technology trends in order to start standard setting processes when opportunities present themselves. This is a difficult process and government leadership is generally considered inferior to industry leadership.[110]

Third, due to the weaknesses in China's innovation capability, many of China's leading indigenous standards relied heavily on foreign core technology. Thus China must deal with the tradeoff between timely accession to advanced technology by operating within the bounds of established foreign technical standards and continued technological dependence and vulnerability to high licensing fees since foreign technology remains at the core of the standards.[111] Finally, the 1989 Standardisation Law was obsolete after 30 years of economic

[107] Wang and Liang (n 103) 315.

[108] M Murphree, 'The China Standards Engine', 12 (2) *China Currents* (2013), www.chinacenter.net/2014/china_currents/12-2/the-china-standards-engine/ accessed 1 March 2020.

[109] S Weithmann, *The Evolvement of Standards in China: Insights from the Electric Vehicle Sector* (Nomos, 2017) 220–236.

[110] JL Funk and DT Methe, 'Market and Community-Based Mechanism in the Creation and Diffusion of Global Industry Standards: The Case of Mobile Communication' (2001) 30(4) *Research Policy* 589, 610.

[111] D Ernst, 'Indigenous Innovation and Globalization: The Challenge for China's Standardization Strategy', UC Institute on Global Conflict and Cooperation and the East West Centre (2011) 21.

reforms. At the time when the law was adopted, there were only health and safety standards. Technology standards such as IEEE or IEC standards for interoperability were not widely discussed and many issues in modern technology standardisation, such as intellectual property or the means by which it could be incorporated into technology standards, were not even envisioned by the legislators.[112]

On January 1, 2018, the amended Standardisation Law of the People's Republic of China has come into force. The new law modernises and reforms the previous standardisation system established by the 1988 Standardisation Law. As part of a comprehensive market-oriented reform, the standardisation reform in China essentially involves reducing government involvement and enhancing the role of the market in standard setting. The most striking highlight of the reform scheme lies in its clear provisions for reducing the number of government-set mandatory standards and fostering the development of market-driven voluntary standards by non-governmental organisations.[113]

First, the new Standardisation Law has drastically reduced the scope of mandatory standards (technical regulations in the WTO terminology). Only national standards issued by the SAC and more specifically, only those providing technical requirements concerning safeguarding human health, life and property safety, national security, eco-environment security, and satisfying the basic needs of social and economic administration, can now be mandatory.[114] National standards may also be voluntary, namely GB/T standards, in contrast to mandatory GB national standards. Industry and local standards can no longer be mandatory and they must be voluntary now. All voluntary standards (national, industry, local, association and enterprise) also must provide for technical requirements not lower than those required by mandatory national standards.[115] To encourage the adoption of enterprise standards, the law eliminates the requirements that they must be filed with the standardisation administration and a self-disclosure system of the standards on a dedicated online platform was established.

Second, in order to promote market-driven standards, the law gives legal status to 'association standards' adopted by lawfully established social groups, such as academies, associations, chambers of commerce, federations and industry technology alliances. Association standards do not require governmental approval but their formulation is subject to the regulation, guidance and supervision of the SAC and relevant state council department.[116]

[112] Breznitz and Murphree (n 104) 19.

[113] L Hui and CF Cargill, 'Setting Standards for Industry: Comparing the Emerging Chinese Standardization System and the Current US System', *East-West Centre Policy Studies* 75 (2017) 2–3.

[114] Art 10 of 2018 Standardisation Law.

[115] Ibid, Art 21.

[116] Ibid, Art 18.

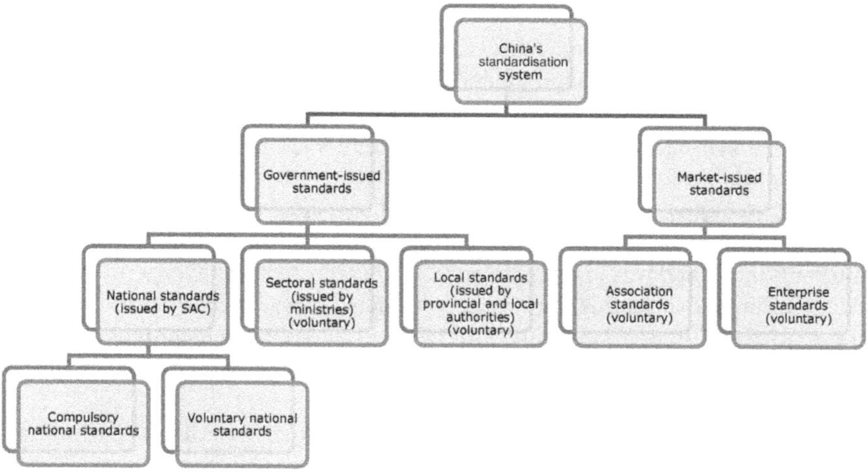


(*Source*: Fagersten and Ruhlig (2019))

Consequently, China has shifted from the previous model of government leading the development of standards to a module of coexistence of both governmental and non-governmental standards. However, there are very few private standardisation organisations in China. The vast majority of associations registered in the information platform for national association standards are government-backed. These organisations are associated with, or to a certain extent, products of government reform and dependent on government support. Their main resources are provided by government agencies and they sometimes adopt an administrative, top-down bureaucracy simulating the government. Therefore even market approaches to standardisation often include significant state support and influence. China still lacks the equivalent to the multitude of consortia composed of large enterprises that are found in the US.[117]

Though China has achieved rapid economic growth over the past 40 years, its low-wage, capital-intensive, and export-oriented strategies using China as a final assembly platform are providing diminishing returns. Operating at the lowest value-added level in many industries, the overall contribution of Chinese firms to the wholesale price of products is usually only a few percentage points. For example, the value of work performed by the Chinese workers accounts for just 3.6 per cent of the total price of the iPhone, whilst the highest value components, chips and software are designed and manufactured overseas and imported by Chinese assemblers.[118] It is therefore imperative for Chinese firms to move up the value chain and become more innovative.[119] However, moving up from the low value-added position is difficult as the technologies being used

[117] Hui and Cargill (n 113) 23.
[118] A Batson, 'Not Really 'Made in China', *Wall Street Journal* (December 15, 2010).
[119] The World Bank & China Development Research Centre of the State Council, *China 2030: Building a Modern, Harmonious, and Creative Society* (2013) 34.

in global production networks are subject to established and clearly defined technology standards. Standards define the basic features of products in international trade and they usually incorporate standards essential patents (SEPs). US and European firms frequently seek to maximise their returns from SEPs by setting licensing fees as high as possible, subject to the reasonable and non-discriminatory principle (RAND). Alternatively, firms with major SEPs enter into technology-sharing agreements with other major SEP contributors, lowering mutual licensing fees.[120] Having not contributed to the development of major international standards in many sectors, Chinese firms must accept internationally determined standards for various products, license technology to produce standards-compliant goods while also being excluded from technology-sharing agreements. These licence payments reduce the already low profits for Chinese manufacturers.[121]

In response to this dilemma, the Chinese Government has identified the development of new technology standards as an innovation strategy to help Chinese firms to move up the value chain and become independently innovative. As Premier Li Keqiang remarked: 'standardization is a reflection of a country's core competitiveness and overall strength'.[122] China's new standards development strategy includes the integration of standards development into China's broader industrial policy goals, China's active participation in the making of international standards, and China's efforts to internationalise Chinese standards through the belt and road initiative.[123] China's ultimate ambition is to transform its domestic industries from 'standards takers' to 'standards makers'.[124]

To begin with, a defining characteristic of China's standardisation strategy is to use standardisation for 'indigenous innovation'. As the guiding principle for national scientific and technological development, indigenous innovation involves a dual-track strategy of encouraging Chinese firms to file more patents and propose more domestic and international standards. An important objective of indigenous innovation is to use homegrown standards to develop innovative national champions and to protect domestic industry.[125] Second, in conjunction with its efforts to use standards as a mechanism for reforming its domestic industrial policy, China has been actively participating in the international standards development process as well as pursuing leadership roles in international

[120] D Ernst, 'China's Standard-Essential Patents Challenge: From Latecomer to (Almost) Equal Player?', Centre for International Governance Innovation special report (2017) 22–26.

[121] Murphree (n 108).

[122] 'Premier Li Keqiang calls for improvements in standardization', State Council of the People's Republic of China (September 14, 2016).

[123] M Sutherland, 'CSR 2019: Setting a New Standard: Implications of China's Emerging Standardization Strategy', *The SIAS China Studies Review* (October 29, 2019).

[124] D Ernst, 'Indigenous Innovation and Globalization: The Challenge for China's Standardization Strategy', UC Institute on Global Conflict and Cooperation and the East West Centre (2011) 21.

[125] DCK Chow, 'China's Indigenous Innovation Policies and the World Trade Organization' (2013) 34(1) *Northwestern Journal of International Law & Business* 81, 88–90.

standardising organisations. For example, China is a participating member in 730 ISO technical committees, compared to Germany's membership in 724 technical committees, which is widely considered to be the ISO's most active western country. China has been given more and more leadership positions on councils, technical management boards, technical committees, sub-committees and working groups in the leading international standardisation institutions such as the ISO, the IEC and ITU.[126] Chinese technology companies have been actively shaping and leading international standards setting in international standardisation bodies in areas such as artificial intelligence, facial recognition, video monitoring, and city and vehicle surveillance.[127] The purpose of China's active participation in international standardising bodies is incorporating Chinese technology into global standards in order to strengthen its bargaining power and reduce its payment of high licence fees, while at the same time promoting its own new international standards in an effort to change the international standards system over time.[128] Third, and more recently, China's belt and road initiative is seen by the Chinese policymakers to export Chinese standards to other countries and enhance Chinese standards' influence overseas.[129]

As China's standardisation reform is an integral component of China's broader industrial policy, there are growing concerns that the development and adoption of unique Chinese standards may pose a significant challenge to TBT Agreement, including the CGP. In particular, the 2018 amendment of the Standardization Law did not incorporate China's WTO TBT obligations, nor did it mandate fair and open participation in standards development activities for foreign stakeholders. To begin with, China's attitude towards international standard has changed from active adoption to increased participation in the development of international standards, adoption of international standards 'in light of actual conditions in China', and the promotion of conversion between Chinese and foreign standards.[130] The absence of any provision in the new law to give preference to international standards and instead striving to promote the application of Chinese standards abroad may result in the adoption of unique Chinese standards which are at adds with relevant international standards. In its 2018 report to congress on China's WTO compliance, for example, the Office of the United States Trade Representative (USTR) noted that China seems to be actively pursing the development of unique technical standards in autos, telecommunication equipment, Internet protocols, wireless local area networks, software encryption, mobile batteries and data security, despite the existence

[126] B Fagersten and T Ruhlig, 'China's Standard Power and its Geopolitical Implications', *The Swedish Institute of International Affairs Policy Brief* 2/2019, at 9–13.

[127] A Gross, 'Chinese Tech Groups Shaping UN Facial Recognition Standards', *Financial Times* (1 December 2019).

[128] Ernst (n 124) 20–21.

[129] 'Action Plan on Belt and Road Standard Connectivity' (2018–2020), www.scio.gov.cn/xwfbh/xwbfbh/wqfbh/37601/39274/xgzc39280/Document/1641459/1641459.htm Accessed 1 March 2020.

[130] Art 8 of 2018 Standardization Law.

of well-established international standards, as a means of protecting domestic companies from competing foreign standards and technologies.[131] The misalignment of Chinese standards with international standards has the potential to create significant barriers for foreign producers to enter into China's market, and raises issues with their consistency with the TBT Agreement. Moreover, the TBT Agreement requires that standards should be developed and applied transparently and on a non-discriminatory basis by WTO Members. Despite the Standardization Law's emphasis on open, transparent and fair standard setting process, foreign business appears to be afforded minimal opportunity to provide input into the setting of Chinese standards. The European Chamber concluded that: 'although there has been some improvement, foreign-invested enterprises and their joint ventures (JVs) are sometimes only granted observer status in Technical Committees (TCs), or even excluded from membership altogether'.[132]

## IV. THE STATUS OF PRIVATE STANDARDS UNDER WTO LAW

### A. Possible Attribution of Private or Hybrid Standards to Government

Since the WTO is an international treaty, only actions (or omissions) by WTO Members can be challenged in the WTO dispute settlement system. Nevertheless, it is well established in WTO jurisprudence that private actions may be attributable to a WTO Member because of some governmental connections to or endorsement of those actions.[133] If a private standard is deemed to be a governmental (public) standard, then the WTO Member will be fully responsible for its compliance with the WTO disciplines. In *Japan – Film*, the panel commented:

> ... the fact that an action is taken by private parties does not rule out the possibility that it may be deemed to be governmental *if there is sufficient government involvement with it*. It is difficult to establish bright-line rules in this regard, however. Thus, that possibility will need to be examined on a case-by-case basis.[134]

The main function of the rule is to prevent a WTO Member from circumventing WTO disciplines by instructing or simply allowing private entities to carry out activities that are normally prohibited.[135] As noted by the WTO Secretariat,

[131] USTR, *2018 USTR Report to Congress on China's WTO Compliance* (February 2019) 84.

[132] European Chamber of Commerce in China, 'China Manufacturing 2025: Putting Industrial Policy ahead of Market Forces' (2017) 58.

[133] WTO Panel Report, *Japan – Measures Affecting Consumer Photographic Film and Paper*, WT/DS44/R (22 April 1998) para 10.52; WTO Appellate Body Report, *United States – Sunset Review of Anti-Dumping Duties on Corrosion-Resistant Carbon Steel Flat Products from Japan*, WT/DS244/AB/R (9 January 2004) para 81.

[134] Ibid, para 10.56.

[135] SM Villalpando, 'Attribution of Conduct to the State: How the Rules of State Responsibility May be Applied within the WTO Dispute Settlement System' (2002) 5 (2) *Journal of International Economic Law* 408.

possible examples include where a government authority decides to incorporate a standard developed by a private body into its SPS regulation or a government permits the entry of imports that are certified to comply with a private standard that incorporates or even exceeds the official SPS requirements.[136]

Precisely under what circumstances will a private conduct trigger the application of WTO rules and render a WTO Member liable to its trading partners? In *Japan – Semiconductors*, a GATT panel held that two criteria are critical to the attribution analysis: whether there are reasonable grounds to believe that sufficient incentives or disincentives by the government exist for the measures to take effect; and whether the operation of the measures is essentially dependent on government action or intervention.[137] The first inquiry can be understood as a refined version of the effectiveness test first outlined in *Japan – Agricultural Restrictions* in which the panel held that if some degree of governmental involvement is present in private actions, the fundamental concern is to evaluate whether private measures are as effective as legally binding ones.[138] Arguably, the effectiveness can be discerned from an examination of the incentives or disincentives associated with the compliance with a private measure.[139] In addition, societal structure, cultural expectations and other circumstances which help shape incentives or disincentives in a particular society play an important role when evaluating the effectiveness of a private measure. For instance, given the deferential disposition of the private sector to the wishes of governmental authorities in Japan, the panel in *Japan – Agricultural Restrictions* found that the measures at issue proved as effective as legally mandatory directives.[140]

The second inquiry focuses on the level of government involvement in the private action. The panel in *Japan – Film* required *sufficient* government involvement to render a private action as a governmental action. However, it remains unclear how 'sufficient' ought to be determined in practice. The panel held in *Japan – Film* that the conditions were met when it found that the Japanese Government collaborated with the photographic film and paper industry in formulating the practices at issue, and then endorsed such practices once developed.[141] The panel also stated that it would be insufficient to merely prove the government provision of some organisational assistance, including the provision of initial start-up funds, or a simple government expression of hope that a private measure be respected and observed by those to whom it was to be applicable.[142] From the

[136] WTO Secretariat (n 3) para 17.

[137] GATT Panel Report, *Japan – Trade in Semiconductors*, GATT Doc. L/6309, 35th Supp. BISD 116 (4 May 1988) para 109.

[138] GATT Panel Report, *Japan – Restrictions on Imports of Certain Agricultural Products*, GATT Doc. L/6253, 35th Supp. BISD 163 (18 November 1987) para 5.4.1.4.

[139] Zadalis (n 7) 341.

[140] GATT Panel Report, *Japan – Agricultural Restrictions* (n 138) para 5.4.1.1.

[141] WTO Panel Report, *Japan – Film* (n 133) paras 10.176–10.180.

[142] Ibid, paras 10.190–10.194.

panel's approach in *Japan – Film*, in order to render an otherwise private standard governmental in nature, it appears essential for the government to play a role in developing and then providing its stamp of approval on the standard under scrutiny, or for there to be evidence of some other kind of involvement showing an actual contribution to the creation of the standard accompanied by supporting expressions which demonstrate it is government-sanctioned.[143]

Other than the general attribution principle articulated in the GATT/WTO jurisprudence, the SPS Agreement and the TBT Agreement contain more specific provisions addressing standards developed and implemented by non-governmental entities. The next two parts of this chapter will explore the applicability of these provisions to private standards.

## B. Private Standards in the SPS Agreement

### *i. Do Private Standards Fall within the Scope of the SPS Agreement?*

As discussed above, the traditional view holds that private standards that have no governmental involvement fall outside the regulatory scope of the SPS Agreement. Indeed, most provisions of the SPS Agreement, including the preamble and the basic rights and obligations in Article 2, explicitly refer to the rights and obligations of WTO Members, which suggests that the SPS Agreement deals exclusively with the actions of WTO Members. Moreover, in *EC – Biotech Products*, the panel held that the form of an SPS measure can only be 'laws, decrees or regulations', ie governmental acts.[144]

As some WTO Members pointed out, the major difficulty with the traditional position is that it is not unambiguously supported by a textual reading of the relevant SPS provisions.[145] Article 1.1 provides that the SPS Agreement applies to all SPS measures 'directly or indirectly affecting international trade' without explicitly limiting its application to governmental SPS measures.[146] Likewise, both the definition and the illustrative list of SPS measures stipulated in Annex A(1) do not seem to exclude measures imposed by private entities. Finally, it is not clear on what basis the panel in *EC – Biotech Products* considered that an SPS measure could only take the form of a governmental act. A textual reading of the second paragraph of Annex A(1) does not lead to a distinction between the form element and the nature element as the panel did in its ruling.[147]

[143] Zadalis (n 7) 346.

[144] WTO Panel Report, *European Communities – Measures Affecting the Approval and Marketing of Biotech Products (EC – Biotech)*, WT/DS291/R (21 November 2006) para 7.149.

[145] Note by the Secretariat, 'Summary of the SPS Committee Meeting of 30 June – 1 July 2016', G/SPS/R/83 (9 August 2016), Para 13.7.

[146] WTO Secretariat (n 3) para 15.

[147] A Arcuri, 'The TBT Agreement and Private Standards' in T Epps and MJ Trebilcock (eds), *Research Handbook on the WTO and Technical Barriers to Trade* (Edward Elgar, 2013) 516.

However, there is some circumstantial evidence which supports the traditional position. First, Annex A(1) refers to SPS measures as 'all relevant laws, decrees, regulations, requirements and procedures'. Though there is no relevant case law under the SPS Agreement, all past GATT/WTO panel reports interpreted these terms, including the term 'requirement', under Article III:4 of the GATT, as demanding some degree of government involvement.[148] Second, the emergence of private standards largely postdates the negotiation of SPS Agreements in the 1980s. Thus, the trade law issues related to private standards were simply unforeseen by the drafters of the SPS Agreement.[149] Lastly, the regulatory scope of the SPS Agreement should also be considered in light of its objective and purpose. If the objective of the SPS Agreement is understood as to achieve a balance between the sovereign right of WTO Members to protect health and safety in their territories and the need to prevent protectionism under the guise of SPS regulation, then the application of the SPS disciplines to private standards would not seem to further this objective as there is no evidence that private standards are motivated by protectionism. Their actions may raise concerns under competition law but the SPS Agreement is not designed to address such a problem.[150] On the other hand, if we understand the objective of the SPS Agreement as to eliminate all unnecessary barriers to trade, then a strong argument may be made that private standards fall within the ambit of the SPS Agreement. However, it is frequently argued that this is not the objective of the SPS Agreement.[151]

### *ii. Article 13 of the SPS Agreement*

A key provision in the SPS Agreement which is directly relevant to private standards is Article 13 which provides:

> Members shall formulate and implement positive measures and mechanisms in support of the observance of … the agreement by *other than central government bodies*. Members shall take such *reasonable measures* as may be available to them to ensure that non-governmental entities within their territories, as well as regional bodies in which relevant entities within their territories are members, comply with the *relevant provisions* of this agreement. In addition, Members shall not take measures which have the effect of, directly or indirectly, requiring or encouraging such regional or non-governmental entities … to act in a manner inconsistent with the provisions of this Agreement.

[148] GATT Analytical Index www.wto.org/english/res_e/booksp_e/gatt_ai_e/art3_e.pdf 173–174.

[149] Submission by the UK, 'Private Voluntary Standards within the WTO Multilateral Framework' (9 October 2007), G/SPS/GEN/802, at 21.

[150] Ibid, 91.

[151] B Rigod, 'The Purpose of the WTO Agreement on the Application of Sanitary and Phytosanitary Measures (SPS)' (2013) 24 (2) *European Journal of International Law* 529–30.

Three questions in Article 13 need to be answered. First, do the terms 'other than central government bodies' and 'non-governmental entities' cover private standards bodies such as retailers and supermarkets? If so, then WTO Members have a legal obligation to take positive or reasonable measures to ensure that they comply with the SPS Agreement. It is therefore irrelevant whether private standards bodies have accepted the SPS Agreement.

With regard to 'other than central government bodies', three types of organisations could potentially be included: regional bodies, non-governmental entities and local government bodies.[152] Given that Article 13 contains a more specific obligation relating directly to non-governmental entities, 'other than central government bodies' should be narrowly interpreted as including only the other two categories. In the *Australia – Salmon* 21.5 panel report, the panel held that sanitary measures taken by the state government of Tasmania, being an 'other than central government' body as recognised by Australia, were subject to the SPS Agreement.[153]

The meaning of 'non-governmental entities' in Article 13 is not defined in the SPS Agreement, nor is there any WTO case law offering much guidance. Some suggest that useful reference might be made to a similar definition contained in its sister TBT Agreement.[154] Annex 1.8 of the TBT Agreement defines 'non-government body' as a '[b]ody other than a central government body or a local government body, *including* a non-governmental body which has legal power to enforce a technical regulation'. One commentator commented:

> Although this definition is rather vague and open-ended, it is possible to argue that, in the light of the context and purpose of the SPS and TBT Agreements, 'non-governmental entities' are not individual economic operators (or their associations) but rather private entities which have been entrusted by government with the performance of certain tasks or which have otherwise a special status as regards the development and implementation of SPS/TBT rules.[155]

This narrow reading of 'non-governmental entity' not only echoes the traditional view that WTO law does not regulate private market behaviours with no governmental interference but also seems to be congruent with the negotiating history of the SPS Agreement. Private standards were quite rare in the 1980s and the WTO negotiators never anticipated the application of the SPS Agreement to private standards during the Uruguay Round.[156] They were more concerned with evasion by WTO Members of the SPS disciplines by developing SPS requirements through independent agencies or regional networks of

[152] Submission by the UK (n 149) 54.

[153] WTO Panel Report, *Australia – Measures Affecting Importation of Salmon – Recourse to Article 21.5 of the DSU by Canada*, WT/DS18/RW (20 March 2000) para 7.13.

[154] Stagiaire (n 43) 34–35; Henson (n 44) 76.

[155] J Pauwelyn, 'Non- Traditional Patterns of Global Regulation: Is the WTO Missing the Boat?' in C Joerges and EU Petersmann (eds), *Constitutionalism, Multilevel Trade Governance and Social Regulation* (Hart Publishing, 2006) 210.

[156] Submission by the UK (n 149) 78.

regulators with government links. Since these agencies and networks operate independently of government in many WTO Members, they may be regarded as non-governmental entities.[157]

This narrow reading of 'non-governmental entities' also dovetails with a systemic and harmonious interpretation of the relationship between Annex A(1) and Article 13 of the SPS Agreement. Arcuri argues that the pre-requisite of the application of Article 13 is that the measures at issue are SPS measures because Article 13 only applies to SPS measures as defined in Annex A (1). If one takes the view that private SPS standards fall outside the scope of the SPS Agreement, then it becomes unnecessary to discuss the application of Article 13 to them.[158] If this reading is correct, then it only makes sense if the scope of 'non-governmental entities' is restricted to those private entities which have been delegated with certain governmental functions.[159]

Nevertheless, a narrow interpretation of 'non-governmental entities' is not well supported by a textual reading of the relevant provisions. It is clear that the use of the word 'including' in Annex 1.8 of the TBT must be taken to mean that the provision only provides an example of what may constitute a 'non-governmental body'. By implication, it acknowledges the existence of non-governmental bodies which do not have the legal power to enforce a product standard. Therefore, it may be argued that 'non-governmental entity' under the SPS Agreement also includes other private bodies that are not trusted by government with certain tasks but which operate or are established within the territories of a Member.[160]

In summary, although the argument that Article 1.1, Annex A(1) and Article 13 only cover governmental and quasi-governmental SPS measures is highly plausible, it is not conclusive. An alternative interpretation could be that Article 13 is independent of Annex A (1) of the SPS Agreement. Whereas Annex Article 1.1 and Annex A(1) *may* refer only to government acts, Article 13 may well extend the obligation of WTO Members to monitor private SPS standards of all non-governmental entities. In *Australia – Salmon*, the panel held that the term 'measure' contained in Article 1.1 SPS must be construed in the light of the obligation contained within Article 13.[161] It could at least be argued that a narrow reading of non-governmental entities is not completely justified by a textual analysis of the SPS Agreement.

[157] S Bernstein and E Hannah, 'Non- state Global Standard Setting and the WTO: Legitimacy and the Need for Regulatory Space' (2008) 11 *Journal of International Economic Law* 578; Prevost (n 8) 19–20.

[158] Arcuri (n 147) 518.

[159] A Herwig, 'The Application of the SPS Agreement to Transnational, Private Food Standards' (2016) 3 *European Journal of Risk Regulation* 610, 615.

[160] D Casey, 'Private Food Safety and Quality Standards and the WTO' (2007) 7 *University College Dublin Law Review* 81–82; SR Gandhi, 'Regulating the Use of Voluntary Environmental Standards within the World Trade Organization's Legal Regime: Making a Case for Developing Countries' (2005) 39 *Journal of World Trade* 867–868.

[161] Art 21.5 Panel Report, *Australia – Salmon* (n 153) para 7.13.

The second question is, assuming that all private standards-setters are non-governmental entities covered by Article 13, what are the 'reasonable measures' that WTO Members are obliged to take? In the first place, it should be noted that this is a best-endeavour obligation rather than an obligation of outcome in the sense that the limits of the obligations a WTO Member bears must take into account various factors which may be Member-specific.[162] For example, such a determination must take into account the legal and constitutional arrangements of a particular WTO Member. What is reasonable for one WTO Member, for example, because the central government has legal authority to coerce private standards-setters, may not be reasonable for another Member that has different legal and constitutional arrangements.[163]

Some suggest that inspiration may be drawn from Article XXIV:12 of the GATT 1994 which imposes a similar obligation on WTO Members to ensure compliance with the GATT by regional and local governments and other authorities within its territories. In *Canada – Gold Coins*, the GATT panel held that the basic principle in determining which measures are reasonable for the purposes of this article is that the consequences of the non-observance of the provisions of the GATT by local government for trade relations with other contracting parties 'are to be weighed against the domestic difficulties of securing compliance'.[164] The GATT panel in *Canada – Alcoholic drinks* further held that, in order to examine whether Canada had demonstrated that it had taken all reasonable measures available, it would have to show that 'it had made *a serious, persistent and convincing effort* to ensure compliance … with the provisions of the GATT Agreement'.[165] It is not clear to what extent the GATT panels' findings on 'reasonable measures' as embodying an onerous positive duty in Article XXIV:12 GATT are relevant in the context of Article 13 of the SPS Agreement. The key difference between these two provisions is clear: while GATT Article XXIV:12 addresses a GATT member's obligation regarding *regional and local governments* which exercise governmental authority, Article 13 deals with non-governmental entities without governmental authority. It may be assumed that, to the extent that the central government authority has constitutional power or influence over a local government body, it would be reasonable to expect it to exercise it. However, a higher level of central government intervention may be inappropriate in the case of non-government entities without government links. Otherwise, it would put private SPS standards in the same position as governmental SPS measures, an outcome which seems to be

[162] J Wouters and D Geraets, 'Private Food Standards and the World Trade Organization: Some Legal Considerations' (2012) 11 (3) *World Trade Review* 486.

[163] Submission by the UK (n 149) 33.

[164] GATT Panel Report, *Canada – Measures Affecting the Sale of Gold Coins*, L/5863 (17 September 1985, unadopted) paras 68–9.

[165] GATT Panel Report, *Canada – Import Distribution and Sale of Alcoholic Drinks by Canadian Provincial Marketing Agencies*, DS17/R (18 February 1992) para 5. 37.

contrary to the requirement of WTO Members, taking only reasonable measures to ensure compliance.[166]

Finally, assuming that private standards are covered by the SPS Agreement and that WTO Members have a positive obligation to ensure that all non-governmental entities comply with the relevant provisions of the SPS Agreement, what are these relevant provisions? For the TBT Agreement, Article 4.1 makes it clear that all recognised non-governmental standardising bodies should follow the Code of Good Practice (CGP). However, there is no corresponding part of the CGP in the SPS Agreement. It may be argued that relevant provisions do not refer to all provisions of the SPS Agreement as this would result in a set of absurd and disproportionate requirements for non-government bodies.[167]

## C. Private Standards in the TBT Agreement

### *i. Are Private Standards Covered by the TBT Agreement?*

The SPS Agreement only applies to SPS measures as defined in Annex A(1). Given that many private standards pursue objectives not covered by the SPS Agreement, such as environmental protection, labour standards and other ethical issues, elements of these standards potentially fall within the TBT Agreement.[168] To apply the TBT Agreement, a threshold question is whether private standards fall within the definition of 'standard'. Annex 1(2) of the TBT Agreement defines 'standard' as:

> Document approved by a recognised body, that provides, for common and repeated use, rules, guidelines or characteristics for products or related process and production methods, with which compliance is not mandatory. It may also include or deal exclusively with terminology, symbols, packaging, marking or labeling requirements as they apply to a product, process or production method.

To meet the definition of 'standard', three elements must be met: first, the standard must be approved by a 'recognised body'; second, it must provide rules, guidelines or characteristics for product or related PPMs; and third, the compliance with a standard is not mandatory. This definition, in particular the last two elements, is discussed in Chapter 2. For private standardisation schemes, the most controversial element is likely to be whether the non-governmental body that approved a private standard is a 'recognised body'.

The term 'body' is defined by reference to the International Organization for Standardization/International Electrotechnical Commission (ISO/IEC) Guide 2 as a 'Legal or administrative entity that has specific tasks and composition'.[169]

[166] Prevost (n 8) 23.
[167] Submission by the UK (n 149) 57.
[168] Art 1.5 of the TBT Agreement.
[169] Explanatory Note to Annex 1 of the TBT Agreement; Art 4.1 of ISO/IEC Guide 2 (1991).

Both a government body (be it central, local or regional) and a non-governmental body could be a recognised body. In particular, some classical non-governmental standardising bodies at both international level, such as ISO and IEC, and national level, such as the ANSI and the European Standards Organisations, are undoubtedly recognised bodies.[170] However, given that there is no definition of a 'recognised body' in the TBT Agreement, whether a particular non-governmental body other than the classical non-governmental standardising bodies is a 'recognised body' is difficult to determine. In particular, more clarity on what features these non-governmental, private bodies should possesses and who can recognise such bodies will be useful guidance to make the judgement. It is suggested that useful reference might be drawn from the WTO Appellate Body's (AB) interpretation of 'recognised activities' in defining an international standardising body in *US – Tuna II*.[171] For the purpose of the TBT Agreement, the AB held that evidence of recognition by WTO Members as well as evidence of recognition by national standardising bodies is relevant.[172] Contrary to what some argued, evidence of recognition by the market and industry would not suffice. The meaning of the term 'recognise', as the AB reasoned, ranges from a factual end (acknowledgement of the existence of something) to a normative end (acknowledgement of the validity or legality of something). The factual and normative dimension of the concept constitutes cumulative requirements.[173] The factual dimension of 'recognition' appears to require, at a minimum, that a WTO Member is aware or has reason to expect that the body in question is engaged in standardisation activities.[174] For the normative dimension of the concept, a WTO Member's participation in the standardising body's standardising activities or the recognition of the resulting standard could suggest that the body's activities are recognised.[175] It is not necessary for the preparation and adoption of standards to be a principal function of a recognised body.[176] Finally, it is easier for a standardising body to be recognised if it has complied with the CGP and the TBT Committee Decisions in developing standards.[177]

If the AB's interpretation of 'recognised activities' offers any useful guidance for the interpretation of 'recognised bodies', it is that for a private standard to meet the definition of 'standard' the non-governmental entity that approves the standard must be *recognised* by WTO Members. This official recognition is critical in the determination of whether the TBT Agreement is applicable

[170] P Delimatsis, 'Relevant International Standards and Recognised Standardization Bodies under the TBT Agreement' in P Delimatsis (eds), *The Law, Economics and Politics of International Standardization* (Cambridge University Press, 2015) 127.

[171] Ibid, 128.

[172] WTO Appellate Body Report (n 28) para 363.

[173] Ibid, para 361.

[174] Ibid, para 362.

[175] Ibid, para 392.

[176] Ibid, para 394.

[177] Ibid, para 377.

to a specific private standard. It further leads to the conclusion that a determination of whether a standardising body is a 'recognised body' and having recognised activities must be made on a case-by-case basis as non-governmental entities differ and WTO Members view them differently. The relevant factors to be considered may include (i) whether the entity's incorporation documents include the power to formulate and issue standards, (ii) whether the entity is established or endorsed by one or more WTO Members as a standardisation body, (iii) whether the entity is involved in the standardisation activities of international standardisation organisations such as ISO and the IEC, (iv) whether any WTO Members apply standards promulgated by the entity, (v) whether the body is open to the involvement of other WTO Members, (vi) whether the body has accepted the CGP and compliance with subsequent guidance on the development of international standards, as laid out in the TBT Committee's Second Triennial Review of the TBT Agreement (Annex 4), (vii) whether the aim of the standard furthers a legitimate TBT objective, and perhaps (viii) whether the organisation is included in the World Standards Services Network listing, which is headed 'International Standardising Bodies'.[178] This is not necessarily a complete list, nor is it necessary for a private standard entity to meet all these requirements. However, it provides a useful guidance. Applying this analytical framework to private standards, it is unlikely that private standards with little or no governmental involvement or endorsement fall within the definition of 'standard' in the TBT Agreement.

One view argues that while it is necessary to attach normative criteria to an international standardising body because international standards play a quasi-judicial role in the TBT Agreement, these considerations do not apply for regular private standards. For the latter, a much lower threshold of recognition could be expected. 'Recognition' could therefore mean that a WTO Member must simply be aware of standardisation activities being carried out by a non-governmental standardising body in its territory.[179] This argument is not convincing. A 'recognised body' cannot be interpreted as any body that is legally registered and operates its business in a lawful manner as this overly-broad interpretation will deprive it of its meaning. In this regard, it is interesting to note that in Annex 1 of the final text of the Standards Code after the Tokyo Round an Explanatory Note provides that 'the definition of "standard" does not cover technical specifications prepared by an individual company for its

[178] CIEL and ISEAL Alliance, 'International Standards and Technical Barriers to Trade Legal Opinion Summary' (July 2006) 4, www.isealalliance.org/sites/default/files/resource/2017-12/ISEAL_CIEL_Legal_Opinion.pdf, accessed 20 April 2020; AE Appleton, 'Private Climate Change Standards and Labelling Schemes under the WTO Agreement on Technical Barriers to Trade' in T Cottier, O Nartova and SZ Bigdeli (eds) *International Trade Regulation and the Mitigation of Climate Change* (Cambridge University Press, 2009) 137, 144.

[179] E Partiti, 'What Use is an Unloaded Gun? The Substantive Disciplines of the WTO TBT Code of Good Practice and its Application to Private Standards Pursuing Public Objectives' (2017) 20 (4) *Journal of International Economic Law* 829, 835.

own production or consumption requirements'. The note was later dropped from the final TBT text.[180] It is not clear why this important clarification was later removed. Nevertheless, it is not convincing to argue that such an omission may indicate that WTO Members wanted to leave the concept of 'standard' more open-ended to include standards developed or implemented by retailers or distributors such as Tesco and Marks and Spencer as explained above. These firm standards are for private use and commercial in nature, thus falling outside of the TBT Agreement.

### *ii. Article 4.1 of the TBT Agreement*

One crucial difference between TBT Article 4.1 and SPS Article 13 is that Article 4.1 obliges WTO Members to *take such reasonable measures as may be available to them* to ensure that non-governmental standardising bodies within their territories *accept and comply with the CGP*.[181] It is important to note that Article 4.1 imposes an enforceable obligation on WTO Members, not on standardising bodies. While standardising bodies may not accept the CGP, Members are nevertheless responsible for their compliance with the provisions contained therein. Moreover, the obligation for WTO Members to ensure compliance with the CGP refers to standardising bodies, and not to the standards they draft. Standardising bodies that accept the CGP assume many obligations that also apply to technical regulations, including transparency and stakeholder participation, non-discrimination, least-trade restrictiveness, use of international standards as benchmarks, and avoidance of duplication or overlap with the work of other standardising bodies in the national territory or with the work of relevant international or regional standardising bodies. These are proven good practices in standard-setting and are particularly useful to private standards developers to make reference to. However, what constitute 'non-governmental standardising bodies' and 'reasonable measures' are undefined in the TBT Agreement.

Even though a textual reading of Annex 1(8) may indicate the term 'non-governmental body' includes *any standardising body* other than a central government body or a local government body, a more plausible interpretation is that the existence of an appropriate nexus between a non-governmental entity (and/or its measure) and a WTO Member is required to impose responsibility on the Member for activities of the entity. Such a nexus may be reflected in governmental

[180] WTO Secretariat, 'Negotiating History of the Coverage of the Agreement on Technical Barriers to Trade with regard to Labeling Requirements, Voluntary Standards, and Processes and Production Methods Unrelated to Product Characteristics', WT/CTE/W/10 (29 August 1995) 11–13.

[181] EP Bartenhagen, 'The Intersection of Trade and the Environment: An Examination of the Impact of the Technical Barriers to Trade Agreement on Eco-labeling Programs' (1997) 17 *Vanderbilt Journal of International Law* 72.

involvement, or support or incentives provided to a non-governmental measure at issue.[182] Thus, if there is not any meaningful governmental involvement or incentives in private standards applied by non-governmental entities, a WTO Member does not have a legal obligation to take reasonable measures to make these entities comply with the CGP. This interpretation is consistent with the definition of standard as discussed in part C(i) above as well as the negotiating history of the TBT Agreement and the CGP. The national standardising bodies of many countries are incorporated as non-governmental entities, such as the ANSI in the US and the British Standards Institution (BSI) in the UK. Both are private, non-profit bodies supported by a diverse constituency of private and public sector organisations. They nevertheless play a vital role in shaping, developing, and implementing domestic technical regulations and standards. Obviously, if their non-governmental body status would allow some WTO Members to circumvent the disciplines of the TBT Agreement, that would be unfair to other WTO Members.[183] Therefore, the term 'non-governmental body' in the TBT Agreement is better interpreted as covering only national standardising bodies and other non-governmental entities performing public regulatory functions.

There seems to be a disassociation of the scope of a WTO Member's legal obligation and who may accept the CGP. The TBT Annex 3:B of the TBT Agreement provides that the CGP is open to *any standardising body*. In practice, a few purely private firms have accepted the CGP, such as Calconnect in the US and Seafood Services Australia Ltd.[184] This is also encouraged by the TBT Committee, which has expressly called on Members to ensure compliance with the CGP's provisions from 'bodies which are not commonly considered as standardising bodies and which have not accepted the CGP'.[185]

For private standards applied by non-governmental bodies, a WTO Member's obligation is limited to 'take reasonable measures as available to it'. The standard of reasonable availability does not entail any obligation of result but, far from being hortatory, imposes an obligation of conduct on the part of the state to actively attempt to address in good faith possible deviations by standardising bodies from TBT discipline.[186] The WTO case law has provided a

[182] A Kudryavtsev, *Private-Sector Standards as Technical Barriers in International Trade in Goods: In Search of WTO Disciplines* (Wolf Legal Publishers, 2015) 290; Appleton (n 177) 147–148. On works insisting on a textual reading of Annex 1 (8), see C Vidal-Leon, 'Corporate Social Responsibility, Human Rights, and the World Trade Organization' (2013) 16 *Journal of International Economic Law* 893, 905.

[183] Revised Proposal by the European Economic Community, 'A Code of Good Practice for Non-Governmental Bodies in the Agreement on Technical Barriers to Trade', MTN/GNC/NG8/W/71 (20 Feb 1990).

[184] WTO ISO Standards Information Gateway, www.tbtcode.iso.org accessed 1 March 2020.

[185] TBT Committee, 'Third Triennial Review on the Implementation and Operation of the TBT Agreement' G/TBT/13 (11 November 2003) para 25.

[186] J Bohanes and I Sandford, 'The (untapped) Potential of WTO Rules to Discipline Private Trade Restrictive Conduct', Paper presented at the Society of International Economic Law Inaugural Conference (Geneva, 15–17 July 2008).

number of guidelines to determine whether measures are reasonably available.[187] 'Reasonable' implies 'a degree of flexibility that involves consideration of all of the circumstances of a particular case'.[188] Difficulties in ensuring compliance by the Member in question are to be weighed against the consequences on the obligations of other WTO Members.[189] A measure would not be available if it entails substantial costs or technical difficulties in its implementation and enforcement. A reasonably available measure must also leave an appropriate scope of autonomy and freedom to the private actors concerned.[190]

It also seems what are reasonable measures depend on the constitutional relationship in a WTO Member. Although nearly all non-governmental national standards bodies have some form of institutionalised collaboration with central government bodies, the extent of this collaboration varies greatly from one country to another.[191] While it may be reasonable for all WTO Members to adopt measures which aim at familiarising standardising bodies with the provisions of the TBT Code, under what circumstance would it be reasonable to expect a central government body to withdraw or reduce a subsidy to a national standards body as a result of non-compliance with the CGP remains unclear at the moment.

## V. THE NORMATIVE DIMENSION OF PRIVATE STANDARDS IN THE WTO

### A. Is there a Normative Case for WTO Oversight over Private Standards?

As can be seen from the discussions above, the legal analysis cannot take us very far in delineating the role of the WTO in regulating private standards. A more fundamental question that emerges is whether there is a normative case for the WTO to regulate private standards. Why is it not desirable to leave private standards unregulated? One view holds that, in view of their market-driven nature and complex economic welfare effects, WTO Members should ensure that the trade regime leaves transnational policy space for private standards-setting rather than trying to create additional rules on what private standards to accept.[192] By contrast, the opposing view argues that private standards may distort trade as much as government conduct and that the governance role of such private standards is too great to allow them to remain reclusive.[193] In failing to explicitly

[187] Kudryavtsev (n 182) 298–310.

[188] Appellate Body Report, *Anti-Dumping Measures on Certain Hot-Rolled Steel Products from Japan*, WT/DS184/AB/R, adopted 24 July 2001, para 84.

[189] Panel Report, *Canada- Measures Affecting the Sale of Gold Coins*, L/5863, 17 September 1985 (unadopted), para 69.

[190] Partiti (n 179) 837.

[191] RW Middleton, 'The GATT Standards Code' (1980) 14 *Journal of World Trade* 201, 208–209.

[192] Bernstein and Hannah (n 157) 604–605.

[193] Mavroidis and Wolfe (n 21) 2.

address the increasingly important non-traditional patterns of regulation, such as those reflected in soft norms created by non-state actors, there is a risk that WTO law becomes 'under-inclusive'.[194]

The starting point to discuss the potential role of the WTO in private standards is to appreciate the important regulatory function of private standards in international trade and international standardisation harmonisation. As detailed in Part II of this chapter, private standards have far-reaching consequences in global trade patterns and affect a wide range of actors. In particular, although private standards tend to have positive effects on food safety and quality to some extent, they also create negative trends toward the marginalisation of small farmers and retailers and subsequently an increase in economic inequality in developing countries.[195] Further, the proliferation of private standards has undermined the process of international harmonisation of standards through international governmental organizations, introducing a new layer of governance that further fragments national markets with which exporters must comply. As Argentina complained bitterly at the SPS Committee:

> International disciplines have been negotiated to limit the trade restrictive effects of SPS measures and members have devoted time and financial and human resources to attending all the international meetings where standards were discussed, developed and implemented. If the private sector could impose unnecessarily trade restrictive standards, and members had no forum in which to advocate some rationalization of these standards, twenty years of discussions in international fora would have been wasted.[196]

The OIE shared Argentina's concerns and warned that private standards may undermine the science-based and democratically-adopted standards of public international organisations. It also said that there was reason to believe that 'many private standards are not consistent with SPS obligations'.[197]

It is precisely because of the significant regulatory power of private standards and their associated economic and social costs that the legitimacy of private standards should be assessed. Drawing on Weber, power relations are legitimate where those engaged in them perceive or believe them to be so.[198] In a regulatory context, a claim to legitimacy requires that the regulator is perceived

[194] Pauwelyn (n 155) 219.

[195] S Ponti, 'Greener than thou: The Political Economy of Fish Ecolabeling and its Local Manifestations in South Africa' (2007) 36(1) *World Development* 159–175; D Fuchs, K Agni and A Maarten, 'Retail Power, Private Standards and Sustainability in the Global Food System', in J Clapp and D Fuchs (eds), *Corporate Power in Global Agrifood Governance* (MIT Press, 2009).

[196] Note by the Secretariat, 'Summary of the SPS Committee Meeting Held on 29–30 June 2005', G/SPS/R/37/Rev.1 (18 August 2005), para 20.

[197] Submission by the OIE, 'Considerations Relevant to Private Standards in the Field of Animal, Health, Food Safety and Animal Welfare', G/SPS/GEN/822 (25 February 2008) 1.

[198] M Weber, HH Gerth and CW Mills (eds), *From Max Weber: Essays in Sociology* (Routledge, 2007) 213.

as having a right to govern both those it seeks to govern and those on behalf of whom it purports to govern.[199] In view of their powerful governance role, naturally there are legitimacy concerns about private standards along the same lines as government regulations, such as whether it is proportionate to the risk; whether it is scientifically-based; whether it is adopted through a democratic and open process; and whether the burden of compliance is distributed fairly. The underlying proposition is that all power-wielders within any regulatory regime, regardless of whether they are to be qualified as public or private, should be viewed as legitimate by those who are affected by their rule-making.[200]

This inquiry throws into sharp relief acute legitimacy concerns about private standards. The term 'legitimacy' has a plurality of models, and actors deploy it at all levels of the international system to refer to different meanings.[201] Nevertheless, the existing research on legitimacy in global governance often explicitly or tacitly understands it as democratic legitimacy. Democracy is 'the touchstone of legitimacy in the modern world' and it is the democratic character of a norm that makes it legitimate.[202] Therefore, public regulation is considered legitimate because of the congruence between an elected government and the public through democratic mechanisms to ensure that a government is accountable to its citizens who can participate in rule-making through representations and can punish the elected government by voting it out of office.[203] By contrast, private regulations are widely claimed to suffer from a 'legitimacy deficit' because of their lack of electoral mandate or democratic representativeness.[204]

Scholars have designed various analytical frameworks to appraise the democratic legitimacy of different forms of global governance arrangements beyond the state. This article does not intend to introduce a full checklist of possible indicators for such a legitimacy assessment but just highlights the two most often cited indicators used in all analytical frameworks – participation and accountability. The notion of democratic legitimacy, at its core, is a simple idea that regulatory authority ultimately rests with the people (government by the people). It is therefore concerned with the relationship between a governing

[199] J Black, 'Constructing and Contesting Legitimacy and Accountability in Polycentric Regulatory Regimes' (2008) 2 *Regulation and Governance* 144.

[200] D Curtin and L Senden, 'Public Accountability of Transnational Private Regulation: Chimera or Reality?' (2011) 38 (1) *Journal of Law and Society* 169.

[201] CA Thomas, 'The Uses and Abuses of Legitimacy in International Law' (2014) 34(4) *Oxford Journal of Legal Studies* 733.

[202] DM Bodansky, 'The Legitimacy of International Governance: A Coming Challenge for International Environmental Law' (1999) 93 *American Journal of International Law* 599; N Hachez and J Wouters, 'A Glimplse at the Democratic Legitimacy of private Standards: Assessing the Public Accountability of GLOBALG.A.P.' (2011) 14 (3) *Journal of International Economic Law* 683.

[203] T Risse, 'Transnational Governance and Legitimacy' in A Benz and Y Papadopoulos (eds), *Governance and Democracy: Comparing National, European and International Experiences* (Routledge, 2006) 183–185.

[204] S Bernstein and B Cashore, 'Can Non-State Global Governance be Legitimate? An Analytical Framework' (2007) 1 (4) *Regulation & Governance* 351.

institution and the public it intends to govern.[205] For norms with regulatory impact to be viewed as legitimate, *prospectively*, the governing institution must allow inclusive and egalitarian participation of the stakeholders in its governing activities in order to take account of the public's preferences, interests and concerns and seek to reflect public deliberations in making governance decisions. *Retrospectively*, the public must be entitled to require the governing institution to render account of its activities and to exercise effective control and sanction over the governing institution for the way it has conducted its governance functions.[206] The prospective dimension of participation and the retrospective dimension of accountability, if effectively implemented, are more likely to generate norms that are viewed as legitimate.[207]

As a normative yardstick, participation should include all stakeholders who are affected by the decisions of the governing entities.[208] In the field of private food governance, for example, one could argue that business actors, including food retailers, food producers and processors, and third party certification companies as well as the general public, arguably represented by civil society organisations, are directly impacted by private food standards. Ideally, all stakeholders affected by the private food governance institutions have an equal chance of participation in the decision-making process in the central governing organ of the institution. In addition, one needs to consider the equal representation of all regions of the globe, ie the distribution of decision-making power between representatives of the south and those of the north. It is true that the use of the 'all affected principle' in practice may lead to challenging questions of identification, representation and feasibility in designing functional democratic governance processes, for example, because of the problem of many hands.[209] However, not all these problems are insurmountable[210] and in any case they should not be used as excuses to disregard the public's entitlement to democratic governance.[211] Turning to accountability, at its core it is a particular type of relationship between different actors in which one gives account and another has the power or authority to impose the resulting consequences.[212] In the regulatory

[205] P Nanz and J Steffek, 'Global Governance, Participation and the Public Sphere' (2004) 39 *Government and Opposition* 314.

[206] R Grant and R Keohane, 'Accountability and Abuses of Power in World Politics' (2005) 99 (1) *American Political Science Review* 29–30.

[207] Hachez and Wouters (n 202) 693.

[208] M Koenig-Archibugi, 'How to Diagnose Democratic Deficits in Global Politics: The Use of the "All Affected Principle"' (2017) 9 (2) *International Theory* 172.

[209] T Macdonald and K Macdonald, 'Non-Electoral Accountability in Global Politics: Strengthening Democratic Control within the Global Garment Industry' (2006) 17 *European Journal of International Law* 91.

[210] GD Burca, 'Developing Democracy beyond the State' (2008) 46 *Columbia Journal of Transnational Law* 221; S Wheatley, 'Democratic Governance beyond the State: The Legitimacy of Non-state Actors as Standard Setters' in A Peters et al (eds), *Non-State Actors as Standard Setters* (Cambridge University Press, 2009) 226–7.

[211] Hachez and Wouters (n 202) 690.

[212] R Mulgan, 'Accountability: An Ever Expanding Concept?' (2000) 78 (3) *Public Administration* 556.

context, it is a fundamental idea of democratic legitimacy that the affected stakeholders should be able to hold the governing institution accountable to its decisions through various control and sanction mechanisms, including removing decision-makers from office if they perform poorly.[213]

Applying these two criteria to a range of private food standards, researchers found that they are either lacking or in need of major improvement.[214] The case study of GlobalGAP, the most widely implemented farm certification scheme worldwide, is particularly illuminating. In respect of participation, research shows that, whereas certain categories of internal stakeholders such as producers and retailers are awarded direct participation in the decision-making process, other stakeholders such as consumers, small producers from developing countries, environmental and labour organisations, are confined to participate through informal and non-binding consultation procedures.[215] The disparity with respect to participation is more apparent considering that the geographical distribution of members is quite unequal. The result is the overwhelming domination of European producers in the decision-making process.[216] Similarly, with regard to accountability, only fully-fledged registered members, such as retailers, producers and suppliers, have access to strong accountability mechanisms. In contrast, the accountability of GlobalGAP to the public at large, ie the stakeholders not included within its corporate structure, is diffuse and only operates along erratic market and reputational lines. Certain categories of stakeholders such as small producers from developing countries are even excluded from any retrospective accountability relationship.[217] These features do not guarantee inclusive and egalitarian participation by all affected stakeholders, nor do they ensure strong accountability relationships as required by democratic legitimacy standards.

It should be noted that participation and accountability are not related to output legitimacy, which refers to the problem-solving quality of a governance institution and addresses the effectiveness and efficiency of norms in remedying collective problems.[218] This is simply because it is extremely difficult to assess output legitimacy or the effectiveness of a private standard. As a precondition to assess effectiveness, it is essential to define the objectives against which the performance of the governance institution can be evaluated. Yet different stakeholders will tend to define different objectives or even similar objectives

[213] M Bovens, 'Analyzing and Assessing Public Accountability: A Conceptual Framework' (2007) 13 (4) *European Law Journal* 450.

[214] Fuchs (n 59) 359–365.

[215] Hachez and Wouters (n 202) 702–704.

[216] Fuchs (n 59) 361.

[217] Hachez and Wouters (n 202) 709.

[218] A Uhlin, 'Democratic Legitimacy of Transnational Actors: Mapping out the Conception Terrain' in E Erman and A Uhlin (eds), *Legitimacy beyond the State? Re-examining the Democratic Credentials of Transnational Actors* (Palgrave Macmillan, 2010) 17–39.

differently.[219] As such, who gets to decide what objectives a private standard should seek? In practice, one may expect that the interests of the strong will turn into officially-desired objectives, leaving the weaker fringes of global society to bear the burden of the costs thereof. For example, large food retailers may pursue objectives of food safety and the turnover of their supply chains while paying little consideration to the necessary balance with the equally legitimate objective of enhancing developing countries' market access or reducing unnecessary costs for consumers. Therefore, output legitimacy as a normative value would require a norm or institution to pursue the public or general interest, not merely self-interest. Accordingly, input legitimacy and throughput legitimacy, reflected by a participatory, transparent and responsive deliberation process involving all affected stakeholders, are expected to result in output legitimacy in an ideal situation.[220]

Admittedly, many of the accusations levelled against the legitimacy of private standards are at least debatable. To begin with, for reasons of limited resources and efficient operations, it will never be realistic to ensure a fully open and participatory process for all potential stakeholders in setting standards, public or private. Even inter-governmental standardising organisations do not meet the requirements used to assess the legitimacy of private standard-setters.[221] Take the Codex as an example. It has long been questioned to what extent the Codex is truly representative of stakeholder interests, particularly within developing countries. An independent evaluation of it found that 69 per cent of low-income countries and 87 per cent of middle-income countries participate less than they would like.[222] While the Codex does allow significant participation from non-governmental organisations as observers, various procedural and power-allocating practices at the Codex skew the decision-making in favour of state interests. Within the non-state groups present at the Codex, there is a heavy bias towards industry interests, with many fewer active consumer and public interest groups.[223] The elevation of Codex standards to being quasi-binding in an effort to harmonise heterogeneous product standards in international trade in the SPS and TBT Agreements has further exacerbated the existing deficiencies in Codex decision-making.[224] On the other hand, some private organisations such as

[219] Fuchs (n 59) 359.

[220] M Walter and N Woods, 'In Whose Benefit? Explaining Regulatory Change in Global Politics' in W Mattli and N Woods (eds), *The Politics of Global Regulation* (Princeton University Press, 2009) 13–15.

[221] SF Halabi and CF Lin, 'Assessing the Relative Influence and Efficacy of Public and Private Food Safety Regulation Regimes: Comparing Codex and GlobalGAP Standards' (2017) 72 *Food & Drug Law Journal* 27–29.

[222] WB Traill et al., 'Report of the Evaluation of the Codex Alimentarious and Other FAO and WHO Food Standards Work' (FAO, 2002) para 24.

[223] MA Livermore, 'Authority and Legitimacy in Global Governance: Deliberation, Institutional Differentiation and the Codex Alimentarius' (2006) 81 *New York University Law Review* 783–786.

[224] Du and Deng (n 32) 115.

GlobalGAP, GFSI and the International Social and Environmental Accreditation and Labelling Alliance (ISEAL) have become significantly more open over time and come to incorporate a wider range of stakeholders to the extent that some argue that the interests of developing country-producers are heard more loudly in GlobalGAP than in the Codex.[225]

Furthermore, even though too much focus on output legitimacy has some inherent conceptual difficulties, there is evidence that private standards are more efficient and effective than public standards in a number of ways. For example, the lack of speed and complexity of the standards-setting process within the Codex has long been a cause of concern. By contrast, with the limited membership, narrower focus and more common interests of the firms and organisations involved, private standards are often developed more rapidly and are more agile in responding to a wide range of continually evolving consumer preferences than Codex standards are, and at a rate that standard-adopters require them.[226] In addition, as discussed above, despite their negative trade effects on some producers, it is also widely acknowledged that private standards have made a positive contribution to enhanced food safety and quality in the food supply chain, as well as producing spillover effects into the domestic markets of the exporting country. Some even argue that the positive impact of private standards may actually outweigh the costs to comply with them.[227]

Moving on to the allegation that the rise of private standards has undermined public regulations, in particular international standards adopted by intergovernmental standardising organisations, this is far from a foregone conclusion. To begin with, it is important to ascertain whether the relation between public standards and private schemes is competitive or complementary.[228] Existing research reveals that by and large private standards are considered to be complementary to, rather than a substitute for, public standards. In many cases, private standards build on the existing public standard infrastructure. Public standards usually establish the minimum requirements for food products and the results to be achieved while private standards translate the requirements into specific tools and operationalising processes, laying out a roadmap to be followed by private firms in order to meet or even exceed public standards.[229] Moreover, private standards frequently 'fill a void' as a substitute for missing or ineffective public regulations. For example, private standards may extend to ethical trade, environmental impact and social accountability which are not covered or not effectively

[225] Henson and Humphrey (n 26) 40; A Loconto and E Fouileux, 'Politics of Private Regulation: ISEAL and the Shaping of Transnational Sustainability Governance' (2014) 8 *Regulation & Governance* 168–170.

[226] Ibid, 40.

[227] ITC (n 70) 23–24.

[228] Y Naiki, 'The Dynamics of Private Food Safety Standards: A Case Study on the Regulatory Diffusion of GLOBALG.A.P.' (2014) 63 *International and Comparative Law Quarterly* 146.

[229] Henson and Humphrey (n 26) 2–13.

governed by public regulations.[230] It has also been reported that private standards developed by some multinational food retailers for their home markets have been applied in less developed countries where public regulations are ineffective and not to the advantage of local consumers. In this way, private and public standards are less antagonistic and can be mutually reinforcing, contributing to total system efficacy and resulting in higher quality food being available in national and global markets.[231] Finally, the fact that public and private standards overlap as potentially competing regulatory spheres at the transnational level may actually help enhance the legitimacy of private standards because the regulatory competition is arguably a source of continuous improvement of private standards, pushing them to be more accountable by displaying a high commitment to food safety and other values preferred by consumers.[232]

These paradoxes do not necessarily indicate that private standards are free from legitimacy concerns but they may call for a reconceptualisation of the legitimacy of non-state actors in global governance. It is obviously not possible to discuss critically all possible alternative bases of legitimacy for private standards even though the article hinted above at the possibility of output legitimacy as well as how a private actor may utilise various techniques to enhance its legitimacy in a particular institutional setting. Instead, I will make the argument that, if properly designed, the WTO may play a legitimacy-enhancing role for private standards as a governance tool in international trade without excessive legalisation.

First, due to the lack of effective public regulation, private bodies often have greater power and importance in the global sphere than in the national law context. Indeed, despite the lack of any relevant delegation of authority, their acts may not be much different in kind from many public norms based on delegations of authority, and may often be more effective.[233] This is precisely the case for private food standards adopted by private bodies such as the GlobalGAP. In view of their significant regulatory role and profound impact, at least some private standards can be regarded as a functional equivalent to a public regulation. Consequently, it may no longer be appropriate to view these private standards as 'private' but they should be reconceptualised as 'public' in character precisely because these private standards are exercising international public authority.[234] If this holds true, then those private standards should be amendable

[230] C Scott, F Cafaggi and L Senden, 'The Conceptual and Constitutional Challenge of Transnational Private Regulation' (2011) 38 (1) *Journal of Law and Society* 8.

[231] J Scott, *The WTO Agreement on Sanitary and Phytosanitary Measures: A Commentary* (Oxford University Press, 2007) 310.

[232] E Meidinger, 'Competitive Supragovermental Regulation: How Could It Be More Democratic' (2008) 8 *Chicago Journal of International Law* 518.

[233] B Kingsbury, N Krisch and RB Stewart, 'The Emergence of Global Administrative Law' (2005) 68 *Law and Contemporary Problems* 23.

[234] AV Bogdandy, P Dann and M Goldmann, 'Developing the Publicness of Public International Law: Toward a Legal Framework for Global Governance Activities' (2008) 9 *German Law Journal* 1384.

according to public law controls, such as participation, transparency, reasoned decisions, proportionality, means-ends rationality and avoidance of unnecessary restrictive means, within a model of global administrative law.[235]

The TBT and SPS Agreements and their associated decisions impose extensive global administrative law requirements of transparency, participation and accountability on standard-setting bodies in order to ensure both a rigorous standard-developing process and high quality standards. These requirements constitute what is probably the most highly developed and profoundly transformative administrative law programme of any global regime and are widely adhered to by international standardising organisations.[236] Therefore, it is appropriate to use the TBT and the SPS Agreements as a benchmark against which some private standards are gauged.

Second, voluntary compliance with WTO disciplines will help boost the legitimacy of private standards. Due to the absence of enforcement power by way of a hierarchical relationship, legitimacy is particularly crucial to non-state regulators because they depend on the voluntary cooperation of others to be effective.[237] A central dimension of the legitimacy of a private regulator is the acceptance and recognition by those in its sphere, including other rival regulators cohabiting the same regulatory space and in particular states and intergovernmental organisations.[238] One strategy used by private actors to facilitate such recognition is to demonstrate equivalence (not sameness) to accepted procedural norms of standard-setting in international institutions. To illustrate this point, although WTO Members have been reluctant to pressure private standards bodies to comply with the CGP, private standard-setting bodies who aspire to make their standards recognised by the WTO have been engaging in increasingly proactive efforts to show that they develop their standards through an open, transparent and accountable process.[239] They voluntarily comply with, or even go beyond, the specific requirements of the CGP and TBT Principles where appropriate. For example, ISEAL claims that its own Code of Good Practice, which defines effective standards-setting processes for setting social and environmental standards, is consistent with the CGP and TBT Principles.[240] Similarly, in order to win WTO recognition, ISO has consistently emphasised that its standards are developed according to the CGP and TBT Principles.[241] Their motivation is of course in the expectation that such normative connectivity

[235] Kingsbury et al (n 233) 37–42.

[236] RB Stewart and MR Sanchez Badin, 'The World Trade Organization: Multiple Dimensions of Global Administrative Law' (2011) 9 *Journal of International Constitutional Law* 569–571.

[237] Black (n 199) 149.

[238] J Bomhoff and A Meuwese, 'The Mega-regulation of Transnational Private Regulation' (2011) 38(1) *Journal of Law and Society* 139.

[239] Bernstein and Hannah (n 157) 588.

[240] ISEAL Alliance, *Setting Social and Environmental Standards: ISEAL Code of Good Practice* (Version 6.0, 2014) 5–6.

[241] ISO (n 30) 5.

will enhance their own legitimacy as a transnational regulatory actor. In this sense, WTO disciplines may be regarded as a 'meta-regulation' for all private standard-setting schemes, providing guidelines on best practices and lending them legitimacy to realise better regulation objectives.[242]

If there is a normative case for the WTO to play an oversight role on private standards, then how could such a function work in practice? To answer this question, it is essential to review the discussions by WTO Members at the SPS Committee on possible actions regarding SPS-related private standards. This is addressed in the next section.

## B. The Prospect of Private Standards Governance in the WTO Framework

In response to widespread concerns raised by WTO Members regarding private standards in the agri-food trade sector, an ad hoc working group was established in 2008 to identify possible actions for the SPS Committee regarding SPS-related private standards. In 2010, twelve possible actions, ranging from the development of a working definition of private standards to an examination of the regulatory scope of the SPS Agreement, were set out.[243] The SPS Committee later agreed in March 2011 to pursue five practical actions recommended whilst no consensus could be reached on the other seven possible actions.[244]

Apart from action 1 which relates to the development of a working definition of SPS-related private standards, the other four adopted actions are exclusively about information exchange between the SPS Committee and other entities that are relevant to the development of SPS-related private standards. Since 2011 the SPS Committee's discussions on private standards have been limited to the five actions and, in particular, to Action 1. The SPS Committee also discussed how to address the seven outstanding proposed actions on which consensus had not been reached. Some Members were keen to move forward on outstanding Actions 6 to 12 through a voluntary working group.[245] However, other Members indicated that they were not prepared to work on those actions as there had been no consensus.

Action 8 recommends that the SPS Committee should develop guidelines on the implementation of Article 13 of the SPS Agreement, in particular the terms 'non-governmental entities' and 'reasonable measures as may be available to Members'. Action 10 encourages WTO Members to explore the prospect of

[242] Bomhoff and Meuwese (n 238) 159.

[243] Note by the Secretariat, 'Possible Actions for the SPS Committee Regarding Private Standards', G/SPS/W/247/Rev.3 (11 October 2010).

[244] SPS Committee, 'Decision of the Committee – Actions Regarding SPS-Related Private Standards', G/SPS/55 (6 April 2011).

[245] SPS Committee, 'Actions Regarding SPS-Related Private Standards- Communication from Belise', G/SPS/GEN/1291 (16 October 2013).

introducing a Code of Good Practice, similar to the CGP of the TBT Agreement, for all private SPS standards to enable Members to better implement SPS provisions and improve market access.[246] It is hard to disagree that these are sensible proposals. The proponents for WTO intervention in private standards have strong evidence demonstrating that private standards are too significant to be left unregulated. Concurrently, the proposals will leave sufficient transnational regulatory space for private standards without excessive legalisation suppressing its development and operation. The essence of the proposal is merely to replicate widely accepted minimum criteria and best practices that standards-setters are expected to follow and to make the WTO play the role of a 'meta-regulator' with no enforcement power.[247] Indeed, this is also the role that international standardising organisations expect the WTO to play in responding to the adverse effects of private standards. The OIE, for example, suggested that the SPS Committee should be used as a forum for countries to identify and discuss specific problems that they have experienced relating to private standards. On the basis of such a discussion, the SPS Committee may develop recommendations on future action for consideration by Members.[248]

Nevertheless, there seems to be little chance of this proposal being accepted by all WTO Members. During the Third Review of the SPS Agreement, China reported that it was in the process of drafting a paper on 'Best Practice Guidelines regarding Private Standards' and argued that its application by private standard-setters and Members hosting them would help private standards make positive contributions while avoiding the creation of unnecessary barriers to trade.[249] However, the EU, US and Canada indicated that they were not prepared to support the initiative, citing fundamental divergences among WTO Members on private standards.[250]

More recently, Mavroidis and Wolfe tabled a similar proposal that WTO Members interested in regulating private standards should draft a standards 'Reference Paper' on the model of the Telecom Reference Paper that can be inscribed in the services schedules of participating Members. These additional commitments are binding on countries that made them and are enforceable through WTO dispute settlement.[251] However, applying this approach to private standards in practice will meet the same practical hurdles as discussed above. Under Article XVIII of GATS, parties are allowed to schedule commitments in addition to market access and national treatment commitments. The only issue is to find a legal mechanism that allows new regulatory principles in the

[246] WTO SPS Committee, 'Third Review of the WTO SPS Agreement, Proposal by India', G/SPS/W/236 (17 April 2009).

[247] Bomhoff and Meuwese (n 238) 141.

[248] OIE Submission (n 197) para 15.

[249] WTO Secretariat (n 145) para 13.1.

[250] Ibid, paras 13.4–13.6.

[251] Mavroidis and Wolfe (n 21) 17–19.

reference paper to be legally binding. Rather than amending the WTO text, the choice of treating the regulatory principles as additional commitments that Members can choose to include in their schedules under Article XVIII was a good approach and had the advantage of containing built in-flexibility which allows countries to pick and choose from a common set of rules.[252] By contrast, the SPS Agreement does not contain a similar provision to XVIII of GATS, and it is even controversial among WTO Members whether, without a proper mandate, the SPS Committee is the proper venue to discuss potential regulatory approaches.

Looking forward, given the challenge of reconciling divergent views on private standards, it might be challenging to impose binding rules on private standards in the WTO. To curb the trade-restrictive nature of private standards, one feasible way is for WTO Members to draft procedural guidelines on private standards in collaboration with intergovernmental organisations and multi-stakeholder standard-setting bodies. The guidelines should focus on transparency and simplifying the certification process to make it easier for producers to comply with the private standard.[253] Another practical way forward is to take a plurilateral approach, bringing together only like-minded WTO Members to draft a Code of Good Practice or reference paper for private standards, based on the CGP and the TBT Principles.[254] These additional commitments could then be built into the bilateral or regional free trade agreements. Similar to the Telecommunication Reference Paper approach, states should be allowed flexibility in picking and choosing from the best practices contained in the Code of Good Practice. However, if states agree to be bound, the relevant provisions are enforceable through the dispute settlement mechanism. It is further hoped that the inclusion and voluntary compliance may serve as a lever to achieve a snowball effect, leading it to be debated and followed by other international instruments and in other international fora. It is also useful for a developing country to identify a specific private standard which is arguably not consistent with the SPS disciplines, such as by not being based on science and being excessively restrictive of international law, and bringing the dispute before the WTO dispute settlement body.[255] The dispute will create an opportunity for the AB to shed more light on the ambiguous SPS provisions and uncertain boundary of the obligation of WTO Members regarding private standards.

[252] B Guermazi, 'Exploring the Reference Paper on Regulatory Principles' (2000) www.wto.org/english/tratop_e/…e/…/guermazi_referencepaper.doc accessed 20 April 2020.

[253] EVD Zee, 'Disciplining Private Standards under the SPT and TBT Agreement: A Plea for Market-State Procedural Guidelines' (2018) 52 (3) *Journal of World Trade* 393, 412–414.

[254] B Hoekman and PC Marvoidis, 'Embracing Diversity: Plural Agreements and the Trading System' (2015) 14 (1) *World Trade Review* 101–116.

[255] Submission by the UK (n 149) 94.

## VI. CONCLUSION

Although private standards have been in existence since the early 1990s, the phenomenon gathered momentum only from the early 2000s. This development away from mandatory government regulation towards voluntary, non-governmental standards should be seen in the context of the broader contemporary shifts in the locus of governance from the public to the private.[256] As it came much later than the formal establishment of the WTO, the proliferation of private standards has posed novel questions about the role of the WTO in addressing soft law norms created by different non-state actors and the utility of government-to-government diplomacy.[257] This chapter provides a comprehensive review of concerns expressed by some WTO Members regarding the effects of private standards on international trade as well as different structures of private standardisation systems in the US, EU and China. It shows that WTO Members are deeply divided on a number of fundamental issues, including whether private standards are covered by the TBT and SPS Agreements, the different roles private standards play in domestic standardisation systems and the extent they comply with the TBT CGP, the legitimacy and accountability of private standards in global governance, as well as possible pathways to move the issue forward within the WTO legal framework. Despite the complexity in debating the pros and cons of private standards in international trade and the current deadlock in the TBT and SPS Committees, it is submitted that private standards should not be permitted to operate entirely outside the purview of WTO disciplines. It is possible to reduce the adverse effects of private standards on international trade while maintaining a transnational regulatory space for them. Indeed, it could even be argued that proper WTO oversight would enhance, rather than undermine, the legitimacy of private standards as a market-based mechanism of transnational private regulation.

[256] AC Cutler, V Haufer and T Porter (eds), *Private Authority and International Affairs* (SUNY Press, 1999) 3–4.
[257] Scott (n 231) 302.

# 6

# *Case Studies*

## I. ISO, INTERNATIONAL STANDARDS AND THE TBT AGREEMENT

As discussed in Chapter 4, neither the TBT Agreement nor the WTO Appellate Body (AB) has defined the key term 'international standards'. The AB ruled in *US – Tuna II* that for the purpose of the TBT Agreement, an international standard is 'a standard adopted by an international standardizing body'.[1] The AB further defined an international standardising body as 'a body that has recognised activities in standardization and whose membership is open to the relevant bodies of at least all WTO Members'.[2] In other words, when examining the international nature of a standard, attention should centre on the traits of the institution promulgating it, rather than the very content of the standard at issue.[3] Moreover, the AB held that the TBT Committee Decision on principles for the development of international standards bears specifically on the interpretation and application of the concept of 'recognised activities in standardisation'. In particular, it would be easier for an international standardising body to be 'recognised' to the extent that it has complied with the principles and procedures of the TBT Committee Decision which WTO Members have decided 'should be observed' in the development of international standards.[4]

The International Organization for Standardization (ISO) and the International Electrotechnical Commission (IEC) account for about 85 per cent of international product standards.[5] While the TBT Agreement does not define international standards exclusively as the products of ISO and IEC standardisation, it assigns these private standardisation organisations a prominent role that amounts at least to an implicit delegation of regulatory authority. The WTO has built a strategic partnership with ISO, IEC and the International

[1] WTO Appellate Body Report, *United States – Measures Concerning the Importation, Marketing and Sale of Tuna and Tuna Product (US – Tuna II)*, WT/DS381/AB/R, adopted 13 June 2012, para 356.

[2] Ibid, para 359.

[3] Panagiotis Delimatsis, 'Global Standard-Setting 2.0: How the WTO Spotlights ISO and Impacts the Transnational Standard-Setting Process' (2018) 28 *Duke Journal of Comparative & International Law* 273, 282.

[4] AB Report, *US – Tuna II* (n 1) para 376.

[5] T Buthe, 'Engineering Uncontestedness? The Origins and Institutional Development of the International Electrotechnical Commission (IEC)' (2010) 12 *Business and Policy* 1, 5.

Telecommunication Union (ITU).[6] Annex 1 of the TBT Agreement provides that the terms used in the TBT Agreement shall have the same meaning as given in the sixth edition of the ISO/IEC Guide 1: 1991. The ISO holds an observer status in both the TBT committee and the SPS committee. Any standardising body which would like to accept the TBT's Code of Good Practice (CGP) is required to notify the WTO ISO Standards Information Gateway.[7] ISO, IEC and ITU are recognised as the only international standardisation bodies in the field of technical standards for certain WTO Members, such as the EU.[8] Then to what extent should standards adopted by ISO be recognised as international standards for the purpose of the TBT Agreement? In particular, do ISO standards development processes fulfil the six principles of transparency, openness, impartiality and consensus, relevance and effectiveness, coherence and developing country interests outlined in the TBT Committee Decision?

## A. An Introduction of the ISO and ISO Standard-setting Processes

The ISO was the first general international standardising body (ISB) ever created. As the world's largest and most widely recognised developer of international standards, it is an independent, non-governmental international organisation with a membership network of 164 national standards bodies and more than 22,500 international standards published by August 2019.[9] ISO develops voluntary, consensus-based, market-relevant international standards that support innovation and provides solutions to global challenges. These standards cover almost every industry, from technology to food safety, to agriculture and healthcare. Though ISO initially focused on developing technical standards for specific products, it has expanded its scope significantly, and now develops management systems standards and other protocols that have significant environmental and social policy implications.[10] The object of the ISO is to promote the development of international standards with a view to facilitating the international exchange of goods and services, to improving the management of business processes, to supporting the dissemination of social and environmental best practices and to developing cooperation with respect to intellectual, scientific, technological, and economic activity.[11]

[6] IEC, 'Liaison between WTO and IEC' www.iec.ch/about/globalreach/partners/wto/ Accessed 8 March 2020.

[7] F Temmerman, *Trade in Water under International Law* (Edward Elgar, 2017) 230.

[8] EU Regulation 1025/2012 of the European Parliament and of the Council of 25 October 2012, on European Standardisation, Art 2(9).

[9] ISO, 'ISO in Brief' (2019) 3.

[10] M Morikawa and J Morrison, 'Who Develops ISO Standards? A Survey of Participation in ISO's International Standards Development Process', Pacific Institute for Studies in Development, Environment, and Security (October 2004) 6.

[11] Art 2.1 of ISO Statutes (18th edn, 2018).

ISO membership is organised by country and strictly limited to one member body per country.[12] The member bodies shall be those national standards bodies most broadly representative of standardisation in their respective countries.[13] States and governments as such cannot be ISO members. The nature of ISO's members is more diversified compared to other international organisations. Many ISO members are part of the government structure in their country or mandated by government whilst others are private-sector organisations. In the US for instance, the ANSI is a private, not-for-profit organisation responsible for coordinating the US voluntary standardisation and conformity assessment system and representing the US in the ISO. In China, by contrast, it is the Standardization Administration of the People's Republic of China, a governmental entity authorised by the State Council to exercise administrative responsibilities of standardisation work in China and represent the Chinese interests at the ISO. The vast majority of private standardisation bodies at the ISO have some kind of institutional link with their government through either legal instrument or contract, so that they are usually given privileges to pursue their public interest function as national standard-setting bodies and to represent the country in ISBs.[14] This flexible approach preserves the freedom of each country to organise standardisation at the domestic level.

All ISO members, whether public or private, have the same obligations towards the ISO, depending on their type of membership. There are three member categories in ISO. Each enjoys a different level of access and influence over the ISO system. Full members (or member bodies) enjoy unconditional rights in influencing ISO standards development and strategy by participating and voting in ISO technical and policy meetings. They can participate in all ISO technical committees (TCs) as participating members (P-members) or observing members (O-members). They are eligible to be members of the Council and the Technical Management Board, the two main non-plenary governance organs of the ISO.[15] There are currently 121 member bodies. Nevertheless, the degree of participation in ISO activities among full members varies: some ISO members (such as Afghanistan, Dominic Republic and Fiji) only participate in several TCs, while other ISO members (such as China, Germany, UK and France) participate in over 700 technical bodies, including TCs, subcommittees and working groups.

Correspondent members amount to observers to ISO. They receive all ISO publications and observe the development of ISO standards and strategy by attending ISO technical and policy meetings. The least active category is subscriber members. They keep up to date on ISO's work but cannot participate in it, nor can they sell or adopt ISO international standards nationally as the other two

[12] Ibid, Arts 3.2.

[13] Ibid, Arts 3.1.1.

[14] OECD/ISO, 'International Regulatory Co-operation and International Organizations: The Case of the International Organization for Standardization (ISO)' (2016) 22.

[15] ISO, *ISO Membership Manual* (2015) 16–17.

categories of memberships. There are currently 39 correspondent members and 4 subscriber members in the ISO.[16] In an effort to facilitate their learning and gaining experience in ISO standards development work, the ISO Council has approved a new rights pilot programme for correspondent and subscriber members. They are exceptionally allowed to participate as P-members in up to five TCs with full commenting and voting rights for the period 2014–2019.[17]

TCs are the forums where ISO standards are actually discussed and formed. These forums are where national member bodies, and their expert delegates, provide their input into the standards. The proposal to a new TC in a new field of work requires a two-thirds majority of the national bodies voting in favour of the proposal and at least five national bodies who voted in favour expressed their intention to participate actively.[18]

Each TC deals with a different subject or specialist area. Altogether there are more than 300 active TCs in the ISO today.[19] In order to participate in the work of TCs, a national member body expresses to the ISO Central Secretariat whether it intends to act as a P-member or O-member. P-members actively take part in the work: they are expected to attend meetings and have an obligation to vote on all formal questions, enquiry drafts, and final draft international standards. By contrast, O-members agree to follow the TC's work and to receive committee documents. O-members have the right to submit comments and to attend meetings. A national body may choose neither P-member nor O-member status for a given committee, in which case it will have neither the rights nor the obligations in that TC, but maintains the right to vote on inquiry drafts and on final draft international standards.[20]

The ISO's standards development process is based on a project approach, consisting of a sequence of project stages through which the technical work is developed. These project stages include preliminary stage, proposal stage, preparatory stage, committee stage, enquiry stage, approval stage and publication stage. Most of the stages may be omitted if certain conditions are fulfilled.[21] At the preliminary stage, technical committees may introduce preliminary items into their work programmes by a simple majority vote of their P-members, which are not yet sufficiently mature for processing to further stages and for which no target dates can be established such as subjects dealing with emerging technologies.[22] Preliminary work items may then develop into a new work item proposal for a new international standard or a new part of an existing

[16] ISO, *Annual Report 2018: Advancing the Global Agenda* (2019) 41.
[17] OECD/ISO (n 14) 23.
[18] ISO/IEC Directives, Part 1 Consolidated ISO Supplement- Procedures Specific to ISO (10th edn, 2019), Art 1.5.7.
[19] ISO Technical Committees www.iso.org/technical-committees.html?s=BUILDING accessed on 2 March 2020.
[20] Morikawa and Morrison (n 10) 7.
[21] ISO/IEC Directives (n 18) Art 2.1.3.1.
[22] Ibid, Art 2.2.1.

standard. It is possible to omit the preliminary stage and move to proposal stage directly by making a new work item proposal to an existing TC. The request for a new standard can originate from a national body, a TC, the technical management board or even an organisation outside ISO. Acceptance of a new work item proposal requires (1) approval of the work item by a two-thirds majority of the P-members of the technical committee voting and (2) a commitment to participate actively in the development of the project by at least 4 P-members in committees with 16 or fewer P-members, and at least 5 P-members in committees with 17 or more P-members.[23]

In the preparatory stage, a working draft will be prepared for circulation to the members of the TC as the first committee draft.[24] For this purpose, the creation of a working group under the TC may be necessary. The project leader of the working group is responsible for the development of the standard, working with technical experts nominated by those P-members having agreed to participate actively as well as nominated experts from other P-members or liaison organisations. As soon as the first committee draft is available, it shall be circulated to all P-members and O-members of the TC for comments. The TC secretariat shall then compile, circulate and respond to all comments received. Consideration of successive drafts may continue until consensus of the P-members of the TC has been obtained. In case of doubt concerning consensus, approval by two-thirds majority of the P-members of the TC voting may be deemed sufficient for the committee draft to be accepted for registration as an enquiry draft. It is important to note that the committee stage is the principal stage at which comments from national bodies are taken into consideration, with a view to reaching consensus on the technical content.[25]

At the enquiry stage, the enquiry draft shall be circulated to all national bodies for a 12-week vote. Crucially this is the first time that ISO members that do not participate in the relevant TC will see the draft standard.[26] An enquiry draft is approved if (1) a two-thirds majority of the votes cast by the P-members of the TC are in favour and (2) not more than one-quarter of the total number of votes cast are negative. Negative votes not accompanied by technical reasons will not be counted, as well as abstentions.[27] Both positive and negative votes may be accompanied by technical comments. When the approval criteria are met and no technical changes are to be included, the enquiry draft will proceed directly to publication. But if technical changes are to be included, the modified enquiry draft will be registered as a final draft international standard.

At the approval stage, the final draft international standard shall be distributed to all national bodies for an eight-week vote. The same criteria for approval

[23] Ibid, Art 2.3.5.
[24] Ibid, Art 2.4.8.
[25] Ibid, Arts 2.5.1 and 2.5.6.
[26] Delimatsis (n 3) 297.
[27] ISO/IEC Directives (n 18), Art 2.6.3.

apply at this stage as the inquiry stage. Technical changes to an approved final draft of international standard are not allowed. The approved standard shall proceed to the publication stage and be printed and distributed as an international standard. If the criteria are not met, the draft standard shall be referred back to the TC with a view to resubmit, be published as a technical specification, or even be cancelled entirely.[28]

In terms of the timeframe, ISO has established the deadlines for various stages within four development tracks, 18 months, 24 months, 36 months or 48 months to publication. A fast-track procedure is also established, for instance, in cases of a standard developed in another international standardising body that is recognised by the ISO council.[29]

### B. ISO as an 'International Standardising Body'

It is submitted that the ISO fulfils the definition of an ISB in the TBT Agreement. First, the ISO/IEC Guide 2 defines 'body' as a 'legal or administrative entity that has specific tasks and composition'. ISO is created as a legal entity under the Swiss Civil Code.[30] Second, it has specific tasks of promoting the development of international standards with a view to facilitating the international exchange of goods and services.[31] Finally, ISO also has a specific composition that includes national standards bodies as members and a classic governance structure that is composed of Organs (General Assembly, Council, President's Committee, Technical Management Board, Technical Committee and Central Secretariat) and Officers (President, Vice-presidents, Treasurer, Secretary-General).[32]

Second, ISO has 'recognised' activities in standardisation. Even if the AB stressed in *US – Tuna II* that the development of standards does not need to be the main function of an ISB,[33] it is clear that standardisation is the principal function of ISO. The AB has also indicated a contextual analysis to find whether a given body has recognised activities in international standardisation, including the level of participation of WTO Members in the development of a given standard; wide recognition of the validity and legality of even a single standard by WTO Members and national standardising bodies; and adherence to the TBT Committee Decision on principles for the development of international standards.[34] Applying this analytical framework to the ISO, WTO Members are undoubtedly aware of and normatively recognise the standardisation activities of

[28] Ibid, Art 2.7.6.
[29] Ibid, Annex F.2.
[30] Art 18 of ISO Statutes.
[31] Ibid, Art 2.
[32] Ibid, Art 5.
[33] Appellate Body Report, *US – Tuna II* (n 1) para 360.
[34] Ibid, para 390.

the ISO. To begin with, the ISO has 164 members, with 121 full members actively participating in the development of standard and all members are updated of the ISO standardisation work. Most of ISO members are also WTO Members. Furthermore, ISO has an observer status at the WTO TBT Committee; and ISO regularly informs the TBT Committee of its activities. Finally, the ISO Code of Conduct endorses explicitly the six TBT Committee principles as the key principles of international standardisation guiding its technical work.[35]

Third, it is debatable whether the ISO is open to the relevant bodies of at least all WTO Members. In *US – Tuna II*, the AB held that accession to an ISB should not de jure or de facto disadvantage the relevant bodies of any WTO Members, and if there are any accession requirements, they should be a mere formality. In addition, the ISB must be open to all stages of the standards-development process. The ISO Statutes provide that only the national standards bodies from those countries officially recognised by the United Nations (UN) may become members of ISO. The national standards bodies shall be most broadly representative of standardisation in their respective countries and only one body in each country may be admitted to ISO membership. According to ISO staff, the accession process is only a mere formality as membership has always been granted.[36] However, two problems have emerged. First, the UN and the WTO have different memberships as the latter is also open to 'separate customs territories possessing full autonomy in the conduct of their external commercial relations' such as Chinese Taiwan, Hong Kong and Macau.[37] Therefore, the ISO may shut the door on at least some WTO Members such as Chinese Taiwan, which is not a UN member. Nevertheless, the ISO manages to be open to a wider membership than only UN members. For example, both Hong Kong and Macau, which are not UN members, are correspondent members of ISO, and Hong Kong has participated in 248 ISO technical committees. Second, some scholars pointed to the fact that only full members can participate in all TCs whilst correspondent and subscriber members can participate in only up to five TCs as a basis to argue that ISO provisions disadvantage the relevant bodies of some members.[38] This argument is not convincing as full membership and full participation rights in all stages of standards development are automatically open to all qualified national standardising bodies. The fact that some ISO members *voluntarily* choose not to be full members and thus not participate in all stages of standards development cannot be equalised as being disadvantaged by the ISO.

In summary, at least reading from the paper, ISO has largely fulfilled the definition of ISB in the TBT Agreement.

[35] ISO, *Code of Conduct for the Technical Work* (2019) 5.

[36] AB Villarreal, *International Standardization and the Agreement on Technical Barriers to Trade* (Cambridge University Press, 2018) 193.

[37] Art XII, Marrakesh Agreement Establishing the World Trade Organization (1994).

[38] Villarreal (n 36) 194.

## C. ISO and WTO TBT Committee Decision

In *US – Tuna II*, the AB held that an examination of the procedural and substantive guarantees of the ISB at issue is necessary if its output are to play a decisive role in finding inconsistency of a national standard with the relevant international standard. This judicial finding essentially demands scrutiny of mechanics through which standards are adopted by particular ISBs. The ISO endorsed the TBT Committee Decision as containing the key principles of international standardisation and the ISO Code of Conduct specifies that its standard development adheres strictly to the six TBT principles: transparency, openness, impartiality and consensus, effectiveness and relevance, coherence, and the development dimension.[39] The TBT Committee Decision has had a substantial impact on standards-setting processes within the ISO, such as ensuring due process in standards development, accommodating more intensively the concerns of developing countries and broadening the circle of stakeholder participation.[40] Nevertheless, a more rigorous investigation of whether the standards development process at the ISO is consistent with the TBT Committee Decision is warranted.

### *i. Transparency*

With regard to transparency, the TBT Committee Decision requires that all essential information regarding current work programmes, proposals for standards and the final results should be made easily accessible to all interested parties in all WTO Members. Procedures should be established so that adequate time and opportunities be provided for written comments. At a minimum, the transparency procedures should include (a) the publication of a notice at an early appropriate stage that the ISB proposes to develop a particular standard; (b) the notification through established mechanisms to members of the ISB of the draft standard at an early stage when amendments can still be introduced and comments taken into account; (c) prompt provision to members of the ISB of the text of the draft standard upon request; (d) the provision of adequate time for interested parties of all members of the ISB to make comments in writing and take these written comments into account in the further consideration of the standard; (e) prompt publication of a standard upon adoption and (f) publish periodically a working programme containing information on standards being prepared or adopted.

ISO members are constantly notified of the work of the TCs in which they participate as P-members or O-members, including the work programme, the proposal for a new ISO standard, the draft standard and the final standard adopted.[41] However, all ISO members (except O and P-members of the

[39] ISO, 'Code of Conduct for the Technical Work' (2019) 5.
[40] Delimatsis (n 3) 284.
[41] Arts 2.3.4, 2.5.2, 2.6.1 and 2.7.1 of *ISO/IEC Directives*.

relevant TC) will not be able to see the draft standard until the enquiry stage. By that time, they merely have three months to raise objections on only technical aspects of the standard. Two problems may arise. First, it is questionable why comments should be limited to technical aspects of a standard. Procedural deficiencies should be permitted to be raised by the membership as well since these objections could not be raised earlier. Moreover, the limitation to raising technical objections accentuates the capability gap between technologically more sophisticated ISO members and less informed members. This is because those members without technical capability usually tend to abstain or cast a positive vote since negative votes without technical justification and abstentions are not considered in the final count.[42] This may disguise the real level of rejection of a standard. Second, as the inquiry stage is the first time many ISO members see the draft standard, it is doubtful whether three months provide sufficient time for at least some of ISO members to digest complex technical matters contained in the proposed standard. In this regard, it seems sensible for ISO to require relevant TCs to share information on draft standards at early stages such as when the first draft standard becomes available at the committee stage. Such information could be easily put on ISO website so all members can be alerted early on.[43]

### *ii. Openness*

The openness principle requires that membership of an ISB should be open on a non-discriminatory basis to relevant bodies of at least all WTO Members, including participation at the policy development level and at every stage of standards development, such as new work item proposal, technical discussion, submission of comments, reviewing existing standards, voting and adoption of standards and dissemination.

ISO membership is open to one national standardisation body per country and member bodies have the right to participate in all the procedures, including making proposals for new fields of work or new work items, participating in TCs, sending experts, submitting comments and voting. However, only P-members can enjoy the full range of these rights and it is up to ISO members themselves to assess their technical capacity and accordingly decide their membership status (P-member, O-member, subscriber or correspondent membership). While it is true that it is neither effective nor efficient to have all developing countries participate in all standard-setting activities, the different memberships have effectively created second-class members within the ISO. Moreover, the ISO has operated a ranking system of ISO members to determine if and how members can participate in its governance bodies such as the ISO council. Currently the ranking criteria reflects 'the size of the economies

[42] G Levy, 'Decision Making in Committees: Transparency, Reputation, and Voting Rules' (2007) 97 *American Economic Review* 150, 152.

[43] Delimatsis (n 3) 306–308.

of their countries and the degree of their involvement in ISO's technical work, both quantitatively and qualitatively' and hence take into account the financial contribution to the organization, the number of TC secretariats and the number of P-memberships in committees. As a result, developed countries have occupied most of the positions in the Council.[44] Finally, the distribution of technical work and leadership tasks within ISO is highly imbalanced with much of the work within TCs dominated by industry-driven developed country interests.[45] This raises the question of whether developing countries could effectively participate in ISO work despite of the formal openness of the standard development process.

### *iii. Impartiality and Consensus*

The principle of impartiality requires that all relevant bodies of WTO Members should be provided with meaningful opportunities to contribute to the elaboration of an international standard so that the standard development process will not privilege any particular interests, suppliers, countries or regions. Impartiality should be accorded throughout all the standards development process. Consensus procedures should be established that seek to take into account the views of all parties concerned and to reconcile any conflicting arguments.

The impartiality of ISO's standard development has been criticised on several grounds. First, there is no balanced participation between members from developed countries and those from developing countries. All correspondent and subscriber members, most of whom are from developing countries, do not enjoy full participation rights. National standards bodies from developed countries represent the majority of P-members in ISO's TCs, the fora where ISO actually develops its standards, and thus exert much greater influence on the standard development.[46] Second, the US has long complained that ISO is dominated by European standardising bodies through the Vienna Agreement allowing for mutual consultation, joint TC meetings, common planning of the new work and parallel approval of standards. However, it is controversial whether empirical data supports this claim.[47] Finally, ISO has not adequately engaged with at least some of the key stakeholders such as consumer or labour associations and NGOs.[48] Therefore ISO is still very much economic, trade-oriented and in particular, producer-oriented. This is particularly problematic for ISO. In *US – Tuna II*,

[44] Villarreal (n 36) 212.

[45] N Roht-Arriaza, '"Soft Law" in a "Hybrid" Organization: The International Organization for Standardization' in D Shelton (ed), *Commitment and Compliance- The Role of Non-Binding Norms in the International Legal System* (Oxford University Press, 2000) 263, 267.

[46] Morikawa and Morrison (n 10) 10.

[47] JM Witte, 'A single European Voice in International Standardization? American Perceptions, European Realities'. AICGS/DAAD Working paper Series (2003) 17.

[48] Delimatsis (n 3) 309.

the US argued that the AIDCP was not a relevant international standard because, inter alia, it did not allow for the participation of consumer and conservation interests in its standard-related activities. The AB stressed that the TBT Committee Decision relating to impartiality stipulates that an ISB must not privilege any particular interests when developing international standards.[49]

Currently stakeholders are not allowed to directly participate in the ISO standards development processes, but through ISO's members and its liaison organisations. ISO members are supposed to engage all relevant categories of stakeholders to build the national position, which will then be defended by the national standards body at the ISO level. This situation can prevent the participation of stakeholders if their national standards body is not a P-member in the relevant TC.[50] While stakeholder engagement is an obligation for ISO members, they are free to design their own mechanisms appropriate to their national context to organise the participation of stakeholders with no interference from the ISO. One frequent complaint in this regard is that stakeholder participation is dominated by industry.[51] Nevertheless, the ISO has issued two brochures on best practices for stakeholder engagement to ensure impartiality.[52]

ISO defines consensus as 'general agreement, characterised by the absence of sustained opposition to substantial issues by any important part of the concerned interests and by a process that involves seeking to take into account the view of all parties concerned and to reconcile any conflicting arguments'. A note to the ISO definition clarifies that consensus does not imply unanimity. This is the same language used in the TBT Committee Decision. The ISO runs a 'double level consensus' at national and the ISO levels. As introduced above, at the national level, national standardising bodies are required to form a national position that reflects and reconciles the views of the range of its national stakeholders that have a legitimate interest in the ISO subject. For this purpose, national standardising bodies are required to inform and seek input from all relevant national stakeholders and give them equal access to information and equal opportunities to provide input.

At the ISO level, according to the ISO definition, the key criterion to determine whether consensus exists is whether there is 'sustained opposition', which is defined as 'views … maintained by an important part of the concerned interests and which are incompatible with the committee consensus'. The notion of concerned interests will vary depending on the dynamics of the TC and shall

[49] Appellate Body Report, *US – Tuna II* (n 1) paras 383–4.

[50] OECD (n 14) 48–49.

[51] M Balzarova and P Catska, 'Stakeholders' Influence and Contribution to Social Standards Development: The Case of Multiple Stakeholder Approach to ISO 26000 Development' (2012) 111 *Journal of Business Ethics* 277.

[52] ISO, 'Guidance to ISO National Standards Bodies Engaging Stakeholders and Building Consensus' (December 2010); ISO, 'Guidance to ISO Liaison Organizations Engaging Stakeholders and Building Consensus' (December 2010).

be determined by the TC leadership on a case by case basis. The TC leadership has responsibility for assessing whether or not consensus has been reached and if there is sustained opposition, the leadership is required to try and resolve it in good faith. Nevertheless, a sustained opposition is not akin to a right to veto. If the sustained opposition cannot be successfully resolved, the TC leadership will register the opposition and continue to work. Moreover, ISO doesn't allow members to wield consensus as a basis to cause unnecessary delays or even hold out the standard development process. For example, if there is doubt as to whether consensus was reached for registration as an enquiry draft, a two-thirds majority of the P-members in the TC approving it would suffice.[53] To approve an enquiry draft and a final draft of an international standard, in addition to the two-thirds of the votes cast in favour by P-members of the TC, not more than one-quarter of all votes casted by all ISO members can be negative.

### *iv. Effectiveness and Relevance*

The principle of effectiveness and relevance is essentially about international standards being fit for purpose. International standards need to be relevant and to effectively respond to regulatory and market needs, as well as scientific and technological developments. They should not distort the global market, have adverse effects on fair competition, stifle innovation and technological development, or give preference to the characteristics or requirements of specific countries when different needs or interests exist in other countries. For this purpose, the TBT Committee Decision requires that ISBs (1) take into account relevant regulatory or market needs, and scientific and technological developments; (2) to put in place procedures aimed at identifying and reviewing standards that have become obsolete, inappropriate or ineffective; and (3) establish or maintain communication channels with the WTO.

A new international standard must respond to a market need. One key principle of ISO standard development is that the ISO does not decide when to develop a new standard, but responds to a request from industry or other stakeholders such as consumers.[54] Over 90 per cent of proposals for new standards originate from industry sectors. They communicate the need for a standard to its national member who then contacts ISO. Once a proposal is made, the procedure to approve it, either as a new field of work or a new work item, ensures that ISO only develops standards that there is a clear market requirement for. For example, any proposal for a new standard must be adequately detailed and justified by the body proposing it.[55] A list of documents such as statement explaining the technological, economic, societal and environmental benefits of the proposed standard may be submitted to make a substantial business case for its market

[53] ISO/IEC Directives (n 18) Art 2.5.6.
[54] ISO, 'Developing Standards' www.iso.org/developing-standards.html accessed 2 March 2020.
[55] ISO/IEC Directives (n 18) Art 2.3.4.

relevance. A new standard can only be developed if a two-thirds majority of the P-members of the TC are in favour and if four or five members, depending on the size of the committee, commit to actively participate and nominate experts to develop the draft.[56]

A new standard must not only respond to a market need, it should also be developed in a timely manner to tackle it. When a proposed new project is approved, the TC must choose a standards development track: 24 months for an accelerated track, 36 months for a normal track or 48 months for an enlarged track and it must also establish target dates for the completion of each step in the standards development process. The target dates shall be continuously reviewed to confirm that projects are still market relevant. If not, the project shall be cancelled.[57]

In order to facilitate international trade, international standards must be globally relevant, rather than responding to the needs of only a few countries. A relevant well-known case is the TC 159- Ergonomics, whose standards were not suitable for use in some countries, particularly Asian and Latin American countries, as the standards were based on anthropometric parameters appropriated to the populations in Europe and the US.[58] To address this problem, the ISO Technical Management Board established global relevant policy as early as 2003. Global relevance is defined within ISO as 'required characteristics of an international standard that it can be used/implemented as broadly as possible by affected industries and other stakeholders in markets around the world'.[59] ISO requires that its TCs present one unique international solution and that they only present options in specific provisions to accommodate existing and legitimate market differences where they are justified. The latter should be approved by P-members of the relevant TC as early as possible and at the latest at the committee draft stage.[60]

The global relevance would best be achieved by the widest possible participation of ISO members and of categories of stakeholders in the standards development process. If only a small number of countries vote on the adoption of an ISO standard, then it is doubtful whether it is globally relevant. It is therefore directly linked to the openness principle of the TBT Committee Decision discussed above.

ISO includes a review mechanism of adopted international standards. The systemic review can be initiated by a TC, a national standard body or the ISO Secretary-General. Every adopted international standard is subject to systematic review at least every five years to determine whether it should be confirmed,

[56] Ibid, Art 2.3.5.

[57] Ibid, Art 2.1.6.

[58] Villarreal (n 36) 220.

[59] ISO, *ISO/TMB Implementation Guidance: Global Relevance of ISO Technical Work and Publications* (2004).

[60] ISO, 'ISO/TMB Policy and Principles Statement: Global Relevance of ISO Technical Work and Publications' (2004).

revised or amended or withdrawn. A committee may at any time between systemic reviews pass a resolution initiating a revision or amendment of a standard.[61] This systemic review falls short of a systematic impact assessment as used in other ISBs such as ISEAL.[62] However, the TBT Committee Decision has not imposed an impact assessment requirement. If an international standard is used by at least five countries, a simple majority of the P-members of the committee voting is required to confirm or modify the standard. The purpose of the systemic review is to ensure the global relevance of a standard.[63]

The key weakness of the systemic review is that it relies on the quality and quantity of replies by ISO Members. This may not be accurate if few members reply to the review or if they have not done sufficient stakeholder consultation to find about the national use of the standard in question.[64] For this reason the ISO review rules changed in 2016 requiring all P-members of a given committee to vote on all systemic review ballots.

### *v. Coherence*

The principle of coherence is not concerned with the standard-setting processes *within* a single ISB. It requires that ISBs cooperate and coordinate with other relevant ISBs to avoid the development of duplicative or conflicting international standards. This principle is particularly relevant to ISO in view of its broad mandate in standardisation and its recent expansion of the substantive subject matter to include less technical areas such as social responsibility.[65]

ISO has cooperative mechanisms in place with other ISBs at the international level, in particular IEC and ITU. The jurisdiction of ISO and IEC started to overlap in the 1970s when products began to have both electric and electronic features. As early as 1976, ISO and IEC reached an agreement to form together a system for international standardisation as a whole. Annex B of the ISO/IEC Directives has established detailed procedures for coordination and allocation of work between the technical committees of both organisations. They further decided to create a joint TC (ISO/IEC JTC1) in 1987 with the mission of providing a single, comprehensive standardisation committee in which to address information technology standardisation.[66] Currently there are 3,237 published ISO/IEC standards developed by committees in JTC1 comprised of some 4,500 registered technical experts from around the world.[67] The three ISBs exchange

[61] ISO/IEC Directives (n 18) Art 2.9.1.

[62] Communication from India, 'Principles of International Standard Setting', G/TBT/W/345 (10 November 2011) 3.

[63] ISO/IEC Directives (n 18) Art 2.9.2.

[64] OECD (n 14) 54–55.

[65] ISO, 'ISO 26000:2010 Guidance on Social Responsibility' (November 2010); R Werle, 'Institutional Aspects of Standardization- Jurisdictional Conflicts and Choice of Standardization Organizations' (2011) 8 *Journal of European Public Policy* 392, 395.

[66] ISO/IEC, 'ISO/IEC JTC 1: Vision, Mission and Principles' (April 2014).

[67] ISO/IEC JTC 1 Information Technology www.iso.org/isoiec-jtc-1.html accessed on 2 March 2020.

their new work items every month in order to avoid duplication of effort.[68] Moreover, ISO, IEC, ITU and the United Nations Economic Commission for Europe (UNECE) signed an MOU in 2000 on coordinating the standards development in the field of electronic business.[69] ISO, IEC and ITU also established the World Standards Cooperation, a high-level collaboration with the goal of strengthen and advancing the voluntary consensus-based international standards system.[70]

Nevertheless, there is evidence that the ISO work may be in some cases duplicative or overlapping with other ISBs. For example, the ISO 22005: 2007 standard on Traceability in the Feed and Food Chain developed within TC 34 – Food was an overlap with Codex's work, despite Codex's liaison status with the TC. Similarly, the ISO working item on a standard in Chain of Custody of Wood and Wood-Based Products seems to be overlapping with the standard already adopted by the Forest Stewardship Council (FSC).[71]

### *vi. Development Dimension*

The last principle that the TBT Committee Decision identifies is addressing the concerns of developing countries. Because of limited resources, developing countries continue to struggle to participate in the development of international standards and to participate in governance structures of ISBs. However, participation of developing countries in international standardisation is essential to ensure the global relevance of ISO standards and to contribute to developing countries' access to world markets, technical progress and sustainable development.[72] To address these challenges, ISO has a number of programmes that promote the participation of developing countries.

First, ISO established the Committee on developing country matters (DEVCO) in 1961. DEVCO membership is open to interested member bodies as either participating or observer members, and to interested correspondent members as observer members. The objectives of DEVCO are to identify the needs and requirement of developing countries in the field of standardisation and to recommend actions to ISO Council to assist the developing countries.[73]

A central piece of ISO' efforts to assist developing countries is a five-year action plan, the implementation of which is monitored by DEVCO. The most recent is an action plan for developing countries for the period of 2016–2020. The new action plan envisages a combination of activities such as dissemination of

[68] OECD (n 14) 53.

[69] IEC, ISO, ITU and UNECE, 'Memorandum of Understanding Concerning Standardization in the Field of Electronic Business' (24 March 2000).

[70] World Standards Cooperation worldstandardscooperation.org/about/ accessed on 2 March 2020.

[71] Villarreal (n 36) 221–223.

[72] ISO, 'ISO Action Plan for Developing Countries 2016-2020' (2016) 2.

[73] See www.iso.org/devco.html accessed on 2 March 2020.

materials, awareness raising, sponsorship, training and technical assistance, and capacity building including strengthening the national quality infrastructure, which is the country's institutional framework that establishes and implements the practice of standardisation, conformity assessment services, metrology and accreditation.[74] DEVCO meet annually to review needs and assess progress. The DEVCO Chair's Advisory Group meets twice a year and assists DEVCO in monitoring the implementation of the Action plan for developing countries.

Second, ISO and its members have also developed the concept of twinning by which an ISO member, usually a developing country, seeking to build its capacity may enter into an arrangement with another ISO member, usually a developed country, that is in a position to share its knowledge, provide training, guidance and assistance to build the capacity of the twinned partner. There are four types of twining arrangements: between P-members so that the developing member can participate actively in the technical work of standards development and gain specific targeted experience related to the work of a committee at the international and national levels, between convenors and twinned convenors, between chairs and vice-chairs and between Secretariats and twinned Secretariats. The latter three types of twinning arrangements are referred to as 'leadership twinning' arrangements because they involve learning the competences relevant to leadership roles.[75] ISO shall be notified of all new twinning agreements.

The objectives of twinning arrangements are to improve the standardisation infrastructures and capacities of the twinned partner, to increase the participation of the twinned partner in the governance and technical work of ISO, and to promote the exchange of experience between members, optimise the use of resources through cooperation, and develop long-term strategic partnerships. Despite the concept of twinning having been established for a few years, the number of actual cases being implemented is relatively low. Common challenges include lack of communication and information sharing, insufficient access to Internet/IT tools, cultural differences in meeting techniques, observance of deadlines, ways of thinking; English-language barriers, insufficient financial resources for full participation on the part of the twinned member, and fluctuation of staff during the twinning arrangement.[76]

## D. Conclusion

Overall, ISO is an 'international standardising body' and its activities and processes appear to be to a large extent in line with the basic tenets of the TBT Committee Decision. Nevertheless, it seems that there is significant room for ISO to improve or even reform its standard-setting practices in efforts to

[74] ISO Action Plan (n 72) 5–12.
[75] ISO, 'Guidance on Twinning in ISO Standards Development Activities' (March 2019) 4–7.
[76] ISO Action Plan (n 72) 39–41.

make it more open, transparent and inclusive. In particular, developing countries and some key stakeholders remain underrepresented in the ISO standard development process.[77] Nevertheless, as discussed in Chapter 4, most of the six principles contained in the TBT Committee Decisions are aspirational in nature. Although they are relevant factors to be taken into account when deciding whether a relevant international standard is to be recognised, the AB has never ruled that all six principles must be strictly complied with or that any failure in adherence to one of the principles will automatically render a standard unfit to be an international standard. The AB is more likely to conduct a case-by-case assessment of the practices of the relevant ISB as well as an analysis of the procedures that led to the adoption of a particular standard in question before a final conclusion is reached.

## II. THE CONSISTENCY OF THE EU ECOLABELLING SCHEME WITH THE TBT AGREEMENT

### A. The Role of Ecolabelling in International Trade

In many countries but especially developed countries, consumers' concerns with the state of the environment are on the rise. In parallel to this concern, awareness of the relationship between consumption patterns and sustainable or unsustainable production of goods and services is growing. Thus, consumers intending to actively contribute to sustainable production through their individual consumption demand information about the environmental impact of the product they purchase, allowing them to make an informed choice.[78] Armed with such information, the informed purchasers would theoretically opt for more environmentally friendly products, providing incentives for manufacturers to increase production that meet consumer demand. The 'right to know' has become a rallying cry for consumers who care about how products are produced.

Ecolabelling is precisely a policy tool that is used by the issuing entity as a medium of distinguishing between products based on their relative impact on the environment in an attempt to influence consumer purchasing decisions in favour of environmentally-friendly products.[79] Ecolabels are usually designed to achieve four policy goals: (1) improve the sale or image of a labelled product; (2) raise the environmental awareness of consumer; (3) provide accurate and timely information for consumers to make informed judgments; and (4) direct manufacturers to account for the environmental impacts of their products.[80]

[77] Delimatsis (n 3) 320; Villarreal (n 36) 224–225.

[78] Committee of Trade and Environment, 'Labelling for Environment Purposes', Submission by Switzerland, WT/CTE/W/219 (14 October 2002), paras 6–7.

[79] Note by the Secretariat, 'Market Access Impact of Eco-Labelling Requirements', WT/CTE/W/79 (9 March 1998), para 4.

[80] Ibid, para 5.

These schemes are usually voluntary in nature, ie, they all use market incentives to promote 'green' products with the ultimate goal of influencing behaviour among both consumers and producers.[81] Increasingly, ecolabels are being based on an environmental policy-making tool known as life-cycle assessment (LCA).[82] According to ISO, LCA considers the environmental impact along the continuum of a product's life (ie, cradle-to-grave) from raw materials acquisition to production, use and disposal.[83] The federal government of Germany issued the first environmental label 'Blue Angel' in the world in 1978 and today, around 12,000 products and services from around 1,600 companies carry the Blue Angel ecolabel.[84] According to the website of ecolabel.com, there are now more than 400 ecolabels in 199 countries, and 25 industry sectors in the world.[85]

With the increasing use of ecolabels by governments, industry and NGOs, the international trade implications of ecolabelling programs have emerged as a hot issue in various international fora.[86] It is part of an item 3(b) on the Committee on Trade and Environment (CTE) Committee of the WTO work program in which the committee is assigned to consider 'the relationship between the provisions of the WTO's agreements and the requirements governments make for environmental purposes relating to products, including standards and technical regulations, packing, labelling and recycling'. The examination and analysis of voluntary ecolabelling schemes and their relationship to the WTO provisions in general, and the TBT Agreement in particular, constitute major parts of the CTE work.[87] Paragraph 32(iii) of the 2001 Doha Declaration tasked the CTE to focus on, inter alia, environmental labelling.[88] Also, environmental labelling, as potential non-tariff barriers, is regularly discussed in the TBT Committee under 'specific trade concerns'.[89]

Labelling can generally be seen as a 'trade friendly' approach to regulation, tending to be less restrictive to trade than many other regulatory measures. The CTE summarises WTO Members' opinions on this issue: 'most Members agreed that voluntary, participatory, market-based and transparent environmental labelling schemes were potentially efficient economic instruments in order to

[81] EP Bartenhagen, 'The Intersection of Trade and the Environment: An Examination of the Impact of the TBT Agreement on Ecolabeling Programs' (1997) 17 *Virginia Environmental Law Journal* 51, 56.

[82] Note by the Secretariat (n 79), para 6.

[83] ISO/Technical Committee 207/ Sub-Committee 5 (1995), Environmental Management- Life Cycle Assessment- Principles and Guidelines.

[84] www.blauer-engel.de/en/our-label-environment accessed on 9 March 2020.

[85] www.ecolabelindex.com/ accessed on 9 March 2020.

[86] See generally, Eco-Labelling: Overview of Current Work in Various International Fora- Note by the Secretariat (29 September 2010) JOB/TE/9.

[87] Report of the Committee on Trade and Environment, WT/CTE/1 (12 November 1996) para 185.

[88] Doha Ministerial Declaration, WT/MIN(01)DEC/1 (14 November 2001).

[89] Eg, Members raised concerns at the TBT Committee about the negative trade impact of France's Grenelle 2 Law which included provisions on product carbon footprint labelling and environmental lifecycle analysis. See www.wto.org/english/news_e/news11_e/tbt_15jun11_e.htm accessed 8 March 2020.

inform consumers about environmentally friendly products. As such they could help move consumption on to a more sustainable footing'.[90] Nevertheless, the rise of eco-labelling as a policy tool for environmental governance has brought about some difficult questions to international trade law. There are concerns that certain labelling measures have not been without consequences to the international flow of goods.[91] Despite their environmental benefits, ecolabel programs have been frequently criticised as disguised non-tariff barriers.

Developing countries and industry representatives frequently criticise eco-labelling schemes as disguised non-tariff trade barriers. In the CTE, other international organisations such as the United Nations Conference on Trade and Development (UNCTAD), the Organization for Economic Cooperation and Development (OECD) and NGOs, developing countries and researchers have identified common themes of concern about ecolabelling programs on market access and highlighted the potentially discriminatory effects of ecolabelling.[92] The challenge is thus how to respond to consumers' information needs for environmentally friendly products without unduly burden international flow of goods by creating unnecessary trade barriers.

Among the common concerns about ecolabelling programs, one of the biggest challenges to developing countries is the great variety of divergent national or regional labelling requirements. Exporters have to obtain information to adjust to the requirements of different markets if they want to qualify for an ecolabel.[93] Compliance with the criteria laid down for environmental labels in some countries was extremely costly and that those costs far exceeded the potential benefits of compliance with the set requirements. This is particularly the case for small- and medium-sized enterprises (SMEs).[94] In addition, the process-related criteria, which tend to be based on environmental and technological conditions in the importing country, may imply high costs for foreign producers and may be environmentally inappropriate in the context of their local conditions.[95] Ecolabelling schemes may discriminate between imported and domestically produced goods if local industry influences the selection of the products to which the ecolabel would apply, as well as the selection of criteria

[90] WTO, 'Report to the Fifth Session of the WTO Ministerial Conference in Cancun', WT/CTE/8 (11 July 2003) 8.

[91] WTO, 'Labelling and Requirements of the Agreement on Technical Barriers to Trade (TBT): Framework for Informal Structured Discussions, Communication from Canada', WT/CTE/W/229 (23 June 2003), para 2.

[92] H Ward, 'Trade and Environment Issues in Voluntary Eco-labeling and Life Cycle Analysis', 6 RECIEL (1997) 139.

[93] WTO, 'Environmental Labels and Market Access: Case Study on the Colombian Flower-Growing Industry', WT/CTE/W/76 (9 March 1998).

[94] Background Note by the Secretariat, 'Technical Barriers to the Market Access of Developing Countries', WT/CTE/W/101 (25 January 1999), paras 9–15.

[95] CUTS Centre for International Trade, Economics and Environment Discussion Paper, 'Eco-Labels: Trade Barriers or Trade Facilitators?' (2009) 1 www.cuts-citee.org/pdf/DP-Eco-labels.pdf accessed 28 February 2020.

for the award of the eco-label. Even well-designed eco-labelling schemes may discriminate against foreign producers in conformity assessment procedures if the exporters have to seek certification from the certification bodies in an importing country. Developing countries tend to be 'standard-takers' rather than 'standard-setters'. Fewer standards are developed by developing countries than are by their developed counterparts.[96] While transparency is the basic criteria, it is not considered adequate, as inability to comply with the labels restricts their market access.

On the other hand, the labelling requirements also offer interesting opportunities to developing countries.[97] Initiated by the increasing environmental awareness in industrial countries, a new market for products from developing countries has emerged during the last few years. If exporters do gain access to these markets, the benefits in terms of long-term trade relations can be significant. More broadly, the challenges associated with compliance with strict ecolabelling programs can be fundamental catalysts for developing countries to processes of up-grading and capacity development, while providing opportunities to position themselves strategically in key export markets.[98]

In practice, it is difficult to estimate precisely the environmental effectiveness of eco-labelling programs. There is no easily accessible, independent body of data even on the most renowned ecolabels to support definitive claims for eco-labelling, positive or negative.[99] In addition, it is currently difficult to isolate the effects of eco-labelling from other variables that could lead to more sustainable production and consumption. Nevertheless, it is generally accepted that many types of eco-labels are not likely to be successful in the absence of complementary public or private policies. The main value of eco-labels could lie in its ability to catalyse or operationalise other public or private policies. Also, the mere existence of ecolabels can stimulate a process of environmental awareness-raising in companies and the general public.[100]

## B. An Overview of the EU Ecolabelling Scheme

Originally established in 1992 and most recently amended in 2010, the EU ecolabel is a label of environmental excellence that is awarded to products and services meeting high environmental standards throughout their life-cycle: from

[96] Background Note by the Secretariat, 'Technical Barriers to the Market Access of Developing Countries', WT/CTE/W/101 (25 January 1999), para 4.

[97] Submission from Switzerland, 'Marking and Labelling Requirements' WT/CTE/W/192 (19 June 2001), para 9.

[98] S Jaffee and S Henson, 'Standards and Agri- food Exports from Developing Countries: Rebalancing the Debate', World Bank Policy Research Working Paper 3348 (June 2004) 1, 37.

[99] United Nations Environment Programme, *The Trade and Environmental Effects of Ecolabels: Assessment and Response* (2005) 3.

[100] Ibid, 10–11.

raw material extraction, to production, distribution and disposal.[101] The EU ecolabel scheme is based on a voluntary basis, with the objective 'to promote products with a reduced environmental impact during their entire life cycle and to provide consumers with accurate, non-deceptive, science-based information on the environmental impacts of products'.[102] The EU ecolabel scheme is an integrated part of a wider package of product instruments to change current consumption and production patterns in efforts to achieve the transition to a circular economy.[103]

The functioning of the EU ecolabelling scheme is set through a regulation of the European Parliament and of the Council. It is managed by the European Commission in cooperation with the European Union Eco-Labelling Board (EUEB) and competent bodies of the Member States. The European Commission manages the scheme at the EU level to ensure that the Ecolabel Regulation is implemented correctly. It is responsible for preparing the final draft of the criteria documents and adopts EU ecolabel criteria for each product group as 'Commission decisions'.[104] The Commission shall establish a common register of products awarded EU ecolabels and update it regularly. The Commission shall promote the use of the EU ecolabel.[105] The EUEB is composed of the representatives of the competent bodies of the all the EU Member States and of other interested parties such as the European Consumer Organization and European Environmental Bureau. The EUEB contributes to the development and revision of EU ecolabel criteria and to any review of the implementation of the EU ecolabel scheme. It also provides the Commission with advice and assistance and in particular, issues recommendations on minimum environmental performance requirements.[106] Competent bodies are independent and impartial organisations designated by Member States within government ministries or outside the ministries. They are responsible for implementing the EU ecolabel scheme at the national level. They specifically assess applications and award the EU ecolabel to products that meet the criteria in a consistent, neutral and reliable manner.[107]

Following consultation with the EUEB, which considers it suitable to propose a new product/service group for the EU ecolabel scheme, both public authorities, such as the Commission, Member States and competent bodies, and private bodies such as industrial consortiums may initiate and lead the development or revision of EU ecolabel criteria. However, private stakeholders who are put in charge of leading the development of criteria must demonstrate both expertise

[101] http://ec.europa.eu/environment/ecolabel/index_en.htm accessed on 3 March 2020.

[102] Recital (1) of Regulation (EC) No 66/2010 of the European Parliament and of the Council of 25 November 2009 on the EC Ecolabel.

[103] European Commission, 'Closing the Loop- An EU Action Plan for the Circular Economy', COM(2015) 614 final.

[104] Art 8(2) and (3) of EU Ecolabel Regulation.

[105] Ibid, Art 12.

[106] Ibid, Art 5.

[107] Ibid, Art 4.

in the product area and the ability to lead the process with neutrality.[108] In the development of the criteria, a balanced participation of all relevant interested parties concerned with a particular product group, such as industry and service providers, including SMEs, trade unions, retailers, importers, environmental and consumer organisations has to be guaranteed.[109] The development and revision of EU ecolabel criteria shall follow the procedure laid down in Annex 1 of the Regulation.[110] Even if this process can be led by parties other than the EU Commission, the Commission is in any case responsible for preparing the final draft of the criteria documents and adopts EU ecolabel criteria for each product group as 'Commission decisions'.[111]

The EU ecolabel scheme is intended to promote those products which have a higher level of environmental performance during their entire life cycle than other similar products and services. The relevant criteria include 'the most significant environmental impacts', in particular the impact on climate change, the impact on nature and biodiversity, energy and resources consumption, generation of waste, emissions of environmental pollution, the substitution of hazardous substances by safer substances, the potential to reduce environmental impacts, and social and ethical implications. Only products that fulfil stringent environmental requirements within a product group may be awarded the EU ecolabel.[112] Any operator who wishes to use the EU ecolabel shall apply to the national competent bodies. Even a product originating outside of the Community is eligible to apply for the label. Upon award of the label, the competent body shall conclude a contract with the operator covering the terms of use of the EU ecolabel.[113]

Under the EU Procurement Directives, ecolabels may be used to promote green public procurement (GPP), through which public authorities seek to procure goods, services and works with a reduced environmental impact throughout their life cycle.[114] However, a number of conditions must be met. For example, the label requirements are based on objectively verifiable and non-discriminatory criteria; are established in an open and transparent procedure and accessible to all interested parties etc.[115]

A previous impact assessment of the revised 2000 EU Ecolabel scheme showed that it didn't fully achieve its objectives because of the low awareness of the label and slow uptake by industry.[116] The European Commission again assessed the function and performance of the revised 2010 EU Ecolabel scheme in 2017.

[108] Art 7.1,

[109] Ibid, Para A.2, Annex 1.

[110] Ibid, Arti 8 (1).

[111] Ibid, Art 8 (2).

[112] Ibid, Art 6(3).

[113] Ibid, Art 9.

[114] A Rainville, 'Standards in Green Public Procurement- A Framework to Enhance Innovation' (2017) 167 *Journal of Cleaner Production* 1029, 1030.

[115] Art 43 of Directive 2014/24/EU and Art 61 of Directive 2014/25/EU.

[116] European Commission, 'Proposal for a Regulation of the European Parliament and of the Council on a Community Ecolabel Scheme', COM(2008) 401 Final, at 4.

The Commission concluded that the scheme has contributed to reducing the environmental impact of consumption and production. However, this contribution was substantially limited by the low level of uptake of the EU ecolabel by producers and organisations. Consequently, the EU ecolabel was not sufficient to achieve significant changes in overall consumption and production pattern and, through this, deliver significant environmental benefits beyond the companies and organisations deciding to be part of the schemes.[117] The limits in uptake are linked to limited awareness of the label by external stakeholder including business partners and consumers; limited market and administrative award for participation; lack of recognition in public policy and significant compliance and verification costs.[118]

### C. The Consistency of the EU Ecolabelling Scheme with the TBT Agreement

Given that the EU Ecolabelling scheme is administered by public authorities including the European Commission, the EUEB and competent bodies of EU Member States (many of which are designated government ministries), is voluntary by nature as market access is not dependent on the carrying of the label and that it includes NPR-PPM-based requirements because it pursues a life-cycle approach, the EU 2010 Ecolabel scheme is best described as a voluntary government-administered labelling scheme based on NPR-PPMs.[119] The fact that most of the existing ecolabelling programmes have some degree of government involvement is sometimes argued as evidence to support the proposition that government involvement would provide the necessary level to ensure that these programmes conform to internationally agreed norms or disciplines.[120]

#### *i. The Applicability of the TBT Agreement*

The first legal issue to be examined is the applicability of the TBT Agreement to the EU ecolabelling scheme. To begin with, even though it is still controversial whether NPR-PPMs fall within the definition of 'standard' in Annex 1.2 of the TBT Agreement,[121] the TBT Committee has clarified in the First Triennial Review of the TBT Agreement that voluntary labelling requirements based on

[117] European Commission, 'Report from the Commission to the European Parliament and the Council', COM(2017) 355 Final, at 4.

[118] Ibid, 4–6; F Iraldo and M Barberio, 'Drivers, Barriers and Benefits of the EU Ecolabel in European Companies' Perception' (2017) 9(5) *Sustainability* 751, 757.

[119] E Vranes, 'Climate Labelling and the WTO: The 2010 EU Ecolabelling Programme as a Test Case under WTO Law', in C Hermann and JP Terhechte (eds), *European Yearbook of International Economic Law* 205 (Springer-Verlag Berlin and Heidelberg GmbH & Co. KG, 2011) 212–213.

[120] Communication from Canada, G/TBT/W/9 (5 July 1995) 2.

[121] TBT Committee & CTE Committee, 'Eco- Labelling Programmes', WT/CTE/W/23 (19 March 1996) 17; M Josh, 'Are Eco-labels Consistent with World Trade Organization Agreements?' (2004) 38(1) *Journal of World Trade* 69, 80.

NPR-PPMs are subject to the notification obligation under paragraph L of the CGP.[122] Next, the most important criteria of the EU labelling scheme concerns the environmental impact of the product, which arguably has 'a sufficient nexus' to the characteristics of the product.[123] Thus the EU ecolabelling may be considered as a 'related PPM', falling within the definition of standard. Finally, the WTO case law has also confirmed that labelling requirements, regardless of the information contained, should be scrutinised under the TBT Agreement. In other words, the labelling scheme *as such* constitutes a product characteristic and is covered by the TBT Agreement.[124] In *US – Tuna II*, the US 'dolphin-safe' labelling requirements were based on NPR-PPM criteria of fishing processes. In *US – Cool*, country of origin labelling requirements did not bear any connection with physical characteristics or PPMs. However, no WTO Member has ever raised issues of applicability of the TBT Agreement in both cases and the AB supported the panel's evaluation that both labelling schemes fell within the scope of the TBT Agreement.[125] Therefore, the EU labelling scheme should be categorised as a 'standard' in the TBT terminology. As Article 4.1 of the TBT Agreement imposes obligations on WTO Members to ensure that their central government standardising bodies accept and comply with the CGP for the preparation, adoption and application of standards, the EU must ensure that its Ecolabelling scheme is consistent with the disciplines embodied in the CGP.

As the EU Ecolabelling scheme falls into the category of 'standard', it should be dealt with under the TBT Agreement first because it deals 'specifically, and in detail' with such measures.[126] However, a finding of consistency with the TBT Agreement would not automatically lead to the conclusion that it is consistent with the GATT 1994 as the GATT 1994 and the TBT are cumulative and WTO Members must comply with both agreements simultaneously.[127] In this regard, WTO panels have consistently refused to limit the coverage of the GATT 1994 to mandatory measures. Voluntary government standards such as the EU Ecolabelling scheme are not exempt from the scrutiny of GATT 1994, in particular if there are advantages from the government by complying with the labelling requirements.[128]

[122] TBT Committee, 'First Triennial Review of the Operation and Implementation of the Agreement on Technical Barriers to Trade', G/TBT/5 (19 November 1997), para 12.

[123] WTO Appellate Body Report, *European Communities – Measures Prohibiting the Importation and Marketing of Seal Products (EC – Seal Products)*, WT/DS400/AB/R, adopted on 18 June 2014, para 5.12.

[124] Report of the Panel, *EC – Trade Marks and Geographical Indications*, WTO/DS290/R (20 April 2005), para 7.451.

[125] Appellate Body Report, *United States – Measures Concerning the Importation, Marketing and Sale of Tuna and Tuna Product (US – Tuna II)*, WT/DS381/AB/R (13 June 2012), para 199; Panel Report, *United States – Certain Country of Origin Labelling (COOL) Requirements*, WT/DS384/R, adopted 18 November 2011, para 7.212.

[126] WTO Panel Report, EC – *Asbestos*, WT/DS135/R, adopted 5 April 2001, as modified by Appellate Body Report WT/DS135/AB/R, paras 8.15–8.17.

[127] Appellate Body Report, *Korea – Definitive Safeguard Measures on Imports of Certain Dairy Products*, WT/DS98/AB/R, adopted 12 January 2000, para 81.

[128] Panel Report, *Canada – Certain Measures Affecting the Automotive Industry*, WT/DS139/R (11 February 2000), para 10.73.

### *ii. The MFN and NT Treatment*

Paragraph D of the CGP embodies both an MFN and an NT obligation for standardising bodies. It provides that in respect of standards, the standardising body shall accord treatment to imported products no less favourable than that accorded to domestic like products and to like products from any other country. As discussed in Chapter 1, Paragraph D of the CGP provides exactly the same MFN and NT obligation as those in TBT Article 2.1 and therefore the jurisprudence under the TBT Article 2.1 is in principle applicable to paragraph D of the CGP.

There is no evidence that the EU ecolabelling scheme might de jure violate the MFN obligation. Article 9 makes it clear that any foreign producer, irrespective of national origin, who wishes to use the EU ecolabel could present the application to a competent body in any of the EU Member States in which the product is to be placed on the market, and the EU ecolabel will be awarded on the condition that they meet the criteria for their respective product group. It is theoretically possible that the competent bodies may de facto discriminate against producers from certain countries compared to other countries in implementing the ecolabelling scheme but any such allegation would require factual and empirical evidence, which does not appear to exist. I will therefore focus on the NT obligation.

As the AB found in *US – Tuna II*, Article 2.1 (and by analogy paragraph D of the CGP) sets out a three-tier test of consistency with the NT obligation: (1) the measure at issue must be a technical regulation/standard; (2) the imported products from other WTO Members are 'like products' and (3) the imported products are accorded 'treatment no less favourable' than domestic like products.[129] As the EU ecolabelling scheme is a standard falling within the regulatory scope of the CGP as analysed in part II.C.i above, I will focus on the other two inquiries.

#### a. "Like Products"

The EU Ecolabel is awarded to those products within a given product group that fulfil the labelling criteria defined by the EU. A product group is defined as 'a set of products that serve similar purposes and are similar in terms of use, or have similar functional properties, and are similar in terms of consumer perception'.[130] This has raised an important legal issue: are products carrying the EU ecolabel and those products not fulfilling the labelling criteria 'like products'? As explained in Chapter 3, the determination of 'like products' in paragraph D of the CGP, similar to TBT Article 2.1 and GATT Article III:4,

[129] Appellate Body Report, *United States-Measures Affecting the Production and Sale of Clove Cigarettes*, WT/DS406/AB/R, adopted 24 April 2012, para 87.

[130] Art 3(1) of the EU Ecolabel Regulation.

is fundamentally a determination about the nature and extent of a competitive relationship between and among products in the marketplace.[131] To assess this competitive relationship, four factors must be examined, including the properties, nature and quality of products, the end-uses of the products, consumers' tastes and habits, and the international classification of the products for tariff purposes.[132] The AB also clarified that it was not a *closed* list of criteria. A panel should have examined the evidence relating to *each* of those four criteria and then, weighed all of that evidence, along with any other pertinent evidence, in making an overall determination of whether the products at issue could be characterised as 'like products'.[133]

The key difference between products qualified for the EU ecolabel and those that are not so qualified is that the former group have a higher environmental performance, which is mainly based on NPR-PPMs. Then, applying the AB's analytical approach to determining like products, is it possible to cite different environmental performance as a basis to conclude that two otherwise identical products are unlike? This depends on how flexible the AB will use the different factors for the determination of 'like products', in particular whether consumer tastes and habits may be used to distinguish products with different environmental implications that would otherwise be seen as like products as they have similar properties and functions.[134] It is true that some consumers may perceive products with higher environmental performance unlike similar products without such quality and that the government may have a legitimate concern of environmental degradation. However, it is one thing to argue that an increasing number of consumers are interested in, and sensitive to, environmental concerns embodied in a product, it is quite another to *demonstrate* that such concerns truly shape consumer preferences and guide consumer choices in the market place. In reality, more often consumers are primarily guided by the price and quality of the products in their choice between products.[135] If so, it is unlikely to overturn the 'like products' determination between two otherwise identical products with only divergent environmental impact. In *US – Tuna II*, for example, the panel's finding that dolphin-friendly tuna and dolphin-unfriendly tuna are 'like products' was not appealed. Moreover, even if this factor is satisfied, it must be balanced with other relevant factors which are in favour of like products determination. In short, it is only in exceptional cases that two otherwise like products are rendered unlike due to their different environmental performance.

[131] Appellate Body Report, *US – Clove Cigarettes* (n 129), para 99.

[132] WTO Appellate Body Report, *European Communities – Measures Affecting Asbestos and Asbestos-Containing Products (EC – Asbestos)*, WT/DS135/AB/R, adopted 5 April 2001, para 101.

[133] Ibid, paras 102–103.

[134] E Partiti, 'The Appellate Body Report in *US – Tuna II* and Its Impact on Eco-Labelling and Standardization' (2013) 40 (1) *Legal Issues of Economic Integration* 73, 81.

[135] P Van den Bossche and W Zdouc, *The Law and Policy of the World Trade Organization* 4th edn (Cambridge University Press 2017) 393.

It is not clear whether the definition of 'product group' covers the same scope as 'like products' in the CGP. At any case, as the determination of 'like products' in WTO law is a context-related value judgement, it is possible that products which are not meeting the EU ecolabelling criteria may be considered as like products under WTO law as the products encompassed in the ecolabelling scheme.[136]

### b. 'No Less Favourable Treatment'

Similar to TBT Article 2.1, for a finding of less favourable treatment under paragraph D of the CGP, a panel must not only find that the EU Ecolabelling scheme modifies the conditions of competition in the relevant market to the detriment of imported products vis-à-vis domestic like products, but also that the detrimental impact does not stem exclusively from a legitimate regulatory distinction but reflects discrimination against imported products.[137]

There is no evidence that the EU ecolabelling scheme might de jure discriminate against foreign imported products. Article 9 does not explicitly differentiate between products on the basis of national origin and makes it clear that the EU ecolabel may be awarded to any foreign or domestic operator under the same conditions. However, as has been explained above, there is a strong possibility that, products that are not eligible for the ecolabel under the EU ecolabelling scheme and those that are awarded the label may be considered as 'like products' under the WTO law. This gives rise to a real risk that the EU labelling scheme may de facto discriminate against imported like products if foreign like products are disproportionately affected by it. Unfortunately this is exactly what quite a number of the EU's trading partners claimed. For example, the US, Canada and Brazil have argued for a long time that the EU Ecolabel scheme is not transparent enough and only takes into account environmental priorities and conditions in Europe, resulting in discrimination against foreign producers whose production processes and methods differ from those used in the EU while having comparable environmental impact.[138] The US and Brazil have been particularly upset over the EU's criteria for products such as toilet paper and kitchen rolls. Brazilian exporters have claimed that the criteria favouring the use of recycled pulp penalise Brazilian manufacturers, which use virgin wood from 'sustainably managed' forest plantations. In addition, the concept of 'consumption of renewable resources' has been defined so as to exclude wood waste, sawdust, trimmings from saw mills, thinnings and thin wood, thus exempting these materials from load points. This is discriminatory against planted forest

[136] Vranes (n 119) 223.

[137] Appellate Body Report, *US – Tuna II* (n 1) para 215.

[138] D Vogel, *Barriers or Benefits? Regulation in Transatlantic Trade* (Brookings Institute Press, 1997) 48.

and the Brazilian plantation forests have been particularly affected.[139] Moreover, the criteria do not take into account the fact that Brazilian producers largely use hydroelectricity and that the criteria concerning SO2 emissions are of less relevance in Brazil, where acid rain is not a problem.[140]

The award of an EU ecolabel tends to provide products covered by the scheme competitive advantages. For example, Article 12 of the EU ecolabelling regulation imposes a duty on Member States and the Commission, in cooperation with the EUEB, to agree on a specific action plan to promote the use of the EU label, and encourages Member States to consider the setting of targets for the purchasing of products meeting the EU label criteria. In short, there is a real risk that the EU ecolabelling scheme may afford less favourable treatment to like products that are not eligible for the ecolabel.

Similar to TBT Article 2.1, the existence of such a possible detrimental effect, by itself, is not sufficient to demonstrate less favourable treatment under paragraph D of the CGP. In the second step, a panel must further analyse whether the detrimental impact on imports stems exclusively from a legitimate regulatory distinction.[141] If a regulatory distinction is not designed and applied in an even-handed manner because, for example, it constitutes a means of arbitrary or unjustifiable discrimination, that distinction cannot be considered 'legitimate'.[142] In assessing even-handedness, a panel must scrutinise the design, architecture, revealing structure, operation and application of the technical regulation at issue.[143] Applying the legitimate regulatory test to the EU ecolabelling scheme, the key question is whether the regulatory distinction between domestic products, which are awarded an ecolabel and like foreign products, which do not qualify for an ecolabel, is 'legitimate'. As *US – Shrimp* and *US – Tuna II* illustrated, important considerations here are whether the EU has adequately considered different PPMs used to achieve similar environmental excellence and different circumstances in other non-EU WTO Members in designing and implementing the EU Ecolabelling regulation. Given that the legitimate regulatory distinction is interpreted rather stringently, there is a high risk that the EU ecolabelling regulation may be found inconsistent with paragraph D if foreign PPMs and unique circumstances were not considered. In this regard, it is worth noting that the EU ecolabel criteria for specific products are revised from time to

[139] ABECEL, 'Eco-Labelling of Tissue and Towel Paper Products in the EU: A Brazilian Perspective', in S Zarrilli, V Jha and R Vossenaar (eds) *Eco-Labelling and International Trade* 84 (Palgrave Macmillan, 1997) 85.

[140] R Piotrowski and S Kratz, 'Eco-Labelling in the Globalised Economy', in A Pfaller and M Lerch (eds), *Challenges of Globalization* 217 (Transaction Publishers, 2005) 227.

[141] Appellate Body Report, *US – Clove Cigarettes* (n 129), para 182.

[142] Appellate Body Report, *United States – Certain Country of Origin Labelling (COOL) Requirements* (*US – Cool*), WT/DS384/AB/R (29 June 2012), para 271.

[143] Appellate Body Report, *US – Clove Cigarettes* (n 129), para 182.

time considering stakeholders' input. The revision process offers opportunities for unjustifiable regulatory distinction to be dealt with.[144]

### *iii. Unnecessary Obstacles to International Trade*

Paragraph E of the CGP provides that the standardising body shall ensure that standards are not prepared, adopted or applied with a view to, or with the effect of, creating unnecessary obstacles in international trade. To find whether the EU Ecolabelling scheme is consistent with paragraph E, a number of analytical steps must be followed. First, it must be determined whether the EU scheme pursues a legitimate objective. The aim of the EU scheme is to protect the environment and to provide consumers with accurate information on the environmental impact of products.[145] Both objectives are explicitly listed in TBT Article 2.2 and GATT Article XX as legitimate. Second, it is necessary to evaluate the degree to which the EU scheme 'fulfills' the objectives it pursues. The TBT Agreement does not impose a pre-determined threshold of contribution that the EU scheme must make. It suffices that the scheme has made some contribution.[146] On this inquiry, the Commission concluded in 2017 that the scheme was only partly effective in reducing the environmental impact of consumption and production.[147] Still, one must take into account that the effectiveness of labels may increase over time when they are combined with other policies.[148]

Finally, it must be determined whether the EU scheme is more trade-restrictive than necessary to fulfil the legitimate objective. Such a determination requires considering factors that include the degree of contribution made by the EU scheme to the objectives pursued, the trade-restrictiveness of the EU scheme, the nature of the risks at issue and the existence of alternative measures which makes an equivalent contribution to the objective, less trade restrictive and reasonably available. To begin with, as the EU Commission found, the scheme has made an important but limited contribution to the objectives. Furthermore, the trade-restrictiveness of the EU scheme seems to be limited as voluntary labelling is commonly seen as the most suitable and least trade distorting of the instruments for pursuing environmental goals.[149] Next, the protection of

[144] Eg, European Commission JRC Technical Report: Revision of the EU Ecolabel Criteria for Paper Products, Final Technical Report (January 2019).

[145] Recital (1) of the EU Regulation (n 102).

[146] M Du, 'The Necessity Test in World Trade Law: What Now?' (2016) 15 *Chinese Journal of International Law* 817, 841.

[147] European Commission, 'Report from the Commission to the European Parliament and the Council', COM (2017) 355 Final, at 4.

[148] Ibid, at 8.

[149] A Green, 'Climate Change, Regulatory Policy and the WTO: How Constraining are Trade Rules?' (2005) 8(1) *Journal of International Economic Law* 143, 186.

environment is generally seen as an important regulatory objective explicitly recognised by the WTO as well as numerous international treaties. Lastly, on the possible alternative means to achieve the objective, there is some proposal on the privately sponsored ecolabelling scheme replacing state-administered voluntary labelling. However, it is not clear if privately sponsored schemes may be less trade restrictive than state-administered ones; state-administered schemes may be more effective in achieving their regulatory objectives.[150] In short, it is highly unlikely that the EU Ecolabelling scheme is found to be an unnecessary obstacle to international trade.

### *iv. The Relevant International Standard*

Although environmental labels can provide information about a product in terms of its overall environmental benefits and positively influence consumer choices, the increasing proliferation of environmental labelling has led to concerns of 'greenwashing' and exaggerated marketing claims. International standards on environmental labelling are therefore needed to provide a credible and level playing field. Paragraph F of the CGP provides that where international standards exist, the standardising body shall use them, or the relevant parts of them, as a basis for the standards it develops, except where such international standards or relevant parts would be ineffective or inappropriate. The ISO 14020 series of standards provide an internationally recognised and agreed set of benchmarks against which environmental labels can be prepared.[151] For our purpose, the most relevant are ISO 14020, which outlines the guiding principles for the development and use of environmental labels that underpin all the other standards in the 14020 series,[152] and ISO 14024, which outlines the requirements for developing Type 1 environmental labelling programmes.[153] Type 1 environmental labelling is defined by ISO as 'a voluntary, multiple-criteria based, third party programme that awards a licence which authorises the use of environmental labels on products indicating overall environmental preferability of a product within a particular product category based on life cycle considerations'.[154] EU ecolabelling is one of the best known Type 1 environmental labels.[155] During the drafting process, there was express concern for disciplining the potential abuse of the environmental labelling scheme as unjustified barriers to international trade.[156]

[150] Vranes (n 119) 240–241.

[151] ISO Central Secretariat, 'Environmental Labels' (2019) 2.

[152] ISO 14020, Environmental Labels and Declarations- General Principles (15 September 2000).

[153] ISO 14024:2018, Environmental labels and declarations- Type 1 environmental labeling – Principles and procedures (2018-02).

[154] Ibid, Art 3.1.

[155] O Brilhante and JM Skinner, 'Promoting Sustainable Construction in the EU: Green Labels, Certification Systems and Green Procurement' (June 2015) 23.

[156] DA Wirth, 'The International Organization for Standardization: Private Voluntary Standards as Swords and Shields' (2009) 36 *Boston College Environmental Affairs Law Review* 79, 98.

ISO 14020 establishes guiding principles for the development and use of environmental labels and declarations. The overall goal of environmental labels is through communication of verifiable and accurate information on environmental aspects of products to encourage the demand for and supply of those products that cause less stress on the environment, thereby stimulating the potential for market-driven continuous environmental improvement.[157] These general principles include: environmental labels shall be accurate, relevant and not misleading; procedures and requirements for environmental labels shall not create unnecessary obstacles to international trade; based on scientific methodology; life cycle analysis; open, participatory consultation with interested parties; availability of relevant information on environmental labels to purchasers from the party making the environmental label.[158] ISO 14024 establishes more specific principles and procedures for developing Type 1 environmental labelling programmes, including the selection of product categories, product environmental criteria, product function characteristics, and for assessing and demonstrating compliance.[159] Key guiding principles of Type 1 labels include: voluntary nature of the programme; a third party sets the criteria and grants licences to use the label; verifiable; criteria are set to enable products to be distinguished by measurable environmental impacts; consistent with the requirements of ISO 14020; transparency process; a product's fitness for purposes and general performance are considered; label certificate subject to regular review.[160]

Both ISO standards were approved by CEN as European Standards and CEN members are bound to comply with the CEN Internal Regulations which stipulates the conditions for giving this European Standard the status of a national standard without any alteration.[161] As a Type I ecolabel, the EU Ecolabelling scheme makes it clear that it works in accordance with the ISO standard 14024.[162] Nevertheless, some problems have emerged from the European Commission Report on the review of implementation of the EU Ecolabel regulation. For example, according to ISO standards, ecolabels must be 'accurate, verifiable, relevant and not misleading' and 'based on scientific methodology that is sufficiently thorough and comprehensive to support the claim'. The Commission report shows that the quantitative benchmark of EU ecolabel's environmental excellence cannot be verified due to the lack of an agreed methodology for comparison. In some cases, when the validity of EU ecolabel criteria is extended without a thorough analysis of the evolution of the market situation, the EU ecolabel may no longer reflect environmental excellence.[163]

[157] ISO 14020: 2001, Art 3.

[158] Ibid, Art 4.

[159] ISO 14024:2018, Art 1.

[160] Ibid, Art 5–7.

[161] ISO 14024:2018 was approved by European Committee for Standardization (CEN) as EN ISO: 14024 on 21 March 2018.

[162] The EU Ecolabelling Regulation, Art 6(f), 7(2) and 11.

[163] European Commission, 'Report from the Commission to the European Parliament and the Council', COM(2017) 355 Final, at 4.

### D. Conclusion

The EU Ecolabel scheme is intended to promote products which have a higher level of environmental performance during their entire life cycle than other similar products and services. As the features of the EU Ecolabelling scheme meet the definition of 'standard', it falls within the regulatory scope of the TBT Agreement. The EU Ecolabel scheme is on paper consistent with ISO standard 14024, the relevant international standard governing Type 1 ecolabels. As a voluntary scheme, it is also highly unlikely that the scheme may be considered as unnecessary trade barriers. However, there is legal uncertainty whether products qualified for the EU ecolabel and those that are not so qualified simply because of inferior environmental performance are 'like products'. If they are considered 'like products', then the government support and promotion of products with EU ecolabels may run the risk of modifying the conditions of competition in the relevant market to the detriment of like imported products without EU ecolabels. It is possible to argue that the EU Ecolabelling scheme makes a legitimate regulatory distinction between like products with different environmental performance as reflected in the award of ecolabels, but that conclusion will be based on a number of factors such as the labelling criteria can be verified by scientific evidence; foreign PPMs and unique foreign circumstances were adequately considered in making decisions on whether ecolabel may be awarded etc. Given that the legitimate regulatory distinction is interpreted rather stringently in WTO case law, there remains a real risk that the EU ecolabelling regulation may be found inconsistent with the CGP.

## III. FOREST STEWARDSHIP COUNCIL (FSC) CERTIFICATION AND THE WTO LAW

### A. An Overview of the FSC

For centuries, foresters have used their sustainable management skills to balance competing demands on the forest, ensuring its ability to produce wood and deliver other forest products, without infringing on the resilience of ecosystems. In recent years, the critical role of forests as carbon sinks and as sources of renewable materials and energy has been clearly recognised. The significance of deforestation worldwide as one of the main contributors to greenhouse gas emissions, exceeding the impact of all other sectors, is also well recognised.[164]

In this broad context, the FSC was established in 1993 as a follow-up to the United Nations Conference on Environment and Development, the Earth

[164] VC Martons and F Romig, 'Trade in Energy and Forestry: A perspective from the United Nations Economic Commission for Europe', www.wto.org/english/res_e/publications_e/wtr10_forum_e/wtr10_11may10_e.htm accessed on 20 April 2020.

Summit at Rio de Janeiro, 1992 with the mission to promote environmentally appropriate, socially beneficial, and economically viable management of the world's forests through a system of certification and labelling.[165] Although the Rio Summit adopted Agenda 21, it failed to produce a legally binding commitment on forest management. Disillusioned with the effectiveness of government regulation and legislation to address forest sustainability challenges, a group of NGOs concerned with the sustainability of forest came together to create the FSC, an international NGO that develops and approves FSC Stewardship Standards, a voluntary certification and labelling programme for forest products from sustainably harvested and verified sources, which are based on the FSC Principles and Criteria.[166] The market impact of the FSC is constantly growing. By 3 December 2018, more than 200 million hectares of forest, distributed in 85 countries worldwide, were certified to FSC standards. This is an area roughly corresponding to 14 per cent of the world's managed forests. In addition, there are almost 35,772 chain-of-custody certificates issued in 123 countries.[167]

The FSC is established as a multi-stakeholder membership organisation with both individuals and organisations as members, including private enterprises, NGOs, international organisations, indigenous groups and educational institutions.[168] Although state-owned or -controlled companies can participate in the FSC (in the economic chamber only) as members and the FSC in various ways collaborates with states and intergovernmental organisations, it is considered a private body because countries cannot participate as such, nor governmental agencies.[169] Members are divided into three chambers – environmental, economic, and social. Each chamber has one-third of the voting power. In addition, the voting power is divided equally between developed (referred to as 'Northern') and developing ('Southern') country members in each chamber.[170] The FSC thus makes room for both business interests (the economic chamber), social (eg labour unions and representatives of local communities and indigenous groups) and environmental NGOs. The FSC membership has been steadily growing from its inception. At the end of December 2018, the FSC membership stood at 1,087. Yet, it has struggled to achieve a balanced representation of members from the different chambers. There is still less representation of social stakeholders.[171] The FSC is governed by a General Assembly (GA) of these members and the GA elects the nine-member Board of Directors, comprising three members from each of the three chambers.[172]

[165] Art 4 of FSC Statutes (2017).
[166] Villarreal (n 36) 17.
[167] FSC Annual Report 2018 (2019) 52-53.
[168] Article 11 of FSC Statutes (2017).
[169] Villarreal (n 36) 24.
[170] Art 12 of FSC Statutes (2017).
[171] M Bostrom and KT Hallstrom, 'Global Multi-Stakeholder Standard Setters: How Fragile are they?' (2013) 9 (1) *Journal of Global Ethics* 93, 95.
[172] Art 13 of FSC Statutes (2017).

The basic FSC standards are known as the FSC 'Principles and Criteria', which are formulated at a general, abstract level, and must be worked out in more concrete regional or national processes of standard setting and certification. The framework has 10 principles, and each principle is coupled with a number of criteria. Certification is carried out by an accredited third-party certifier, which can use either a national/regional adjusted FSC standard or the FSC's Principles and Criteria directly in countries lacking such locally adjusted standards. Through chain-of-custody certification, the products that come from certified forests are given the FSC label.[173]

## B. The FSC Certification in the Eyes of the World Trade Organisation

There is recognition among some WTO Members and civil society that certain private environmental standards and labels, such as the FSC label, are becoming widely accepted both at the international level and by consumers. But there is much uncertainty as to whether WTO rules apply to the FSC standard.[174] In this section, I will first discuss whether the FSC label, a private certifications scheme, is a 'standard' and thus covered by the TBT Agreement. Then, I will explore whether the FSC standard is an 'international standard' for the purpose of the TBT Agreement.

### *i. Is the FSC Label Covered by the TBT Agreement?*

As analysed in Chapter 2, to meet the definition of 'standard', three elements must be met: first, the standard must be approved by a 'recognised body'; second, it must provide rules, guidelines or characteristics for product or related PPMs; and third, the compliance with a standard is not mandatory. First, as a private global multi-stakeholder standard setter, the FSC certification scheme is entirely voluntary. It involves an audit of a forest's management by an independent organisation to check that it meets internationally and nationally agreed standards of responsible forest management. Forest products like timber can then carry the FSC label, guaranteeing that it comes from a well-managed forest.[175]

Second, an award of the FSC label is based on non-product-related production and process methods (NPR-PPMs) as it seeks to promote forest products from

[173] FSC, 'FSC Principles and Criteria for Forest Stewardship', FSC-STD-01-001 V5-2 EN (22 July 2015) 6.

[174] Natural Resources Institute, 'Forest Certification in the Eyes of the World Trade Organization', Ethical Trade Policy Watching Brief 1 (October 1999) 1-4. AE Appleton, 'Private Climate Change Standards and Labelling Schemes under the WTO Agreement on Technical Barriers to Trade' in T Cottier, O Nartova and SZ Bigdeli (eds) *International Trade Regulation and the Mitigation of Climate Change* (Cambridge University Press, 2009) 137, 144.

[175] FSC, Forest Management – Fact Sheet (05 March 2018) 1.

sustainably harvested and verified sources and encourages responsible management of the world's forests. From the perspective of end-use suitability, forest products sourced from sustainably managed forests are unlikely to differ from those harvested from a less-sustainable manner.[176] Although it remains uncertain to what extent NPR-PPMs fall under the purview of the TBT Agreement as developing countries are strongly opposed to them, it is well settled in the WTO law that a labelling requirement, regardless of the information contained, *as such* constitutes a product characteristic and is covered by the TBT Agreement. Therefore, the FSC certification and labelling cannot be ruled out of the TBT regulatory scope simply because it is based on NPR-PPMs.

Third, the thorniest issue is whether the FSC is a 'recognised body'. There is no doubt that the FSC is a 'body' as it is a properly incorporated legal entity under Mexican law that has specific tasks of promoting environmentally appropriate, socially beneficial, and economically viable management of the world's forests and composition, including Members, the General Assembly, the Board of Directors and the Director General.[177] But is the FSC a 'recognised' body? Both a government body (be it central, local or regional) and a non-governmental body could be a recognised body. In Chapter 5, the analysis shows that the relevant factors to be considered may include, inter alia, (i) whether the entity is established or endorsed by one or more WTO Members as a standardisation body, (ii) whether the entity is involved in the standardisation activities of international standardisation organisations such as ISO and the IEC, (iii) whether any WTO Members apply standards promulgated by the entity, (iv) whether the body is open to the involvement of other WTO Members, (v) whether the body has accepted the CGP and compliance with subsequent guidance on the development of international standards, as laid out in the TBT Committee's Second Triennial Review of the TBT Agreement (Annex 4), (vi) whether the aim of the standard furthers a legitimate TBT objective.[178]

It is submitted that the FSC standard meets most of these criteria. First, whilst it is unlikely that private standards with little or no governmental involvement or endorsement fall within the definition of 'standard' in the TBT Agreement, there is strong evidence demonstrating that at least some WTO Members are not only aware of the standardisation activity at the FSC, but also recognise its normative value. To begin with, a number of countries, particularly in Europe, have incorporated FSC standards into their national technical regulations or procurement policies. For example, the UK Government Timber Procurement

[176] C Tollefson, F Gale and D Haley, *Setting the Standards: Certification, Governance, and the Forest Stewardship* (University of British Columbia Press, 2008) 258.

[177] Art 6 of FSC Statutes (2017); Explanatory Note to Annex 1 of the TBT Agreement; Art 4.1 of ISO/IEC Guide 2 (1991).

[178] CIEL and ISEAL Alliance, 'International Standards and Technical Barriers to Trade Legal Opinion Summary' (July 2006) 4, www.isealalliance.org/sites/default/files/resource/2017-12/ISEAL_CIEL_Legal_Opinion.pdf, accessed 20 April 2020; Appleton (n174) 144.

Policy (TPP) requires that only timber and wood-derived products originating from an independently verifiable Legal and Sustainable source will be demanded for use on the government estate. In order to demonstrate compliance with the TPP requirement, the FSC certification is recognised by the UK Government as meeting the criteria and delivering requirements for both legality and sustainability.[179] Some countries, like Mexico, have based their national technical regulations on FSC standards, and others, like South Africa, have committed to have their forests certified according to FSC standards.[180]

Furthermore, some WTO Members explicitly seek FSC certification and pay fees to the FSC. This is a common practice in some eastern European countries with large state-owned forests, including Estonia, Latvia, and Poland.[181] Other WTO Members, including Austria, Germany, UK, Switzerland, Denmark and the Netherlands, have provided funding for the FSC through donations.[182] Still, the standardization activities of the FSC are not recognised by all WTO Members.

Finally, even if the FSC has nongovernmental authority, it often serves to support governmental authorities. For example, a growing number of countries and regions – including the European Union, US and Australia – have legislation banning the trade and use of illegally harvested timber and derived products. FSC certification can be used as part of a due diligence system to meet the mandatory European Timber Regulation (EUTR).[183] When Bolivia passed a requirement that forest concessionaries meet certain sustainability standards, the FSC was identified as the only certification body that met those standards. It became the de facto auditor for Bolivia while the government worked toward developing its own auditing scheme.[184]

Second, the FSC is open to involvement of all individuals and entities of all WTO Members. However, its membership excludes governments and governmental agencies and only state-owned or -controlled companies can participate in the Economic Chamber. One good example is the Joint Stock Company 'Latvia's State Forests', whose stakeholder is the state represented by the Ministry of Agriculture of the Republic of Latvia. Therefore, one may argue that governments can participate in the FSC indirectly.[185]

[179] Department for Environment Food and Rural Affairs, 'Results of the Evaluation of Category A Evidence: Forest Certification Schemes', Defra Project ID EV0481 (October 2015).

[180] K Dingwerth, 'North-South Parity in Global Governance: The Affirmative Procedures of the Forest Stewardship Council' (2008) 14 (1) *Global Governance* 53, 59.

[181] E Meidinger, 'The Administrative Law of Global Private-Public Regulation: The Case of Forestry' (2006) 17 *European Journal of International Law* 47, 59.

[182] MN Moody, 'Warning: May Cause Warming Potential Trade Challenges to Private Environmental Labels' (2012) 65 (5) *Vanderbilt Law Review* 1401, 1436.

[183] NEPCon, 'How Forest Certification Systems Meet the EUTR Requirements' (Version 2.0, January 2019) 13–14.

[184] Rainforest Alliance, 'Toward Sustainability: The Roles and Limitations of Certification' (June 2012) 33.

[185] Villarreal (n 36) 194.

Third, the FSC has comprehensively revised its principles and criteria in developing standards and made it clear that they are developed in compliance with the CGP of the WTO TBT Agreement.[186] As my analysis will show in the next section, the FSC standard-setting procedures are also to some extent consistent with the TBT Committee Decision on the development of international standards. It may also be argued that responsible management of forest is a legitimate purpose supported by the TBT Agreement.

### *ii. Is the FSC Standard an 'International Standard'?*

In *US – Tuna II*, the AB concluded that an international standard is 'a standard adopted by an international standardizing body'[187] Thus, it is primarily the characteristics of the international standardising body (ISB) that lends a standard its international character. The AB further held that for the purpose of the TBT Agreement, an ISB must have *recognised activities* in standardisation and whose membership is open to the *relevant bodies* of at least all WTO Members.[188] In part B(i) above, I have already argued that the FSC is a recognised standardisation body for at least some WTO Members. To meet the definition of an ISB, it must also be shown that (1) the membership of the FSC is 'open' to all relevant bodies of at least all WTO Members and (2) the FSC standard-setting is consistent with the TBT Committee Decision on the development of international standards.

For the open requirement, the AB reasoned in *US – Tuna II* that the accession provision of the ISB should not disadvantage the relevant bodies of some Members, either or de jure or de facto, and if there are procedures or requirements, they should be a mere formality. Also, an ISB should be open at all stages of the standards-development process. First, the accession provision in the FSC is largely a mere formality as in practice almost all applications are accepted.[189] All Members can participate in all the subsidiary bodies created by these bodies and through all the development process of each standard or at any step they decide to. Second, the FSC is open to individuals and legal entities of all WTO Members, which may result in a number of bodies from one single WTO Member. The FSC excludes government agencies from its membership but allows state-owned or state-controlled companies to participate in the Economic Chamber.[190] This exclusion may raise questions as to whether the FSC is open to all the relevant bodies of WTO Members, in particular if the relevant body of a WTO Member is a government agency. It may be argued that

[186] FSC (n 173) 5.
[187] AB Report, *US – Tuna II* (n 1) para 356.
[188] Ibid, para 359.
[189] F Gale and M Haward, *Global Commodity Governance: State Response to Sustainable Forest and Fisheries Certification* (Palgrave, 2011) 53.
[190] Art 12 of FSC Statutes (2017).

WTO Members can still make their way into participating through state-owned and -controlled companies and therefore the FSC complies with the definition of ISB in the TBT Agreement.[191] But this argument may be tenuous as not all WTO Members have state-owned or controlled companies interested in forest sustainable management.

There is also some evidence that the FSC has complied with the six principles embodied in the TBT Committee Decision on the development of international standards. First, transparency. The FSC is highly transparent with regards to its standardisation activities. The FSC informs all the draft standards and standards that are under review through its publication in the FSC newsletters and website. All the interested parties are provided with adequate time (30 days) to make comments in writing, which are taken into consideration. Meetings are open to all interested parties and the final standards are publicly available.[192]

Second, openness. The FSC is a completely open body as any interested party can participate in the standardisation process and submit comments. However, at the policy level, certification bodies, industry associations and government-owned or controlled companies cannot be elected to the Board of Directors.[193] This exclusion might be explained as an attempt to help safeguard the credibility of the FSC standard. Certification bodies and industry are actual users of the standard so they may have a conflict of interest problem. The exclusion of state-owned or controlled firms may be explained by the lack of trust toward governments who failed to reach international agreements and national policies to protect the forests. Moreover, the majority of the FSC members come from European and North American countries; stakeholders from African and Asian countries are underrepresented, so are smallholders.[194]

Third, impartiality and consensus. The FSC was created with the aim of providing a voice for all stakeholders that should be included in the development of a particular standard, including that are normally underrepresented or excluded from the debate such as social and environmental stakeholders.[195] For this purpose, the FSC has set up a chamber and sub-chamber system to ensure a balanced representation of all affected interests, including the divergent interests between Northern and Southern interests.

Despite the FSC's structure and efforts, it has struggled to achieve a balanced representation of members from the different chambers. There is still less representation of social stakeholders at the FSC.[196] Moreover, in general, stakeholders from the developing countries are underrepresented.[197]

[191] Villarreal (n 36) 196, 243. FSC, 'Standard Setting in FSC' (7 July 2016).
[192] FSC, The Development and Revision of FSC Normative Documents (25 March 2015).
[193] Art 24 of FSC Statutes (2017).
[194] FSC, 'FSC Annual Report 2018', at 24.
[195] FSC, 'Global Strategic Plan 2015-2020' (2015) 15.
[196] Bostrom and Hallstrom (n 171) 96.
[197] T Cadman, *Quality and Legitimacy of Global Governance: Case Lessons from Forestry* (Palgrave, 2011) 61.

FSC standards are developed through a sophisticated consultation process that includes all interested parties. The coordinator shall plan for two rounds of public consultation and a public consultation round shall consist of a period of at least 60 days, which may be reduced to 30 in exceptional circumstances. All valid comments received should be made publicly available and be answered with an indication of how the issues raised were addressed.[198] The working group makes recommendation for approval of FSC standards through consensus. Main issues and concerns raised during the consultation process should be explained and addressed in the report for the FSC board of directors. Lack of consensus on a specific issue should be recorded.[199]

Fourth, effectiveness and relevance. Several studies provide evidence that FSC certification have generated an ecological impact in certified forests in terms of forest management, enhancing biodiversity, social improvements, and economic benefits. However, the methodologies of these studies are questioned, and other studies have identified some contradictory results. Consequently, it is impossible to draw any definitive conclusion on the basis of the existing evidence so far.[200] Moreover, as of December 2018, only 14 per cent of the world's managed forests were certified by FSC standards. Most of the certified forests are located in Western Europe and North America (83 per cent), while developing countries only account for 17 per cent. The lack of interest in FSC certification in developing countries may be due to exorbitant FSC certification, false expectations regarding price premium for certified timber, and difficulty in accessing to Northern markets.[201] Finally, FSC standards are periodically reviewed after its publication to ensure its relevance.[202]

Fifth, coherence. The proposal for new work at FSC requires considering what other standards exist or are in the process of development which meet all or part of the expressed need.[203] However, it is not clear how the FSC will consider the existence of other similar standards to avoid overlap and duplication. The FSC's competitor is the Programme for Endorsement of Forest Certification Schemes (PEFC), another major global forestry certification scheme created mainly by industry and government with the similar mission of the FSC. Compared with the PEFC, FSC members represent more countries and

[198] FSC (n 192), Arts 5.5–5.12.

[199] Ibid, Art 7.2.

[200] A Marx, E Becault and J Wouters, 'Private Standards in Forestry: Assessing the Legitimacy and Effectiveness of the Forest Stewardship Council', in A Marx, M Maerrtens, J Swinnen and J Wouters (eds), *Private Standards and Global Governance: Economic, Legal and Political Perspectives* 153 (Edward Elgar, 2012) 60, 82–83.

[201] DH Schepers, 'Challenges to Legitimacy at the Forest Stewardship Council' (2009) 92 *Journal of Business Ethics* 279; 286; F Carrera et al, 'Forest Certification in Guatemala', in B Cashore at al (eds), *Confronting Sustainability: Forest Certification in Developed and Transitional Countries* (Yale School of Forestry & Environmental Studies, 2006) 406.

[202] FSC (n 192) Art 9-11.

[203] Ibid, Art 2.2.

are more inclusive. It is also claimed that FSC standards are stricter and offer a higher level of assurance.[204]

Sixth, development dimension. The FSC has given some consideration to facilitating developing countries' participation in standards development. For example, the FSC has a structure in which stakeholders from developing and developed countries are differentiated. Stakeholders from the South pay lower fees while enjoying the same rights as Northerners. The Southern stakeholders also have their own sub-chamber in each chamber. When developing standards, the working groups need to have a balanced stakeholder representation. The FSC also provides some financial and assistance to stakeholders from developing countries to participate in its standardisation activities.[205]

## IV. CONCLUSION

There is a lot of uncertainty concerning the status of FSC Standards in the WTO law. An argument could be made that the FSC certification and accreditation falls within the regulatory scope of the TBT, and that the FSC standard may fulfil the definition of international standard for the purpose of the TBT Agreement as well. Indeed, even the FSC claims that its standard development principles and criteria are consistent with the CGP of the TBT Agreement. That said, it must be cautioned that this conclusion is highly tentative and controversial. The best evidence is yet to come to firm up the conclusion and the burden of proof falls on the people who argue that the TBT Agreement is applicable and that FSC standards are 'international standards'. This is a tall order.

[204] NEPCon, 'Comparative Analysis of the PEFC System with FSC Controlled Wood Requirements' (May, 2012) 17; Cadman (n 197) 59.

[205] Villarreal (n 36) 243.

# 7

# Conclusion

WITH TARIFFS, QUOTAS and other traditional instruments of protectionism increasingly unimportant in international trade, the predominant concern of the GATT/WTO regime has shifted to standards and technical regulations that exist behind the national borders.[1] A 'standard' is defined in the TBT Agreement as 'a document approved by a recognised body laying down product characteristics or related processes and production methods with which compliance is not mandatory'. A typical example is voluntary sustainability standards which are rules that producers, traders, manufacturers, retailers or service providers may be asked to follow so that the things they make or grow do not hurt people and the environment.[2] Over the past few decades, a great number and wide range of product standards have been applied to international trade.[3] Increased standardisation activity reflects, among other factors, demand by consumers for safer and higher quality products, rising living standards, technological innovations, the expansion of global economic integration and the increased concern paid by many governments and non-governmental organisations to social issues and the environment.[4]

The proliferation of product standards has presented an important policy dilemma to international rule-makers. On the one hand, standards play an important role in ensuring the functioning of the market, increasing economic efficiency, correcting market failures and fostering innovation. They vary sometimes tremendously among countries, and very often for good reasons such as different levels of development, technology, environmental requirements and preferences.[5] On the other hand, standards may be captured by well-organised

[1] WTO Trade Report, *Trade and Public Policy: A Closer Look at Non-Tariff Measures in the 21st Century* (2012) 37.

[2] UN Forum on Sustainability Standards (UNFSS), *Voluntary Sustainability Standards, Trade and Sustainable Development* (2018) 3.

[3] K Purnhagen, 'Mapping Private Regulation- Classification, Market Access and Market Closure Policy and Law's Response' (2015) *Journal of World Trade* 309; SI Akhtar and VC Jones, 'Proposed Transatlantic Trade and Investment Partnership (TTIP): In Brief', Congressional Research Service (11 June 2014) 8.

[4] European Commission, *A Strategic Vision for European Standards: Moving forward to Enhance and Accelerate the Sustainable Growth of the European Economy by 2020*, EC Communication COM (2011) 311 Final (June 1, 2011); World Trade Report, *Exploring the Links between Trade, Standards and the WTO* (2005).

[5] AO Sykes, 'The (limited) Role of Regulatory Harmonisation in International Goods and Service Markets' (1999) 2 *Journal of International Economic Law* 49, 57.

interest groups or narrow constituencies at the expense of the general interests of the whole society at large. They may be designed to the effect of discriminating the imported products vis-à-vis domestic like products de jure or de facto. Even if product standards are not intended to provide protection to domestic producers, these standards may be opaque, duplicative, poorly designed, badly implemented, or simply unreasonably burdensome on trade.[6] Though effects of heterogeneous product standards on international trade are difficult to quantify, there is strong evidence supporting the proposition that they could potentially constitute substantial barriers to international flow of goods. This is especially the case for small- and medium-size enterprises in the developing countries.[7] Accordingly, if WTO rules are applied too strictly, a broad intrusion into the regulatory space of standardising bodies might place unnecessary limits on non-protectionist standards and thwart legitimate policy decisions and value choice of domestic consumers. On the other hand, if WTO disciplines are applied too laxly, a failure to consider seriously the possibility of covert protectionism arising from the proliferation of product standards undermines the integrity of trade disciplines, providing a ready means of cheating with impunity on explicit trade commitments.

In light of the foregoing, the purpose of this book is to explore to what extent should WTO disciplines penetrate into the regulatory space of WTO Members, non-governmental bodies and other international standardising bodies (ISBs) in setting product standards based on their alleged trade concerns. By answering this question, this book intends to provide a comprehensive and critical analysis of how governmental, private and hybrid product standards are regulated under GATT/WTO law, as well as to explore the implications of regime interaction between the WTO and other standard-setting bodies at both national and international levels.

The TBT Agreement makes a clear distinction between a 'standard' and a 'technical regulation'. While the compliance with a technical regulation is mandatory, the compliance with a standard is only voluntary. Four elements must be fulfilled to meet the definition of standard. First, a standard must provide product characteristics or related process and production methods (PPMs). Second, a standard must be approved by a 'recognised body'. Third, a standard must apply to an *identifiable* product or group of products. Finally, the compliance with a standard must not be mandatory. For the first element,

[6] OECD, *International Regulatory Cooperation and Trade: Understanding the Trade Costs of Regulatory Divergence and the Remedies* (2017) 16–18; A Marx and J Wouters, 'Competition and Cooperation in the Market of Voluntary Sustainability Standards', in P Delimatsis (eds), *Law, Economics and Politics of International Standardization* 215 (Cambridge University Press, 2015), 221–231.

[7] L Fontagne, G Orefice, R Piermartini and N Rocha, 'Product Standards and Margins of Trade: Firm Level Evidence', WTO Staff Working Paper ERSD-2013-04 (2013) 4; I Sheldon, 'North-South Trade and Standards: What can General Equilibrium Analysis Tell us?' (2012) 11(3) *World Trade Review* 376, 388.

product characteristics include not only any objectively definable features and qualities *intrinsic* to the product, such as a product's composition, size, hardness, flammability and density, but also 'distinguishing marks' of a product, such as the means of identification, the presentation and the appearance of a product. They may be prescribed in either a positive or a negative form.[8] The AB usually had no difficulty in holding that the measure at issue set out product characteristics until *EC – Seal Products* in which the AB ruled that for a multi-faceted measure, a panel must carefully examine the design and operation of the measure while seeking to identify its 'integral and essential' aspects. It is these features of the measure that are to be accorded the most weight for the purpose of characterising the measure.[9] It remains unsettled to what extent PPMs fall under the purview of the TBT Agreement. Although the negotiating history appears to support the position that only product-related PPMs are covered in the definition of a standard, it is not clear whether the AB will adhere to such a narrow interpretation. At least for labelling requirements, the debate has become increasingly irrelevant in practice. In several recent cases, such as *US – Tuna II* and *US – Cool*, in which the labelling requirements at issue were based on non-product-related PPMs, the AB nevertheless held that they should be scrutinised under the TBT Agreement.[10] The AB's rulings have confirmed that a labelling requirement, regardless of the information contained, *as such* constitutes a product characteristic and is covered by the TBT Agreement. For the 'identifiable' requirement, it does not suggest that those products need to be named or otherwise expressly identified. Even though a product standard does not expressly identify products by name, they may be still identifiable through the characteristic that is the subject of the standard.[11]

What is a 'recognised body' is not defined in the TBT Agreement. Both a government body (be it central, local or regional) and a non-governmental body could be a recognised body.[12] However, for a private standard to meet the definition of 'standard', the non-governmental entity that approves the standard must be recognised by WTO Members. This official recognition is critical in the

[8] WTO Appellate Body Report, *European Communities – Measures Affecting Asbestos and Asbestos-Containing Products (EC – Asbestos)*, WT/DS135/AB/R, adopted 5 April 2001, paras 66–70.

[9] WTO Appellate Body Report, *European Communities – Measures Prohibiting the Importation and Marketing of Seal Products (EC– Seal Products)*, WT/DS400/AB/R, adopted on 18 June 2014, para 5.19.

[10] Panel Report, *United States- Certain Country of Origin Labelling (COOL) Requirements*, WT/DS384/R, adopted 18 November 2011, para 7.212; Appellate Body Report, *United States – Measures Concerning the Importation, Marketing and Sale of Tuna and Tuna Product (US – Tuna II)*, WT/DS381/AB/R, adopted 13 June 2012, para 199.

[11] WTO Appellate Body Report, *European Communities – Trade Description of Sardines (EC – Sardines)*, WT/DS231/AB/R, adopted 23 October 2002, para 185.

[12] P Delimatsis, 'Relevant International Standards and Recognised Standardization Bodies under the TBT Agreement' in P Delimatsis (eds), *The Law, Economics and Politics of International Standardization* (Cambridge University Press, 2015) 127.

determination of whether the TBT Agreement is applicable to a specific private standard.[13] To determine whether a standardising body is a 'recognised body', the relevant factors to be considered may include, inter alia, (i) whether the entity's incorporation documents include the power to formulate and issue standards, (ii) whether the entity is established or endorsed by one or more WTO Members as a standardisation body, (iii) whether the entity is involved in the standardisation activities of international standardisation organisations such as ISO and the IEC, (iv) whether any WTO Members apply standards promulgated by the entity, (v) whether the body is open to the involvement of other WTO Members, (vi) whether the body has accepted the Code of Good Practice and compliance with subsequent guidance on the development of international standards, as laid out in the TBT Committee's Second Triennial Review of the TBT Agreement (Annex 4), and (vii) whether the aim of the standard furthers a legitimate TBT objective.[14] Applying this analytical framework to standardising bodies, it is unlikely that private standards with little or no governmental involvement or endorsement fall within the definition of 'standard' in the TBT Agreement.[15]

Conventional wisdom holds that the compliance is mandatory when a technical requirement, such as a label, is required for market access, The AB has clarified that, after *US – Tuna II*, in addition to the traditional understanding, an 'exclusive' label, in the sense that it is the only way to meet the requirement and is enforced by the governmental power, will transform what would otherwise be a 'standard' into a 'technical regulation'[16]

Though product standards could be significant non-tariff barriers, they are also in essence public goods used by governments and private firms to address market failures such as network externalities, information asymmetry, and negative externalities, improve welfare and achieve public policy objectives.[17] The effects of standards on the volume and direction of trade flows tend to be complex and there is only rather limited empirical literature on the subject. An important point emerging from both economic theory and the empirical evidence is that there is no monotonic relationship between standardisation and

[13] M Du and F Deng, 'International Standards as Global Public Goods in the World Trading System' (2016) 43 (2) *Legal Issues of Economic Integration* 113, 132.

[14] CIEL and ISEAL Alliance, 'International Standards and Technical Barriers to Trade Legal Opinion Summary' (July 2006) 4, www.isealalliance.org/sites/default/files/resource/2017-12/ISEAL_CIEL_Legal_Opinion.pdf, accessed 20 April 2020; AE Appleton, 'Private Climate Change Standards and Labelling Schemes under the WTO Agreement on Technical Barriers to Trade' in T Cottier, O Nartova and SZ Bigdeli (eds) *International Trade Regulation and the Mitigation of Climate Change* (Cambridge University Press, 2009) 137, 144.

[15] A Kudryavtsev, *Private-Sector Standards as Technical Barriers in International Trade in Goods: In Search of WTO Disciplines* (Wolf Legal Publishers, 2015) 290

[16] Appellate Body Report, *US – Tuna II* (n 10) para 199; H Schepel, 'Between Standards and Regulation: On the Concept of 'de facto mandatory standards' after Tuna II and Fra.bo' in P Delimatsis (ed), *The Law, Economics and Politics of International Standardization* 199 (*Cambridge University Press*, 2015) 211.

[17] WTO Trade Report (n 4) 42–51.

trade flows. Standards can be both trade creating and trade hampering.[18] It is thus important to distinguish different types of standards and to analyse their effects on trade flows on a case-by-case basis.

Product standards could be categorised as public standards and private standards, mandatory standards and voluntary standards; product standards and PPMs; and national, regional and international standards.[19] This book focuses on three types of standards: voluntary standards administered by central government standardising bodies, international standards and standards sponsored by non-governmental bodies. To deal with the problems presented by heterogeneity in product standards, the WTO regime has adopted a sophisticated legal framework to curtail their adverse effects on international trade. The legal framework has evolved significantly from the Tokyo Round to the Uruguay Round. Currently, Article 1.1, III:4 and XX of the GATT 1994, the TBT Agreement, in particular its Annex 3 Code of Good Practice and the relevant TBT Committee Decisions, and the SPS Agreement constitute the core WTO disciplines on product standards. The search for the right balance between trade liberalisation while protecting important social values has characterised the evolution and interpretation of WTO disciplines on product standards.

All public and private standards falling within the definition of Annex 1.2 of the TBT Agreement are subject to the disciplines of the TBT Code of Good Practice (CGP) in Annex 3. The CGP is open to acceptance to all governmental, local and non-governmental standardising bodies which are active in the territory of a WTO Member. There is evidence that the CGP has been playing an important role in regulating how standards are set at both national and international levels. Between 1995 and 2019, 192 standardising bodies from 144 Members or observers have accepted the CGP.[20] The non-government standardising bodies that have accepted the CGP include not only those which enjoy a government franchise/mandate to coordinate standards in their respective countries such as the American National Standards Institute (ANSI), but also private industry consortiums. At the international level, many ISBs such as the International Organisation for Standardisation (ISO), the Forest Stewardship Council (FSC) and the ISEAL Alliance have revised their standardisation procedures or their code of good practice to incorporate the principles outlined in the CGP.[21]

[18] RL Pinto de Andrade, 'The Positive Consequences of Non-Tariff Barriers' (2009) 43(2) *Journal of World Trade* 363, 363–378. Y Li and JC Beghin, 'A Meta-analysis of Estimates of the Impact of Technical Barriers to Trade' (2012) 34 (3) *Journal of Policy Modelling* 497, 511.

[19] E Vranes, 'Climate Labelling and the WTO', *European Yearbook of International Economic law* (Springer, 2011) 211–213.

[20] Note by the Secretariat, 'Twenty-Fifth Annual Review of the Implementation and Operation of the TBT Agreement', G/TBT/44 (19 February 2020) 20.

[21] ISO/IEC Guide 59:2019; FSC Principles and Criteria for Forest Stewardship (22 July 2015); ISEAL Code of Good Practice (December 2014).

Article 4 of the TBT Agreement has imposed different levels of legal obligations on WTO Members depending on the nature of the standardising bodies. For central government standardising bodies, WTO Members are obliged to ensure that they accept and comply with the CGP. For local government and non-governmental standardising bodies, by contrast, WTO Members shall take 'reasonable measures' as may be available to them to ensure that they accept and comply with the CGP. Neither Article 4 of the TBT Agreement nor the CGP has been tested before the WTO dispute settlement body. Nevertheless, there is no doubt that TBT Article 4 has imposed enforceable obligations on WTO Members. Moreover, WTO Members have committed to largely identical disciplines to reduce the negative impact of standards in the CGP as they have done with regard to technical regulations. Given the similarities of trade law disciplines governing standards and technical regulations, it is reasonable to argue that the AB's extensive interpretative guidance over the substantive obligations on technical regulations is in principle transposable to standards in the CGP.[22]

Based on such an assumption, Chapter 3 has provided a critical analysis of key WTO disciplines governing product standards, including national treatment, most-favoured nation treatment, necessity test, transparency and scientific justifications, drawing on the rich WTO case law on technical regulations in the GATT, TBT and SPS Agreements. One important conclusion emerging from the extensive review of the WTO case law is that the WTO jurisprudence has been constantly evolving. The AB has kept refining and retuning its rulings to address the criticisms and to provide clarity to the scope and nature of relevant WTO disciplines. Nevertheless, uncertainties remain and these unresolved uncertainties are critically examined in chapter 3.

It is a basic undertaking by WTO Members not to use product standards in a protectionist fashion. This obligation is enshrined in the national treatment (NT) provision in Article III:4 of the GATT 1994 and Article 2.1 of the TBT Agreement. Despite the important role played by the NT obligation in constraining national regulatory measures, the AB has never formulated a clear and consistent criterion for its application.[23] The interpretation of Article III:4 hinges principally on three key terms. First, 'like products'; second, 'no less favourable treatment' and third, 'not applied so as to afford protection'. It is now firmly established that a determination of 'like products' under Article III:4 is fundamentally a determination about the nature and extent of a competitive

[22] E Partiti, 'What Use is an Unloaded Gun? The Substantive Disciplines of the WTO TBT Code of Good Practice and its Application to Private Standards Pursuing Public Objectives' (2017) 20 (4) *Journal of International Economic Law* 829, 833; A Davies, 'Technical Regulations and Standards under the WTO Agreement on Technical Barriers to Trade' (2014) 41(1) *Legal Issues of Economic Integration* 37, 43.

[23] NF Diebold, 'Standards of Non-Discrimination in International Economic Law' (2011) 60 (4) *International and Comparative Law Quarterly* 831, 832–833; S Lester, 'Finding the Boundaries of International Economic Law' (2014) 17 (1) *Journal of International Economic Law* 3, 9.

relationship between and among products.[24] Notably, the AB has repeatedly rejected the 'aims and effects' test and instead held that the regulatory purpose in Article III:1 should *not* be considered as part of the 'like products' inquiry.[25]

A violation of 'treatment no less favourable' obligation would be found when a measure modified the conditions of competition in the market place to the detriment of imported products.[26] Similar to the interpretation of 'like products', there has been a long-standing debate on whether the regulatory purpose in Article III:1 should be considered in the interpretation of 'treatment no less favourable' in Article III:4.[27] The AB has finally stated unequivocally in *EC – Seal Products* that a finding of detrimental impact on imported like products, without more, is a violation of 'treatment no less favourable' requirement and will automatically send the measure to be justified under GATT Article XX.[28] The AB's ruling shows that the AB attaches great importance to the *effects* of the measure and defines protectionism solely by disparate impact on imported products. Despite the AB's stringent interpretation of the NT obligation, there are still a few possible buffers which allow WTO Members more regulatory space than conventionally assumed for non-protectionist product standards. These buffers include the AB's 'genuine relationship' requirement between the measure at issue and its adverse impact on competitive opportunities between like products; the role of 'the design, structure and expected operations of the measure' in the NT analysis and how flexible the AB will be in using the different factors for the determination of 'like products'.[29]

Product standards inconsistent with substantive WTO obligations, such as Article I (most favoured nation treatment) and Article III (national treatment) may be justified by Article XX on 'General Exceptions'. The AB has established a two-tiered analysis to Article XX. A measure must first be provisionally justified under one of the legitimate objectives listed in subparagraphs of Article XX before it is further appraised under the chapeau.[30] The essential requirement of

[24] WTO Appellate Body Report, *European Communities – Measures Affecting Asbestos and Asbestos-Containing Products (EC – Asbestos)*, WT/DS135/AB/R, adopted 5 April 2001, para 99.

[25] WTO Panel Report, *Japan – Taxes on Alcoholic Beverages (Japan – Alcoholic Beverages)*, WT/DS8/R, adopted 1 November 1996, paras 6.16–6.18; WTO Appellate Body Report, *United States – Clove Cigarettes*, WT/DS406/AB/R, adopted 24 April 2012, paras 113–115.

[26] GATT Panel Report, *United States Section 337 of the Tariff Act of 1930*, L/6439, adopted 7 November 1989, BISD 36S/345, para 5.11; Appellate Body Report, *Korea – Measures Affecting Imports of Fresh, Chilled and Frozen Beef*, WT/DS161/AB/R, adopted 10 January 2001, paras 137–144.

[27] M Du, 'The Rise of National Regulatory Autonomy in the GATT/WTO Regime' (2011) 14 (3) *Journal of International Economic Law* 639, 655–664.

[28] WTO Appellate Body Report, *European Communities – Measures Prohibiting the Importation and Marketing of Seal Products (EC– Seal Products)*, WT/DS400/AB/R, adopted on 18 June 2014, paras 5.105–5.115.

[29] M Du, 'Treatment No Less Favourable and the Future of National Treatment Obligation in Article III:4 of the GATT 1994 after EC-Seal Products' (2016) 15 (1) *World Trade Review* 139, 155–163.

[30] WTO Appellate Body Report, *United States – Standards for Reformulated and Conventional Gasoline*, WT/DS2/AB/R, adopted 20 May 1996, 29–30; WTO Appellate Body Report,

the chapeau is that a measure provisionally justified under one of the subparagraphs of Article XX must not be applied in a manner that 'would constitute a means of arbitrary or unjustifiable discrimination between countries where the same conditions prevail'. This requirement is in essence an anti-discrimination provision. To find a violation of this requirement, three elements must exist. First, the application of the measure must result in *discrimination*. Second, the discrimination must be '*arbitrary or unjustifiable*' in character. Third, this discrimination must occur 'between countries where the same conditions prevail'. For the first element of 'discrimination', the AB clarified that the circumstances that bring about the discrimination under the chapeau may be the same as those that led to the finding of a violation of a substantive provision of the GATT 1994'. Still, the AB may consider a wider range of the circumstances that bring out the discrimination under the chapeau.[31] For example, in *EC – Seal Products*, the AB considered whether the measure has any discriminatory effects on different indigenous communities, an issue that had not been considered in the discrimination analysis under Article 1.1 of the GATT 1994.

The second element is to examine whether the discrimination is 'arbitrary or unjustifiable'. In *Brazil – Retreated Tyres*, the AB held that such a determination is essentially an analysis that relates primarily to the *cause or the rationale* of the discrimination put forward to explain its existence.[32] If the measure could be rationally related to a legitimate policy objective, then there is no arbitrary or unjustifiable discrimination. However, such an analytical framework turned out to be problematic for measures with multiple purposes in *EC – Seal Products*. Therefore, the AB modified its position in *Brazil – Retreated Tyres*, stating that it is not the sole test that is relevant to the assessment of arbitrary or unjustifiable discrimination.[33] This is an implicit recognition that *the rationales behind the exceptions* could still provide justification to discrimination, even if they do not relate to the immediate policy objective of the measure at issue. By doing so, the AB has opened the door for considering a broader scope of policy rationales under the chapeau, beyond the list of policy objectives specified in Article XX.[34] Moreover, the measure at issue must be 'necessary' in the sense that no reasonably available alternative measures exist that would achieve the legitimate objective in a *less discriminatory manner*.[35] This implicit necessary

*United States – Import Prohibition of Certain Shrimp and Shrimp Products* (*US – Shrimp*), WT/DS58/AB/R, adopted 6 November 1998, para 119 and 120.

[31] AB Report, *EC – Seal Products* (n 28) para 5.316.

[32] Appellate Body Report, *Brazil – Measures Affecting Imports of Retreaded Tyres* (*Brazil – Retreaded Tyres*), WT/DS332/AB/R, adopted 17 December 2007, paras 225–6.

[33] Appellate Body Report, *EC – Seal Products* (n 28) para 5.321.

[34] J Qin, 'Accommodating Divergent Policy Objectives under the WTO Law: Reflections on *EC – Seal Products*', in AJIL Unbound (25 June 2015).

[35] GM Duran, 'Measures with Multiple Competing Purposes after EC-Seal Products: Avoiding a Conflict between GATT Article XX-Chapeau and Article 2.1 TBT Agreement' (2016) 19 *Journal of International Economic Law* 467, 481–482.

test in the chapeau should be distinguished from the explicit necessity test (*least trade restrictive*) in the subparagraphs.

For the last element, 'between countries where the same conditions prevail', the AB held that the identification of the relevant conditions should be understood by reference to the relevant regulatory objectives of Article XX under which the measure was provisionally justified and the substantive obligations under the GATT 1994 with which a violation has been found.[36] It remains unclear how wide/narrow the concept of 'the same conditions prevail' is. To date, the AB has never found that 'conditions' were not the same in different countries. Going forward, how will the AB interpret 'the same conditions' may be the key to open up more policy space for a regulating WTO Member.

For a long time, Article XX and its early GATT/WTO jurisprudence were accused of demonstrating a strong pro-trade bias at the expense of WTO Members' national regulatory autonomy.[37] More recently, the evolving jurisprudence developed by the WTO AB has shown a more sophisticated approach towards domestic regulatory priorities, suggesting that a more nuanced understanding of Article XX jurisprudence is required.[38]

The NT obligation in TBT Article 2.1 (and paragraph D of the CGP) is similar to GATT Article III:4 except one principal difference: whilst GATT Article XX provides affirmative defences for violation of Article III:4, the TBT Agreement does not contain any similar provisions. For a violation of the NT obligation in Article 2.1 (paragraph D) to be established, three elements must be satisfied: (i) the measure at issue must be a technical regulation/standard; (ii) the imported and domestic products at issue must be 'like products'; and (iii) the treatment accorded to imported products must be less favourable than that accorded to like domestic products.

The AB held that the determination of 'like products' under TBT Article 2.1 should adopt the same competition-oriented approach as GATT Article III:4. It is a determination about the nature and extent of a competitive relationship between and among products at issue.[39] Since the TBT Agreement does not contain a general exceptions clause similar to GATT Article XX, the AB found that a finding of 'treatment no less favourable' under Article 2.1 requires a two-step analysis. First, a panel must find that the measure at issue modifies

[36] Appellate Body Report, *EC – Seal Products* (n 28) paras 5.300–5.301; L Bartels, 'The Chapeau of the General Exceptions in the WTO GATT and GATS Agreements: A Reconstruction' (2015) 109 *American Journal of International Law* 95, 112.

[37] S Gaines, 'The WTO's Reading of the GATT Article XX Chapeau: A Disguised Restriction on Environmental Measures' (2001) 22 *University of Pennsylvania Journal of International Law* 739, 739–862; D McRae, 'GATT Article XX and the WTO Appellate Body' in M Bronckers and R Quick (eds), *New Directions of International Economic Law* (Kluwer International, 2000) 226.

[38] M Du and QJ Kong, 'EC – Seal Products: A New Baseline for Global Economic Governance and National Regulatory Autonomy Debate in the Multilateral Trading System' (2016) 13 (1) *Manchester Journal of International Economic Law* 2, 2–21.

[39] Appellate Body Report, *US – Clove Cigarettes* (n 25) para 120.

the conditions of competition in the relevant market to the detriment of like imported products. It is submitted that the first step is the same analysis as GATT Article III:4. However, different from GATT Article III:4, the existence of such a detrimental effect, by itself, is not sufficient to demonstrate less favourable treatment in Article 2.1 of the TBT Agreement. In the second step, a panel must further analyse whether the detrimental impact on imports *stems exclusively from a legitimate regulatory distinction*.[40] If a regulatory distinction is not designed and applied in an even-handed manner, then it constitutes a means of arbitrary or unjustifiable discrimination and the distinction cannot be considered 'legitimate'.[41]

For the second step of ascertaining whether the detrimental impact on imported products stems exclusively from a legitimate regulatory distinction, the analytical approach of identifying a rational connection between the disputed measure and a legitimate regulatory objective outlined by the AB in *Brazil – Retreaded Tyres* has informed the recent TBT cases. This is not surprising given the similarity of the legitimate regulatory distinction test in TBT Article 2.1 and the chapeau test of GATT Article XX. Similar to the chapeau test in GATT Article XX, the detrimental impact under Article 2.1 of the TBT Agreement is not restrained by a rigid rational connection requirement. If a disputed measure pursues multiple competing objectives, it may also be justified by reference to reasons other than the main objective of the measure. Moreover, the 'legitimate regulatory distinction' test in TBT Article 2.1 not only requires a rational connection between ends and means, but also *no less discriminatory* alternative measure is available that would be at least equally effective in fulfilling the objective pursued by the disputed measure.[42] Intentionally or unintentionally, the AB may examine elements of the measure under Article 2.1 what it is supposed to be done under Article 2.2.[43]

The MFN treatment obligation prohibits a WTO Member from favouring products from another WTO Member without extending the same favour to like products from any other WTO Members. The object and purpose of the MFN treatment obligation is to ensure all WTO Members equality of competitive opportunities to import from, or export to, all other WTO Members, with the effect that like imported products from all WTO Members are treated equally.[44] To determine whether or not there is a violation of the MFN obligation of

[40] Ibid, para 182.

[41] Appellate Body Report, *United States – Certain Country of Origin Labeling (COOL) Requirements (US – Cool)* WT/DS384/AB/R, adopted 29 June 2012, para 271; Appellate Body Report, *US – Cool (Recourse to Article 21.5 by Canada and Mexico)*, WT/DS384/AB/RW, adopted 29 May 2015, para 5.93.

[42] Duran (n 35) 484.

[43] J Carlone, 'An Added Exception to the TBT Agreement after Clove, II and Cool' (2014) 37 *Boston College International & Comparative Law Review* 103, 136.

[44] Appellate Body Report, *EC-Seal Products* (n 28) para 5.87; Appellate Body Report, *EC – Bananas III*, WT/DS27/AB/R, adopted 25 September 1997, para 190.

GATT Article 1:1, a panel must determine whether the measure at issue grants a trade advantage; whether the products concerned are 'like products'; and whether the advantage at issue is granted immediately and 'unconditionally' to all like products concerned. For the first question, the AB has given a broad definition to the term 'advantage', including any more favourable competitive opportunities or commercial relationships between like products of different origins.[45] For the second question, what has never been solved is the extent to which the term 'like product' under Article I:1 should be given the same meaning as the term 'like product' in GATT Article III. Notwithstanding their textual differences, both provisions are concerned with prohibiting discriminatory measures and ensuring equality of competitive opportunities between products that are in a competitive relationship.[46] For the third question on the meaning of 'unconditionally', it does not mean that a WTO Member is prohibited from attaching any conditions to the granting of an advantage within the meaning of Article I:1. Instead, it inquires whether an advantage, once it has been granted to the product of any country, is accorded 'unconditionally' to the like products of all other Members.[47] It prohibits only those conditions that have a detrimental impact on the competitive opportunities for like imported products from any Member.[48]

Different from GATT Article I.1, Article 2.1 (and paragraph D of the CGP) of the TBT Agreement provides that in respect of technical regulations/standards, products imported from any WTO Member shall be accorded treatment *no less favourable than* that accorded to like products originating in any other country, similar to the NT obligation. Moreover, the MFN treatment obligation in the TBT Agreement does not have a general exception provision of its own. In view of the similarities of MFN treatment obligation and NT obligation in the TBT Agreement, all the analysis relating to 'like products' and 'treatment no less favourable' in the NT obligation is relevant to MFN obligation in the TBT Agreement as well. Specifically, for a finding of less favourable treatment, a panel must not only find that the technical regulation at issue modifies the conditions of competition in the relevant market to the detriment of imported products vis-à-vis like products originating in any other country, but also that the detrimental impact on imports does not stem exclusively from a legitimate regulatory distinction but reflects discrimination against imported products.

At first glance, there does not exist one uniform necessity test in the WTO law. The necessity test under GATT Article XX is to justify a measure found

[45] Panel Report, *United States – Certain Measures Affecting Imports of Poultry from China (US-Poultry)* (29 September 2010), para 7.415.

[46] Appellate Body Report, *EC – Seal Products* (n 28) para 5.82.

[47] WTO Panel Report, *Canada – Autos*, WT/DS139/R (11 February 2000) paras 10.22–10.24.

[48] Appellate Body Report, *European Communities – Conditions for the Granting of Tariff Preferences to Developing Countries*, WT/DS246/AB/R (7 April 2004) para 190; Appellate Body Report, *United States – Measures Concerning the Importation, Marketing and Sale of Tuna and Tuna Products (Recourse to Article 21.5 of the DSU by Mexico)* (20 November 2015) para 7.338.

to be inconsistent with the GATT substantive obligations, whilst the necessity test under Article 2.2 (and paragraph E of the CGP) of the TBT Agreement and Article 5.6 of the SPS Agreement is an independent obligation applicable to all TBT and SPS measures. Nevertheless, beyond technicalities, the essence of the necessity test in WTO law is the same. The key question is whether there is an alternative measure not only less trade restrictive, but also reasonably available and able to achieve the regulatory objective pursued by the regulating WTO Member. The weighing and balancing test first outlined in *Korea – Beef* was precisely designed to perform this essential inquiry in a reasonable and transparent manner. Despite their textual and structural differences, the AB has successfully pushed for a broad convergence in necessity tests across WTO Agreements in the sense that the necessity test across the WTO Agreements considers identical elements and follows the same line of inquiry.[49] The AB's necessity test has been heavily criticised for its ambiguous and unpredictable legal standard and a disconcerting dependence on the AB's discretion for the survival of domestic regulatory choices.[50] However, these oft-repeated criticisms are no longer justifiable in light of the recent developments in WTO case law. The AB has provided clear instructions on how to examine each element of the necessity test, how different elements interact and how to draw a conclusion after weighing and balancing these elements. Furthermore, the AB has substantially relaxed the necessity test over the past decade under GATT Article XX. This is particularly the case when the values or interests pursued by the disputed measures are important, such as human life or safety. Similarly, the AB found that the defending party had not violated Article 2.2 in all TBT disputes up to date. In a general sense, one might conclude that the AB is likely to grant more leeway to Members in determining what is necessary to achieve a legitimate policy goal.[51]

Compared to the necessity test in the GATT and the TBT Agreement, Article 5.6 of the SPS Agreement and its related footnote are more specific and arguably more protective of domestic regulatory autonomy. Nevertheless, a phase of stricter application has begun after 2012 in which in all SPS cases Article 5.6 violations were found.[52] This observation must be understood in its proper context. The SPS Agreement regulates specific categories of risks

[49] M Du, 'The Necessity Test in WTO Law: What Now?' (2016) 15 (4) *Chinese Journal of International Law* 817, 846–847.

[50] DH Regan, 'The Meaning of 'Necessary' in GATT Article XX and GATS Article XIV: The Myth of Cost- Benefit Balancing' (2007) 6 *World Trade Review* 347, 348; CP Bown and JP Tratchman, '*Brazil – Measures Affecting Imports of Retreated Tyres*: A Balancing Act' (2009) 8 *World Trade Review* 85, 129–131.

[51] T Voon, A Mitchell and C Gascoigne, 'Consumer Information, Consumer Preferences and Product Labels under the TBT Agreement', in T Epps and M Trebilcock (eds), *Research Handbook on the WTO and Technical Barriers to Trade* (Edward Elgar, 2013) 473.

[52] H Schebesta and D Sinopoli, 'The Potency of the SPS Agreement's Excessivity Test: The Impact of Article 5.6 on Trade Liberalization and the Regulatory Power of WTO Members to Take Sanitary and Phytosanitary Measures' (2018) 21 *Journal of International Economic Law* 123, 148.

and explicitly designates relevant international standards. For most recent SPS disputes, there was little controversy about either the relevant international standard or scientific evidence. Thus the panel was more confident about supporting the less trade restrictive measure.

Scientific evidence plays a central role in assessing the rationality and legality of SPS standards. The SPS Agreement contains detailed provisions such as the risk assessment with respect to the scientific justification of a measure.[53] Even though scientific evidence is not mentioned in the TBT Agreement (including the CGP) or the GATT, the AB has frequently referred to science in the determination of 'like products' and whether the standard in question is an 'unnecessary obstacle to international trade', in particular whether there is a genuine risk to be addressed, the nature of such risk, the extent of contribution of a measure to the achievement of the regulatory objective, and the feasibility of alternative less trade restrictive measures.[54] However, it must be stressed that the AB has not sought to extend the extensive scientific requirements of the SPS Agreement to the other two agreements.

With the rise of product standards in international trade, transparency has been playing a key role in reducing information asymmetry and enhancing the effectiveness of the WTO law. Transparency at the WTO has undergone substantial transformations through three generations. The first-generation transparency is mainly concerned with the obligation of publication of all proposed and adopted measures. The second generation refers to the monitoring and surveillance mechanisms. It is implemented through notification as well as regulatory dialogues among WTO Members, such as raising specific trade concerns (STCs) at the TBT and SPS Committees. The third-generation transparency focuses on efficiency of procuring information by the public. The major tools provide by the WTO are the requirements to establish enquiry points and the use of new technologies.[55] Extensive transparency obligations in the TBT Agreement (including paragraphs J to Q of the CGP) and SPS Agreement make ambiguous technical regulations and standards known and publicly available. They have enhanced the consultation processes domestically, allow other Members, in particular developing countries, to adapt to newly adopted standards, and help to avoid conflict and prevent disputes.[56] Whilst Chapter 3 focuses on the traditional GATT-style negative integration approach to reduce unnecessary regulatory diversity, Chapter 4 moves to positive integration in the form of

[53] D Winickoff at al, 'Adjudicating the GM Food Wars: Science, Risk and Democracy in World Trade Law' (2005) 30 *Yale Journal of International Law* 81, 84.

[54] L Gruszczynski, 'Science and the Settlement of Trade Disputes in the World Trade Organization', in B Mercurio and K-J Ni, *Science and Technology in International Economic Law: Balancing Competing Interests* 11 (Routledge, 2014) 29.

[55] R Wolfe, 'Letting the Sunshine in at the WTO: How Transparency Brings the Trading System to Life', WTO Staff Working Paper ERSD-2013-03, at 7–14.

[56] MB Karttunen, *Transparency and Dispute Settlement: Complements or Substitutes* (EUI PhD Thesis, 2016).

regulatory cooperation in the WTO. Regulatory cooperation has the potential to transfer good regulatory practices, to level the playing field, to reduce costs, and to contribute to the reduction of unnecessary barriers to trade as well as mitigate the economic impact of necessary trade barriers.[57] Regulatory cooperation can take various forms. In the WTO context, the TBT and SPS Agreements contain substantive provisions on harmonisation through international standards, and mutual and unilateral recognition of foreign standards. In addition, the adoption of good regulatory practices has been regularly discussed at the TBT Committee and incorporated in free trade agreements.[58]

Since international standards assume special legal significance under the TBT Agreement, which standards may be recognised as international standards have become an important threshold question. The AB has changed its original hands-off approach in *EC – Sardines* to a more intrusive approach in *US – Tuna II*, applying global administrative law principles embodied in the TBT Committee Decision to vet international standards before they are afforded quasi-legislative status. It is submitted that the AB's new approach to international standards marks a distinctive pathway for the development of global administrative law in producing global public goods. The elevation of international standards to 'first preference' status in the TBT Agreement involves a delegation of regulatory power from the WTO to international standardising bodies and such a delegation creates classic agency problems over whether these 'agents' are faithful to the WTO's objectives. This is all the more striking if we consider the nature, composition and working processes of some international standardisation bodies. The capture of international standardising bodies (ISBs) by industry interests, the duplicative and competing standards, the lack of consideration of developing countries' interests are among the most common criticisms of ISBs.[59] The scrutiny from the WTO panels helps ensure that only standards that are impartial, effective, well reasoned, and generated through transparent and open procedures are given legal effect. These procedural and substantive requirements would help ensure that the resulting standards embody a fair consideration of all affected interests, and thereby would reduce the risk of suppressing local regulatory autonomy through invocation of international standards that may lack public legitimacy.

[57] OECD, *International Regulatory Cooperation: Addressing Global Challenges* (OECD Publishing, 2013) 19.

[58] B Hoekman, 'Trade Agreements and International Regulatory Cooperation in a Supply Chain World', (EUI Robert Schuman Centre for Advanced Studies 2015/04) 4.

[59] AB Villarreal, *International Standardisation and the Agreement on Technical Barriers to Trade* (Cambridge University Press, 2018); H-W Liu, 'International Standards in Flux: A Balkanised ICT Standards-Setting Paradigm and its Implications for the WTO' (2014) 17 (3) *Journal of International Economic Law* 551, 553–558. G Mayeda, 'Developing Disharmony? The SPS and TBT Agreement and the Impact of Harmonisation on Developing Countries' (2004) 7 (4) *Journal of International Economic Law* 737, 746–749.

The TBT Committee Decision on International standard and the CGP have been universally and voluntarily accepted by all types of ISBs and they have had a profound influence on the development of standards at international and national levels. By recognising the TBT Committee Decision as a subsequent agreement, the AB has in effect transformed what would be at best the 'soft law' of the TBT Committee Decision into a code of administrative procedure and practice for international standardisation.[60] Still, the nature of the obligations embodied in the TBT Committee Decisions is unclear. Whilst some principles in the TBT Committee Decision have created specific norms that ISBs must observe and the violation of which may lead to the rejection of a standard as a relevant international standard, other principles are akin to merely procedural requirements and may represent only 'best efforts' obligations.[61]

WTO Members hold diametrically different views on what are 'relevant international standard' in the TBT Agreement. One group of Members led by the EU supports a 'centralised approach', arguing that relevant ISBs should be explicitly named and only standards adopted or approved by such bodies can be recognised as international standards for the purpose of the TBT Agreement. Another group of Members led by the US argues the exact opposite 'decentralised approach'. In this view, ISBs should not be confined to certain institutions. The EU's centralised approach would run counter to the TBT Committee Decision as it would essentially endorse all standards that such designated bodies produce without reviewing their content, even if in cases where the standards might not reflect the interests of all Members, or, disproportionately reflects those of only a few.[62] The divergence of approaches towards international standard setting between the EU and the US is a reflection of different institutional endowments and local political and economic cultures.[63] The TBT Committee Decision does little to clarify the WTO's position on the competing approach to international standards setting. On the one hand, it is highly unlikely that standards adopted in traditional ISBs such as the ISO and IEC will be disqualified as international standards for the purpose of the WTO. On the other hand, the TBT Agreement doesn't name any specific ISBs and leaves open the possibility that standards developed by private organisations may be recognised as international standards. In practice, the WTO retains a judicial role in determining whether a standard at issue is an international standard on a case-by-case basis. Besides international standards, mutual recognition agreements and equivalence are

[60] MA Crowley and R Howse, 'Tuna – Dolphin II: A Legal and Economic Analysis of the Appellate Body Report' (2014) 13 (2) *World Trade Review* 321, 342.

[61] M Du and F Deng (n 13) 132–138.

[62] Erik Wijkstrom and Devin McDaniels, 'Improving Regulatory Governance: International Standards and the WTO TBT Agreement' (2013) 47(5) *Journal of World Trade* 1013, 1015. Communication from the European Union, TN/MA/W/129/Rev.1 (23 June 2010).

[63] JK Winn, 'Governance of Global Mobile Money Networks: the Role of Technical Standards' (2013) 8 *Washington Journal of Law, Technology and Art* 197, 203–204.

also highly desirable policy tools in reducing product standards heterogeneity, as the European Union experience has shown.[64] However, these two policy tools are only technically feasible and politically acceptable on a bilateral, country to country basis. There are practical problems for WTO Members to make the full use of these tools on a multilateral basis. As a result, they have only limited use in the WTO.[65] On the other hand, new and additional requirements on regulatory cooperation have emerged in free trade agreements. A careful review of the FTAs has showed that they indeed go beyond the WTO obligations in certain aspects, such as the new rules on regulatory coherence and transparency obligations.[66]

In the context of the broader contemporary shifts in the locus of governance from the public to the private, private standards have also emerged as potential trade barriers to international trade. As they came much to the attention of WTO Members only in 2000s, much later than the establishment of the WTO in 1995, the proliferation of private standards has posed novel questions about the role of the WTO in addressing soft law norms created by different non-state actors. Indeed, WTO Members could not even agree on a definition of private standards at the SPS Committee. The disagreement reflected a fundamental divergence of views regarding private standards between developed and developing countries. In particular, most producers and retailers in developed countries benefit from the widespread adoption of private standards whilst the cost of complying with private standards mainly falls on exporters from developing countries. Moreover, the adoption of private standards is considered normal market behaviour of private economic actors which a government has little control over in domestic law.[67] The distinction between private and public standards has become increasingly blurred in the context of profound changes in the role of government in market regulation. As a good governance strategy, modern governments have actively used private standards to achieve certain policy goals. There are diverse ways through which public regulations and private standards may interact.[68]

[64] R Schutze, *From Dual to Cooperative Federalism: The Changing Structure of European Law* (Oxford University Press, 2009).

[65] L Bartels, 'The Legality of the EU Mutual Recognition Clause under the WTO Law' (2005) 8 (3) *Journal of International Economic Law* 691, 703; JA Zell, 'Just Between You and Me: Mutual Recognition Agreements and the Most-Favored Nation Principle' (2016) 15(1) *World Trade Review* 3.

[66] AC Molina and V Khoroshavina, 'Technical Barriers to Trade Provisions in Regional Trade Agreements: To What Extent do They Go beyond the WTO TBT Agreement?', in R Acharya (ed), *Regional Trade Agreements and the Multilateral Trading System* 371 (Cambridge University Press, 2016) 373; C-F Lin and HW Liu, 'Regulatory Rationalisation Clauses in FTAs: A Complete Survey of the US, EU and China' (2018) 19 (1) *Melbourne Journal of International Law* 149, 150–151; E Sheregold and AD Mitchell, 'The TPP and Good Regulatory Practices: An Opportunity for Regulatory Coherence to Promote Regulatory Autonomy?' (2016) 15(4) *World Trade Review* 587, 590–593.

[67] PC Mavroidis and R Wolfe, 'Private Standards and the WTO: Reclusive No More' (2017) 16 (1) *World Trade Report* 13.

[68] A Marx, 'The Public-Private Distinction in Global Governance: How Relevant is it in the Case of Voluntary Sustainability Standards?' (2017) 3 *The Chinese Journal of Global Governance* 14.

Private standards are institutionalised market instruments to address governance challenges. They appear to be simultaneously a useful tool for the private sector to regulate supply chains, a substitute for inadequate public regulation, a response to increasingly stringent government regulation and potential litigation, and a means of exceeding public regulations to provide credible product differentiation.[69] The effects of private standards on international trade are complex. On the one hand, they can be significant trade barriers, especially for small-scale producers or exporters in developing countries.[70] On the other hand, there is empirical evidence demonstrating that private standards can claim credit for facilitating international trade and result in a positive social, economic and environmental impact and a better livelihood for producers and their surrounding community.[71]

The standardisation system varies substantially among WTO Members. While most other countries adhere to a 'top-down' approach to standardisation where the government serves as the standards setter or mandates what standards will be developed, the US standardisation system is characterised by its high degree of decentralisation.[72] In contrast to the decentralised, flexible, sector-based, and market-driven US standardisation system, the European standardisation system is hierarchical, centralised, closely tied to the public authorities, and relatively well endowed with resources. What is more, standards systems are converging towards what could be termed a 'European Model' featuring centralised private associations enjoying public recognition and monopoly power, elaborating and promulgating standards according to a rather homogenous set of procedures built on the core principles of consensus, openness, and transparency.[73] As the institutional fragmentation in the US impedes efficient information flows between domestic standards development organisations and makes the aggregation of technical preferences at the national level more difficult, it is alleged that the US standardisation system may be at a disadvantage in positioning their domestic firms for exerting influence in global standard-setting.[74]

The Chinese standardisation system has undergone massive transformation over the past three decades, from a rigid top-down, state-controlled system to a system featured by the co-existence of government-controlled and market-based standard development organisations.[75] Nevertheless, the role of the government

[69] L Fulponi, 'Final Report on Private Standards and the Shaping of the Agro- Food System' (2006) OECD Doc AGR/CA/APM (2006)9/Final.

[70] Note by the Secretariat, 'Effects of SPS- Related Private Standards- Compilation of Replies', G/SPS/GEN/932/Rev.1 (10 December 2009) 2.

[71] S Jaffe, 'Food Safety and Agricultural Health Standards: Challenges and Opportunities for Developing Country Exports' (2005) World Bank Report No 31207, XI–XII.

[72] ANSI, *Overview of the U.S. Standardization System* 3rd edn (2010).

[73] H Schepel, *The Constitution of Private Governance: Product Standards in the Regulation of Integrating Markets* (Hart Publishing, 2005).

[74] T Buthe and W Mattli, *The new Global Rulers: The Privatization of Regulation in the World Economy* (Princeton University Press, 2011) 147.

[75] L Hui and CF Cargill, 'Setting Standards for Industry: Comparing the Emerging Chinese Standardization System and the Current US System', *East-West Centre Policy Studies* 75 (2017).

remains strong. There are increasing concerns that China may be using standardisation as a strategic industrial policy tool, with the ambition of changing China from standard-takers to standard-setters.[76]

WTO Members are deeply divided on a number of fundamental issues relating to private standards, including whether private standards are covered by the TBT and SPS Agreements, and the scope of relevant TBT and CGP disciplines, the legitimacy and accountability of private standards in global governance and possible pathways to move the issue forward within the WTO legal framework. It is unlikely that private standards with little or no governmental involvement or endorsement fall within the definition of 'standard' in either the TBT or SPS Agreement.[77] However, there is a disassociation of the scope of a WTO Member's legal obligation and who may accept the CGP. The TBT Annex 3:B of the TBT Agreement provides that the CGP is open to *any standardizing body*, including purely private standardisation bodies and firms. For private standards applied by non-governmental bodies that are covered by the TBT Agreement, a WTO Member's obligation is limited to 'take reasonable measures as available to it'. The extent of such reasonable measures is not clear. Certain inspirations may be drawn from the WTO case law. It also seems what are reasonable measures depend on the constitutional relationship within a WTO Member.[78]

Despite the complexity in debating the pros and cons of private standards in international trade and the current deadlock in the TBT and SPS Committees, it is submitted that WTO disciplines may play a role in reducing their adverse effects on international trade while maintaining a transnational regulatory space for them. Indeed, it could even be argued that proper WTO oversight would enhance, rather than undermine, the legitimacy of private standards as a market-based mechanism of transnational private regulation.[79]

After clarifying the relevant WTO disciplines on product standards, Chapter 6 applies the legal doctrines to examine whether the standards development process in the International Organization for Standardization (ISO) fulfils the WTO requirements of international standards, whether the EU ecolabelling regulation is consistent with the WTO TBT Agreement and the interaction between FSC standards and the WTO.

Overall, ISO is an 'international standardising body' and its activities and processes appear to be to a large extent in line with the basic tenets of the

[76] D Ernst, 'Indigenous Innovation and Globalization: The Challenge for China's Standardization Strategy', UC Institute on Global Conflict and Cooperation and the East West Centre (2011); B Fagersten and T Ruhlig, 'China's Standard Power and its Geopolitical Implications', *The Swedish Institute of International Affairs Policy Brief* 2/2019.

[77] A Kudryavtsev, *Private-Sector Standards as Technical Barriers in International Trade in Goods: In Search of WTO Disciplines* (Wolf Legal Publishers, 2015).

[78] WTO Secretariat, 'Negotiating History of the Coverage of the Agreement on Technical Barriers to Trade with regard to Labeling Requirements, Voluntary Standards, and Processes and Production Methods Unrelated to Product Characteristics', WT/CTE/W/10 (29 August 1995) 11–13.

[79] M Du, 'WTO Regulation of Transnational Private Authority in Global Governance', 67 (4) *International and Comparative Law Quarterly* 867, 902.

TBT Committee Decision. Nevertheless, it seems that there is significant room for ISO to improve or even reform its standard-setting practices in efforts to make it more open, transparent and inclusive. In particular, developing countries and some key stakeholders remain underrepresented in ISO standard development process.[80]

The EU ecolabel scheme falls within the regulatory scope of the TBT Agreement. It is on paper consistent with ISO standard 14024, the relevant international standard governing Type 1 ecolabels. As a voluntary scheme, it is highly unlikely that the scheme may be considered as unnecessary trade barriers. However, there is legal uncertainty whether products qualified for the EU ecolabel and those that are not so qualified simply because of inferior environmental performance are 'like products'. If they are considered 'like products', then the government support and promotion of products with EU ecolabels may run the risk of modifying the conditions of competition in the relevant market to the detriment of like imported products without EU ecolabels.[81] It is possible to argue that the EU ecolabel scheme makes a legitimate regulatory distinction between like products with different environmental performance as reflected in the award of ecolabels. Nevertheless, that conclusion will be based on a number of factors such as whether the labelling criterion can be verified by scientific evidence; whether foreign PPMs and unique foreign circumstances are adequately considered in making decisions on whether ecolabel may be awarded etc. Given that the legitimate regulatory distinction is interpreted rather stringently in WTO case law, there remains a real risk that the EU ecolabelling regulation may be found inconsistent with the CGP.

There is a lot of uncertainty concerning the status of Forest Stewardship Council (FSC) Standards in the WTO law. An argument could be made that the FSC certification and accreditation falls within the regulatory scope of the TBT, and that the FSC standard may fulfil the definition of international standard for the purpose of TBT Agreement as well.[82] Indeed, even the FSC claims that its standard development principles and criteria are consistent with the CGP of the TBT Agreement. That said, it must be cautioned that this conclusion is highly tentative and controversial. The best evidence is yet to come to firm up the conclusion and the burden of proof falls on the people who argue that the TBT Agreement is applicable and that FSC standards are 'international standards'. This is a tall order.

[80] P Delimatsis, 'Global Standard-Setting 2.0: How the WTO Spotlights ISO and Impacts the Transnational Standard-Setting Process' (2018) 28 *Duke Journal of Comparative & International Law* 273, 320; OECD/ISO, 'International Regulatory Co-operation and International Organizations: The Case of the International Organization for Standardization (ISO)' (2016).

[81] E Vranes, 'Climate Labelling and the WTO: The 2010 EU Ecolabelling Programme as a Test Case under WTO Law', in C Hermann and JP Terhechte (eds), *European Yearbook of International Economic Law* 205 (Springer-Verlag Berlin and Heidelberg GmbH & Co. KG, 2011) 212–213; European Commission, 'Report from the Commission to the European Parliament and the Council', COM(2017) 355 Final.

[82] Andrea (n 59) 237–244.

The analysis shows that the balance between the regulatory autonomy of states and standardising bodies on the one hand, and the trade liberalisation mandate of the WTO on the other hand, has been constantly evolving. The line demarcating the relevant regulatory scope has been drawn, erased and redrawn over the past several decades. The debate is still ongoing, and it is hoped that this book provides a firm basis to take the debate forward.

# *Bibliography*

## A. BOOKS

J Alvarez, *International Organizations as Lawmakers* (Oxford University Press, 2005)

S Barrett, *Why Cooperate? The Incentive to Supply Global Public Goods* (Oxford University Press, 2007)

P Van den Bossche and W Zdouc, *The Law and Policy of the World Trade Organization* 4th edn (Cambridge University Press, 2017)

LD Brandeis, *Other People's Money and How the Bankers Use it* (Frederick A Stokes Company, 1914)

N Brunsson and B Jacobson, *A World of Standards* (Oxford University Press, 2002)

T Buthe and W Mattli, *The New Global Rulers: The Privatization of Regulation in the World Economy* (Princeton University Press, 2011)

T Cadman, *Quality and Legitimacy of Global Governance: Case Lessons from Forestry* (Palgrave, 2011)

F Cafaggi and HMW Elgar, *The Regulatory Function of European Private Law* (Edward Elgar, 2009)

B Cashore, G Auld, D Newsom, *Governing through Markets: Forest Certification and the Emergency of Non-State Authority* (Yale University Press, 2004)

S Cho, *Free Markets and Social Regulation: A Reform Agenda of the Global Trading System* (Kluwer Law International, 2003)

W-Mog Choi, *Like Products in International Trade Law: Towards a Consistent GATT/WTO Jurisprudence* (Oxford University Press, 2003)

CR Conrad, *Processes and Production Methods (PPMs) in WTO Law: Interfacing Trade and Social Goals* (Cambridge University Press, 2011)

AC Cutler, V Haufer and T Porter (eds), *Private Authority and International Affairs* (SUNY Press, 1999)

DW Drezner, *All Politics is Global: Explaining International Regulatory Regimes* (Princeton University Press, 2007)

D Esty, *Greening the GATT: Trade, Environment, and the Future* (Institute for International Economics, Washington, DC, 1994)

ME Footer, *An Institutional and Normative Analysis of the World Trade Organization* (Martinus Nijhoff Publishers, 2006)

F Gale and M Haward, *Global Commodity Governance: State Response to Sustainable Forest and Fisheries Certification* (Palgrave, 2011)

A Hammoudi et al, *Food Safety, Market Organization, Trade and Development* (Springer, 2015)

JH Jackson, *World Trade and the Law of GATT* (The Bobbs- Merrill Company, 1969)

TE Josling, S Tangerman and TK Warley, *Agriculture in the GATT* (Macmillan, 1996)

S Krislov, *How Nations Choose Standards and How Standards Change Nations* (University of Pittsburg Press, 1997)

A Kudryavtsev, *Private-Sector Standards as Technical Barriers in International Trade in Goods: In Search of WTO Disciplines* (Wolf Legal Publishers, 2015)

R Lawrence, *Regionalism, Multilateralism, and Deeper Integration* (The Brookings Institute, 1995)

B McGrady, *Trade and Public Health: The WTO, Tobacco, Alcohol, and Diet* (Cambridge University Press, 2011)

F Ortino, *Basic Legal Instruments for the Liberalization of Trade: A Comparative Analysis of EC and WTO Law* (Hart Publishing, 2004)

Robert Schutze, European Union Law (Cambridge University Press, 2018)

HZ Schroder, *Harmonization, Equivalence and Mutual Recognition of Standards in WTO Law* (Wolters Kluwer, 2011)

J Scott, *The WTO Agreement on Sanitary and Phytosanitary Measures: A Commentary* (Oxford University Press, 2007)

H Schepel, *The Constitution of Private Governance: Product Standards in the Regulation of Integrating Markets* (Hart Publishing, 2005)

O Shy, *The Economics of Network Industries* (Cambridge University Press, 2001)

C Struck, *Product Regulation and Standards in WTO Law* (Wolters Kluwer, 2013)

AO Sykes, *Product Standards for Internationally Integrated Markets* (The Brookings Institute, 1995)

F Temmerman, *Trade in Water under International Law* (Edward Elgar, 2017)

C Tollefson, F Gale and D Haley, *Setting the Standard: Certification, Governance and the Forest Stewardship Council* (University of British Columbia Press, 2008)

M Trebilcock, R Howse and A Eliason, *The Regulation of International Trade* 4th edn (Routledge, 2012)

AB Villarreal, *International Standardization and the Agreement on Technical Barriers to Trade* (Cambridge University Press, 2018)

D Vogel, *Barriers or Benefits? Regulation in Transatlantic Trade* (Brookings Institute Press, 1997)

E Vranes, *Trade and the Environment: Fundamental Issues in International Law, WTO Law, and Legal Theory* (Oxford University Press, 2009)

M Weber, HH Gerth and CW Mills, *From Max Weber: Essays in Sociology* (Routledge 2007)

S Weithmann, *The Evolvement of Standards in China: Insights from the Electric Vehicle Sector* (Nomos, 2017)

J Wieland, *Governance Ethics: Global Value Creation, Economic Organization and Normativity* (Springer, 2014)

## B. BOOK CHAPTERS

ABECEL, 'Eco-Labelling of Tissue and Towel Paper Products in the EU: A Brazilian Perspective', in S Zarrilli, V Jha, R Vossenaar (eds) *Eco-Labelling and International Trade* 84 (Palgrave Macmillan, 1997)

AE Appleton, 'The Agreement on Technical Barriers to Trade', in PFJ Macrory (ed), *The World Trade Organization: Legal, Economic and Political Analysis* (Springer, 2005)

—— 'Private Climate Change Standards and Labelling Schemes under the WTO Agreement on Technical Barriers to Trade' in T Cottier, O Nartova and SZ Bigdeli (eds) *International Trade Regulation and the Mitigation of Climate Change* 131 (Cambridge University Press, 2009)

A Arcuri, 'The TBT Agreement and Private Standards' in T Epps and MJ Trebilcock (eds), *Research Handbook on the WTO and Technical Barriers to Trade* (Edward Elgar, 2013)

NR Arriaza, 'Soft Law in a Hybrid Organization: The International Organization for Standardization', in DL Shelton (ed), *Commitment and Compliance- The Role of Non-binding Norms in the International Legal System* (Oxford University Press, 2000)

TJ Bollyky, 'Regulatory Coherence in the TPP Talks', in CL Lim, DK Elms, and P Low (eds), *The Trans-Pacific Partnership: A Quest for a Twenty-first Century Trade Agreement* (Cambridge University Press, 2012)

T Buthe and W Mattli, 'International Standards and Standard-Setting Bodies', in D Coen, W Grant and G Wilson (eds), *The Oxford Handbook of Business and Government* (Oxford University Press, 2009)

F Carrera et al., 'Forest Certification in Guatemala', in B Cashore at al (eds), *Confronting Sustainability: Forest Certification in Developed and Transitional Countries* (Yale School of Forestry & Environmental Studies, 2006)

S Charnovitz, 'Improving the Agreement on Sanitary and Phytosanitary Standards' in GP Sampson and WB Chambers (eds), *Trade, Environment and the Millennium* 2nd edn (United Nations University Press, 2001)

P Delimatsis, 'Relevant International Standards and Recognized Standardization Bodies under the TBT Agreement' in P Delimatsis (ed), *The Law, Economics and Politics of International Standardization* (Cambridge University Press, 2015)

TM Egyedi, 'Institutional Dilemma in ICT Standardization: Coordinating the Diffusion of Technology', in K Jakobs (ed), *Information Technology Standards and Standardization: A Global Perspective* (IGI Global Book, 2000)

D Fuchs, A Kalfagianni and A Maarten, 'Retail Power, Private Standards and Sustainability in the Global Food System', in J Clapp and D Fuchs (eds), *Corporate Power in Global Agrifood Governance* (MIT Press, 2009)

L Gruszczynski, 'Science and the Settlement of Trade Disputes in the World Trade Organization', in B Mercurio and K-Jung Ni, *Science and Technology in International Economic Law: Balancing Competing Interests* (Routledge, 2014)

H Horn and JHH Weiler, 'EC- Asbestos' in H Horn and PC Mavroidis (eds), *The WTO Case Law of 2001* (Cambridge University Press, 2003)

—— 'European Communities – Trade Description of Sardines: Textualism and its Discontent', in H Horn and PC Mavroidis (eds), *The WTO Case Law of 2002* (Cambridge University Press, 2005)

R Howse, 'A New Device for Creating International Legal Normativity: The WTO Technical Barriers to Trade Agreement and International Standards' in C Joerges and E-Ulrich Petersmann (eds), *Constitutionalism, Multilevel Trade Governance and Social Regulation* (Hart Publishing, 2006)

—— 'Managing the Interface between International Trade Law and the Regulatory State: What Lessens Should (and should not) Be Drawn from the Jurisprudence of the United States Dormant Commerce Clause' in T Cottier and PC Mavroidis (eds), *Regulatory Barriers and the Principle of Non-Discrimination in World Trade Law* (Michigan University Press, 2000)

A Kudryavtsev, 'The TBT Agreement in Context', in TE and M Trebilcock (eds), *Research Handbook on the WTO and Technical Barriers to Trade* (Edward Elgar, 2013)

S Lester and I Manak, 'Addressing Regulatory Trade Barriers in Mega-Regional Trade Agreements', in T Rensmann (ed), *Mega-Regional Trade Agreements* (Springer, 2017)

M Maertens and J Swinnen, 'Private Standards, Global Food Supply Chains and the Implications for Developing Countries' in A Marx, M Maerrtens, J Swinnen and J Wouters (eds), *Private Standards and Global Governance: Economic, Legal and Political Perspectives* (Edward Elgar, 2012)

A Marx and J Wouters, 'Competition and Cooperation in the Market of Voluntary Sustainability Standards', in P Delimatsis (eds), Law, Economics and Politics of International Standardization 215 (Cambridge University Press, 2015)

A Marx, E Becault and J Wouters, 'Private Standards in Forestry: Assessing the Legitimacy and Effectiveness of the Forest Stewardship Council', in A Marx, M Maerrtens, J Swinnen and J Wouters (eds), *Private Standards and Global Governance: Economic, Legal and Political Perspectives* 153 (Edward Elgar, 2012)

PC Mavroidis, 'Come Together? Producer Welfare, Consumer Welfare, and WTO Rules', in E-Ulrich Petersmann (eds) *Reforming the World Trading System: Legitimacy, Efficiency, and Democratic Governance* (Oxford University Press, 2005)

D McRae, 'GATT Article XX and the WTO Appellate Body' in M Bronckers and R Quick (eds), *New Directions of International Economic Law* (Kluwer International, 2000)

PA Messerlin and D Palmeter, 'Technical Regulation and Industry Standards', in T Cottier, PC Mavroidis and P Blatter (eds), *Regulatory Barriers and the Principle of Non-Discrimination in World Trade Law* (University of Michigan Press, 2000)

AC Molina and V Khoroshavina, 'Technical Barriers to Trade Provisions in Regional Trade Agreements: To What Extent do They Go beyond the WTO TBT Agreement?' in R Acharya (ed), *Regional Trade Agreements and the Multilateral Trading System* (Cambridge University Press, 2016)

N Moran, 'The First Twenty Cases under GATT Article XX: Tuna or Shrimp Dear' in G Adinolfi et al (eds), International Economic Law: Contemporary Issues (Springer, 2017)

J Pauwelyn, 'Does the WTO Stand for "Deference to" or "Interference with" National Health Authorities When Applying the SPS Agreement'? in T Cottier and PC Mavroidis (eds), *The Role of Judge in International Trade Regulation* (The University of Michigan Press, 2003)

—— 'Non- Traditional Patterns of Global Regulation: Is the WTO Missing the Boat?' in C Joerges and E-Ulrich Petersmann (eds), *Constitutionalism, Multilevel Trade Governance and Social Regulation* (Hart Publishing, 2006)

R Piermartini and M Budetta, 'A Mapping of Regional Rules on Technical Barriers to Trade', in A Estevadeordal, K Suominen and R Teh (eds), *Regional Rules in the Global Trading System* (Cambridge University Press, 2009)

R Piotrowski and S Kratz, 'Eco-Labelling in the Globalised Economy', in A Pfaller and M Lerch (eds), *Challenges of Globalization* 217 (Transaction Publishers, 2005)

DH Regan, 'Regulatory Purpose and "Like Products" in Article III:4 of the GATT' in GA Bermann and PC Mavroidis (eds), *Trade and Human Health and Safety* (Cambridge University Press, 2006)

T Risse, 'Transnational Governance and Legitimacy' in A Benz and Y Papadopoulos (eds), *Governance and Democracy: Comparing National, European and International Experiences* (Routledge 2006)

H Schepel, 'Between Standards and Regulation: On the Concept of 'de facto mandatory standards' after Tuna II and Fra.bo' in P Delimatsis (ed), *The Law, Economics and Politics of International Standardization* (Cambridge University Press, 2015)

—— 'The Empire's Drains: Sources of Legal Recognition of Private Standardization under the TBT Agreement', in C Joerges and E-Ulrich Petersmann (eds), *Constitutionalism, Multilevel Trade Governance and Social Regulation* (Hart Publishing, 2006)

LTamiotti, 'Article 2 TBT', in R Wolfrum, P-Tobias Stoll and A Seibert-Fohr (eds), *WTO, Technical Barriers to Trade and SPS Measures* (Nijhoff, 2007)

J Trachtman, 'Addressing Regulatory Divergence through International Standards' in A Mattoo and P Sauve (eds), *Domestic Regulation and Service Trade Liberalization* (World Bank/Oxford University Press, 2003)

MJ Trebilcock and JA Soloway, 'International Trade Policy and Domestic Food Safety Regulation: The Case for Substantial Deference by the WTO Dispute Settlement Body under the SPS Agreement' in DM Kennedy and JD Southwick (eds), *The Political Economy of International Trade Law* (Cambridge University Press, 2002)

A Uhlin, 'Democratic Legitimacy of Transnational Actors: Mapping out the Conception Terrain' in E Erman and A Uhlin (eds), *Legitimacy beyond the State? Re-examining the Democratic Credentials of Transnational Actors* (Palgrave Macmillan, 2010)

T Voon, A Mitchell and C Gascoigne, 'Consumer Information, Consumer Preferences and Product Labels under the TBT Agreement', in T Epps and M Trebilcock, *Research Handbook on the WTO and Technical Barriers to Trade* (Edward Elgar, 2013)

E Vranes, 'Climate Labelling and the WTO: The 2010 EU Ecolabelling Programme as a Test Case under WTO Law', in C Hermann and JP Terhechte (eds), *European Yearbook of International Economic Law* (2011)

W Mattli and N Woods, 'In Whose Benefit? Explaining Regulatory Change in Global Politics' in W Mattli and N Woods (eds), *The Politics of Global Regulation* (Princeton University Press, 2009)

P Wang and Z Liang, 'Beyond Government Control of China's Standardization System- History, Current Status and Reform Suggestions' in D Ernst and MG Plummer (eds), *Megaregionalism 2.0- Trade and Innovation within Global Networks* (World Scientific, 2018)

S Wheatley, 'Democratic Governance beyond the State: The Legitimacy of Non-state Actors as Standard Setters' in A Peters et al (eds), *Non-State Actors as Standard Setters* (Cambridge University Press, 2009)

AB Zampetti, 'Mutual Recognition in the Transatlantic Context: Some Reflections on Future Negotiations', in T Cottier and PC Mavroidis (eds), *Regulatory Barriers and the Principle of Non-Discrimination in World Trade Law* (University of Michigan Press, 2000)

## C. ARTICLES

KW Abbot and D Snidal, 'International 'Standards' and International Governance', (2001) 8 *European Public Policy Journal* 345

D Acemoglu et al, 'Competing Engines of Growth: Innovation and Standardization' (2012) 147 *Journal of Economic Theory* 570

S Alshareef, 'Technical Standards Liberalization in FTAs of the United States, the European Union and China' (2019) 53(3) *Journal of World Trade* 433

AC Aman, 'The Limits of Globalization and the Future of Administrative Law: From Government to Governance' (2001) 8(2) *Indianan Journal of Global Legal Studies* 379

M Andenas and S Zlepting, 'Proportionality: WTO Law in Comparative Perspective' (2007) 42 *Texas Journal of International Law* 371

SM Anders and JA Caswell, 'Standards as Barriers Versus Standards as Catalysts: Assessing the Impact of HACCP Implementation on U.S. Seafood Imports' (2009) 91(2) *American Journal of Agricultural Economics* 310

R Pinto de Andrade, 'The Positive Consequences of Non-Tariff Barriers' (2009) 43(2) *Journal of World Trade* 363

LJ Ankersmit and JC Lawrence, 'The Future of Environmental Labelling: *US – Tuna* II and the Scope of the TBT' (2012) 39 *Legal Issues of Economic Integration* 127

NR Arriaza, 'Shifting the Point of Regulation: The International Organization for Standardization and Global Law Making on Trade and the Environment' (1995) 22 *Ecology Law Quarterly* 479

JJ Barcelo III, 'Product Standards to Protect the Local Environment- the GATT and the Uruguay Round Sanitary and Phytosanitary Agreement' (1995) 27 *Cornell International Law Journal* 755

S Barrett, 'Rethinking Climate Change Governance and Its Relationship to the World Trading System' (2011) 34 (11) *World Economy* 1863

RE Baldwin, 'Regulatory Protectionism, Developing Nations, and a Two-Tier World Trade System' (2000) *Brookings Trade Forum* 237

EP Bartenhagen, 'The Intersection of Trade and the Environment: An Examination of the Impact of the Technical Barriers to Trade Agreement on Eco-labeling Programs' (1997) 17 *Virginia Journal of International Law* 72

L Bartels, 'The Legality of the EU Mutual Recognition Clause under the WTO Law' (2005) 8 (3) *Journal of International Economic Law* 691

—— 'The Chapeau of the General Exceptions in the WTO GATT and GATS Agreements: A Reconstruction' (2015) 109 *American Journal of International Law* 95

M Balzarova and P Catska, 'Stakeholders' Influence and Contribution to Social Standards Development: The Case of Multiple Stakeholder Approach to ISO 26000 Development' (2012) 111 (2) *Journal of Business Ethics* 265

R Basedow, 'The WTO and the Rise of Plurilateralism – What Lessons can we Learn from European Union's Experience with Differentiated Integration?' (2018) 21(2) *Journal of International Economic Law* 411

J Beghin, A-Celia Disdier, S Marette and F Van Tongeren, 'Welfare Costs and the Benefits of Non-tariff Measures in Trade: A Conceptual Framework and Application' (2012) 11(3) *World Trade Review* 356

S Bernstein and B Cashore, 'Can Non-State Global Governance be Legitimate? An Analytical Framework' (2007) 1 (4) *Regulation & Governance* 351

S Bernstein and E Hannah, 'Non- state Global Standard Setting and the WTO: Legitimacy and the Need for Regulatory Space' (2008) 11 *Journal of International Economic Law* 575

K Blind, 'The Impacts of Innovations and Standards on Trade of Measurement and Testing Products: Empirical Results of Switzerland's Bilateral Trade Flows with Germany, France and the UK' (2001) 13(4) *Information Economics and Policy* 439

DM Bodansky, 'The Legitimacy of International Governance: A Coming Challenge for International Environmental Law' (1999) 93 *American Journal of International Law* 599

AV Bogdandy, 'The European Lesson for International Democracy: The Significance of Articles 9–12 EU Treaty for International Organizations' (2012) 23 *European Journal of International Law* 315

AV Bogdandy, P Dann and M Goldmann, 'Developing the Publicness of Public International Law: Toward a Legal Framework for Global Governance Activities' (2008) 9 *German Law Journal* 1384

M Bovens, 'Analyzing and Assessing Public Accountability: A Conceptual Framework' (2007) 13 (4) *European Law Journal* 450

J Bomhoff and A Meuwese, 'The Mega-regulation of Transnational Private Regulation' (2011) 38(1) *Journal of Law and Society* 139

J Bohanes, 'Risk Regulation in WTO Law: A Procedure-Based Approach to the Precautionary Principle' (2002) 40 *Columbia Journal of Transnational Law* 323

EW Bond and J Trachtman, 'China – Rare Earths: Export Restrictions and the Limits of Textual Interpretation' (2016) 15 (2) *World Trade Review* 189

M Bostrom and KT Hallstrom, 'Global Multi-Stakeholder Standard Setters: How Fragile are they?' (2013) 9 (1) *Journal of Global Ethics* 93

CP Bown and JP Tratchman, '*Brazil – Measures Affecting Imports of Retreated Tyres*: A Balancing Act' (2009) 8 *World Trade Review* 85

TJ Bollyky and PC Mavroidis, 'Trade, Social Preferences and Regulatory Cooperation: The New WTO-Think' (2017) 20 (1) *Journal of International Economic Law* 1

T Broude and PI Levy, 'Do you Mind if I do not Smoke? Products, Purpose and Indeterminacy in US – *Measures Affecting the Production and Sale of Clove Cigarettes*' (2014) 13 (2) *World Trade Review* 357

T Buthe, 'The Globalization of Health and Safety Standards: Delegation of Regulatory Authority in the SPS Agreement of the 1994 Agreement Establishing the World Trade Organization' (2008) 71 *Law and Contemporary Problem* 219

—— 'Engineering Uncontestedness? The Origins and Institutional Development of the International Electrotechnical Commission (IEC)' (2010) 12 *Business and Policy* 1

G de Burca, 'Developing Democracy beyond the State' (2008) 46 *Columbia Journal of Transnational Law* 221

D Casey, 'Private Food Safety and Quality Standards and the WTO' (2007) 7 *University College Dublin Law Review* 81

J Carlone, 'An Added Exception to the TBT Agreement after Clove, Tuna II and Cool' (2014) 37 *Boston College International & Comparative Law Review* 103

S Cassese, 'Administrative Law without the State? The Challenge of Global Regulation' (2005) 37 *New York University Journal of International Law and Politics* 663

B Cashore, 'Legitimacy and the Privatization of Environmental Governance: How Non-state Market-Driven Governance Systems Gain Rule-Making Authority' (2002) 15(4) *Governance* 503

S Charnovitz, 'The Law of Environmental "PPMs" in the WTO: Debunking the Myth of Illegality' (2002) 27 *Yale Journal of International Law* 59

MX Chen and A Mattoo, 'Regionalism in Standards: Good or Bad for Trade?' (2008) 41 (3) *Canadian Journal of Economics* 838

T Christoforou, 'Settlement of Science-Based Trade Disputes in the WTO: A Critical Review of the Developing Case Law in the Face of Scientific Uncertainty' (2000) 8 *New York University Environmental Law Journal* 622

DCK Chow, 'China's Indigenous Innovation Policies and the World Trade Organization' (2013) 34(1) *Northwestern Journal of International Law & Business* 81

JA Clougherty and M Grajek, 'The Impact of ISO 9000 Diffusion on Trade and FDI: A New Institutional Analysis' (2008) 39(4) *Journal of International Business Studies* 613

A Cosbey and PC Mavroidis, 'Heavey Fuel? Trade and Environment in the GATT/WTO Case Law' (2014) 23(3) RECIEL 288

MA Corvaglia, 'Public Procurement and Private Standards: Ensuring Sustainability under the WTO Agreement on Government Procurement' (2016) 19 *Journal of International Economic Law* 608

MA Crowley and R Howse, 'Tuna – Dolphin II: A Legal and Economic Analysis of the Appellate Body Report' (2014) 13 (2) *World Trade Review* 321

D Curtin and L Senden, 'Public Accountability of Transnational Private Regulation: Chimera or Reality?' (2011) 38 (1) *Journal of Law and Society* 169

MR Darby and E Karni, 'Free Competition and the Optimal Amount of Fraud' (1973) 16 (1) *The Journal of Law & Economics* 67

PA David and S Greenstein, 'The Economics of Compatibility Standards: An Introduction to Recent Research' (1990) 1 *Economics of Innovation and New Technology* 3

A Davies, 'Interpreting the Chapeau of GATT Article XX in Light of the 'New' Approach in Brazil-Tyres' (2009) 43 *Journal of World Trade* 507 (2009)

—— 'Technical Regulations and Standards under the WTO Agreement on Technical Barriers to Trade' (2014) 41 (1) *Legal Issues of Economic Integration* 37

K Dawar and E Ronen, 'How "Necessary"? A Comparison of legal and Economic Assessments -GATT Disputes Settlements under Article XX (B), TBT 2.2 and SPS 5.6' (2016) 8 (1) *Trade, Law and Development* 1

P Delimatsis, 'Standardization in Services- European Ambitions and Sectoral Realities' (2016) 41(4) *European Law Review* 513

—— 'Global Standard-Setting 2.0: How the WTO Spotlights ISO and Impacts the Transnational Standard-Setting Process' (2018) 28 *Duke Journal of Comparative & International Law* 273

NF Diebold, 'Standards of Non-Discrimination in International Economic Law' (2011) 60 (4) *International and Comparative Law Quarterly* 831

N DiMascio and J Pauwelyn, 'Nondiscrimination in Trade and Investment Treaties: Worlds apart or Two Sides of the Same Coin' (2008) 102 *American Journal of International Law* 48

K Dingwerth, 'North-South Parity in Global Governance: The Affirmative Procedures of the Forest Stewardship Council' (2008) 14 (1) *Global Governance* 53

C Dolan and J Humphrey, 'Governance and Trade in Fresh Vegetables: The Impact of UK Supermarkets on the African Horticulture Industry' (2000) 37 (2) *Journal of Development Studies* 169

M Du, 'Domestic Regulatory Autonomy under the TBT Agreement: From Non-Discrimination to Harmonization' (2007) 6 (2) *Chinese Journal of International Law* 269

—— 'Autonomy in Setting Appropriate Level of Protection: Rhetoric or Reality?' (2010) 13 *Journal of International Economic Law* 1077

—— 'The Rise of National Regulatory Autonomy in the GATT/WTO Regime' (2011) 14 (3) *Journal of International Economic Law* 639

——'Explaining China's Tripartite Strategy towards the TPP' (2015) 18 (2) *Journal of International Economic Law* 407

——'The Necessity Test in World Trade Law: What Now?' (2016) 15 *Chinese Journal of International Law* 817

—— 'What is a "Technical Regulation" in the TBT Agreement?' (2016) 6 (3) *European Journal of Risk Regulation* 396

—— 'Treatment No Less Favourable and the Future of National Treatment Obligation in Article III:4 of the GATT 1994 after EC-Seal Products' (2016) 15 (1) *World Trade Review* 139

—— (with Qingjiang K), 'EC – Seal Products: A New Baseline for Global Economic Governance and National Regulatory Autonomy Debate in the Multilateral Trading System' (2016) 13 (1) *Manchester Journal of International Economic Law* 2

—— (with F Deng), 'International Standards as Global Public Goods in the World Trading System' (2016) 43 (2) *Legal Issues of Economic Integration* 127

GM Duran, 'Measures with Multiple Competing Purposes after EC-Seal Products: Avoiding a Conflict between GATT Article XX-Chapeau and Article 2.1 TBT Agreement' (2016) 19 *Journal of International Economic Law* 467

L Ehring, 'De Facto Discrimination in World Trade Law: National and Most-Favored-Nation Treatment- or Equal Treatment?' (2002) 36 (5) *Journal of World Trade* 921

DC Esty, 'Good Governance at the Supranational Scale: Globalizing Administrative Law' (2006) 115 *Yale Law Journal* 1490

M Fairbrother, 'Externalities: Why Environmental Sociology should Bring them in' (2016) 2(4) *Journal of Environmental Sociology* 375

J Flett, 'WTO Space for National Regulation: Requiem for a Diagonal Vector Test' (2013) 16 (1) *Journal of International Economic Law* 37

F Fontanelli, 'ISO and Codex Standards and International Trade Law: What Gets Said is not What's Heard' (2011) 60 (4) *International and Comparative Law Quarterly* 895

—— 'Necessity Killed the GATT Article XX and the Misleading Rhetoric about 'Weighing and Balancing' (2012) 4(2) *European Journal of Legal Studies* 39

L Fontagne, M Mimouni and J-Michel Pasteels, 'Estimating the Impact of Environmental SPS and TBT on International Trade' (2005) 22(9) *Integration and Trade* 7

L Fulponi, 'Private Voluntary Standards in the Food System: The Perspective of Major Food Retailers in OECD Countries' (2006) 31 (1) *Food Policy* 6

JL Funk and DT Methe, 'Market and Community-Based Mechanism in the Creation and Diffusion of Global Industry Standards: The Case of Mobile Communication' (2001) 30(4) *Research Policy* 589

D Fuchs, A Kalfagianni and T Havinga, 'Actors in Private Food Governance: the Legitimacy of Retail Standards and Multistakeholder Initiatives with Civil Society Participation' (2011) 28 *Agriculture and Human Values* 362

SE Gaines, 'The WTO's Reading of the GATT Article XX Chapeau: A Disguised Restriction on Environmental Measures' (2001) 22 University *of Pennsylvania Journal of International Law* 739

SR Gandhi, 'Regulating the Use of Voluntary Environmental Standards within the World Trade Organization's Legal Regime: Making a Case for Developing Countries' (2005) 39 *Journal of World Trade* 867

N Gandal and O Shy, 'Standardization Policy and International Trade' (2001) 53 (2) *Journal of International Economics* 363

R van Gestel and H-W Micklitz, 'European Integration through Harmonization: How Judicial Review is Breaking down the Club House of Private Standardization Bodies' (2013) 50 *Common Market Law Review* 145

EL Glaeser and A Shleifer, 'The Rise of the Regulatory State' (2003) 41 XLI *Journal of Economic Literature* 401

A Green, 'Climate Change, Regulatory Policy and the WTO: How Constraining are Trade Rules?' (2005) 8(1) *Journal of International Economic Law* 143

L Gruszczynski, 'Re-Tuning Tuna? Appellate Body Report in *US –Tuna II*', 2012 (3) *European Journal of Risk Regulation* 430

N Grijp, T Marsden and J Cavalcanti, 'European Retailers as Agents of Change towards Sustainability: The Case of Fruit Protection in Brazil' (2005) 2 (4) *Environmental Sciences* 445

AT Guzman, 'Against Consent' (2012) 52 *Virginia Journal of International Law* 747

N Hachez and J Wouters, 'A Glimplse at the Democratic Legitimacy of private Standards: Assessing the Public Accountability of GLOBALG.A.P.' (2011) 14 (3) *Journal of International Economic Law* 683

C Harlow, 'Global Administrative Law: The Quest for Principles and Values' (2006) 17 *European Journal of International Law* 187

T Havinga, 'Private Regulation of Food Safety by Supermarkets' (2006) 28 (4) *Law and Policy* 522

SF Halabi and C-Fu Lin, 'Assessing the Relative Influence and Efficacy of Public and Private Food Safety Regulation Regimes: Comparing Codex and Global G.A.P. Standards' (2017) 72 *Food & Drug Law Journal* 1

HH Jia, 'The Legitimacy of Exceptions Containing Exceptions in WTO Law: Some Thoughts on *EC – Seal Products*' (2015) 14 (2) *Chinese Journal of International Law* 411

LR. Helfer, 'Nonconsensual International Lawmaking' (2008) *University of Illinois Law Review* 71

Spencer Henson and Thomas Reardon, 'Private Agri- Food Standards: Implications for Food Policy and the Agri- Food System' (2005) 30 Food Policy 241

S Henson and S Jaffee, 'Understanding Developing Country Strategic Responses to the Enhancement of Food Safety Standards' (2008) 31 (4) *The World Economy* 552

S Henson and J Humphrey, 'Understanding the Complexity of Private Standards in Global Agri-Food Chains as They Impact Developing Countries' (2010) 46 (9) *The Journal of Development Studies* 1641

S Henson, 'The Role of Public and Private Standards in Regulating International Food Markets' (2008) 4 *Journal of International Agricultural Trade and Development* 67

A Herwig, 'Too much Zeal on Seals? Animal Welfare, Public Morals and Consumer Ethics at the Bar of the WTO' (2016) 15(1) *World Trade Review* 109

—— 'The Application of the SPS Agreement to Transnational, Private Food Standards' (2016) 7(3) *European Journal of Risk Regulation* 610

M Hilf, 'Power, Rules and Principles- Which Orientation for WTO/GATT Law?' (2001) 4 *Journal of International Economic Law* 111

AL.Hillman and HW Ursprung, 'Domestic Politics, Foreign Interests, and International Trade Policy' (1988) 78(4) *The American Economic Review* 729

H Horn and JHH Weiler, 'European Communities- Measuring Affecting Asbestos and Asbestos-Containing Products' (2004) 3(1) *World Trade Review* 129

H Horn, PC Mavroidis and EN Wijkstrom, 'In the Shadow of the DSU: Addressing Specific Trade Concerns in the WTO SPS and TBT Committees' (2013) 47 (4) *Journal of World Trade* 729

B Hoekman and PC Marvoidis, 'Embracing Diversity: Plural Agreements and the Trading System' (2015) 14 (1) *World Trade Review* 101

R Howse, 'Human Rights in the WTO: Whose Rights? What Humanity? Comments on Petersmann' (2002) 13 *European Journal of International Law* 651

—— 'Regulatory Cooperation, Regulatory Trade Agreements, and World Trade Law: Conflict or Complementarity' (2015) 78 (4) *Law and Contemporary Problems* 137

—— (with J Langille and K Sykes), 'Pluralism in Practice: Moral Legislation and the Law of the WTO after Seal Product' (2015) 48 *George Washington International Law Review* 81

J Houston–McMillan, 'The Legitimate Regulatory Distinction Test: Incomplete and Inadequate for the Particular Purpose s of the TBT Agreement' (2016) 15(4) *World Trade Review* 543

D Hurst, 'Hormones: European Communities- Measures Affecting Meat and Meat Products' (1998) 9 *European Journal of International Law* 182

RE Hudec, 'GATT/WTO Constraints on National Regulation: Requiem for an "Aim and Effects" Test' (1998) 32 *International Lawyer* 619

—— 'Science and "Post-Discriminatory" WTO Law' (2003) 26 *Boston College International and Comparative Law Review* 185

JH Jackson, 'Afterword: The Linkage Problem- Comments on Five Texts' (2002) 96 *American Journal of International Law* 118

M Josh, 'Are Eco-labels Consistent with World Trade Organization Agreements?' (2004) 38(1) *Journal of World Trade* 69

G Kapterian, 'A Critique of the WTO Jurisprudence on Necessary' (2010) 59 *International and Comparative Law Quarterly* 89

J Karbowski, 'Grocery Store Activism: A WTO-Compliant Means to Incentivize Social Responsibility' (2009) 49 (3) *Virginia Journal of International Law* 727

I Kaul, 'Global Public Goods: Explaining Their Underprovision' (2012) 15 (3) *Journal of International Economic Law* 729

M Kim, 'The 'Standard' in the GATT/WTO TBT Agreements: Origin, Evolution and Application' (2018) 52 (5) *Journal of World Trade* 765

B Kingsbury, N Krisch and RB Stewart, 'The Emergence of Global Administrative Law' (2005) 68 *Law and Contemporary Problems* 15

JH Knox, 'The Judicial Resolution of Conflicts between Trade and the Environment' (2004) 28 *Harvard Environmental Law Review* 1

M Koenig-Archibugi, 'How to Diagnose Democratic Deficits in Global Politics: The Use of the "All Affected Principle"' (2017) 9 (2) *International Theory* 172

N Krisch, 'The Decay of Consent: International Law in an Age of Global Public Goods' (2014) 108 *American Journal of International Law* 1

R Labonte et al, 'USMCA (NAFTA 2.0): Tightening the Constraints on the Right to Regulate for Public Health' (2019) 15 *Global Health* 1

A Lang and J Scott, 'The Hidden World of WTO Governance' (2009) 20(3) *European Journal of International Law* 575

RP Lazo and P Sauve, 'The Treatment of Regulatory Convergence in Preferential Trade Agreements' (2018) 17(4) *World Trade Review* 575

Christian Vidal-Leon, 'Corporate Social Responsibility, Human Rights, and the World Trade Organization' (2013) 16 *Journal of International Economic Law* 893

S Lester and I Barbee, 'The Challenge of Cooperation: Regulatory Trade Barriers in the TTIP' (2013) 16 *Journal of International Economic Law* 847

S Lester, 'Finding the Boundaries of International Economic Law' (2014) 17 (1) *Journal of International Economic Law* 3

Gt Levy, 'Decision Making in Committees: Transparency, Reputation, and Voting Rules' (2007) 97 *American Economic Review* 150

PI Levy and DH Regan, 'EC – Seal Products: Seals and Sensibilities (TBT Aspects of the Panel and Appellate Body Reports)' (2015) 14 *World Trade Review* 337

Y Li and JC Beghin, 'A Meta-analysis of Estimates of the Impact of Technical Barriers to Trade' (2012) 34 (3) *Journal of Policy Modelling* 497

C-Fu Lin, 'SPS-Plus and Bilateral Treaty Network: A 'Global' Solution to the Global Food Safety Problem?' (2012) 29 *Wisconsin International Law Journal* 694

—— 'Public-Private Interaction in Global Food Safety Governance' (2014) 69 (2) *Food and Drug Law Journal* 159

C-Fu Lin and H-Wei Liu, 'Regulatory Rationalization Clauses in FTAs: A Complete Survey of the US, EU and China' (2018) 19 (1) *Melbourne Journal of International Law* 149

H-Wei Liu and C-Fu Lin, 'The Emergence of Global Regulatory Coherence: A Thorny Embrace for China?' (2018) 40 (1) *University of Pennsylvania Journal of International Law* 133

H-Wei Liu, 'International Standards in Flux: A Balkanized ICT Standard-Setting Paradigm and its Implications for the WTO' (2014) 17(3) *Journal of International Economic Law* 551

MA Livermore, 'Authority and Legitimacy in Global Governance: Deliberation, Institutional Differentiation, and the Codex Alimentarius' (2006) 81 *New York University Law Review* 766

A Loconto and E Fouileux, 'Politics of Private Regulation: ISEAL and the Shaping of Transnational Sustainability Governance' (2014) 8 *Regulation & Governance* 168–170

EB Lydgate, 'Consumer Preferences and the National Treatment Principle: Emerging Environmental Regulations Prompt a New Look at an Old Problem' (2011) 10 (2) *World Trade Review* 165

DG Arce M and T Sandler, 'Transnational Public Goods: Strategies and Institutions' (2001) 17 (3) *European Journal of Political Economy* 493

T Macdonald and K Macdonald, 'Non-Electoral Accountability in Global Politics: Strengthening Democratic Control within the Global Garment Industry' (2006) 17 *European Journal of International Law* 91

G Marceau, 'The New TBT Jurisprudence in US – *Clove Cigarettes, US – Tuna II* and *US – Cool*' (2013) 8 *Asian Journal of WTO and International Health Law & Policy* 1

G Marceau and J Trachman, 'A Map of the World Trade Organization Law of Domestic Regulation of Goods: The Technical Barriers to Trade Agreement, the Sanitary and Phytosanitary Measures Agreement, and the General Agreement on Tariffs and Trade' (2014) 48 (2) *Journal of World Trade* 351

A Marx, 'The Public-Private Distinction in Global Governance: How Relevant is it in the Case of Voluntary Sustainability Standards?' (2017) 3 *The Chinese Journal of Global Governance* 14

W Mattli and T Buthe, 'Setting International Standards: Technological Rationality or Primacy of Power?' (2003) 56 *World Politics* 1

PC Mavroidis, 'No Outsourcing of Law? WTO Law as Practiced by WTO Courts' (2008) 102 *American Journal of International Law* 421

—— 'Driftin' too far from Shore- Why the Test for Compliance with the TBT Agreement Developed by the WTO Appellate Body is Wrong, and What Should the AB have Done Instead' (2013) 12 (3) *World Trade Review* 509

—— (with K Saggi) 'What is not so Cool about *US–Cool Regulations?* A Critical Analysis of the Appellate Body's Ruling on *US–Cool*' (2014) 13(2) *World Trade Review* 299

—— (with R Wolfe) 'From Sunshine to a Common Agent: The Evolving Understanding of Transparency in the WTO' (2015) 21(2) *Brown Journal of World Affairs* 117

—— (with R Wolfe) 'Private Standards and the WTO: Reclusive No More' (2017) 16 (1) *World Trade Review* 13

—— 'Last Mile for Tuna (to a Safe Harbour): What is the TBT Agreement All About?' (2019) 30(1) *European Journal of International Law* 279.

G Mayeda, 'Developing Disharmony? The SPS and TBT Agreement and the Impact of Harmonization on Developing Countries' (2004) 7 (4) *Journal of International Economic Law* 737

D McDaniels, AC Molina and EN Wijkstrom, 'A Closer Look at WTO's Third Pillar: How WTO Committees Influence Regional Trade Agreements' (2018) 21 *Journal of International Economic Law* 815

J McDonald, 'Domestic Regulation, International Standards, and Technical Barriers to Trade' (2005) 4 *World Trade Review* 249

JO McGinnis and ML Movsesian, 'The World Trade Constitution' (2000) 114 *Harvard Law Review* 511

B McGrady, 'Necessity Exceptions in WTO Law: Retreaded Tyres, Regulatory Purpose and Cumulative Regulatory Measures' (2008) 12 *Journal of International Economic Law* 153

JH McMillan, 'The Legitimate Regulatory Distinction Test: Incomplete and Inadequate for the Particular Purpose s of the TBT Agreement' (2016) 15(4) *World Trade Review* 543

D McRae, 'MFN in the GATT and the WTO' (2012) 7(1) *Asian Journal of WTO and International Health Law and Policy* 1

EE Meidinger, 'Competitive Supragovermental Regulation: How Could It Be More Democratic' (2008) 8 *Chicago Journal of International Law* 513

—— 'The Administrative Law of Global Private-Public Regulation: The Case of Forestry' (2006) 17 *European Journal of International Law* 47

J Meltzer, 'The WTO Ruling on U.S. Country of Origin Labeling' ("COOL"), 16 (23) *ASIL Insight* (2012)

Jo Meltzer and A Porges, 'Beyond Discrimination? The WTO Parses the TBT Agreement in US-Clove Cigarettes, US-Tuna II (Mexico) and US-Cool' (2013) 14 *Melbourne Journal of International Law* 1

RW Middleton, 'The GATT Standards Code' (1980) 14 *Journal of World Trade* 201

A Mitchell and T Voon, 'Regulating Tobacco Flavors: Implications of WTO Law' (2011) 29 *Boston University International Law Journal* 383

MN Moody, 'Warning: May Cause Warming Potential Trade Challenges to Private Environmental Labels' (2012) 65 (5) Vanderbilt Law Review 1401

WJ Moon and AS Sweet, 'Consensus Analysis, State Practice, and Majoritarian Activism in the WTO', *AJIL Unbound* (June 25, 2015)

PA Moye, 'Private Certification Versus Public Certification in the International Environmental Arena: The Marine Stewardship Council and Marine Eco-Label Japan Fisheries Certification Schemes as Case Studies' (2010) 43 *Vanderbilt Journal of Transnational Law* 533

R Mulgan, 'Accountability: An Ever Expanding Concept?' (2000) 78 (3) *Public Administration* 556

CI Nagy, 'Clash of Trade and National Public Interest in WTO Law: The Illusion of "Weighing and Balancing" and the Theory of Reservation' (2020) 23 (1) *Journal of International Economic Law* 143

Y Naiki, 'The Dynamics of Private Food Safety Standards: A Case Study on the Regulatory Diffusion of GLOBALG.A.P.' (2014) 63 *International and Comparative Law Quarterly* 146

P Nanz and J Steffek, 'Global Governance, Participation and the Public Sphere' (2004) 39 *Government and Opposition* 314

J Neumann and E Turk, 'Necessity Revisited: Proportionality in World Trade Organisation Law after *Korea – Beef, EC – Asbestose* and *EC – Sardines*' (2003) 37 *Journal of World Trade* 199

J Norpoth, 'Mysteries of the TBT Agreement Resolved? Lessons to Learn from Climate Policies and Developing Country Exporters from Recent TBT Disputes' (2013) 47(3) *Journal of World Trade* 575

DA Osiro, 'GATT/WTO Necessity Analysis: Evolutionary Interpretation and Its Impact on the Autonomy of Domestic Regulation' (2002) 29 *Legal Issues of Economic Integration* 123

E Partiti, 'The Appellate Body Report in *US- Tuna II* and Its Impact on Eco-Labelling and Standardization' (2013) 40 (1) *Legal Issues of Economic Integration* 73

—— 'What Use is an Unloaded Gun? The Substantive Disciplines of the WTO TBT Code of Good Practice and its Application to Private Standards Pursuing Public Objectives' (2017) 20 (4) *Journal of International Economic Law* 829

J Pauwelyn, 'Rule-Based Trade 2.0? The Rise of Informal Rules and International Standards and How They may Outperform WTO Treaties' (2014) 17 *Journal of International Economic Law* 739

—— (with RA Wessel and J Wouters) 'When Structures Become Shackles: Stagnation and Dynamics in International Lawmaking' (2014) 25 (3) *European Journal of International Law* 733

S Peltzman, 'Toward a More General Theory of Regulation' (1976) 19 *Journal of Law & Economics* 211

S Ponti, 'Greener than thou: The Political Economy of Fish Ecolabeling and its Local Manifestations in South Africa' (2007) 36(1) *World Development* 159

A Porges and JP Trachman, 'Robert Hudec and Domestic Regulation: The Resurrection of Aim and Effects' (2003) 37 (4) *Journal of World Trade* 783

D Prevost, 'Private Sector Food- Safety Standards and the SPS Agreement: Challenges and Possibilities' (2008) 33 *South African Yearbook of International Law* 6

GV Puig and ED Dalke, 'Nature and Enforceability of WTO-Plus SPS and TBT Provisions in Canada's PTAs: From NAFTA to CETA' (2016) 15(1) *World Trade Review* 51

K Purnhagen, 'Mapping Private Regulation- Classification, Market Access and Market Closure Policy and Law's Response' (2015) *Journal of World Trade* 309

J Qin, 'Accommodating Divergent Policy Objectives under the WTO Law: Reflections on *EC – Seal Products*', in *American Journal of International Law Unbound* (25 June 2015)

A Rainville, 'Standards in Green Public Procurement- A Framework to Enhance Innovation' (2017) 167 *Journal of Cleaner Production* 1029

DH Regan, 'The Meaning of 'Necessary' in GATT Article XX and GATS Article XIV: The Myth of Cost- Benefit Balancing' (2007) 6 *World Trade Review* 347

—— 'Measures with Multiple Purposes: Puzzles from EC – Seal Products', *American Journal of International Law Unbound* (June 25, 2015)

C Riffel, 'The Chapeau: Stringent Threshold or Good Faith Requirement' (2018) 45 (2) *Legal Issues of Economic Integration* 141

B Rigod, 'The Purpose of the WTO Agreement on the Application of Sanitary and Phytosanitary Measures (SPS)' (2013) 24 (2) *European Journal of International Law* 529

—— 'TBT-Plus Rules in Preferential Trade Agreements' (2013) 40(3) *Legal Issues of Economic Integration* 247

D Roberts, 'Preliminary Assessment of the Effects of the WTO Agreement on Sanitary and Phytosanitary Trade Regulations' (1998) 1 *Journal of International Economic Law* 377

MJ Robertson, 'The Fairy Tale of US 'Dolphin Safe' Labelling: False Claims, Unintended Consequences' (2012) 6(1) *BioResources* 14

H Schebesta and D Sinopoli, 'The Potency of the SPS Agreement's Excessivity Test: The Impact of Article 5.6 on Trade Liberalization and the Regulatory Power of WTO Members to Take Sanitary and Phytosanitary Measures' (2018) 21 *Journal of International Economic Law* 123

DH Schepers, 'Challenges to Legitimacy at the Forest Stewardship Council' (2010) 92 (2) *Journal of Business Ethics* 287

TJ Schoenbaum, 'International Trade and Protection of the Environment: the Continuing Search for Reconciliation' (1997) 91 *American Journal of International Law* 268

HZ Schroder, 'Definition of the Concept 'International Standard' in the TBT Agreement' (2009) 43(6) *Journal of World Trade* 1223

C Scott, 'Continuity and Change in British Food Law' (1990) 56 *Modern Law Review* 792

C Scott, F Cafaggi and L Senden, 'The Conceptual and Constitutional Challenge of Transnational Private Regulation' (2011) 38 (1) *Journal of Law and Society* 8

G Shaffer, 'United States – Measures Concerning the Importation, Marketing and Sale of Tuna and Tuna Products' (2013) 107 *American Journal of International Law* 192

—— (with D Pabian) 'The WTO *EC – Seal Products* Decision: Animal Welfare, Indigenous Communities and Trade' (2015) 109 (1) *American Journal of International Law* 154

I Sheldon, 'North-South Trade and Standards: What can General Equilibrium Analysis Tell us?' (2012) 11(3) *World Trade Review* 376

DP Steger, 'Institutions for Regulatory Cooperation in 'New Generation' Economic and Trade Agreements' (2012) 39 (1) *Legal Issues of Economic Integration* 109

RB Stewart and MRS Badin, 'The World Trade Organization: Multiple Dimensions of Global Administrative Law' (2011) 9 *International Journal of Constitutional Law* 556

TP Stewart and DS Johanson, 'The SPS Agreement of the World Trade Organization and International Organizations: The Roles of the Codex Alimentarius Commission, the International Plant Protection Convention, and the International Office of Epizootics' (1998) 26 *Syracuse Journal of International Law and Commerce* 27

RW Stiger and AO Sykes, 'International Trade, National Treatment and Domestic Regulation' (2011) 40 *Journal of Legal Studies* 149

SM Stephenson, 'Mutual Recognition and Its Role in Trade Facilitation' (1999) 33 *Journal of World Trade* 141

DM Sturm, 'Product Standards, Trade Disputes, and Protectionism' (2006) 39 *Canadian Journal of Economics* 564

M Sutherland, 'CSR 2019: Setting a New Standard: Implications of China's Emerging Standardization Strategy', *The SIAS China Studies Review* (October 29, 2019)

P Swann, P Temple and M Shurmer, 'Standards and Trade Performance: The UK Experience', (1996) 106 (438) *The Economic Journal* 1297

J Swinnen and T Vandemoortele, 'Trade and Political Economy of Standards' (2012) 11(3) *World Trade Review* 390

AO Sykes, 'The (limited) Role of Regulatory Harmonization in International Goods and Service Markets' (1999) 2 *Journal of International Economic Law* 49

—— 'Regulatory Protectionism and the Law of International Trade' (1999) 66 *University of Chicago Law Review* 1

—— 'The Least Restrictive Means' (2003) 70 *University of Chicago Law Review* 403

—— 'Economic "Necessity" in International Law' (2015) 109 (2) *American Journal of International Law* 296

—— 'Regulatory Consistency Requirements in International Trade' (2017) 49 *Arizona State Law Journal* 821

MF Teisl, B Roe and RL Hicks, 'Can Eco-Labels Tune a Market? Evidence from Dolphin-Safe Labelling' (2002) 43 *Journal of Environmental Economics and Management* 339

P Temple and G Urga, 'The Competitiveness of UK Manufacturing: Evidence from Imports' (1997) 49 (2) *Oxford Economic Papers* 207

CA Thomas, 'The Uses and Abuses of Legitimacy in International Law' (2014) 34(4) *Oxford Journal of Legal Studies* 733

JP Trachtman. 'Embedded Mutual Recognition at the WTO' (2007) 14 (5) *Journal of European Public Policy* 780

F Valinaki, 'Repairing the Defects of Article 2.1 of the WTO Barriers to Trade Agreement: An Amendment Proposal' (2016) 43 (1) *Legal Issues of Economic Integration* 65

T Vandemoortele and K Deconinck, 'When are Private Standards More Stringent than Public Standards?' (2014) 96 (1) *American Journal of Agricultural Economics* 154

MP Vandenbergh, 'The New Wal-Mart Effect: The Role of Private Contracting in Global Governance' (2007) 54(4) *UCLA Law Review* 913

G Vidigal, 'From Bilateral to Multilateral Law-making: Legislation, Practice, Evolution and the Future of Inter Se Agreements in the WTO' (2013) 24 (4) *European Journal of International Law* 1027

SM Villalpando, 'Attribution of Conduct to the State: How the Rules of State Responsibility May be Applied within the WTO Dispute Settlement System' (2002) 5 (2) *Journal of International Economic Law* 408

DG Victor, 'The Sanitary and Phytosanitary Agreement of the World Trade Organization: An Assessment after Five Years' (2000) 32 *New York University Journal of International Law and Politics* 865

T Voon, 'Flexibilities in WTO Law to Support Tobacco Control Regulation' (2013) 39 *American Journal of Law & Medicine* 199

—— 'Exploring the Meaning of Trade-Restrictiveness in the WTO', 14 (3) *World Trade Review* (2015) 451

D Vogel, 'Private Global Business Regulation' (2008) 11 *Annual Review of Political Science* 265

M Wagner, 'The Future of Sanitary and Phytosanitary Governance: SPS-Plus or SPS-Minus' (2017) 51(3) *Journal of World Trade* 445

VR Walker, 'Keeping the WTO from Becoming the "World Trans-Science Organization: Scientific Uncertainty, Science Policy, and Fact-Finding in the Growth Hormones Dispute' (1998) 31 *Cornell International Law Journal* 251

—— 'The Myth of Science As a "Neutral Arbiter" For Triggering Precautions' (2003) 26 *Boston College International and Comparative Law Review* 197

H Ward, 'Trade and Environmental Issues in Voluntary Eco-labeling and Life Cycle Analysis' (1997) 6 *Review of European Community and International Economic Law* 139

JHH Weiler, 'Comment on *Brazil – Retreaded Tyres*' (2009) 8 *World Trade Review* 137

J Weiss, 'The Regulatory Coherence Chapter of the Trans-Pacific Partnership Agreement: Making the Link between Adherence to Good Regulatory Practice Principles and Promoting International Trade and Regulatory Cooperation, Notice and Comment', *Yale Journal of Regulation* (11 February 2016)

R Werle, 'Institutional Aspects of Standardization- Jurisdictional Conflicts and Choice of Standardization Organizations' (2011) 8 *Journal of European Public Policy* 392

D Winickoff and others, 'Adjudicating the GM Food Wars: Science, Risk and Democracy in World Trade Law' (2005) 30 *Yale Journal of International Law* 81

JK Winn, 'Governance of Global Mobile Money Networks: the Role of Technical Standards' (2013) 8 *Washington Journal of Law, Technology and Art* 197

E Wijkstrom and D McDaniels, 'Improving Regulatory Governance: International Standards and the WTO TBT Agreement' (2013) 47(5) *Journal of World Trade* 1013

DA Wirth, 'The Role of Science in the Uruguay Round and NAFTA Trade Disciplines' (1994) 27 *Cornell International Law Journal* 817

—— 'The International Organization for Standardization: Private Voluntary Standards as Swords and Shields' (2009) 36 *Boston College Environmental Affairs Law Review* 79

T Wlostowski, 'Selected Observations on the Regulation of Private Standards by the WTO' (2010) 30 *Polish Yearbook of International Law* 229

J Wouters and D Geraets, 'Private Food Standards and the World Trade Organization: Some Legal Considerations' (2012) 11 (3) *World Trade Review* 486.

RJ Zadalis, 'When Do the Activities of Private Parties Trigger WTO Rules?' (2007) 10 (2) *Journal of International Economic Law* 337

EVD Zee, 'Disciplining Private Standards under the SPT and TBT Agreement: A Plea for Market-State Procedural Guidelines' (2018) 52 (3) *Journal of World Trade* 393

JA Zell, 'Just Between You and Me: Mutual Recognition Agreements and the Most-Favored Nation Principle' (2016) 15(1) *World Trade Review* 3

W Zhou, 'The Role of Regulatory Purpose under Article III:2 and 4- Toward Consistency between Negotiating History and WTO Jurisprudence' (2012) 11 (1) *World Trade Review* 81

—— '*US – Clove Cigarettes* and *US – Tuna II* (Mexico): Implications for the Role of Regulatory Purpose under Article III:4 of the GATT' (2012) 15 (4) *Journal of International Economic Law* 1075

## D. GOVERNMENT DOCUMENTS, RESEARCH REPORTS AND WORKING PAPERS

ANSI, Overview of the U.S. Standardization System (3rd edn, 2010)

ANSI, United States Standards Strategy (2 December 2015)

ANSI, European Questions about the U.S. Standardization System (July 2018)

ANSI, ANSI Essential Requirements: Due Process Requirements for American National Standards (January 2019)

ANSI, '2018–2019 Annual Report: Expanding to New Horizons' (31 August 2019)

S Ilias Akhtar and VC Jones, 'Proposed Transatlantic Trade and Investment Partnership (TTIP): In Brief', Congressional Research Service (11 June 2014)

S Baller, 'Trade Effects of Regional Standards: A Heterogeneous Firms Approach', World Bank Policy Research Working Paper 4124 (2007)

D Breznitz and M Murphree, 'The Rise of China in Technology Standards: New Norms in Old Institutions', Research Report Prepared on Behalf of the U.S. – China Economic and Security Review Commission (January 16, 2013)

J Bohanes and I Sandford, 'The (untapped) Potential of WTO Rules to Discipline Private Trade Restrictive Conduct', Paper presented at the Society of International Economic Law Inaugural Conference (Geneva, 15–17 July 2008)

AC de Brito, C Kauffmann, J Pelkmans, 'The Contribution of Mutual Recognition to International Regulatory Co-operation', OECD Regulatory Policy Working papers No.2 (OECD Publishing, 2016)

CEN, CENELEC and EFSI, 'Questions and Answers Regarding the European Standardization System' (July 2019)

MX Chen, T Otsuki and JS Wilson, 'Do Standards Matter for Export Success?' World Bank Policy Research Working Paper 3809 (2006)

CIEL & ISEAL Alliance, 'International Standards and Technical Barriers to Trade Legal Opinion Summary' (July 2006)

Codex Alimentarius Commission, Report of the 21st Session, ALINORM 95/37 (July 8, 1995)

CUTS Centre for International Trade, Economics and Environment Discussion Paper, 'Eco-Labels: Trade Barriers or Trade Facilitators?' (2009)

Consultative Board to the Director-General Supachai Panitchpakdi, The Future of the WTO: Addressing Institutional Challenges in the New Millennium (WTO, 2004)

Department for Environment Food and Rural Affairs, 'Results of the Evaluation of Category A Evidence: Forest Certification Schemes', Defra Project ID EV0481 (October 2015)

A-Celia Disdier, B Fekadu, C Murillo, SA Wong, 'Trade Effects of SPS and TBT Measures on Tropical and Diversification Products' (2008) ICTSD Issue Paper No. 12

D Ernst, 'Indigenous Innovation and Globalization: The Challenge for China's Standardization Strategy', UC Institute on Global Conflict and Cooperation and the East West Centre (2011)

—— 'China's Standard-Essential Patents Challenge: From Latecomer to (Almost) Equal Player?', Centre for International Governance Innovation special report (2017)

European Commission, 'Proposal for a Regulation of the European Parliament and of the Council on a Community Ecolabel Scheme', COM(2008) 401 Final

—— Commission Notice on the definition of relevant market for the purposes of Community competition law [1997] OJ C 372/5 (Commission Relevant Market Notice)

—— 'A Strategic Vision for European Standards: Moving forward to Enhance and Accelerate the Sustainable Growth of the European Economy by 2020', EC Communication COM (2011) 311 Final (June 1, 2011)

—— 'Report from the Commission to the European Parliament and the Council', COM(2017) 355 Final

—— 'Closing the Loop- An EU Action Plan for the Circular Economy', COM(2015) 614 final

—— 'Independent Review of the European Standardization System Final Report' (March 2015)

—— JRC Technical Report: Revision of the EU Ecolabel Criteria for Paper Products, Final Technical Report (January 2019)

EU Regulation 1025/2012 of the European Parliament and of the Council of 25 October 2012 on European Standardisation

European Chamber of Commerce in China, 'China Manufacturing 2025: Putting Industrial Policy ahead of Market Forces' (2017)

B Fagersten and T Ruhlig, 'China's Standard Power and its Geopolitical Implications', The Swedish Institute of International Affairs Policy Brief 2/2019

MJ Ferrantino, 'Using Supply Chain Analysis to Analyze the Costs of Non-Tariff Barriers to Trade and the Benefits of Trade Facilitation', WTO Working Paper ERSD 2012-02 (2012)

B Fliess et al., 'The Use of International Standards in Technical Regulation', OECD Trade Policy Papers No. 102 (Paris: OECD Publishing, 2010)

L Fontagne, G Orefice, R Piermartini and N Rocha, 'Product Standards and Margins of Trade: Firm Level Evidence', WTO Staff Working Paper ERSD-2013-04 (2013)

J Francois, 'Reducing Transatlantic Barriers to Trade and Investment: An Economic Assessment', CEPR Final Project Report (March 2013)

FSC, The Development and Revision of FSC Normative Documents (25 March 2015)

FSC, 'FSC Principles and Criteria for Forest Stewardship', FSC-STD-01-001 V5-2 EN (22 July 2015)

FSC, 'Global Strategic Plan 2015–2020' (2015)

FSC, 'Standard Setting in FSC' (7 July 2016)

FSC, FSC Statutes (2017)

FSC, Forest Management – Fact Sheet (05 March 2018)

FSC, Annual Report 2018 (2019)

L Fulponi, 'Final Report on Private Standards and the Shaping of the Agro- Food System' (2006) OECD Doc AGR/CA/APM (2006)9/Final

Global Agenda Council on Trade & FDI, 'Will the Trans-Pacific Partnership Agreement Reshape the Global Trade and Investment System?' (July 2016)

Global Affairs Canada, 'Canada-European Union Joint Report: Towards a Comprehensive Economic Agreement' (5 March 2009)

T Havinga and F van Waarden, 'Enforcing Compliance with Food Regulation: Modalities in the Relationship between Public Enforcement Agencies and Private Parties' (ECPR General Conference, September 2013)

S Henson and J Humphrey, 'The Impacts of Private Food Safety Standards on the Food Chain and on Public Standard-Setting Processes' (2009) Paper Prepared for FAO/WHO 14

B Hoekman and PC Mavroidis, 'Regulatory Spillovers and the Trading System: From Coherence to Cooperation', E15 Task Force on Regulatory Systems Coherence Overview Paper (April 2015)

B Hoekman, 'Trade Agreements and International Regulatory Cooperation in a Supply Chain World', EUI Robert Schuman Centre for Advanced Studies 2015/04

H Horn, 'National Treatment in the GATT' (2006) IFN Working Paper No. 657
L Hui and CF Cargill, 'Setting Standards for Industry: Comparing the Emerging Chinese Standardization System and the Current US System', East-West Centre Policy Studies 75 (2017)
J Humphrey, 'Food Safety, Private Standards Schemes and Trade: The Implications of the FDA Food Safety Modernization Act' (2012) IDS Working Paper No. 403
IEC, ISO, ITU and UNECE, 'Memorandum of Understanding Concerning Standardization in the Field of Electronic Business' (24 March 2000)
Inter-American Institute of Cooperation on Agriculture, Handbook of Good Practices for Participation in Codex Alimentarius Meetings (IICA, 2009)
International Trade Centre, 'The Impact of Private Standards on Producers in Developing Countries: Literature Review Series on the Impacts of Private Standards – Part II' (2011)
International Trade Centre UNCTAD/WTO and Commonwealth Secretariat, Influencing and Meeting International Standards: Challenges for Developing Countries (Geneva, 2003)
ISEAL Alliance, 'Legal Opinion: WTO Conformity of Private Sustainability Standards and the ISEAL Standard-Setting Code' (2017)
ISO, Engaging Stakeholders and Building Consensus (2010)
ISO, 'Guidance to ISO National Standards Bodies Engaging Stakeholders and Building Consensus' (December 2010)
ISO, 'ISO Action Plan for Developing Countries 2016–2020' (2016)
ISO, 'Economic Benefits of Standards: International Case Studies' (2011)
ISO Central Secretariat, 'Environmental Labels' (2019)
ISO, Annual Report 2018: Advancing the Global Agenda (2019)
ISO, 'Code of Conduct for the Technical Work' (2019)
ISO, 'Developing Standards' www.iso.org/developing-standards.html Accessed 2 March 2020
ISO, 'Guidance on Twinning in ISO Standards Development Activities' (March 2019)
ISO, 'ISO/TMB Policy and Principles Statement: Global Relevance of ISO Technical Work and Publications' (2004)
ISO, ISO/TMB Implementation Guidance: Global Relevance of ISO Technical Work and Publications (2004)
ISO, 'International Standards and Private Standards' (2010)
ISO, 'Code of Conduct for the Technical Work' (2019)
ISO, 'ISO 26000:2010 Guidance on Social Responsibility' (November 2010)
ISO, ISO Membership Manual (2015)
ISO 14020, Environmental Labels and Declarations- General Principles (15 September 2000)
ISO 14024:2018, Environmental labels and declarations- Type 1 environmental labeling – Principles and procedures (2018-02)
ISO/CEN, 'Guidelines for the Implementation of the Agreement on Technical Cooperation between ISO and CEN' (the Vienna Agreement) (7th edn, 2016)
ISO/IEC, 'ISO/IEC JTC 1: Vision, Mission and Principles' (April 2014)
ISO/IEC Directives, Part 1 Consolidated ISO Supplement- Procedures Specific to ISO (10th edn, 2019)
ISO/Technical Committee 207/ Sub-Committee 5, Environmental Management- Life Cycle Assessment- Principles and Guidelines (1995)
ISEAL Alliance, Setting Social and Environmental Standards: ISEAL Code of Good Practice (Version 6.0, 2014) 5–6
S Jaffee, 'From Challenges to Opportunities: Transforming Kenya's Fresh Vegetables Trade in the Context of Emerging Food Safety and Other Standards in Europe' (2003) World Bank Agriculture and Rural Development Discussion Paper No. 2, 59
—— (with S Henson), 'Standards and Agri- food Exports from Developing Countries: Rebalancing the Debate', World Bank Policy Research Working Paper 3348 (June 2004)
—— 'Food Safety and Agricultural Health Standards: Challenges and Opportunities for Developing Country Exports' (2005) World Bank Report No. 31207, XI–XII

MB Karttunen, *Transparency and Dispute Settlements: A Study of the Agreements on Sanitary and Phytosanitary Measures and Technical Barriers to Trade* (EUI PhD Thesis, 2016)

J Klabbers, 'Forest Certification and the WTO' (European Forest Institute Discussion Paper 7 (1999)

P Liu, 'Private Standards in International Trade: Issues and Opportunities' (WTO Workshop on Environment-related Private Standards, Certification and Labeling Requirements, Geneva, 9 July 2009)

—— 'Certification in the Value Chain for Fresh Fruits: The Example of Banana Industry' (2009) FAO Commodity Studies No. 4

KE Maskus, T Otsuki and JS Wilson, 'The Costs of Complying with Foreign Product Standards for Firms in Developing Countries: An Econometric Study', World Bank Policy Research Working Paper No. 3590 (2005)

J McBride and A Chatzky, 'What is the Trans-Pacific Partnership (TPP)?', Council on Foreign Relations Backgrounder (4 January 2019)

Ministry of Business, Innovation & Employment of New Zealand, 'Evaluation of Conformity Assessment Mutual Recognition Agreements and Arrangements' (April, 2018)

J Moenius, 'Information versus Product Adaptation: The Role of Standards in Trade' (February 2004)

—— 'Do National Standards Hinder or Promote Trade in Electrical Products' (2006) International Electrotechnical Commission Centenary Challenge Papers 54

M Morikawa and J Morrison, 'Who Develops ISO Standards? A Survey of Participation in ISO's International Standards Development Process', Pacific Institute for Studies in Development, Environment, and Security (October 2004)

M Murphree, 'The China Standards Engine', 12 (2) China Currents (2013)

J Nakagawa, 'Private Standards and Global Governance: Prospects and Challenges' (2017) ISS Research Series No. 62

Natural Resources Institute, 'Forest Certification in the Eyes of the World Trafde Organization', Ethical Trade Policy Watching Brief 1 (October 1999)

NEPCon, 'Comparative Analysis of the PEFC System with FSC Controlled Wood Requirements' (May 2012)

—— 'How Forest Certification Systems Meet the EUTR Requirements' (Version 2.0, January 2019)

OECD,'Processes and Production Methods (PPMs): Conceptual Framework and Considerations on Use of PPM- Based Trade Measures' (1997) OECD/GD (97) 137

OECD, International Regulatory Cooperation: Addressing Global Challenges (OECD Publishing, 2013)

OECD, International Regulatory Cooperation and Trade: Understanding the Trade Costs of Regulatory Divergence and the Remedies (2017)

OECD/ISO, 'International Regulatory Co-operation and International Organizations: The Case of the International Organization for Standardization (ISO)' (2016)

N Meyer-Ohlendorf, C Gerstetter and I Bach, 'Regulatory Cooperation under CETA: Implications for Environmental Policies' (The Ecologic Institute, 1 November 2016)

G Oreficea, R Piermartinib and N Rocha, 'Harmonization and Mutual Recognition: What are the Effects on Trade?', 15th Annual Conference on Global Economic Analysis (Geneva 2012)

Rainforest Alliance, 'Toward Sustainability: The Roles and Limitations of Certification' (June 2012)

Regulation (EC) No. 66/2010 of the European Parliament and of the Council of 25 November 2009 on the EC Ecolabel

J-Daniel Reyes, 'International Harmonization of Product Standards and Firm Heterogeneity in International Trade', The World Bank Policy Research Paper 5677 (2011)

Statement of The IEEE Standards Association Board of Governors, 'An International Standards Developer: IEEE Adheres to the WTO Principles for International Standardization' (12 December 2011)

B Shepherd, 'Product Standards, Harmonization, and Trade: Evidence from the Extensive Margin', World Bank Policy Research Working Paper 4390 (2007)

G Smith, 'Interaction of Public and Private Standards in the Food Chain' (2009) OECD Food, Agriculture and Fisheries Working Paper No. 15

GC-HL Stagiaire, 'Private Food Standards and Their Impacts on Developing Countries' (2006)

The US Chamber of Commerce, 'Regulatory Coherence & Cooperation in the TTIP' (17 February 2015)

The World Bank & China Development Research Centre of the State Council, China 2030: Building a Modern, Harmonious, and Creative Society (2013)

WB Traill et al., 'Report of the Evaluation of the Codex Alimentarious and Other FAO and WHO Food Standards Work' (FAO, 2002)

S Trew, 'International Regulation and the Public Good' (Canadian Centre for Policy Alternative, 2019)

United Nations Environment Programme, The Trade and Environmental Effects of Ecolabels: Assessment and Response (2005)

USTR, 2018 USTR Report to Congress on China's WTO Compliance (February 2019)

UN Forum on Sustainability Standards (UNFSS), *Voluntary Sustainability Standards, Trade and Sustainable Development* (2018)

M Vancauteren and D Weiserbs, 'Intra-European Trade of Manufacturing Goods: An Extension of the Gravity Model', ECON Discussion Papers (2005)

F Veggeland, 'Trade Facilitation through Equivalence and Mutual Recognition: The EU Model', Norwegian Agricultural Economics Research Institute Report 2006-3

F Veggland and SO Borgen, 'Changing the Codex: The Role of International Institutions', Norwegian Agricultural Economics Research Institute Working Paper 2002-16.

MA Villarreal and IF Fergusson, 'NAFTA Renegotiation and the Proposed United States-Mexico-Canada Agreement (USMCA)', Congressional Research Service R44981 (26 February 2019)

S Washington and L Ababouch, 'Private Standards and Certification in Fisheries and Aquaculture: Current Practice and Emerging Issues' (2011) FAO Fisheries and Aquaculture Technical Paper 553

EN Wijkstrom, 'The Third Pillar: Behind the Scenes, WTO Committee Work Delivers', E15 Task Force on Regulatory Systems Coherence Think Piece (August 2015)

A Williams, 'Comparative Study of Cut Roses for the British Market Produced in Kenya and the Netherlands', Precis Report for World Flowers (12 February 2007)

JM Witte, 'A single European Voice" in International Standardization? American Perceptions, European Realities. AICGS/DAAD Working Paper Series (2003)

R Wolfe, 'Letting the Sunshine in at the WTO: How Transparency Brings the Trading System to Life', WTO Staff Working Paper ERSD-2013-03

World Economic Forum, Enabling Trade: Valuing Growth Opportunities (Geneva 2013)

World Trade Report, Exploring the Links between Trade, Standards and the WTO (2005)

World Trade Report, Trade and Public Policies: A Close Look at Non-Tariff Measures in the 21st Century (2012)

WTO, The WTO and Preferential Trade Agreements: From Co-existence to Coherence (2011)

WTO and OECD, Facilitating Trade through Regulatory Cooperation: The Case of the WTO's TBT and SPS Agreements and Committees (2019)

## E. NEWSPAPER AND INTERNET SOURCES

A Batson, 'Not Really 'Made in China', Wall Street Journal (December 15, 2010)

CIEL & ISEAL Alliance, 'International Standards and Technical Barriers to Trade Legal Opinion Summary' (July 2006) www.isealalliance.org/sites/default/files/resource/2017-12/ISEAL_CIEL_Legal_Opinion.pdf

J Clayton, 'Organic Farmers Face Ruin as Rich Nations Agonise over Food Miles, The Times (1 August 2007)

S Donnan, 'EU and ASEAN to pave way for trade pact talks', *Financial Times* (6 September 2004).

*The Economist*, 'A Brief History of Wi-Fi' (June 12, 2004)

GATT Analytical Index www.wto.org/english/res_e/booksp_e/gatt_ai_e/art3_e.pdf

A Gross, 'Chinese Tech Groups Shaping UN Facial Recognition Standards', *Financial Times* (1 December 2019)

R Howse, 'WTO Seals: What is it really that makes the AB think that TBT doesn't apply?' http://worldtradelaw.typepad.com/ielpblog/2014/05/wto-sealswhat-is-it-really-that-makes-the-ab-think-that-tbt-doesnt-apply.html

—— 'The WTO Appellate Body Ruling in Seals: National Treatment Article III:4', http://worldtradelaw.typepad.com/ielpblog/2014/05/the-wto-appellate-body-ruling-in-seals-national-treatment-article-iii4.html (23 May 2014)

J Pauwelyn, 'Cool … but what is Left now for TBT Art. 2.2?', http://worldtradelaw.typepad.com/ielpblog/2012/07/cool-but-what-is-left-now-of-tbt-art-22.html (03 July 2012)

—— 'The Public Morals Exception after Seals- How to Keep it under Check?' http://worldtradelaw.typepad.com/ielpblog/2014/05/the-public-morals-exception-after-seals-how-to-keep-it-in-check.html (27 May 2014)

State Council of the People's Republic of China, 'Premier Li Keqiang calls for improvements in standardization', (September 14, 2016)

'Action Plan on Belt and Road Standard Connectivity' (2018–2020), www.scio.gov.cn/xwfbh/xwbfbh/wqfbh/37601/39274/xgzc39280/Document/1641459/1641459.htm

'Canada, EU Strike Deal on Indigenous-hunted Seal Products', www.nunatsiaqonline.ca/stories/article/65674canada_eu_strike_deal_on_indigenous-hunted_seal_products/ (10 October 2014)

CIEL and ISEAL, 'International Standards and Technical Barriers to Trade' (July 2006) www.isealalliance.org/sites/default/files/R053_ISEAL_CIEL_Legal_Opinion.pdf

B Guermazi, 'Exploring the Reference Paper on Regulatory Principles' (2000) www.wto.org/english/tratop_e/…e/…/guermazi_referencepaper.doc

IEC, 'Liaison between WTO and IEC' www.iec.ch/about/globalreach/partners/wto/

I Manak, 'Regulatory Issues in the New NAFTA', in International Economic Law and Policy Blog (10 October 2018) https://worldtradelaw.typepad.com/ielpblog/2018/10/regulatory-cooperation-in-the-new-nafta.html

VC Martons and F Romig, 'Trade in Energy and Forestry: A perspective from the United Nations Economic Commission for Europe', www.wto.org/english/res_e/publications_e/wtr10_forum_e/wtr10_11may10_e.htm

Studio Legal Stefanelli and Stefanelli, 'New China's Standardization Law: An Overdue Reform' (30 January 2018), www.lexology.com/library/detail.aspx?g=dc14088b-9061-48d6-9ee4-0be8bd610e3d

EA Taub, 'Smart Headlights to Inch Closer to American Road', *New York Times* (21 November 2018)

World Standards Cooperation http://worldstandardscooperation.org/about/

WTO, 'New Global Trade Alert System Launched to Boost Market Access for Developing Countries' (8 November 2016) www.wto.org/english/news_e/pres16_e/pr783_e.htm

WTO, 'WTO Members Adopt Report on Food Safety Agreement' (14 July 2017) www.wto.org/english/news_e/news17_e/sps_13jul17_e.htm

WTO ISO Standards Information Gateway www.tbtcode.iso.org

www.blauer-engel.de/en/our-label-environment

www.ecolabelindex.com/

http://ec.europa.eu/environment/ecolabel/index_en.htm

## F. GATT/WTO DOCUMENTS

GATT Sub-Committee on Non-Tariff Barriers and Other Special Problems, TN.64/3/Rev.2 (3 November 1966)

GATT Doc. COM.IND/W/36, Summary of Proposals in Reports of the Five Working Groups on Non-Tariff Barriers 2-3 (1970)
Committee on Trade in Industrial Products- Report to Council, L/3496 (10 February 1971)
GATT Doc. COM.IND/W/108, Group 3 on Standards: Report (25 June 1973)
GATT Doc. MTN/3B/3, Part 3 of the Inventory of Non-Tariff Measures: Standards Involving Imports and Domestic Goods 11 (14 February 1974)
GATT Doc. MTN/NTM/W/14, Definitions: Working Paper by the Secretariat (26 June 1975)
Note by the Chairman, 'Meeting of January/February 1976', MTN/NTM/12 (24 February 1976)
Proposal by the European Economic Community, 'A Code of Good Practice for Non-Governmental Bodies in the Agreement on Technical Barriers to Trade-', GATT Doc TBT/W/110 (7 July 1988)
Revised Proposal by the European Economic Community, 'A Code of Good Practice for Non-Governmental Bodies in the Agreement on Technical Barriers to Trade', MTN/GNC/NG8/W/71 (20 February 1990)
Revise Proposal by the European Economic Community, 'Code of Good Practice for the Preparation, Adoption and Application of Standards', TBT/W/137 (15 February 1990)
Note by the Secretariat, 'Agreement on Technical Barriers to Trade: Aspects of the Agreement Proposed for Negotiation', MTN.GNC/NG8/W/83/Add.3 (23 July 1990)
Committee on Technical Barriers to Trade, 'Decisions and Recommendations Adopted by the Committee since 1 January 1980', TBT/16/Rev.5 (18 November 1992)
GATT, *Report of the Committee on Technical Barriers to Trade*, L/7107 (3 November 1992)
The TBT Committee, 'Draft Minutes of the Meeting Held on 20 October 1995', G/TBT/W/15 (22 November 1995)
—— 'First Triennial Review of the Operation and Implementation of the Agreement on Technical Barriers to Trade', G/TBT/5 (19 November 1997)
—— 'Environmental Labels and Market Access: Case Study on the Colombian Flower-Growing Industry', G/TBT/W/60 (9 March 1998)
—— 'Second Triennial Review of the Operation and Implementation of the Agreement on Technical Barriers to Trade', G/TBT/9 (13 November 2000)
—— 'Minutes of the Meeting Held on 29 June 2001', G/TBT/M/24 (14 August 2001)
—— 'Fifth Triennial Review of the Operation and Implementation of the Agreement on Technical Barriers to Trade under Article 15.4', G/TBT/26 (13 November 2009)
—— 'Minutes of the Meeting of 15–16 June 2011', G/TBT/M/54 (20 September 2011)
—— 'Sixth Triennial Review of the Operation and Implementation of the Agreement on Technical Barriers to Trade under Article 15.4', G/TBT/32 (29 November 2012)
—— 'Minutes of the Meeting of 10–11 November 2016', G/TBT/M/70 (17 February 2017)
—— 'Eighth Triennial Review of the Operation and Implementation of the Agreement on Technical Barriers to Trade under Article 15.4', G/TBT/41 (19 November 2018)
—— 'Twenty-Fourth Annual Review of the Implementation and Operation of the TBT Agreement', G/TBT/42 (25 February 2019)
—— 'Decisions and Recommendations Adopted by the WTO Committee on Technical Barriers to Trade since 1 January 1995', G/TBT/1/Rev.14 (24 September 2019
—— 'Twenty-Fifth Annual Review of the Implementation and Operation of the TBT Agreement', G/TBT/44 (19 February 2020)
Communication from Canada on Eco- Labeling, G/TBT/W/9 (5 July 1995)
Communication from Canada, 'Labeling and Requirements of the Agreement on Technical Barriers to Trade: Framework for Informal, Structured Discussions' (2003) WT/CTE/W/229
US Paper on the First TBT Triennial Review, G/TBT/W/40 (25 April 1997)
Submission from Japan, 'Issues Concerning International Standards and International Standardization Bodies', G/TBT/W/113 (15 June 1999)
WTO, United States – Olive Oil, G/TBT/N/USA/395 (6 April 2008)
WTO, EC- Marketing Standards for Olive Oil, G/TBT/N/EEC/226 (22 October 2008)
Note from New Zealand, 'Equivalency of Standards: An Interim Measure to Facilitate Trade in the Absence of Relevant International Standards', G/TBT/W/88 (15 September 1998)

Communication from the European Union, 'A Policy Framework for the Facilitation of Trade in the Fields of Standardization and Conformity Assessment: A Toolbox of Instruments', WTO Doc. G/TBT/W/173/Add.1 (19 April 2002)

Communication from the European Union, TN/MA/W/129/Rev.1 (23 June 2010)

WTO Negotiating Group on Market Access, 'Communication from the United States: International Standards', TN/MA/W/138 (28 June 2010)

Market Access for Non-Agricultural Products, International Standards Communication from the Delegation of the European Union, India, Malaysia, Norway, the Philippines, Switzerland and Thailand, Negotiating Group on Market Access, JOB/MA/81 (19 January 2011)

Communication from India, G/TBT/WT/345 (10 November 2011)

WTO Secretariat, 'Negotiating History of the Coverage of the Agreement on Technical Barriers to Trade with regard to Labeling Requirements, Voluntary Standards, and Processes and Production Methods Unrelated to Product Characteristics', WT/CTE/W/10 (29 August 1995)

The CTE Committee, 'Eco-Labelling Programmes', WT/CTE/W/23 (19 March 1996)

WTO Negotiating Group on Market Access, 'Market Access for Non-Agricultural Products-International Standards in Support of Trade and Economic Development: Strengthening the Contribution of the Committee Decision', TN/MA/W/141 (29 March 2011)

SPS Committee, 'Guidelines to Further the Practical Implementation of Article 5.5', G/SPS/15 (18 July 2000)

—— 'Decision on the Implementation of Article 4 of the Agreement on the Application of Sanitary and Phytosanitary Measures', G/SPS/19/Rev.2 (23 July 2004)

—— 'Third Review of the WTO SPS Agreement, Proposal by India', G/SPS/W/236 (17 April 2009)

—— 'Decision of the Committee: Actions Regarding SPS-Related Private Standards', G/SPS/55 (6 April 2011)

—— 'Actions Regarding SPS-Related Private Standards- Communication from Belize', G/SPS/GEN/1291 (16 October 2013)

—— 'Second Report of the Co-Stewards of the Private Standards E-Working Group on Action 1 (G/SPS/55)', G/SPS/W/281 (30 September 2014)

—— 'Actions Regarding SPS-Related Private Standards- Communication from Belize', G/SPS/GEN/1374 (23 October 2014)

—— 'Review of the Operation and Implementation of the SPS Committee- Draft Report of the Committee', G/SPS/W/280/Rev.2 (6 November 2014)

—— 'Report of the Co-Stewards of the Private Standards E-Working Group to the March 2015 Meeting of the SPS Committee on Action 1 (G/SPS/55)', G/SPS/W/283 (17 March 2015)

—— 'Recommended Procedures for Implementing the Transparency Obligations of the SPS Agreement (Article 7)', G/SPS/7/Rev.4 (4 June 2018)

Note by the Secretariat, 'Summary of the SPS Committee Meeting Held on 29–30 June 2005', G/SPS/R/37/Rev.1 (18 August 2005)

—— 'Private Standards and the SPS Agreement', G/SPS/GEN/746 (24 January 2007)

—— 'Effects of SPS- Related Private Standards- Compilation of Replies', G/SPS/GEN/932/Rev.1 (10 December 2009)

—— 'Possible Actions for the SPS Committee Regarding SPS-Related private Standards', G/SPS/W/247/Rev.3 (11 October 2010)

—— 'Proposed Working Definition of SPS-Related Private Standards', G/SPS/W/265/Rev.2 (28 September 2012)

—— 'Existing Definitions of Private Standards in other International Organizations', G/SPS/GEN/1334/Rev.1 (5 August 2014)

—— 'Summary of the SPS Committee Meeting of 30 June – 1 July 2016', G/SPS/R/83 (9 August 2016)

—— 'Summary of the SPS Committee Meeting of 22–23 March 2017', G/SPS/R/86 (1 June 2017)

Statement by Egypt at the Meeting of 7–8 July 1999, G/SPS/GEN/128

Submission from the United States, 'Equivalence', G/SPS/GEN/212 (7 November 2000)

Submission by the United Kingdom, 'Private Voluntary Standards within the WTO Multilateral Framework' G/SPS/GEN/802 (9 October 2007)
Submission by the OIE, 'Considerations Relevant to Private Standards in the Field of Animal, Health, Food Safety and Animal Welfare', G/SPS/GEN/822 (25 February 2008)
Submission by Switzerland, 'Voluntary Standards' G/SPS/GEN/967 (20 October 2009)
Communication from Nigeria, 'Private Standards', G/SPS/GEN/1398 (16 March 2015)
Communication from Belize, 'Belize's Comments on Private Standards', G/SPS/W/288 (14 July 2015)

# Index

Lightning Source UK Ltd.
Milton Keynes UK
UKHW021114180321
380557UK00003B/59

9 781509 931132